OFFICIAL SYBASE INTERNALS

Designing and Troubleshooting for High Performance

JOHN KIRKWOOD

I(T)P®

OFFICIAL SYBASE INTERNALS

INTERNALS

Designing and Troubleshooting for High Performance

JOHN KIRKWOOD

INTERNATIONAL THOMSON COMPUTER PRESS

I(T)P®   An International Thomson Publishing Company

Boston • Bonn • London • Johannesburg • Madrid • Melbourne • Mexico City • New York • Paris
Singapore • Tokyo • Toronto • Albany, NY • Belmont, CA • Cincinnati, OH • Detroit, MI

For more information, contact:

International Thomson Computer Press
20 Park Plaza, 13th Floor
Boston, MA 02116
USA

International Thomson Publishing Europe
Berkshire House 168-173
High Holborn
London WCIV 7AA
England

International Thomson Publishing Gmbh
Königswinterer Strasse 418
53227 Bonn
Germany

International Thomson Publishing Asia
221 Henderson Road #05-10
Henderson Building
Singapore 0315

Thomas Nelson Australia
102 Dodds Street
South Melbourne, 3205
Victoria, Australia

International Thomson Publishing Japan
Hirakawacho Kyowa Building, 3F
2-2-1 Hirakawacho
Chiyoda-ku, 102 Tokyo
Japan

Nelson Canada
1120 Birchmount Road
Scarborough, Ontario
Canada M1K 5G4

International Thomson Editores
Campos Eliseos 385, Piso 7
Col. Polanco
11560 Mexico D.F. Mexico

International Thomson Publishing Southern Africa
Bldg. 19, Constantia Park
239 Old Pretoria Road, P.O. Box 2459
Halfway House, 1685 South Africa

International Thomson Publishing France
1, rue st. Georges
75 009 Paris France

Library of Congress Cataloging-in-Publication Data
A catalogue record for this book is available from the Library of Congress

First Printed 1997

ISBN: 1-85032-334-8

Publisher/Vice President: Jim DeWolf, ITCP/Boston
Project Director: Vivienne Toye, ITCP/Boston
Marketing Manager: Christine Nagle
Printed in the U.S.

Contents

Sybooks™ Installation Guide

The Sybooks™ Installation Guide is located at the end of the book.

Preface

This is not a book for beginners. It is aimed at developers and administrators who have been working with SQL Server for some time and are familiar with its day-to-day usage and requirements. The aim of the book is to make you feel comfortable when developing and administering SQL Server, no matter what problems you are presented with and to provide you with a methodical approach to diagnosing a problem and implementing a solution. The underlying theme of the book is to achieve and monitor high performance. This means that I have not dealt with the day-to-day requirements but have described how the server works; how to design for optimum use of SQL Server features; how to regularly and pro-actively monitor the server; understanding what can go wrong; why it has gone wrong and how to respond to the problem so that you can solve it as effectively as possible.

The book starts with a treatment of the logical to physical design to describe the methods needed to ensure that the implemented design is as efficient as possible; it then looks at SQL Server indexing to show how it works and how to take maximum advantage of it. It then goes into a very detailed description of how the internals of the server operate. This covers storage, the transaction log, automatic and database recovery and locking. The level at which the internals are presented is more detailed than you will need most of the time. However, I feel that knowledge at this level is especially important as it allows you to investigate what is happening when there is a problem. Be careful when you work at this level. You do not always have the safety of well-tested error handling routines; a simple syntax error can cause a stack trace and a failure of the connection. You have been warned!

The rest of the book concentrates on system monitoring and troubleshooting. The System 11 monitoring procedure sp_sysmon is described in detail: what it does, how to interpret the information to determine bottlenecks and which configuration variables to alter to adjust the monitoring figures. The final section on troubleshooting looks at what problems can occur and how to investigate and solve them. This covers indexing, storage, space problems, response time problems, sp_sysmon, the network and SQL.

The material is laid out in a type of question and answer format. Over the years—too many of them in this business—I found that questions have the same theme most of the time. So I have tried not to present a textbook style but to provide a "drill down" format to each section where the most common questions are presented first, and these lead to supplementals with a growing level of detail. Although this format does not apply to all sections, you will not find standard section headings but instead a question about a topic. So instead of "clustered index layout" followed by a description of the index layout, you'll see "What index choices do I have?" and then a description of the SQL Server index types. I hope that you like the approach—not everyone did when it was reviewed. If not, I hope that you still enjoy the read and can find the material you need via the index.

The material is laid out as:follows.

Part I: First Cut Physical Design

Part I discusses the implementation phase of a design: normally called the first cut physical design. This phase takes the logical design model and alters it, if necessary, to provide a physical model which conforms to the requirements of SQL Server and to the performance requirements of the application.

Chapter 1: Logical to Physical Model Mapping

This chapter discusses the criteria of the logical design start point and the need to have a performance goal. The implementation aspect concentrates on the SQL Server choices for domain and referential integrity.

Chapter 2: Choice of Datatype

This chapter discusses the various datatypes available in SQL Server and the criteria for choosing between them. The concentration is on the commonly used character, numeric and datetime datatypes with discussions on the reasons for choosing a particular datatype. The problems with the datetime datatype are discussed in some detail.

Chapter 3: Record Size Considerations

This chapter discusses the SQL Server record layout and storage characteristics. Record size restrictions are detailed with a discussion of overnormalization techniques to cater for large records.

Chapter 4: Table Size Considerations

This chapter discusses overnormalization techniques to reduce the size of very large tables. The problem of large index keys and the use of surrogate keys is also covered.

Part II: SQL Server Indexing

Part II gives a detailed description of SQL Server indexes, the rules for their selection and the overheads of the maintenance commands.

Chapter 5: Types of Index

This chapter describes the types of index available in SQL Server—clustered and non-clustered—and then discusses the differences between them and when to choose one instead of the other.

Chapter 6: Indexing Overheads

This chapter discusses the overheads of insert/update/ delete for the two SQL Server index types. Particular attention is given to the update strategies and the overhead of clustered index page splitting.

Chapter 7: Index Selection

This chapter discusses the rules associated with index selection based on search arguments, index statistics and index density. Execution plan choices are then described for the different types of SQL commands.

Part III: Administrations Internals

Part III gives a detailed description of SQL Server internals for storage, transaction log, recovery and locking.

Chapter 8: Storage

This chapter describes the allocation and management of data space, discussing allocation units, allocation pages, extents, OAM, GAM and the data and index page and record layouts.

Chapter 9: Transaction log and recovery

This chapter describes the layout and usage of the transaction log and how it is used to provide the automatic recovery using roll forward and rollback.

Chapter 10: Database recovery

This chapter describes database dumping and how to recover from lost user and system databases.

Chapter 11: Locking

This chapter describes the types of locks supported by SQL server and how they are used to ensure data consistency. The chapter concludes with suggestions on how to minimize the performance overheads caused by locking.

Part IV: System Monitoring

Part IV describes a methodology for system monitoring which uses a "drill-down" analysis to minimize problem resolution time. It describes the System 11 stored procedure sp_sysmon in detail.

Chapter 12: Methodology

This chapter illustrates how to analyze the symptoms of a problem, how to diagnose the problem from the available symptoms and how to formulate a solution to the problem.

Chapter 13: System monitoring with sp_sysmon

This chapter describes the system 11 monitoring tool, sp_sysmon.

Part V: Troubleshooting

Part V looks at the possible problems you can encounter and suggests approaches to diagnosing and implementing solutions.

Chapter 14: Index troubleshooting

This chapter discusses solutions to why indexes are not being used. The optimizer trace flags are detailed to show how to investigate optimization problems and the techniques used to force specific optimizer behavior are also described.

Chapter 15: Storage troubleshooting

This chapter describes the **dbcc** commands associated with monitoring and troubleshooting the database space allocation. It then discusses the approach to identifying why allocation, OAM, data and index errors have occurred.

Chapter 16: Space problems

This chapter investigates database space problems, looks at diagnostic methods for specific problems and discusses the associated solutions.

Chapter 17: Response time problems

This chapter investigates response time problems by looking at diagnostic methods for specific problems and discussing the associated solutions. The chapter also provides a step-by-step approach to analyzing the SQL optimization plan to effect a "drill-down" method which will identify the most common problems first.

Chapter 18: Troubleshooting with sp_sysmon

This chapter analyzes the sp_sysmon output in a top-down approach to show how to get the most from the principal outputs and what to look for in each output.

Chapter 19: Network troubleshooting

This chapter is about making optimum use of the network mainly by reducing the use of the network.

Chapter 20: High performance SQL

This chapter describes the most common problems of SQL and how to avoid them with specific solutions given to indicate the relative performance merits of the solutions.

And finally: If it is working OK and nobody is complaining…leave it alone.

FIRST CUT PHYSICAL DESIGN

This section discusses the implementation phase of a design: usually called the first cut physical design. This phase takes the logical design model and alters it, if necessary, to provide a physical model which conforms to the requirements of SQL Server and which achieves the performance requirements of the application.

It is important to implement a design which is capable of supporting the application performance requirements. This section describes the steps you might take and the techniques you might use to adjust the logical design to implement it on SQL Server.

It is worth noting that our first cut physical design starts from a logical design which conforms to the relational model. Because SQL Server is a relational database implementation, it is necessary to start physical design based on a relational design model. If you have been following an object oriented analysis and design methodology, you will have a business model which does not support the relational model. It is necessary to introduce another modeling stage to create a logical relational model before you start the physical design.

This chapter discusses the criteria of the logical design start point and the need to have a performance goal. The implementation aspect of the chapter concentrates on the SQL Server implementation choices for domain and referential integrity.

1

Logical to Physical Model Mapping

What do I create a design for implementation from? What do I start from?

Start the physical design implementation from a relational model logical design.

The principal reason for this is that you will be trying to implement a high performance physical design and you need a reference point to gauge your success against. If your changes do not provide an improvement in performance then you simply go back to the logical design and try again. The logical design (sometimes referred to as the conceptual design) is the stage which reflects the business model—data and processing—without any reference to the underlying method or software used to implement the system. So the logical design is independent of any hardware and software used to produce the business functionality.

The logical model will normally be produced as an entity/relationship or object oriented model which then has to be translated into a relational model for implementation. The assumption is that the logical model we are using as a start point for implementation is a form of the entity/relationship model. It represents the business objects as entities with each property of the entity defined by an attribute of the entity. Also, the relationships between the entities will have been reduced to 1:1 and 1:M relationships which do not contain data, allowing them to map directly onto the relational model of SQL Server. If the business model which you are building does not conform to this, you will have to introduce an extra step to produce this model so that you can implement on SQL Server. Non-conformance to a relational model will be most evident with an object based analysis and design methodology where multiple attribute occurrences and M:M relationships are common. These non-relational properties of the business model must be removed before you start your physical modeling phase.

This implemented model is called the **physical design**. The physical design is the stage of the design which is modeled to conform to the characteristics and limitations of the hardware and software used to implement the application. When SQL Server is used as the data storage method, the physical design must conform to the relational model representing the data in tables and columns, the relations as primary—foreign key relationships, and defining and accessing the data using SQL.

Why start from a relational model logical design?

SQL Server is a tool for managing relational databases. While this does not mean that it completely supports the relational model, it does follow it 100% in the use of tables, columns, integrity, and the support of SQL. This means that the optimum start point for implementation is a design which supports this model.

The principal points of the relational model which may require changes from other models are:

- Each attribute must be a single atomic property of the entity

- The relations between the entities must not support attributes

- The relations between the entities must be 1:1 or 1:M—specifically M:M is not supported

Single Atomic Attributes

Any attribute which may have many occurrences must be reduced either to multiple single attributes or to a separate entity with one row per attribute occurrence. Consider an entity with an attribute which may have up to 12 monthly values. This can be reduced to 12 single month attributes or to a separate monthly value entity:

```
Original Entity      Single Entity Solution    Multiple Entity Solution
entity_id            entity_id                 entity 01    entity 02
month_values         month_01_val              entity_id    entity_id
                     month_02_val                           month_number
                       .                                    month_val
                       .
                       .
                     month_12_val
```

In the Multiple Entity Solution the primary key of entity_02 is the composite key (entity_id, month_number). Make your own choice on this. It depends principally on the number of values and associated processing. If the number of values is small and fixed, having multiple attributes in a single entity is probably a better solution. A typical example of this is an address attribute where two lines of address, town, county, and zip on one entity is very common. If the number of values is large and variable then the separate entity is easier to handle as it is a join in SQL. However, do not disregard the multiple attribute approach as it will require less storage than the separate entity. Chapter 20 has a solution to accessing multiple attributes using characteristic functions. A specific problem with the multiple column solution is that you will often have to allow several of the columns to accept null. Especially if the datatype is numeric, this can lead to processing complications when accommodating null values.

No Attributes on Relations

Any relation which supports attributes must be converted into an entity. Consider a delivery relationship between a supplier and a customer as shown in Figure 1.1.

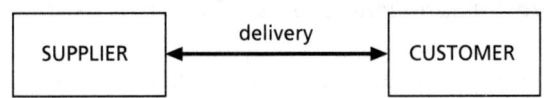

Figure 1.1 *Supplier—Customer Relationship*

If the delivery relation has attributes such as quantity and delivery date then another location must be found for these attributes or a new entity must be created to accommodate them as shown in Figure 1.2.

Figure 1.2 Supplier—Delivery—Customer Relationship

No Many to Many Relations

The relational model does not support M:M relations; these must be converted to link entities with two 1:M relations. Consider an order relation between a supplier and a customer which will be M:M as each customer may be supplied by many suppliers and each supplier may supply many customers.

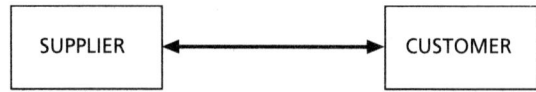

Figure 1.3 Supplier—Customer M:M Relationship

This must be converted into two 1:M relations with a link entity between the supplier and customer.

Figure 1.4 Supplier—Orders—Customer Relationship

Another benefit of the relational model is that it supports integrity of the data; both the inherent properties of the data itself—**entity** and **domain integrity**—and its relationship with other data in the model—**referential integrity**. These integrity rules are based on the concepts of primary and foreign keys.

The **primary key** is one or more columns in a table which comprise a unique identifier for each row in the table. Where there are several candidate columns which can enforce uniqueness, one of these must be chosen as the primary key for the physical design.

```
orders(order no, order_date, customer_no)
```

The order_no is the primary key of the orders entity.

```
order_item(order no, product no, order_qty, net_price)
```

The order_no and product_no combination is the composite primary key for the order_item entity.

```
customer(cust no, name, address_line_1, town, county, zip code)
```

The cust_no has been chosen as the primary key of the customer entity. The name may also have been a candidate for the primary key, although you can obviously find occasions when this is not applicable. However, the combination of name, address_line_1, and zip code is definitely a candidate for primary key. When faced with a choice, choose the candidate which is most familiar to the user of the application; if there is no difference, choose the simplest and/or the smallest.

The **foreign key** is one or more columns in a table which is also a primary key in another table. The primary key—foreign key link forms the relationship between the tables in the relational model.

```
customer(cust no, name, ...)
```

```
orders(order no, order_date, cust_no, ...)
```

The cust_no in the orders table is a foreign key in orders as it is also a primary key in the customer table.

Entity integrity defines that the primary key or any part of the primary key must not be null. Any columns defined as part of the primary key cannot allow null. This is based on the fact that the null value is not an actual value and is unknown. If a value is unknown, there is no way to determine if it is unique and, as primary key values must be unique, there is no way that a null value can take part in a primary key.

Domain integrity covers the validation of data attributes independently of the rest of the data. This includes the type of data such as numeric or character; whether the attribute allows null values; the acceptable range of values which the attribute may accept and any default value assigned to the attribute if no explicit value is supplied.

Referential integrity is the definition and maintenance of the relationships between entities such that the following rules are maintained:

- The foreign key may allow null but if it contains a value then that value must be present as a primary key in the related table

This gives rise to the following referential integrity checks and processing:

Foreign Key Processing

Insert Existence

If a non-null foreign key value is inserted then the value must exist as a primary key on the related table.

Consider the orders, customer relationship:

```
orders(order no, order_date, cust_no, ......)
customer(cust no, name, ......)
```

The orders.cust_no is a foreign key since it is also a primary key of customer. Any insert of orders is allowed only if the cust_no being inserted exists on the customer table.

This is always implemented in referential integrity implementations. Note that it specifically allows null foreign key values to be inserted. You may wish to enhance this rule by not allowing null foreign key values.

Primary Key Processing

Restriction

A deletion or update of a primary key value is not allowed if there are any existing foreign key occurrences for that value.

In the above orders:customer relation we are not allowed to delete a customer record if the cust_no deleted exists on an orders record. We are also not allowed to update a customer.cust_no if the current cust_no has related orders records. Of course you do not allow update of primary keys in your application so this problem does not arise. Theory is nice, so make sure that you check the referential integrity of the deletion phase of the primary key update.

Restriction is the most common approach to primary key referential integrity—it is the easiest to implement and it does cover the majority of business requirements.

Cascade

A deletion of a primary key value is cascaded to all foreign key occurrences with the foreign key rows being deleted. This is less common but not unknown as business requirements will sometimes require the complete removal of an object's data. In the above orders:customer relation a cascade delete of customer would delete all orders records for the deleted cust_no. Clearly, cascade can be quite a performance hit if there are many related foreign key records to be deleted.

Nullify

A deletion or update of a primary key value sets all foreign key values in related rows to null. This is an unusual integrity check and any implementations of this will normally be based on specific business requirements. In my opinion the introduction of specific business requirements to justify this integrity check means that it is no longer a true referential integrity check which should be based purely on the data relationships. Let's not argue about this.

Set Default

A deletion of a primary key value sets all foreign key values in related rows to a specific default value. This is a recent addition to the referential integrity rules and I disagree completely with this one as it requires specific processing to cope with the default values. I spent enough time with pre-relational databases creating exception processing for the special key values without re-introducing it again here.

Relational model drawbacks

A problem with the relational model is that it tends to create many small tables with few attributes per row which increases the need to join the tables together. For example, the name of a customer is present on the customer table only and is uniquely referenced by the primary key of the customer row. However, this means that an inquiry on orders which wishes to display the customer name has to join to the customer table on the customer table primary key. Another drawback of the normalized design is that it does not allow for summary or derived data and again tables have to be joined to create this information. Calculating and displaying summary information for a foreign key will necessitate reading all of the instances of the foreign key. For example, displaying the number of orders for a customer would require a join of the two tables and the reading of all orders records for the cust_no. All this means is that the normalized logical design is an excellent representation of the business application but, in general, does not provide the fastest performance.

What is the first thing I should do to the logical design?

The first physical implementation is simply the logical model.

- Map the entities to tables
- Map the attributes to columns
- Select appropriate datatypes and nullability for the columns
- Map the primary keys to a unique index
- Map the foreign keys to an index

This will give you a physical model identical to the logical model. The important thing to understand here is that if this gives you the required performance then do not mess around with it. One of the hardest things to do is to stop when you are creating a physical design to a required performance specification. There will always be something else which you can do to make it go faster. There is always a point of diminishing return when the effort required to get a small increase in performance is not worth it. Realize that the current design is complete when you have provided the required performance.

If it is not broken, why fix it?

How do I know if it is working adequately?

Insist on specific performance criteria which you can measure the physical implementation against.

You cannot design a physical model unless you have a target. There are any number of physical models which can be generated from one logical model and each of them will be different based on the target performance. In fact, two designers will often come up with different physical models for the same requirement. This does not mean that one of them is wrong: if both of them provide the required performance then they are both correct. Do not get into religious wars about a particular technique: if it works it may just be better than you thought.

What constitutes useful performance criteria?

This is less obvious as there are many ways of expressing performance requirements.

At the initial logical-to-physical mapping stage, they will be along the lines of:

- Single record updates within a second
- Multiple record updates no longer than 10 seconds
- Inquiries which access limited amounts of data from less than 4 tables within 5 seconds
- Other limited data, multi-table inquiries within 10 seconds
- Full table inquiries within 30 seconds

Never accept a design at this stage based on "as fast as possible": you will never finish this one and it will never be to the user's satisfaction. Later on in the system design and implementation—often after the system has been implemented and you are monitoring the performance—you will get more specific requests to make one command go faster. In this situation, it can be acceptable to design to "as fast as possible." This refinement of the above general requirements is quite acceptable and often mandatory as you cannot complete the indexing of the physical design until the SQL commands have been written. In practice, there is no point in trying to index properly until the SQL has been written because the optimizer takes decisions based on the SQL syntax and you cannot prejudge all of these. Even the simplest single table command can show quite a different performance than you expected based on how the optimizer sees the SQL against its evaluation criteria. Do not waste time building sophisticated indexing early in the physical design: you will have to redo most of it when the SQL has been written and the optimizer evaluates it against your indexes. If you must have a reasonably complete physical design early in the design process, then you will have to outline the SQL in advance at a level sufficient to identify the tables and the where clauses. This will allow quite accurate indexes to be built early in the design process, although you must still be ready to do some fine tuning once the actual SQL has been written.

Also, do not accept the performance criteria blindly. Most single record processing in less than a second is quite acceptable—if you cannot achieve this then there is probably something fundamentally wrong with your design—but multiple record/table processing needs to be qualified with some data volumes. A two-table join which does a cartesian product of 10,000 rows with 1,000,000 rows is likely to take more than 5 seconds. I know that is a bit extreme but you need to introduce realism into the user's expectations as early as possible. If the cartesian product is mandatory, and runs every 30 seconds and is crucial to the system acceptance, then you need to achieve it and the normal approach of indexing is not going to do it. (It is more likely you'll use masses of memory and return some results to the user before the command has completed.)

How do I implement integrity?

Use the declarative integrity of the create table command for the primary key and foreign key referential integrity. Use the programmatic user defined datatypes, rules and defaults for column domain integrity.

SQL Server has two choices: declarative integrity using create and alter table clauses and programmatic integrity using rule, default, index and trigger objects.

Declarative Integrity

This is implemented in the create table command using the clauses:

- Primary key
- Foreign key...references
- Default
- Check

The default and check clauses establish default values and validation checks for individual clauses. The primary key and foreign key clauses establish the referential integrity of the model. The primary key defines the unique non-null identifier of each record in the table.

```
create table orders
(ord_no   int   primary key,
ord_date   datetime,
.
.
.)
```

```
create table order_item
( ord_no int,
prod_no int,
.
.
primary key (ord_no, prod_no))
```

This primary key definition automatically creates a unique clustered index on the primary key columns to enforce the uniqueness requirement. Be careful here as the index is being created on an empty table so there will be no index statistics created for this index. You can override the index definition to define it as nonclustered if you wish. Defining the primary key index as nonclustered is recommended as it leaves the clustered index for more worthy columns which normally retrieve more than one record such as the foreign key.

The foreign key defines one or more columns as the foreign key in the table and references it to the primary key occurrence in another table.

```
create table orders                create table delivery
(ord_no  int  primary key,         (ord_no   int,
.                                   prod_no   int,
.                                   delivery_no  int,
.                                   .
cust_no   int                       .
references customer(cust_no),       primary key (ord_no, prod_no,
.                                                 delivery_no)
.)                                  foreign key (ord_no, prod_no)
                                    references order_item (ord_no, prod_no))
```

The foreign key definition automatically enforces insert existence integrity on the foreign key table and restriction integrity on the primary key table. At present, SQL Server does not support cascade, for which you will have to write your own code, usually in a trigger.

The above primary and foreign key definitions allow the name of the index to be created automatically by the server. This is done by concatenating the table name, the column name, and a system generated number. If there are too many characters in the resulting index name, the table and/or column name is truncated to fit. This creates quite a horrendous name and it is recommended that you name the index explicitly in the create table statement.

```
create table orders
(ord_no int constraint pkey_idx primary key,
.
.
.
```

Programmatic

This uses separate SQL Server objects to define the integrity. The rule and default objects define the column validation and any default values.

There is no explicit definition of the primary key and foreign key columns. You could use the system procedures sp_primarykey and sp_foreignkey to note what the primary and foreign keys are but these are documentation only and are not used in any integrity checks. The primary key not null requirement is enforced in the null/not null status of the column definition and the uniqueness is enforced by defining a unique index on the primary key columns. The end effect is the same as the declarative approach but you must remember to create the index.

The foreign key integrity is supported by triggers (or procedures) which you must define. The triggers take advantage of the "inserted" and "deleted" tables to check and see if an insert/update/delete has breached the integrity rules. If it has, the command has to be rolled back.

Which approach should I use for integrity: declarative or programmatic?

This is debatable but my personal preference is:

- Declarative for referential integrity using the primary key and foreign key clauses

- Programmatic for domain integrity using rules and defaults bound to user defined datatypes

Consider the two tables: customer and orders.

Declarative

The table creation statements to provide primary and foreign integrity plus a simple check on the key values are:

```
create table customer
(cust_no id_type primary key
     nonclustered
     check (cust_no > 0),
 .
 .
```

```
create table orders
(ord_no id_type primary key
     nonclustered
     check (ord_no > 0),
 .
 .
```

```
.)                                          cust_no id_type
                                                    references customer(cust_no)
                                                    check (cust_no > 0),
                                              .
                                              .)
```

with the additional object support of:

```
sp_addtype id_type, "int", "not null"
go
create clustered index cust_idx on orders(cust_no)
go
```

Programmatic

The table creation statements to provide primary and foreign integrity plus a simple check on the key values are:

```
create table customer                    create table orders
(cust_no id_type,                        (ord_no id_type,
.                                         .
.                                         .
.)                                        cust_no id_type,
                                          .
                                          .)
```

with the additional object support of:

```
sp_addtype id_type, "int", "not null"
go
create rule id_rule as (@fred > 0)
go
sp_bindrule id_rule, id_type
go

create unique nonclustered index idx1 on customer(cust_no)
create clustered index idx1 on orders(cust_no)
create unique nonclustered index idx2 on orders(ord_no)
go

create trigger order_ins for insert on orders as
declare @recs int, @recs1 int
select @recs = @@rowcount
select @recs1 = count(*) from customer c, inserted i
       where c.cust_no = i.cust_no
if (@recs != @recs1)
       begin
       raiserror 51000"customer does not exist"
       rollback tran
```

```
        return
        end
return
go
create trigger cust_del on customer for delete as
if exists (select * from orders o, deleted d
        where o.cust_no = d.cust_no)
        begin
        raiserror 52000 "cannot delete, orders exist"
        rollback tran
        return
        end
return
go
```

Note the primary key as nonclustered and the foreign key as clustered. This is often the best index choice for a first cut physical design. Obviously more programming work is required to define programmatic integrity, mostly caused by the need to define triggers to enforce referential integrity. Declarative integrity easily wins in this comparison. However, the declarative integrity also applies to the schema which makes it difficult to drop and recreate table definitions as you must follow the integrity rules. In the above customer:orders relation you would not be able to drop the customer until you had dropped the integrity constraints or dropped the orders table. Also, fast bcp requires the tables to be unindexed. This is simple enough when the indexes are separate objects, but it requires you to drop and recreate the integrity constraints to remove the indexes automatically created by the primary key definition. I think that it is marginal and still a debatable issue but I side slightly with the declarative integrity and I would recommend that you define primary key and foreign key integrity using the declarative primary key and foreign key...references clauses in the create table.

The check (and default) integrity requires about the same amount of code. However, you need to define the declarative check and default for every column that it applies to. In the programmatic integrity you can define the rule and default once and then bind them to a user defined datatype which can be used to define the columns. The declarative approach is more prone to error in this case but, more importantly, the programmatic approach causes the user defined datatype with bound rule and default to function as a domain for the columns. I suggest that this gives the programmatic rule and default the edge over the declarative check and default, and I would recommend the use of rule, default, and user defined datatype for domain integrity. The only exception to this is when the check validation is across more than one column on the table. The rule cannot support this but the check clause can and should be used for this exception. There is no real conflict as it is no longer domain integrity but really a programmatic validation being implemented as a check constraint.

Summary

The logical design model may contain certain features which are not supported by the relational nature of SQL Server and these have to be resolved to implement the physical model. The principal features which normally require logical to physical adjustment are:

Single valued atomic attributes

Any logical attributes which support multiple values must be resolved into multiple single valued attributes or into a separate entity with single valued attributes. The former of multiple single valued attributes is more common.

No attributes on relations

If the logical model allows the relations between entities to possess attributes then the relation itself must become an entity to accommodate the attributes or the attributes must be relocated to existing entities. The former of a new entity is more common.

No M:M relations

Any M:M relations in the logical design must be resolved into two 1:M relations with a new entity linking the entities.

The logical model may also support entity, domain, and referential integrity and these must be implemented in SQL Server.

Entity integrity

SQL Server provides a choice of implementation for entity integrity: (1) declarative using the primary key constraint of the create table command which enforces non null values and creates a unique index, or (2) programmatic using the not null status in the create table and a separate create unique index.

Domain integrity

SQL Server provides a choice of implementation for domain integrity: (1) declarative—using the default and check constraints in the create/alter table commands and (2) programmatic—using the default and rule objects. The user defined datatype in SQL Server can be included in the programmatic approach to create a domain object which consists of datatype, null status, default value, and range of valid values.

Referential integrity

SQL Server provides a choice of implementation for referential integrity: (1) declarative—using the foreign key...references constraint in the create/alter table commands (2) and programmatic using triggers. The declarative approach provides only insert existence for the foreign key and deletion restriction for the primary key and will require you to create triggers for any cascade or nullify integrity.

2

Choice of Datatype

This chapter discusses the various datatypes available in SQL Server and the criteria for choosing between them. The concentration is on the commonly used character, numeric, and datetime datatypes with discussions on the reasons for choosing a particular datatype. The problems with using the datetime datatype are discussed in some detail.

What are the best datatypes to use?

There are no real preferences: choose the most suitable for the data. But try to avoid the more unusual ones such as bit and varbinary.

The datatype of a column defines the type of data which may be contained in the column. By defining a column as a specific datatype only that type of data may be entered into the column and the system executes basic type validation to ensure that only valid values can be input into the column. In certain situations, the input values may also be truncated to fit into the datatype of the column.

The normal choices are given in the following table.

Table 2.1

Requirement	Datatype Choice	Storage in Bytes
characters	char(n)	n
	varchar(n)	actual data length

Table 2.1 (continued)

Requirement	Datatype Choice	Storage in Bytes
integer numeric	int	4
	smallint	2
	tinyint	1
non-integer with	numeric(p, s)	2 to 17
fixed number of	decimal(p, s)	
decimal places	float(p)	4 or 8
non-integer with	double precision	8
varying number of	real	4
decimal places		
date and time	datetime	8
	smalldatetime	4
large text	text	multiples of 2K

The less used datatypes are given in the following table. In general, these are not commonly used and you should think carefully before using them. It may appear advantageous to use bit for a yes/no type column but the support for this in SQL is quite programming-orientated and beyond the normal user who might wish to issue ad-hoc SQL on these columns. It is usually much better to suffer the increased space usage and stick to the standard numeric and character datatypes.

Table 2.2

Requirement	Datatype Choice	Storage in Bytes
multi-byte characters	nchar(n)	n*@@ncharsize
	nvarchar(n)	actual data length*
	@@ncharsize	
US dollar currency	money	8
(to 4 decimal places)	smallmoney	4
binary	binary(n)	n
	varbinary(n)	actual data length
large binary	image	multiple of 2K
true/false (any two	bit	1 (holds up to 8 bit
values stored as 0 or 1)		columns)
custom sequence	timestamp	8
datatype	(actually varbinary(8))	

What is the difference between char and varchar?

It is as simple as *char* is fixed length and *varchar* is variable length.

The character datatypes allow a mixture of alphabetic and numeric to a maximum of 255 characters. The difference between these is that the *char* datatype is fixed length and the *varchar* datatype is variable length. The fixed length *char* datatype always occupies the same number of characters—the size specified in the column definition. So char(12) always occupies 12 characters regardless of the number of characters input to the column. All unused characters are padded to the right with spaces. However, varchar(30) is variable length and occupies exactly the number of characters input. So 5 characters input into a varchar(30) column occupies 5 characters. There is a 1 byte overhead associated with a variable length column to hold the start location of the column on the record. The start locations are held at the end of the row in an offset table. Also, a *char* column which allows null is held and behaves as varchar.

It does take a little more processing to unpack a variable length column; its length is not known and has to be determined from the offset table at the end of the row. With a fixed length column, SQL Server always retrieves the same number of characters; with a variable length column, SQL Server has to read the offset table to determine how many characters to read. This is not worth worrying about as it really is minimal. There is a 1 byte overhead associated with a variable length column to hold the start location of the column on the record. The start locations are held at the end of the row in an offset table.

Saving space is the most important criteria and so reasonable rules of thumb are:

- Columns with a variation in length should be *varchar*

- Columns with all values the same length should be *char*

- Large sizes are usually better as *varchar* as even a small number of short lengths will save space

When should I use text?

The text datatype is best used for very large—kilobyte—character fields.

This is the character equivalent of a binary large object (BLOB) and is held differently from the other datatypes. For a *text* datatype the record contains a 16 byte pointer which points to a series of linked pages each containing 2 Kb of text up to a maximum of 2^{31}-1 bytes. The *text* columns are held as separate objects from the data records. When you need to hold thousands of characters the *text* datatype is an obvious choice but there is more to think about at the lower end. As there is a limit of 255 characters on a *char/varchar* datatype, it can be difficult to decide if one text column or several varchar(255) columns is better for large character columns. There is no clear solution here but I think that two factors are important: space usage and text processing.

Space Usage

Text always occupies a minimum of 1 page i.e., 2 Kb. Even if you enter 1 character you will use up 2 Kb. This may be a serious consideration if every record on the table wastes an average of 1 Kb. I do not have a rule of thumb, only a personal preference of multiple *varchar* columns up to 500 characters and text above this. But this is not black and white and the problems of multiple *varchar* columns may be too great for the application and then the waste of space will not be that important.

Text Processing

Probably more important is the unfortunate fact that other software does not always process BLOBs. This is true with the *text* datatype where early releases of both third party and Sybase software (Omni and Replication Server) do not support text. There may be workarounds and subsequent releases of the software will support BLOBs. This is the case with early releases of Replication Server, when Sybase Professional Services can supply a solution which splits the text into multiple *varchar* columns. This is an important consideration if you feel that *text* is the right datatype: make sure that the software you are intending to use can support the BLOB *text* datatype.

What is the difference between the numeric datatypes?

The basic split is between integer and non-integer datatypes. The non-integer datatypes further split into those with a fixed number of decimal places and those with a variable number of decimal places.

Integer Numeric

When the numeric values are whole numbers there is a choice of three datatypes: *int* (integer), *smallint*, *tinyint*. The difference is simply the number of bytes used by each datatype and therefore the value range which can be supported.

Table 2.3

Datatype	Number of Bytes	Value Range
int	4	2^{31} -1 to -2^{31} (2,147,483,647 to -2,147,483,648)
smallint	2	2^{15} -1 to -2^{15} (32,767 to -32,768)
tinyint	1	2^{8} - 1 to 0 (255 to 0)

The choice is quite simply based on the expected value range of the column. Using int for a value in the range 1–100 is simply wasting space. However, if you are not sure at this stage you might as well use *int* and suffer any waste of space or make the change before you go into production. Try to get it right, especially the *tinyint* when you will be more sure of the limit and there is no point in wasting 3 bytes for no reason: 3 bytes in 4 columns in 10,000,000 records is quite a lot of disk space.

Non-Integer Numeric

When numeric values contain decimal places there are two categories to choose from: **exact**, which has a fixed number of digits and decimal places, and **non-exact**, which has a maximum number of digits and a variable number of decimal places.

Table 2.4

Datatype	Category	Number of Bytes	Value Range
float(p)	non-exact	4-8	machine dependent
double precision	non-exact	8	machine dependent
real	non-exact	4	machine dependent
numeric(p, s)	exact	2-17	10^{38} - 1 to 10^{-38}
decimal(p, s)	exact	2-17	10^{38} - 1 to 10^{-38}

The difference between theses categories is that the exact datatypes hold exactly the value entered or displayed. If I define a column as numeric (6, 2) then it will always have 6 digits with 2 decimal places. Therefore, the value 20.12 is held as 20.12, displayed as 20.12 and I can locate it in a *where* clause as **where col_a = 20.12**. If I try to input 20.123 into the column I get a conversion error because the scale of the input value is larger than the scale of the target column. A truncation error is the default action. You can use **set arithabort numeric_truncation off** to override this and truncate the input value to fit the defined scale.

However, if I define a column as *float* then it is held with a varying number of decimal places depending on the hardware and any processing on it. So a float_col may display 20.123 based on the number of display decimal places imposed by the application but it may be held as 20.122999999999998 and you will not be able to retrieve it with a *where* clause of **where float_col = 20.123**. Clearly this is rather important to the SQL you write and you should consider using exact numeric datatypes whenever possible. This level of inaccuracy in the stored value can also introduce inaccuracies in calculations and it is recommended to use the *numeric* datatype in place of *float* whenever possible. If the storage requirements or the math requires it, you will need to consider non-exact but be prepared to have to write range tests in *where* clauses to guarantee retrieving the values which you can see on a display.

A particular problem with *float* in System 11 is that it gives an error when converted to a *char* which does not have enough digits to contain the full value. Taking our above value of 20.122999999999998, a convert to (say) char(10) will give a conversion error.

```
declare @f float
select @f = 20.123
select convert(char(10), @f)
Msg 265, level 16, State 1:
Insufficient result space for explicit conversion of FLOAT value
'20.122999999999998' to a CHAR field.
```

convert(char(25), @f) works fine since there are sufficient digits in the target field. You can overcome this with a two stage conversion via a *numeric* datatype:

```
declare @f float
select @f = 20.123
select convert(char(10), convert(numeric(5, 3), @f))
```

Note that this assigns a numeric (5, 3) literal to the float variable which will require an implicit conversion. You really should use the "e" notation to assign a float value: **select @f = 20123e-3**.

How do I handle dates?

With a great deal of difficulty based on the *datetime* datatype. There are two datatypes—*datetime* and *smalldatetime*—which differ only on the date range supported.

Table 2.5

Datatype	Number of Bytes	Date Range
datetime	8	Jan 1, 1753 to Dec 31, 9999
smalldatetime	4	Jan 1, 1900 to Jun 6, 2079

The date is held as a number of days before or after Jan 1, 1900 with dates before this held as negative. For *datetime* the time is held as a number of server ticks (1/300 millisecs by default) from midnight (12:00 A.M.) and for *smalldatetime* as a number of minutes from midnight. In general, there is little to gain by using the *smalldatetime* datatype.

The problem with the *datetime* datatype is that you cannot separate the two components of date and time. All values stored are allocated a time in addition to the date which can make it difficult to retrieve the record. Input of a date without a time always creates a time portion of 12:00 A.M. Input of a date using the SQL Server getdate() function creates a time portion as of the time of input. Therefore, retrieval from a *datetime* field supplying only the date portion requires different approaches depending on how the date was input.

Consider a table with a *datetime* column and two inputs:

```
insert into date_tab values (1, '22 Nov 1995')
insert into date_tab values (2, getdate())
```

Retrieval of all records from the table shows them stored as:

```
select * from date_tab

pkey   date col
1      Nov 22 1995 12:00AM
2      Nov 22 1995 11:37AM
```

Retrieval from this table to identify specific dates gives:

```
select * from date_tab where date_col = 'Nov 22, 1995'
```

```
pkey    date_col
1       Nov 22 1995 12:00AM    (because both the input and where clause
                               date only values have defaulted the time to
                               12:00AM)

select * from date_tab where date_col = getdate()

pkey    date col

0 records returned     (because even if it is still the 22nd, the time has
                       moved on and does not match with any existing
                       records on the table)
```

Inputting the time still does not retrieve the required record.

```
select * from date_tab where date_col = 'Nov 22, 1995 11:37AM'

pkey    date col

0       records returned    (because although the time has displayed as
                            11:37 it is held to a greater resolution and
                            the full time has to be input to match on
                            equality)
```

To retrieve all Nov 22 records a conversion has to be applied to the date field. Another common approach is to use the between operator **where date_col between "22 Nov 1996 12:00AM" and "22 Nov 1995 11:59PM"** although this has obvious problems at the date range limits.

```
select * from date_tab
        where convert(char(12), date_col, 106) = '22 Nov 1995'

pkey    date col
1       Nov 22 1995 12:00AM
2       Nov 22 1995 11:37AM
```

This has two drawbacks:

1. It is extremely sensitive to matching the style of the conversion and the format of the date string. Altering the above to **where convert(char(12), date_col, 106) = "Nov 22 1995"** does not return any rows.

2. Because the date_col is contained in a function the optimizer cannot use any index on date_col which can be a serious performance problem.

If returning multiple records is acceptable, the *like* operator will locate all records based on date only.

```
select date_col from date_tab where date_col like 'Nov 22 1995%'

pkey    date_col
1       Nov 22 1995 12:00AM
2       Nov 22 1995 11:37AM
```

However, this is extremely sensitive to the format of the supplied date which must be a character match for the display pattern. In this case, the string "22 Nov 1995" does not return any records. This is also not applicable to other selection operations such as greater than and therefore is not a particularly feasible option.

The wildcarding approach is more relevant to equality on time.

```
select * from date_tab where date_col like 'Nov 22 1995 11:37AM%'

pkey    date_col
2       Nov 22 1995 11:37AM
```

The approach taken to date/time storage is therefore sensitive to the processing requirements.

What should I do if processing involves dates only?

Enforce default time on input. (recommended option); or,

Store the date as an integer field with no time; or,

Use the standard datetime datatype.

Enforce default time on input

Store the date field as *datetime* datatype but ensure that all date inputs do not have a time specified in which case they will default to 12:00 AM in all cases.

This means that testing against the date field is simple and may be quoted as:

```
select * from date_tab where date_col = 'Nov 22 1995'
```

However, if the *getdate()* function is used as a shorthand for today it does require conversion as:

```
select * from date_tab where date_col = convert(char(12), getdate(), 106)
```

This is quite easily controlled by having a stored procedure which returns a variable with the appropriately converted output of getdate().

Table 2.6

Pros	Cons
Looks natural with normal dates used everywhere	Must remember not to quote time which will require some global input validation
Can use the system functions such as *datediff, dateadd,* etc. this will require output	Display will automatically show the default time of 12:00 A.M.: suppression of conversion
Works in parallel with normal datetime fields	

Store the date as an integer field with no time

Convert all dates on input to store as an integer—usually in the format *yyyymmdd*.

This means that testing against the date field is more complicated and requires knowledge of the storage format or conversion to the format.

```
select * from date_tab where date_col = '19951122'

   or  select * from date_tab
       where date_col = convert(char(12), '22 Nov 1995', 112)
```

Again, easily controlled with a stored procedure to return the correctly formatted character string.

Table 2.7

Pros	Cons
Still easily recognizable as a date Saves on storage space	Requires input conversion Requires output conversion Requires conversion to be used with the system date functions Requires conversion to work with normal datetime columns

Use the standard datetime datatype

Store the input date as *datetime* with no enforcement of default time.

This simply moves the input validation, which involves enforcing the default time of suggestion 1, to a conversion effort on every test against the date column. The choice is processing dependent but the number of inputs normally is less than the number of inquiries and so this is not normally better than option 1 of enforcing the default time.

What should I do if processing involves both date and time?

Use the standard datetime datatype. (recommended option); or,

Use a separate integer column for the time.

Use the standard datetime datatype

This is the standard approach which allows all system date functionality to be utilized. The principal drawback is an exact match on time as the datatype stores to 1/300 of a millisecond but wildcarding is usually adequate here.

```
select * from date_tab where date_time_col like "Nov 22 95 11:37%"
```

As above, the character string has to be quite specific but this is easier to remember as exact time matches are less frequent than date matches.

Use a separate integer column for the time

This is a similar argument to storing the date as a separate *integer* column and has most merit only when the date has been stored separately.

Summary

The main choices of datatype are:

Character	char(n)	fixed length	always held as maximum length of n bytes space padded to the right
	varchar(n)	variable length	held as exactly the number of input bytes to a maximum of n bytes
Numeric	int, smallint, tinyint	integer	
	numeric(p, s) decimal(p, s)	non-integer with an exact number of decimal places	requires conversion between different scales.
	float, real, double precision	non-integer with a variable number of decimal places	value displayed is an approximation rounded to the number of decimal places displayed
Date and time	datetime	4 byte date and 4 byte time	always contains both date and time which makes date only manipulation difficult
Text blob	text	2 Kb to 2 Gb of free format text	can have a significant performance overhead for update and not always supported by third party software

3

Record Size Considerations

This chapter discusses the SQL Server record layout and storage characteristics. Record size restrictions are detailed with a discussion of overnormalization techniques to cater for large records.

Is there an optimum column placement?

No, the sequence of column definition is not important.

The only practical consideration here is the amount of processing that the system has to do to retrieve a column. SQL Server holds all fixed length columns at the start of the record followed by the variable length columns. And a column which allows null is always held as a variable length column.

The record layout is as shown in Figure 3.1:

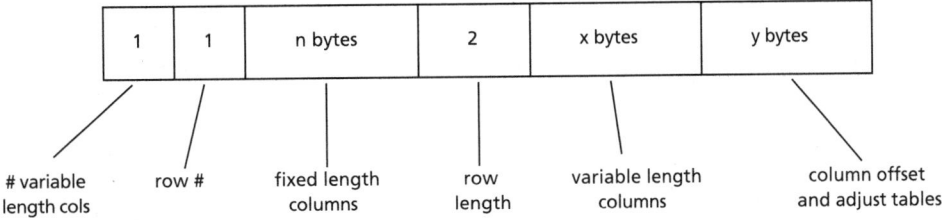

Figure 3.1 Data record layout

All records have a 2 byte overhead at the beginning to hold the number of variable length columns (even if 0) and the row number within the page. If the record contains any variable length columns there is an additional 2 bytes for the record length and 1 byte column location offset entries at the end of the record. To locate a fixed length column the offset of the column from the start of the record is held in the **syscolumns** entry for the column. Therefore, every column is accessed in the same manner by locating the syscolumns entry and going directly to the start of the column as defined by syscolumns.offset. The length of the column is fixed according to the datatype in syscolumns. To locate a variable length column its offset entry number is held in syscolumns.offset as a negative number counting from the end of the column offset table. So the first variable column has offset -1, the second -2 and so on. The offset entry then gives the offset of the column from the start of the row. The length of the variable column is the difference to the next variable column offset value or to the end of the record. The record layout is described in more detail in Chapter 8.

So, the bottom line is that it does not matter but you lose nothing and enhance your documentation by always defining the primary key columns first followed by the most used columns such as foreign keys and high activity columns such as the name on a person record.

Is there an optimum record size?

Not really, but be careful when the record is just greater than half a page.

The records are stored in pages of 2 Kb bytes (except Stratus which is 4 Kb) and a record is not allowed to overflow into a second page. Therefore, each page must contain an integral number of records. When the records do not fit 100% into the page there will be unused space of up to the maximum record size which is not available for new records. The loss of space in a page is most evident when the record is just over half a page. In this case, only one record is allowed per page and the maximum amount of space will be left unused. Every data page has a 32 byte header leaving 2016 bytes available for record storage. Using a record size of just over half of this wastes about 1000 bytes per record page, i.e., effectively doubling the size of the table. Also take into account the record overheads which approximate to 8 bytes + 1 byte per variable length column. The fixed length portion of the record has a 4 byte overhead: 1 byte for record number; 1 byte for number of variable length columns and 2 bytes for the page offset table entry indicating the position of the row in the page. The variable length portion has a minimum overhead of a 2 byte row length plus a row offset table with 2 bytes overhead and 1 byte per variable column. If a variable column starts past 255 bytes in the row there is additional overhead of an adjust table as explained in Chapter 8.

A page is the minimum amount of data transferred to and from disk. The data page is split into three components as illustrated in Figure 3.2.

- A header containing such as: owning object id, next and previous page pointers, free space location, and minimum record size

- The body of the page containing the data rows

- A footer containing row location information (called the **row offset table**)

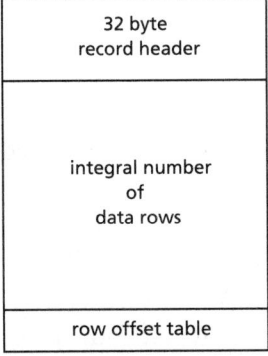

Figure 3.2 Data page structure

Data rows in a page are stored contiguously with all free space at the end of the page. A data row may not cross a page boundary.

The row offset table is a set of entries which contains the byte offset of the record from the start of the page. Three records in a page with lengths of 120, 100, and 115 bytes will have offsets of 32, 152, and 252 respectively: the first record starting immediately after the page header. The internal record identifier or *row_id* is composed of the logical page number and the offset number in the row offset table. This means that the data row may move within the page without changing its row_id as only the byte value in the offset entry changes. This is illustrated in Figure 3.3 where the first row is deleted. The other rows are moved up to take up the free space as all free space in a page always follows the records in the page. The offset value for the deleted record is set to 0. When a new record is added to the page it uses the first free offset entry instead of creating a new one. So this new record becomes row number 0 although it may be placed at the end of the data in the page as shown in Figure 3.3.

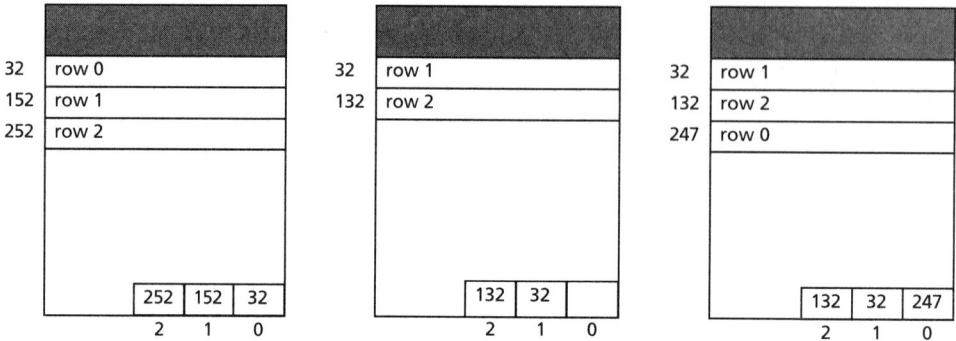

Figure 3.3 *Reuse of row offset entries*

Also be careful when you use a *fillfactor* on a clustered index as this is applied to the data page. In this case, you should make sure that the free space in each page is sufficient for at least one record. A 75% fillfactor will leave a maximum of 500 bytes free in each page. However, the page is filled until the fillfactor is exceeded and so a 350 byte record will fill the page past the 75% full marker and not leave enough space for an insert. This is illustrated in Figure 3.4 where four records take the space to 1432 bytes, just below the fillfactor, and the next record takes the used space to 1782 bytes, not leaving enough free space for 1 record.

Of course the free space is always available for updates to the existing records, so all is not lost but, if you are using a fillfactor, be careful to make sure that you actually have enough space left for record inserts.

Is my record too small?

No, but be careful of the number of records per page as SQL Server currently locks at the page level. Sybase has informed me that record level locking is being developed for inclusion in a later release of System 11.

There is no lower limit on a record. There is a limit of 256 rows per page which means that anything below 8 bytes is not making maximum use of the page space. The row number of the record in the page is a 1 byte column and so the maximum number of

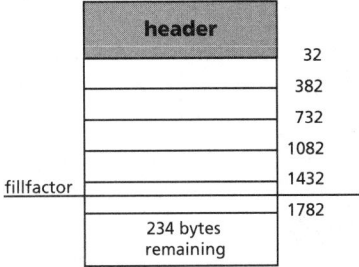

Figure 3.4 Incorrect setting of fillfactor and record size

rows per page is one byte. However, with at least a 4 byte record overhead it is diffi-cult to think of a useful record of less than 8 bytes—not impossible, just difficult. This is the 2 bytes at the start of every record plus the 2 bytes in the offset table at the foot of the page. See the physical storage Chapter 8 for a detailed description of record and page layouts.

A bigger problem with small records is that current SQL Server locking is at the page level which means that, the smaller the record, the more records are locked by a sin-gle maintenance statement. When small records are extremely active an update of one record will block most other transactions from accessing the data. Active tables with small records are effectively single threading bottlenecks which should be eliminated.

How do I ensure less records per page?

Pad the record with dummy columns to the required size, e.g., pad to more than
        half the page size to achieve one record per page; or,

Set the maximum number of rows per page in System 11.

System 11 has a *max_rows_per_page* which can be set at the table level to define a max-imum number of rows in a page for the life of the table.

Prior to System 11, the record had to be padded with dummy columns to make it greater than half the page size and force one record per page—or whatever multiple is suitable. When doing this make sure that you use **char(255) not null** columns as this allows you to input one character to achieve the maximum size of the column. The col-umn has to be not null as columns allowing nulls are held as variable length columns:

a null is actually held as a variable length column of length 0. Fixed length *char* columns occupy the fixed length irrespective of the value input; variable length *varchar* columns occupy the input length. Unless you want to input 255 characters for each dummy column, use char not null.

Is my record too large?

It can be, the maximum record size is 1962 bytes.

As mentioned earlier, the amount of wasted space is the crucial factor here. Anything just over half a page will waste space and should be looked at carefully. A 1250 byte record uses 1 page per record; 100 records use 200 Kb and require 100 I/Os for a table scan. If you could cut the record into 2 of 625 bytes then there are 3 records per page, i.e., 34 pages, saving 132 Kb of storage and 66 I/Os on a table scan. Even on these simple volumes the saving is significant.

However, if the record is close to the maximum size, there is little benefit in reducing it as the benefits are minimal.

How do I make the record smaller?

Split it into more than one record; or,

Use smaller datatypes whenever possible; or,

Codify the large character columns.

Split the record

The optimum solution is to split the large record into two or more smaller records each containing the primary key so that the original record may be reconstructed. This is illustrated in Figure 3.5. This segmentation technique is often referred to as **overnormalization** because already normalized tables are further reduced for physical design purposes. The Sybase training material refers to this as **vertical partitioning**.

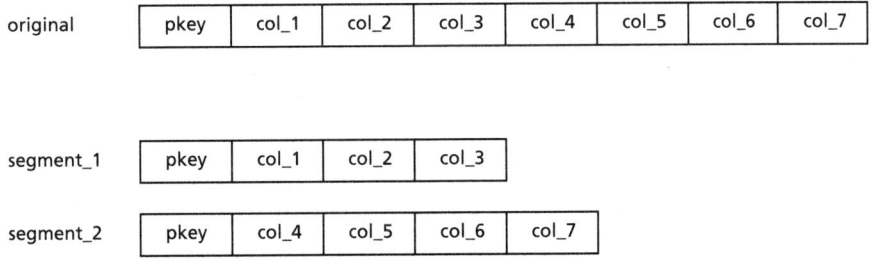

Figure 3.5 *Record segmented vertically into two*

The principal purpose of segmentation is to ensure that each segment may be updated independently. This means there is no joining required to update the data since such updates in SQL Server have a high performance overhead. An update containing a join is always executed as a **deferred** update which requires multiple passes of the data records and the transaction log. This is discussed more fully in Chapter 6. Achieving the segmentation is usually carried out with one of the following approaches: static versus dynamic, application usage or a split by datatype.

Static vs. Dynamic

The columns are split based on usage with all frequently updated (dynamic) columns placed in one record and the low volatility (static) columns in another record. This helps to keep all updates as single records although the inquiries often require columns from both records.

A typical example of this is the person style record, e.g., customer, where there is often a simple static:dynamic split based on the static name and address data and the more dynamic value type columns such as credit_limit, or date_last_ordered. A segmentation of:

```
original          static:dynamic segmentation
cust_no           cust_no              cust_no
name              name                 credit_limit
address           address              date_last_ordered
town              town                 max_order_value
county            county               .
.                 .                    .
.                 .
```

directs most updates to the dynamic table and most inquiries (e.g., for joins to customer name) to the static table. It is extremely unlikely that an update will hit both tables, so the only drawback of this method is the join to merge the two tables together again. Fortunately,, this vertical segmentation is easily hidden from the application/user by a view which contains the join of the two tables on primary key.

Application Usage

The columns are split based on who is using them, with all columns used by application 1 in record 1, by application 2 in record 2, and so on. This helps to minimize the number of occasions when a process requires data from more than one record, but often requires columns other than the primary key to be placed in more than one record. For example, a descriptive column may be required in all records with obvious problems in maintaining data validity if all applications have update rights.

A typical example of this is a product type record where several applications access and update different columns of the record.

```
original product    stock          accounts       design
part_no             part_no        part_no        part_no
description         description     description    description
stock_locn          stock_locn     std_cost       drawing_no
stock_holding       stock_holding  selling_price  parent_part_no
std_cost            .              .              .
selling_price       .              .              .
drawing_no
parent_part_no
.
.
```

This application type split often creates independent tables with little, if any, cross table processing. However, there are often columns—such as description above—which all applications require access to and therefore must be repeated on all segmented tables. This requires application control to ensure that only one occurrence is updated and that this is then replicated on a read-only basis to the other applications. In the above segmentation it is reasonable that the design table is the update source with the others being read only for description.

Again, any cross table access is easily implemented by a view which joins on primary key.

Datatype

The record may also be split by removing columns of specific datatypes into another record. An obvious example of this is **text** where SQL Server achieves this automatically by holding the text column in a separate page chain linked to the parent record via a pointer in the parent. Large *varchar* columns are also likely candidates for this as maximum size reduction is achieved. Apart from *text*, this approach is least useful as there is, little consideration of the frequency of single record updates or of multiple record inquiries.

In all of the above, the decision to segment the record must take into account the overhead of recreating the original record via a join on the primary key. This is extremely important in updates, as a deferred update is carried out when the update contains a join and this can require a significant amount of additional disk accessing.

Use smaller datatypes

Using datatypes which use less space, e.g., *smallint* for *int*, *smalldatetime* for *datetime*, *real* for *double precision* may be sufficient initially, especially if the record is just too large, but this may simply delay value range problems until later. The exception to this is the use of *text* for large character columns. Although the overall space requirement is increased—*text* uses 2 Kb minimum—the text pointer on the record itself is 16 bytes, providing a saving depending on the length of the column, but often in the region of hundreds of characters. The use of *text* does have processing problems as explained earlier, so often it is not a feasible solution.

Codify columns

There may be the opportunity to codify some columns and reduce a large character column to a few characters. Usually these will have already been codified with supporting look-up tables in the logical design and again the saving is often not sufficient. This approach also increases the join activity as the original value will need to be displayed in most inquiries which will require a join on the code value.

Summary

In mapping the entities to tables there are a few size restrictions which you must conform to:

- An integral number of records per 2 Kb page
- The maximum record size of 1962 bytes

- No minimum record size but the maximum number of records per page is 256

- A fixed length record has 4 bytes overhead

- A variable length record has the 4 bytes fixed overhead plus 2 bytes and 1 byte per variable column. (This is slightly inaccurate as the adjust table at the end of the data record has its own overhead bytes depending on the number of adjust tables, but the above is normally sufficiently accurate.)

Small records also suffer from page level locking and it is sometimes advisable to reduce the number of records per page by padding the record with large *char* columns. This is a normal technique to achieve record level locking by padding the record to more than half the page size when the page will be able to contain only one record. Records larger than the maximum record size and large records which waste a high percentage of space in the page may be reduced in size by segmenting the record or by reducing the column size with smaller datatypes.

4

Table Size Considerations

This chapter discusses overnormalization techniques to reduce the size of very large tables. The problem of large index keys and the use of surrogate keys is also covered.

Is my table too small?

No, but you can waste space as SQL Server allocates space to tables in units of 8 pages, i.e., 16 Kb.

There is no lower limit to a table size. One record of one column is sufficient. There is a space waste consideration but you may choose to ignore this.

All space allocated to tables is allocated in units of 8 pages (16 Kb) called extents. A table with one row has 8 pages allocated to it. The space is bound to the table and cannot be used by any other object, so if the table never grows beyond 1 page you are permanently wasting 14 Kb. If there are many such tables you may find it useful to merge them into one larger table to save space. Consider 8 look up tables each with one page of data. The total space allocated will be 8*8*2 Kb, i.e., 128 Kb. Each table is also likely to have an index to enforce uniqueness and each index is a separate object which is allocated an extent. So the reserved space for the 8 look-up tables is 256 Kb. With only 1 page per object, the wasted space is 224 Kb. Merging these into one table—with an addition to the primary key of a table identifier—will use 1–2 extents of data depending on how the records fit into the page and 1 extent for the index, giving a maximum allocation of 48 Kb, or a saving of 208 Kb.

Of course the access to the look-up table is slightly more complicated with a table identifier required in addition to the record primary key. You decide if it is worth it: I do not think so.

Is my table too large?

This is unlikely as the maximum database size is $2^{31}-1$ pages; the maximum size of a device is 2^{24} pages and the maximum number of device fragments per database is 128. You may also be limited in the device size by operating system disk file limits, e.g,. 2 Gb in Unix. However, there are some performance and administration considerations for large tables. This may impose an upper limit which provides realistic processing times for administration functions such as dump and load and creating indexes.

In practice, the database limit of 2 Gb * 2 Kb means that there is no limit to the size of the table. The table size does not include text/image columns so it is difficult to reach the upper limit. You may be constrained by the maximum operating system file size limit—especially for disk dumping purposes. In Unix, the maximum file limit is 2Gb which will restrict the database size if you dump to disk, since the maximum number of dump stripes is 32. This will give you an effective upper limit of 32*2Gb for the database. Since most database objects can be spread across multiple operating system files, this is not really a problem.

The problem of large tables is more related to performance and the time it takes to process all of the data or a large portion of the data. Match up the response time requirements of your queries with the number of pages that have to be read to satisfy the command. If the record is 200 bytes and there are one million records, we have a table size of 100,000 pages. Serial reading of this amount of data with look ahead is unlikely to get the time below three minutes. Range based inquiries accessing 10% of the data will require double-digit figure seconds just for disk I/O. If all of this is unacceptable from a performance viewpoint, you are going to have to reduce the size of the table.

Administration of the table will often require you to limit its size. The ability to reorganize the data or to rebuild a clustered index requires free space of at least the data size and normally greater than the data size. To recreate a clustered index the minimum recommendation is free space of 120% of the table size and the comfortable recommendation is 150%. This is a lot of space to have unused in the database just to support an index rebuild. Of course you can always unload and reload with *bcp* but this will suffer from a serious elapsed time problem because you will be running "slow" bcp as the indexes are still defined on the table.

Usually, it is better to keep the table sizes within a maximum which you can support by the required response times and index build requirements.

How do I make my table smaller?

Break it down into several smaller tables: either vertical segmentation by splitting the record or horizontal segmentation by splitting the table.

It's unlikely that fiddling with the record size will make much difference here as the size of the table is usually caused by a large number of records. So segmenting the table is the normal approach. This may be done vertically to make each table smaller by making the record smaller, or horizontally to make each table smaller by having less records in each table.

Vertical Segmentation

This is identical to the row segmentation discussed in Chapter 3 and will be carried out based on one of the criteria: static versus dynamic, application usage or datatype. Again, the principal criteria is to avoid multiple table updates in the one SQL transaction. This is a useful type of segmentation as the original record may be reconstructed in a view using a join which can hide the underlying segmentation from the user. And as the underlying segmentation is hidden in a view you can easily alter it as the physical design changes with minimum impact on the application code.

Horizontal Segmentation

This leaves the record intact but splits the table based on a column value. The obvious column to use is the primary key so that an even distribution of records is achieved between the segments. For example, place all even primary keys in table_1 and all odd primary keys in table_2. Primary key is advantageous as the value should not change, so the record will remain in one table.

Choosing a meaningful column for horizontal segmentation—such as location—may be an excellent solution from a data distribution aspect but it may not give an even split of the record population. This will leave you with the same problem recurring early in the life of the system as the data volumes grow. You should certainly avoid segmenting on a column whose value is updated frequently as this will cause the record to move between tables.

Often the best choice for horizontal segmentation is based on the usage of the data on a historical basis. Large tables are often caused by large amounts of historical data which is mainly unused and can be split into a separate table which is seldom accessed. An application requirement to retain 10 years information may be satisfied by keeping the recent 2 years an one active table and the older 8 years in a relatively unused table.

The principal problem with horizontal table segmentation is that a union is required to put the original table back together again. This is not a problem in itself as the union operator is supported in SQL, but unfortunately SQL Server does not support union in a view. This means that you cannot protect the application code or the user from the physical segmentation. If further segmentation is necessary as the table grows, you will have to alter application code to support it.

Is there an optimum number of tables to access in one command?

Yes: one. Of course you cannot avoid joins in a relational design but try to keep the number of tables in the join to six or less.

The join is evaluated by a series of nested loops and the more tables you have in the join, the more complicated this can become and the longer it can take. This complexity is not just relevant to the execution but also has an effect on the optimization of the command. To reduce the number of table combinations that the optimizer has to consider, by default SQL Server does not consider all table combinations in a join but limits the number of tables in each tested combination to 4. The best first table for each group of 4 tables is found and this process is repeated with the remaining tables until the complete join sequence is determined. Therefore, it is quite feasible not to get the optimum join sequence when the number of tables is greater than 4 as the optimizer may not check every valid combination. I have seen this effect with 6 tables, so be careful at this level.

System 11 allows you to vary the number of tables grouped together by the optimizer when evaluating join plans. This is a good idea if you suspect a problem but 4 at a time is a reasonable default as the more combinations that the optimizer has to check, the longer it will take it to work out the execution plan. You cannot define a maximum time for optimization in SQL Server; all permissible combinations will be checked.

How do I reduce the number of tables in one command?

Denormalize data by duplicating it onto one or more tables.

The approach is to identify tables which supply one or a few columns of data and to duplicate or denormalize this data onto another table in the command. There are three principal methods of denormalization to achieve this:

- Repeating a column in another table

- Creating summary columns in a header table

- Using repeating groups instead of a separate table

Repeating a column in another table

Used when there is a look up for a single column value. In this case, the trade-off is between the savings of not doing the join and the increased maintenance of the duplicate data. Clearly, the more static the denormalized data the better.

A simple example of this is reading an orders table and showing the customer name for each order. With two tables this requires:

```
select o.ord_no, c.name, ...
    from orders o, customer c
    where o.cust_no = c.cust_no
```

with 10,000 orders this requires at least 10,000 logical I/Os to the customer table to retrieve the name for each order.

If we denormalize the customer name to the orders table we reduce the inquiry to a single table scan:

```
select ord_no, name from orders
```

The clear saving in access to the customer table has to be balanced against the additional maintenance processing when a customer name changes. Not a serious problem in this example but, if you adopt this type of denormalization, make sure that you choose static columns to denormalize. Also remember that the denormalization is specific to the actual SQL and all changes to the application processing will necessitate a review of the denormalization. Simply altering the above requirement to include the customer address in the inquiry requires a join to the customer table to retrieve the address. This negates the denormalization of the name. There are two choices: denormalize the address as well as the name or remove the denormalized name and go back to the join. The choice is not that simple as it introduces a further problem of denormalization—the increase in size of the target record.

Take our above example of the orders table with sizes of:

```
orders record:              150 bytes
name column:                20 bytes average
address column:             40 bytes average
number of orders records:   10,000
```

The number of pages occupied by the orders table is:

	rec size	recs/page	# of pages
original	150	13	770
plus name	170	11	910
plus name and address	210	9	1112

The denormalized name and address has increased the size of the table by about 45% which means that range-based inquiries on the denormalized orders table which read multiple pages will take up to 45% longer. Now you will have to measure the performance gain of the denormalization against both the maintenance overhead and the additional I/O required for the larger records and larger table. Do not neglect this increase in table size when you consider simple denormalization of a column into another table.

Creating summary values in header tables

Used to eliminate the aggregation of multiple record values by holding the aggregate value in a header record. This has a significant advantage as it does not just reduce the number of tables in the join but also reduces the number of records accessed to create the aggregate. Again, the savings must be balanced against the extra effort to maintain the aggregate value but the reduction in records accessed is normally sufficient to make this denormalization a clear winner.

Consider the inquiry which displays the product records with the total quantity on order from the order item records:

```
select p.prod_no, p.description, sum(i.item_qty)
     from product p, order_item i
     where p.prod_no = i.prod_no
     group by p.prod_no, p.description
```

The execution sequence depends on the sizes of the tables, but assuming that there are more items than products, it will probably be executed as a scan of product with a look up of the order_item for each product. If we consider 5000 products and 40,000 items the simple calculation is an average of 8 items per product which gives at least 8*5000 logical I/Os to the item table.

By creating summary data on the product table, we eliminate the order_item I/O and reduce the SQL to a simple scan of the product table.

```
select prod_no, description, total_qty
     from product
```

Note that the aggregation is also removed by this approach but you may have to introduce an order by on prod_no to achieve the same display sequence as the original group by. If this is the case, you should be wary of having to include the aggregation savings to prove your summary value denormalization. However, the savings— 8*5000 logical I/Os in this case—are normally sufficient to ignore any group by versus order by I/O debates.

As with any denormalization you need to balance the savings against the maintenance overheads. In this case, the increase in size of the target record is not normally important. The denormalization this time is being done on a very volatile column and you will have to ensure that you check the overhead of an extra update for every insert and delete to the source table and for most updates. However, it is only the one extra table update and this is not normally as significant as the select savings. But please check it based on your specific application processing and volumetrics; it might be the little additional processing which causes your update to exceed performance requirements.

In general, this technique is widely used as it saves considerable I/O in the inquiries. This denormalization is also evident in covered indexes where the column being aggregated is added to an index already being used. The optimizer is then able to use the index without accessing the data to calculate the aggregate.

Using a repeating group instead of a separate table

Often called **vector data**, this does not necessarily reduce the number of tables in the join but reduces the number of reads to a table by combining multiple records into one large record. It may be used to combine records from different tables but it is more common to combine several records in the same table. A good example of this is calendar-based information such as quantity per month which would be one record per month in a relational model. These could easily be combined into one record with a separate column per month.

```
normalized data
        account(account no, description, ...)
        monthly_costs(account no, month no, cost_value)

vector data
        account(account no, description,
                        jan_cost_value, feb_cost_value, ... dec_cost_value)
```

This reduces the number of disk accesses required to retrieve the cost data and also tends to reduce the amount of processing required to maintain the cost values. However, balance this against the increase in size of the record which can be considerable for vector data.

Also, this is a very specific design solution which is almost impossible to hide from the application/user, so any alteration in the number of occurrences of the data will require a table redefinition and rebuild with potential major code changes required in the application.

Clearly, there are processing problems as SQL is not structured to handle such data easily—although T-SQL CASE statements are being introduced to help here. You need to be careful that the number of occurrences in the repeating group does not increase frequently over the life of the table as this will require application changes. The high performance SQL Chapter 20 has a discussion of characteristic functions which can help when processing vector data.

How big should a key column be?

As small as possible. The maximum size of an index entry is 256 bytes.

The expectation is that a key column—primary or foreign—will take part in an index. Indexes are most efficient with small columns as they reduce the size of the index entry.

This reduces the number of pages in the index which reduces the number of index levels. The size of the index column also determines the number of index statistics entries which has a direct effect on the accuracy of the index statistics. A full treatment of SQL server indexing is given in Chapter 5, SQL Server Indexing. An index entry is the combination of a record or page pointer and the related column value. The size of the column value is the obvious variable and the larger the column size, the larger the index entry. The larger the index entry, the fewer the number of index entries per page, the greater the number of index pages and the greater the number of index levels.

Let's look at the extremes of an integer key and a char(255) key with a non-clustered index on one million records.

```
                                                       integer   char(255)
leaf level index record size (7 byte overhead)            11         262
number of index records per page (2016/record size)     183           7
number of leaf level pages (1,000,000/records per page) 5464      142857
number of intermediate level 1 pages                      30       20409
number of intermediate level 2 pages                                2916
number of intermediate level 3 pages                                 417
number of intermediate level 4 pages                                  60
number of intermediate level 5 pages                                   9
number of intermediate level 6 pages                                   2
root level                                                 1           1

                   total number of pages               5678      166671

                   total number of index levels           3           8
```

The more records you access the more significant the overhead of the large index column becomes. To access one record the integer column index requires 3 index level accesses compared with 8 index level accesses for the char(255) column. To access 100 records the integer column requires (root + 1 intermediate level + 1 or 2 leaf pages) whereas the char(255) index column requires (root + 6 intermediate levels + 15 leaf pages). Because of the lower number of index records per leaf page the overhead of the larger column increases as the number of records retrieved increases.

The column size also affects the index statistics. Each index has one set of column value distribution statistics which are used by the optimizer to estimate how many rows to expect from the specific column values supplied in a where clause. The statistics for an index are collected in a 2 Kb page by sampling and recording the column values at known intervals in the table. The smaller the column size, the more statistics entries will fit into a page, the more statistics samples can be made on the data and the more accurate are the statistics. A nonclustered index will not be used if the optimizer estimates that the number of rows returned is greater than the number of pages in the table. Therefore, the ability to use a nonclustered index is significantly influenced by the accuracy of the index statistics and the smaller the index column, the more accurate these are.

Is there a limit to the number of columns in a key field?

You can have as many columns as you like in the key field at the logical design stage but there is a limit of 16 columns in an index.

If you intend to index the key you must stick to the 16-column limit. The size of the index entry is also important as discussed previously and having too many columns in the index can make the index entry too large. Note that the index statistics accuracy are not directly affected by the size of a compound index as the index statistics are collected on the first column of the compound index only. The space and response time considerations of large index entries are often compounded in this case when the key columns are for a primary key which is present as a foreign key in several other tables.

How do I reduce the number of columns in a key?

Create a **surrogate key** to replace the compound key.

Reduce the compound key to a single column surrogate of an internally generated sequential number. This can be allocated by application code or by using the **identity** property in SQL Server. This approach saves space on the records and reduces the index entry size with the related I/O savings discussed previously.

The surrogate key is a physical design feature for internal use only but can assume meaning if you can get it accepted by the user of the system as a real identifier of the records. This is not uncommon with users being well used to such surrogates as a customer identifier or a product identifier to replace large and possibly complicated descriptive identifiers. If you can persuade the users that your internal identifiers are just as necessary and useful as their existing identifiers, the surrogate becomes meaningful and can be used for access. When the user does not accept the surrogate it remains fully internal and you will have to provide internal look-up tables to cross reference the real key input by the user with the internal surrogate. This causes additional I/O to locate the record, so make sure that you factor this into any savings you use to justify the surrogate. If all you are doing is primary key access, a compound key can be just as efficient as the internal surrogate. The savings in using a surrogate key is always related to the occasions it occurs as a foreign key in another table. The more foreign key occurrences you have, the more important it is to introduce a surrogate key.

A common problem with most database designs is that they are hierarchical by nature and the propagation of the key information down the hierarchy to create primary keys often creates large composite primary keys at the lower levels of the hierarchy.

```
orders(order no, order_date, ...)
order_item(order no, product no, order_qty, ...)
order_delivery(order no, product no, delivery date, delivery_qty ...)
```

By the time we have reached the third level in the hierarchy we have a 3-column composite primary key and it is worth considering introducing a surrogate key for the order_delivery table. The main consideration is saving on space in the indexes and in the tables where the composite key occurs as a foreign key.

If we arbitrarily choose *int* datatype for the order_no and product_no and *datetime* for the delivery_date we have a primary key on order_delivery of 16 bytes. Replacing this with an *int* datatype surrogate key saves 12 bytes for every foreign key occurrence. All we need is 100,000 rows to save 12*100000: 1.2 million bytes. A larger database of 50 million occurrences of the 12 byte saving gives a 600 Mb saving. Such savings are not to be ignored.

We should also consider the saving in index pages and levels to be accessed by use of a surrogate key. However, I find that the reduction in index accesses argument is less important than the space saving and it is normally better to justify surrogate keys on space saving. Using the above 12 byte reduction on a 1 million row table, a non-clustered index would be sized as:

```
16 byte primary key
leaf level index entry 16+7    (key size + index overhead)
non-leaf index entry 16+11

number of leaf level entries per page:              2016/23 = 87
number of intermediate level entries per page:      2016/27 = 74
```

```
number of leaf pages:                              1,000,000/87 = 11495
number of intermediate level 1 pages:              11495/74 = 156
number of intermediate level 2 pages:              156/74 = 2
root level:                                        2/74 = 1
total pages = 11654 in 4 levels
4 byte primary key
leaf level index entry 4+7
non-leaf index entry 4+11
number of leaf level entries per page:             2016/11 = 183
number of intermediate level entries per page:     2016/15 = 134
number of leaf pages:                              1,000,000/183 = 5465
number of intermediate level 1 pages:              5465/134 = 41
root level:                                        41/134 = 1
total pages = 5507 in 3 levels
```

This saves only one level—which is not that important as the larger index size was unfortunate in the two page intermediate level. But a saving of 6147 pages, i.e., 12 Mb is not to be ignored. You need to be a little careful with the index argument as the reduced index size gives more index records per page with more of them locked per access. This can increase the incidence of deadlock in SQL Server which you may need to consider carefully when creating surrogate keys.

The index deadlock situation occurs when one process is sequentially reading the data via index 1 and another process is inserting/updating records via index 2. In this case, the shared lock (SLOCK) will remain on the index page until all records referenced by the index page have been read. If the update process wants to insert an index entry to the SLOCKed index page, there is the possibility of deadlock. This is illustrated in Figure 4.1

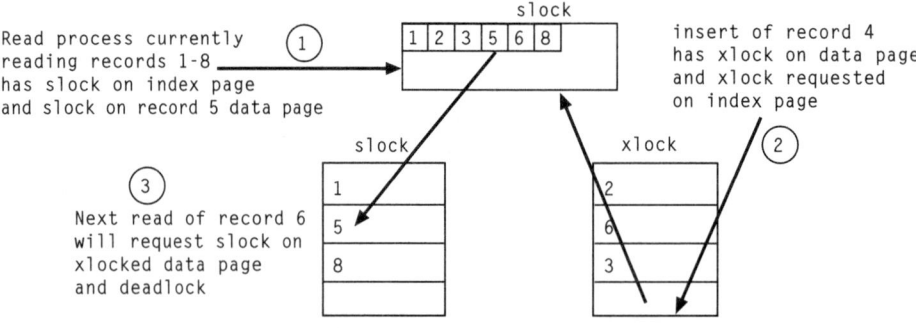

***Figure 4.1** Index processing deadlock*

The read process has an SLOCK on its index page and is reading record 5. A process inserts record 4 and needs to insert an index record for record 4. Therefore, the insert process requests an exclusive lock (XLOCK) on the index page and is blocked by the read process SLOCK. The read process then moves on to the next record in the index—record 6—and requests an SLOCK on the data page for record 6 but is blocked by the insert process XLOCK. This creates a deadlock which is resolved by the server rolling back the process with the least amount of CPU time.

Summary

Any maximum allowable operating system file size does not impose a realistic limit on database or table sizes. However, considerations of the time taken to dump/restore; reorganize data and rebuild indexes will often make very large table processing difficult. It makes administration sense to keep table sizes to a manageable limit. The limit will depend on the physical machine configuration which will constrain the number of processes that you can perform in parallel. Because of these administration limits, you will often want to split the table into several fragments either horizontally or vertically to reduce the physical size and also to reduce multi-user contention when dealing with a single very large resource.

Although table segmentation can be useful with a large table, the relational model usually creates a large number of small to medium size tables. This creates the problem that joins are required to retrieve most data and some of these joins can have many tables in them. The more tables in a command to retrieve a set of data, the more I/O that has to be carried out. Often it is advisable to copy data between tables to reduce the number of tables to be joined. This denormalization has three principal methods:

- Repeating a column in another table

- Creating summary data in a header table

- Using repeating instead of a separate table

The size of a key column can also be important when it is used as a foreign key in many tables. A large key column, or multiple columns in a large composite key, will increase the size of the index record. This requires more space to hold the index and will mean more levels in the index, requiring more I/O to locate the index record. When the large key is used in many tables the space consideration can be significant and it is advisable to replace the large key with a small, single-column surrogate key.

PART **II**

SQL SERVER
INDEXING

Indexing is the principal method of providing high performance for an application. However, it has obvious maintenance overheads and there are a number of situations in which the indexes do not function as you expect them to. This section gives a detailed description of SQL Server indexes, the rules for their selection, maintenance overheads, and then troubleshoots the normal problems that you can get with indexes.

Types of Index

This chapter describes the types of index available in SQL Server—clustered and non-clustered—and then discusses the differences between them and when to choose one instead of the other.

What is an index?

An index is a separate object, defined on a table, which allows access to individual records without having to scan the complete table.

Without an index on a table, all of the data has to be read from the beginning to the end just to locate one record. The full read of the table is called a **table scan** and requires one logical read for every data page in the table. Even if the first record you read is the one you require, there is no way to determine if there is another record of the same value later in the table, until you have read all of the records. The scan of the table is facilitated by a forward and backward page chain held in the page header as illustrated in Figure 5.1.

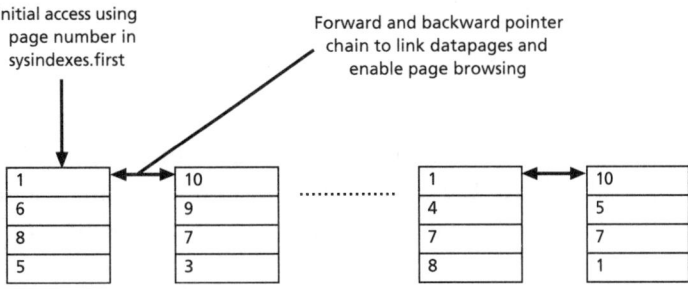

Figure 5.1 Data page chain

The first page of the unindexed table is held in the system table **sysindexes** in the column **first** and the last page of the table in the column **root**. A partitioned table has multiple last pages, one per partition, so the **sysindexes** columns **first** and **root** are meaningless. The partitioned table information is held in the system table **sysparti-tions**. The first page of each partition is held in the column **firstpage** and the partition control page which points to the last page of each partition is held in the column **con-trolpage**. The partition control page is discussed more fully in Chapter 8. All pages in the table can be browsed by following the next page pointers in the page header. Although the page chain has previous pointers there is no current (11.0) ability in SQL Server to scan backwards through the table. Without an index you need to read every record in the table to locate the record you want. With an index on a column you can supply a column value which is used to read the index to obtain the record address and then to access the record directly.

The general approach of all indexing techniques is to create a separate object which contains an index row for every data record. This index row comprises the index column value and the address of the record containing the column value. The index is then accessed on the column value to obtain the record address which is used to access the record directly. The index entries are held in sequence of the index key values to facilitate access. The search knows when to stop as it knows when there are no more records for the supplied value.

There are various indexing techniques but the most common is B-tree which is the only type of indexing supported by SQL Server. SQL Server actually uses the standard B-tree (called the **nonclustered** index) and a variation of this (called the **clustered** index) which still uses the B-tree structure but stores the data differently.

The manner in which the index entries are held minimizes the number of accesses required to find a record. In SQL Server, the minimum number of reads to find a record via an index is 3.

- One to read the system table sysindexes to find the start of the index

- One to read the index entry to get the address pointer to the record

- One to read the record via the pointer

This means that there is no difference between an index access and a table scan when the data in the table occupies up to three pages. In this case, the complete table can be read in as many logical I/Os as it takes to read one record. The index is not considered useful since the table scan is just as fast. Of course, the index may still be required to enforce uniqueness.

Indexes are normally created on columns when you wish to access a few number of records and you wish to avoid a table scan to do this. The SQL command:

```
select name, address, city, state
      from customer
      where name = 'kirkwood'
```

will benefit from an index on name as this index may then be used to retrieve the records for name = 'kirkwood'. There may be more than one row for the input value: the indexing software handles multiple records for an index column value. If you wish to enforce one row per index column value then you can specify the index as being unique.

You may have multiple columns in an index. If the above select statement returned multiple rows and you further restricted the query with a first_name as:

```
select name, address, city, state
      from customer
      where name = 'kirkwood'
      and first_name = 'john'
```

then it would be advantageous to pass the additional restriction into the index by creating an index on (name, first_name). Indexes are structured to reduce the number of accesses required to access one record. The fewer the number of records you retrieve via the index, the more efficient the index is.

What index choices do I have?

SQL Server supports two methods of indexing:

Clustered B-tree   A sparse index with the data records held in the sequence of the index key

Nonclustered B-tree   A standard dense B-tree with record pointers held in the sequence of the index key

B-tree

The B-tree index is a tree-like structure with a single entry point (the **root node**), branching from this to subsequent levels of increasing population through the **leaf level** which contains the record pointers. This is illustrated in Figure 5.2. A feature of the tree structure of the B-tree is that access to any record requires the same number of I/Os. The actual number of I/Os to a record depends on the number of index levels, which is based on the number of data records and the size of the index key. But for a single index, the number of I/Os required to retrieve a record is constant regardless of the index value supplied.

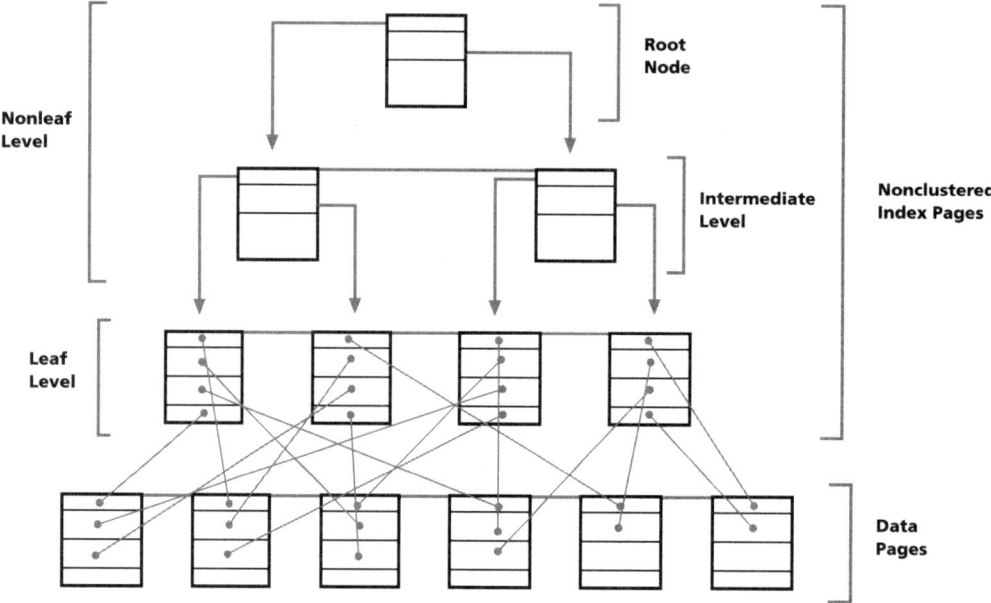

Figure 5.2 *Standard B-tree*

The data rows are stored in a heap fashion in the data pages with no explicit sequencing to the rows. The B-tree creates an index leaf level which contains one index entry for each data record and maintains this leaf level in sequence of the index key values. The leaf level entries are a combination of the index key value and the address of the record for that key value. The leaf level entries are then indexed until the index level is composed of a single index page, the root node. As the leaf level entries are in sequence of the index column values, the non-leaf levels do not need to point to every leaf level entry but only to the first entry in each leaf level page. The non-leaf entries are a combination of the key value of the first entry in the lower level page and the address of that page. Note that in SQL Server, the non-leaf entries also contain the record address of the first record in the page pointed to. This is illustrated in Figure 5.3.

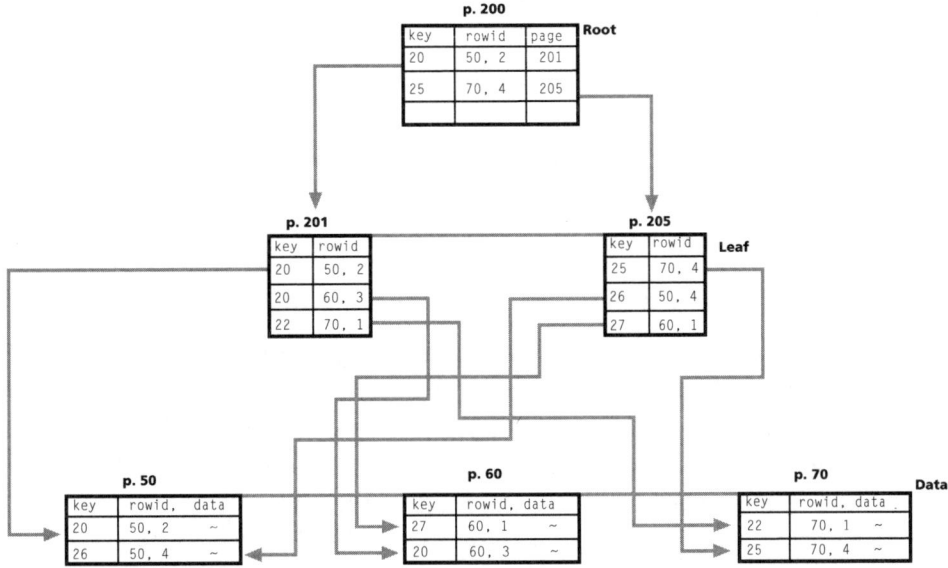

Figure 5.3 *Pointer detail in standard B-tree*

Nonclustered index

This is a standard B-tree as described above. The data rows are in no particular sequence but the leaf level entries are in order of the index key values and contain row_id pointers to each record in the data pages. Because of the leaf level key value sequence, the non-leaf levels need to contain page pointers only based on the first key value in each leaf level page. As the leaf level is maintained in sequence, page 201 above will always contain rows for key values between 20 and 24, and page 205 will always contain rows for key values equal to or greater than 25. Therefore, the non-leaf levels need only point to the first key value in the leaf level page. However, in the SQL Server non-leaf nodes, although only the page pointer is necessary, the index entry also contains the row_id of the first row in the lower level page. This is true for all non-leaf level entries.

The leaf level contains one index record for every data record. This means that access via the index is not always going to be as efficient as a table scan. To locate records 22–26 in Figure 5.3, the following accesses are required.

- Read sysindexes to locate the root page number for the index

- Read the root page to determine the page number of the next level which contains the first record required—record 22

- Read this page which is the leaf level supplying the record pointer of record 22

- Read record 22

- Now the leaf level may be browsed horizontally to obtain the record pointer of the next record—record 25

- Read record 25

- Repeat leaf level:data record reads until all records have been read

Note that once the leaf level has been reached, ranges of records may be retrieved without retraversing the index vertically as the index values are held in sequence of the index key in the leaf level. This is a standard approach to B-tree access of horizontal browsing as often as possible at any level of the index. Each level of the index is linked with a set of pointers in the header of the index page.

Also note that the number of accesses required to locate records 22–26 is:

```
sysindexes + root + Σ intermediate levels + Σ (leaf + record)
```

```
In our example we get        1+1+0+3*2 = 8
```

This is 5 logical I/Os greater than the number of pages in the table (3). When this happens, the optimizer will simply read all of the pages in the table via a table scan which is quicker. This is a very important point when using a nonclustered index. Because the nonclustered index has one index entry per record, it is possible when reading a range of records to generate more I/Os via the index than is required to do a table scan. When this happens the optimizer will always choose to ignore the index and carry out a table scan.

A nonclustered index is advantageous only when the number of records being retrieved is less than the number of pages in the table.

The number of records being retrieved is determined by two factors:

- The selectivity of the *where* clauses, i.e., the range of records being retrieved

- The inherent selectivity of the data, i.e., the amount of duplication

When either of these causes many records to be retrieved, the effectiveness of the nonclustered index is negated. The break point at which this happens is determined by the number of rows in the data page. The discussion does not take all extreme situations into account and ignores index page accesses. You may feel the latter assumption is too loose as it ignores the leaf level accesses but the point is to provide a simple rule of thumb, not a 100% accurate formula.

The data record extremes are uninteresting since with only 1 record per page, the index access will always be less than a table scan (comparing only the data page accesses). With only one page in the table, the table scan will always be better than an index access. The interest is for normal size records: with 2 records per page you will table scan at 50% of the rows; with 4 records per page, 25%; with 8 records, 12.5% and so on. In other words, the breakpoint for choosing a table scan in preference to a non-clustered index is the reciprocal of the number of records per page.

Clustered index

The clustered index in SQL Server is an extremely interesting index. It takes the data and sorts it into the sequence of the index key values. The data pages now become the index leaf level which eliminates the need for a record pointer leaf level as in the non-clustered index. This is illustrated in Figure 5.4.

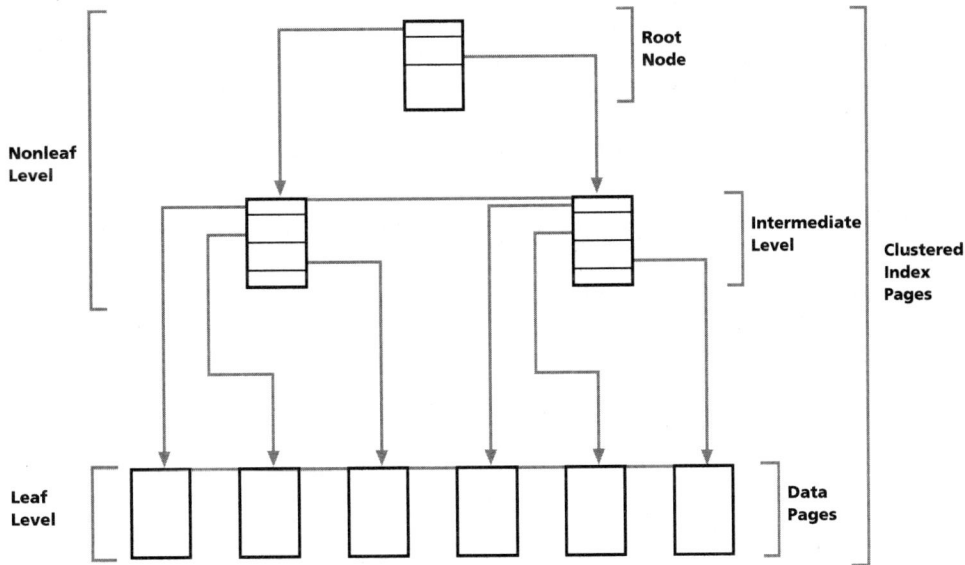

Figure 5.4 SQL Server clustered index

The data pages have become the leaf level of the index and the data records are now in sequence of the index column values. This means that all index entries are page pointers as illustrated in Figure 5.5.

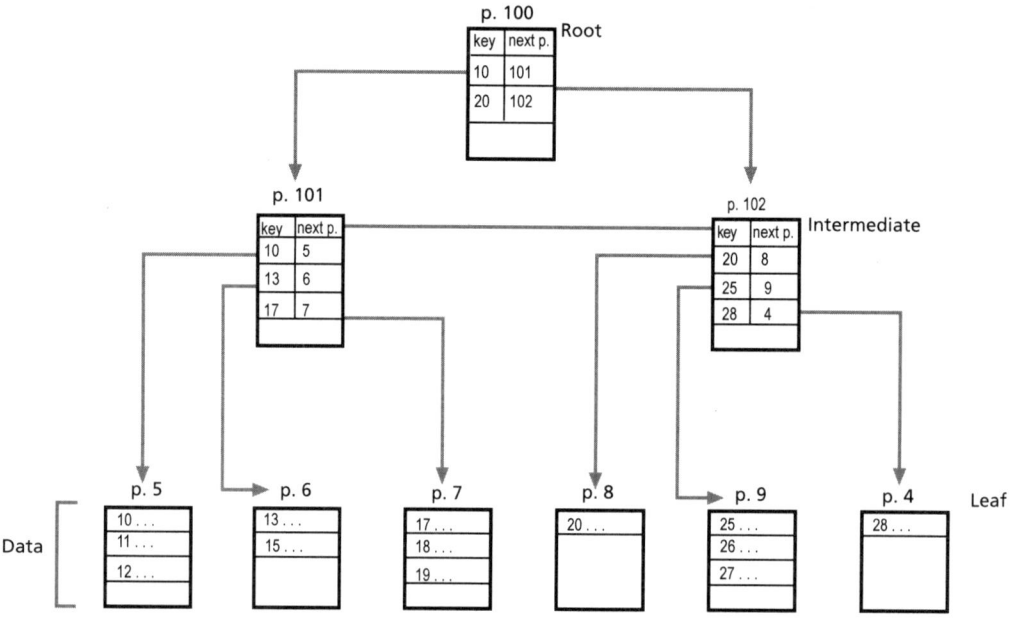

Figure 5.5 *Clustered index pointers*

This is an extremely efficient retrieval index. Once the first record has been located via the index, the data pages may be browsed to locate subsequent records. To locate records 18-25, we require the following accesses:

- Read sysindexes to locate the root page number for the index

- Read the root page to determine the page number of the next level which contains the first record required—record 18 (in this case page 101)

- Read the intermediate level to obtain the data page number containing record 18 (in this case page 7)

- Read the data page and locate record 18

- Now the data pages may be browsed horizontally to locate the other records in the range

The number of logical I/Os required is:

```
sysindexes + root + Σ intermediate levels + Σ data pages
```

```
in our example we get          1+1+1+3 = 6
```

Note that in a large table this will be less than the number of I/Os in a table scan as browsing the data pages between a start and end page will be less I/Os than reading all of the data pages in the table. Except for the extremes of small tables and reading all records in the table, the clustered index access always generates less I/Os than a table scan. This makes the clustered index a very important performance retrieval mechanism in SQL Server. This is illustrated in Figure 5.6.

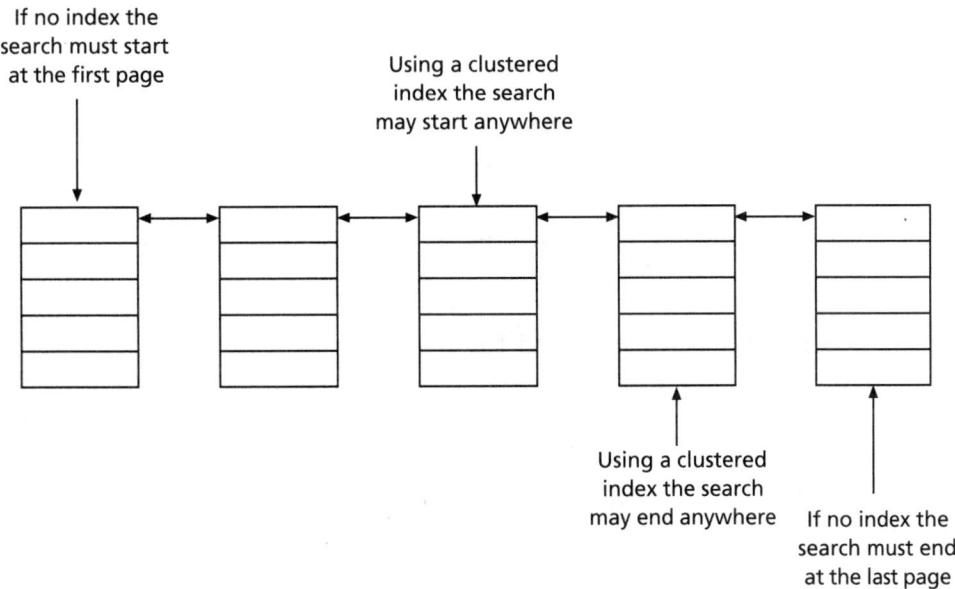

Figure 5.6 *Reduced access using the clustered index*

Quite simply, the clustered index allows access to the first qualifying record and then the end point is known because the records are in sequence of the key.

When should I use the clustered index?

The clustered index should be used for accesses which return multiple records or for inquiries which require the output in sequence of the index key.

The general principle is that a range-based inquiry on a nonclustered index may table scan. It may access more records than pages in the table but the clustered index will always be used. The number of pages accessed is always less than a table scan. Therefore, the clustered index is best considered for:

- Access on a foreign key which may have many rows associated with it

- Access based on where clauses containing the like and between keywords

- Access based on where clauses containing greater than and/or less than operators

Similarly, columns used in order by and group by clauses should be considered for the clustered index. This will avoid sorting the records as they are already in sequence.

Consider clustered indexes when the SQL contains clauses such as:

- Where name like "KIR%"

- Where price between 10 and 100

- Where qty > 10

- Where foreign_key_col = 50

- Group by product_id

- Order by order_id

Be a little careful here, especially when you define the foreign key as the clustered index. Normally, you will have done this because a key value which has many values associated with it may table scan when defined as a nonclustered index. However, you must consider the update activity on a clustered index which has many records with the same value. This will generate many occasions when the data page splitting will be done as an overflow, as described later in this chapter. This has no effect on retrievals but can seriously reduce the response time of the insert, update or delete. Access via the clustered index is to the first occurrence of the value and each record has to be checked in turn until the correct one is located. You must consider this when choosing a clustered index which has a large number of rows per index value.

If you have no specific criteria and there is only one index on the table, make it clustered by default.

When should I use the nonclustered index?

Use the nonclustered index for index columns which return a few rows per index value.

In practice, you will choose the clustered index first and make the rest nonclustered. However, only those keys which return a few rows per index value will be useful as nonclustered indexes. Therefore, the nonclustered index is best considered when the number of rows returned is small and/or the *where* clause operator restricts the number of rows returned.

Nonclustered indexes should be considered for:

* Access on primary key as this returns one row per index value and access is normally on equality

* Access based on *where* clauses containing the *equals* operator

What if I need more than one clustered index?

As the data is in sequence of the key, you can have only the one clustered index on a table. But you may be able to use **index covering** for other clustered candidates.

Because of the data sequencing requirement, you can have only one clustered index on the table. However, there are often occasions when more than one index is unsuitable as a nonclustered index and you must choose between them. In this case, you may be able to resolve the problem by covering the indexes which you cannot cluster.

Index covering is a technique used in retrievals where all of the columns in the SQL command are included in the index. The optimizer recognizes this and realizes that access to the data is not necessary as all of the required columns are in the leaf level of the index. Once the leaf level is reached, the inquiry command may be satisfied by horizontal browsing of the index leaf level without access to the data. As the leaf level of the index is in sequence of the index key, this effectively provides the facilities of clustering on the subset of data contained in the index key.

For example:

```
select prod_no, sum(qty) from order_item
       where prod_no like 'ABC%'
       group by prod_no
```

is better served by a clustered index on prod_no than by a nonclustered index because of the *like* keyword and the *group by* clause. However, if the clustered index has already been defined on other columns in the table, you can best index this command with a nonclustered covered index on (prod_no, qty). Now all of the data is in the leaf level of the index and the command will be satisfied from the leaf level of the index with any group by sort being avoided. This is actually a good index solution as prod_no is likely to be the primary key and in general will be better served by a nonclustered index. Simply adding the *qty* column to the prod_no index has satisfied both indexing requirements. In practice, the covered index is more efficient than a clustered index as the index entry will be smaller than the data record. The covered index gives a performance improvement in the ratio of index entry size to data record size.

Note that only nonclustered indexes may be covered as the clustered index does not contain an index entry for every data record in the table. To avoid accessing the data records, every data record must have an entry in the index which is possible only with the nonclustered index. Also, covering is useful only for retrievals as maintenance commands must access the data record to carry out their function.

Index covering works even when there is no search argument. This is one important occasion when an index will be used without a *where* clause in the search argument format. The simplest example of this is:

```
select count(*) from tab_1
```

This will use a nonclustered index on tab_1 to count the number of records in the table. The command will scan the complete leaf level of the index as there is no *where* clause, but this is still more efficient than a table scan. If there is more than one nonclustered index, the optimizer chooses the index with the fewest leaf pages to minimize I/Os.

Summary

SQL Server uses the B-tree style of indexing to reduce the number of logical I/Os required to retrieve a record. SQL Server uses two types of B-tree index:

Nonclustered

A standard dense B-tree index with every record having an entry in the index.

Clustered

A sparse B-tree index with the data records sorted into the index key sequence. In this case, the data pages have become the leaf level of the index. The actual index contains pointers to the first record in each only and each record in the data pages does not have an entry in the index.

After the nonclustered index is useful when a low number of records is being returned. If too many records are retrieved then the number of logical I/Os may be greater than the number of pages in the table and the optimizer will ignore the index and carry out a table scan. The clustered index is useful when many records are being retrieved in sequence of the index key; the data records are in sequence of the key and so clustered index access is always better than a table scan. Because the data records are held in sequence, only one clustered index may be defined on a table. If there are several candidates for the clustered index, index covering may be used to place every column in the select command in a nonclustered index. This makes the nonclustered index leaf level look like a clustered index to this command; the index record has all of the data columns required by the command and the records are in sequence of the selection criteria.

6

Indexing Overheads

As useful as indexes are in reducing response times, they clearly create extra work for the maintenance commands. This chapter discusses the overheads of insert/update/ delete for the two SQL Server index types. Particular attention is given to the update strategies and the overhead of clustered index page splitting.

What are the overheads of maintaining nonclustered indexes?

All inserts and deletes must update the index entries and some updates also update the index entries.

Inserts and Deletes

Every data record has an entry in a nonclustered index, so all inserts and deletes must update the index. Once a data row has been inserted or deleted its row_id is known and this is then inserted into or deleted from the appropriate leaf level index page to maintain sequence of the index column. An insert is illustrated in Figure 6.1.

An insert of record 21 is made to the appropriate data page, in this case the last page of the table. There is no clustered index defined, and the index entry is inserted to the leaf level page 201 which starts with key value 20 and ends with key value less than 25. The principal problem arises when there is no room for the new index record in the index page. In this case, the index page splits 50:50 to create two index pages as illustrated in Figure 6.2.

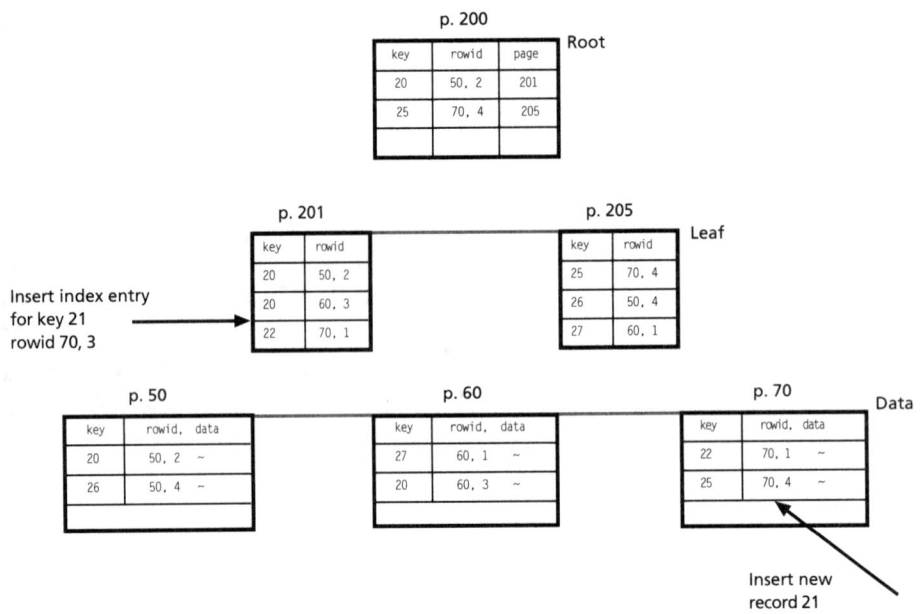

Figure 6.1 *Insert into nonclustered index*

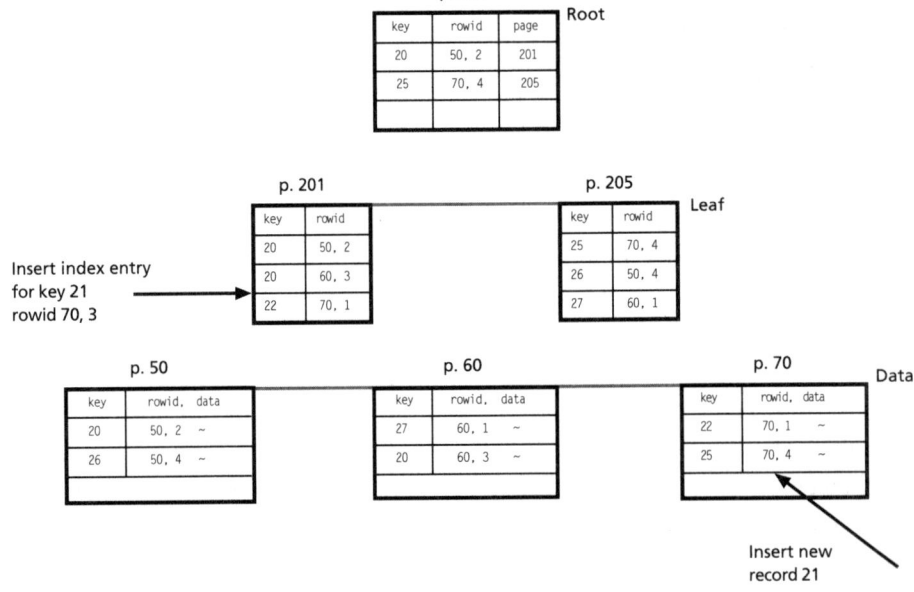

Figure 6.2 *Index page split*

The index record for key 21 has to be inserted into leaf index page 201 but there is no room. This causes the index leaf page to split on a 50:50 basis to make room for the index entry insert. The new page created in the leaf level now has to be indexed in the level above to ensure index consistency. This is an obvious overhead, especially if there is any cascading of the page splitting to the intermediate and node index levels. You can minimize leaf level page splitting by creating the index with a fillfactor to provide room for expansion in the leaf level. SQL Server always leaves a "comfortable" amount of space in the non-leaf levels of the index and you should not see non-leaf level page splitting very often. The information that I have states that there is room for two index entries in the non-leaf levels. It's not that much but it should be enough to prevent a lot of non-leaf index page splitting. Page splitting has a further performance problem as it has to lock several index pages to accomplish the page split. In the above insert of record 21, page 210 has to be inserted into the page chain for the leaf level. To ensure that this is done cleanly, XLOCKs have to be put on page 201, 210 and 205 so that the next and previous page pointers may be updated, and on page 200 so that the new index entry for page 210 can be inserted into page 200. In an active index this increases the potential for index blocking and deadlocking.

Delete overhead is identical to inserts except that there is no page splitting. However, there is page shrinkage when the delete of an index page empties the index page. In this case, the empty page is removed from the index chain and deallocated. Page shrinkage also requires XLOCKs on adjacent index pages to update the next and previous page pointers and on the level above to remove the index entry for the page being deleted.

Update

Update overhead is much more interesting. SQL Server performs updates in one of four ways depending on the SQL and other criteria about the table. We need to discuss the update strategies before we can measure the effect on the indexes.

Update Strategies

There are two classes of update: direct updates—which subdivide into three types and deferred updates. Direct updates are performed in a single pass by:

- Locating each affected row—data and index
- Writing the changes to the transaction log
- Making the actual changes to the data and index pages

Deferred updates are performed in three passes by:

- Locating the affected data rows and writing the inserted and deleted log records to the transaction log
- Reading the log records and actioning the deletes on the data and index pages
- At the commit of the transaction, re-reading the log and actioning the inserts to the data and index pages

Direct updates require less overhead than deferred updates since they action the log and the data and index pages less often. You should always try to avoid deferred updates.

Direct Updates

These split into three types depending on the update requirements.

In Place Direct Update

The data is updated in-place with no movement of data in the page and no change to row ids or offset table values.

For an in-place update to occur, the following criteria must be met:

- The row length must not change
- The updated columns must not be a part of the clustered index
- The updated columns must not take part in referential integrity
- The table must not have a trigger
- The table must not be replicated
- The update must not contain a join

This is a very fast update since nothing but the data changes. You should try to achieve it as often as possible. The principal consideration is that the update does not cause any data location changes either by altering the size of the row or by moving the row to another page. The trigger and replication restrictions are due to the before and after log images of the change. The join and RI restrictions exist because these are both joins, since they are not sure of the number of times a record may be updated, they must be deferred.

Cheap Direct Update

This is the update in-place except that the length of the row changes. The new row is still written back into the same place in the page but, as the size has changed, any rows after it in the page move up or down depending on the size change. In this case, the row ids of all rows in the page remain the same but the offset entries of rows after the updated row will change to reflect their new positions in the page.

For a cheap direct update to occur the following criteria must be met:

- The updated row must fit back into the original page
- The updated columns must not be a part of the clustered index
- The updated columns must not take part in referential integrity
- The update must not contain a join
- If the table has a trigger or is replicated the length of the row must not change

This is still a fast update as the row ids do not change and so no indexes need to be updated. The only addition over the in-place update is the processing required to move the rows in the page and update the offset table entries.

Expensive Direct Update

This is a cheap direct update which causes the row to move to a new page. The row movement may be caused by the updated row not fitting back into the page or a column of the clustered index being changed. The update is actioned as a delete followed by an insert.

For a expensive direct update to occur, the following criteria must be met:

- The index used to find the row is not changed by the update
- The updated columns must not take part in referential integrity
- The update must not contain a join

This is a slow update since it actions as a delete followed by an insert. In this situation, the delete step deletes all index entries for the row and the insert step inserts all index entries for the row. This is necessary since the expensive direct update is being used; the row has moved to a different page and therefore the row id has changed.

Deferred Update

The deferred update is actioned as a delete followed by an insert (as described above). These are done as separate steps using the transaction log to store the changes. The actual data page changes are deferred until the end of the transaction.

Deferred updates occur under the following criteria:

- The update contains a join

- The update is to columns involved in referential integrity

- The update moves the row to a new page while the table is accessed via a table scan or clustered index

- Duplicate rows are not allowed but there is no unique index to enforce this

- The row moves page and the index used to find the row are not unique

On occasion, the data row update will be done as a direct update but the index update must be done as a deferred update. This occurs when:

- The update changes the index used to find the row

- The update changes a unique index

The deferred update is a very slow update as it requires multiple passes of the transaction log, data pages, and index pages. Try to avoid it. The principal restrictions here are the join and RI; the rest are easily avoided by doing single record updates via the primary key.

Nonclustered Index Updates

The various update strategies have the effect on the nonclustered indexes of:

Direct in place   No index changes

Cheap direct	No index changes
Expensive direct	Delete of current index entry
	Insert of new index entry
Deferred	Delete of current index entry
	Insert on new index entry

Note that the expensive direct and deferred strategies action the update as a delete followed by an insert. This will cause the record to move to a new data page if there is no clustered index on the table. With no clustered index, the data is held as a heap structure with all inserts made to the last page of the data page chain. The update will delete the record from its current position and insert it in the last data page. This can cause significant space fragmentation as the space released in each page by deletes is not available for inserts.

What are the overheads of maintaining the clustered indexes?

Because only the first record in each data page is indexed, the only index overhead occurs when the maintenance command causes a new data page to be created or deleted. So, for most insert/ update/ delete activity the overhead is small but when page splitting occurs it can be significant.

Inserts

Inserts into the clustered index pages are similar to the nonclustered leaf level index inserts. This is not surprising as the clustered data pages are actually the leaf level of the index. The important point is that the records must be maintained in key sequence and therefore must be added to specific pages. This is illustrated in Figure 6.3.

If there is enough space in the data page to accept the record then there is no index maintenance required; the clustered index entries are page pointers for the first record in the page only. So inserting record 21 to page 8 (above) does not require any clustered index maintenance, as the entry for page 8 in the intermediate level index page 102 does not change. Any nonclustered indexes defined on the table will require maintenance but there is no overhead in the clustered index if there is room in the data page for the insert.

However, there is significant overhead when there is no room on the data page for the record to be inserted. In this case, the data page splits 50:50 to create free space. This is identical to the nonclustered leaf level index page split. This is illustrated in Figure 6.4 which inserts records 6 and 7 into page 5 of the index configuration shown in Figure 6.3.

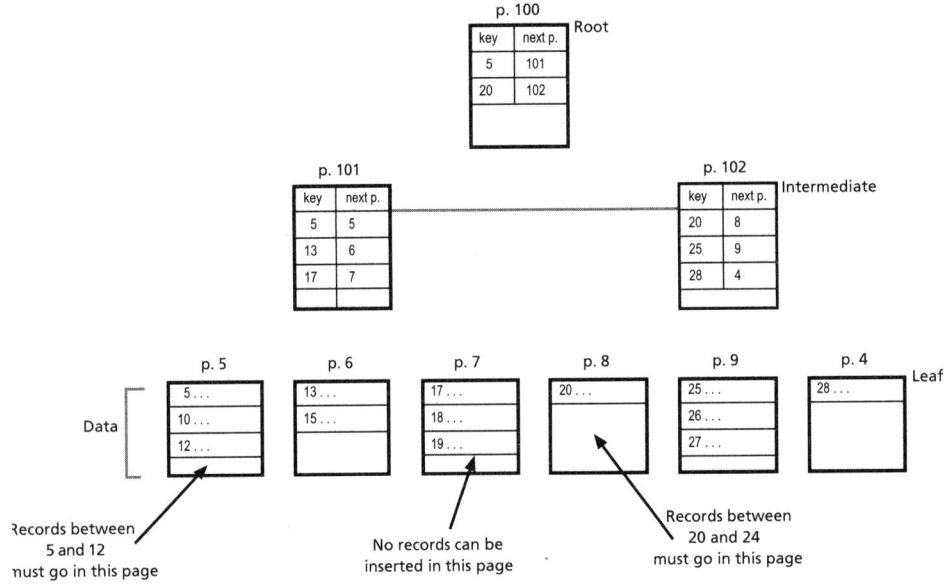

Figure 6.3 *Insert into clustered index*

Again, there is locking overhead on adjacent pages with the possibility of cascading the page, splitting up the index levels. However, there is additional overhead in the clustered data page split; we have now moved some records into a new page which causes their row ids to change. This means that all nonclustered index entries for these records have to be updated. In the above diagram records, 10 and 12 have been moved to page 20 and all nonclustered index entries for these records will have to be updated. This is a significant overhead which you can reduce by creating the clustered index with a fillfactor to leave free space for growth in each data page. This clearly increases the number of pages in the table and will increase the response time of any range-based inquiries. Quite simply, a 75% fillfactor on a clustered index will increase the data size by 25% and any multi-record inquiries via the clustered index by up to 25%.

There are two occasions when the data page does not split 50:50: monotonic data and duplicate data. Index pages always split 50:50.

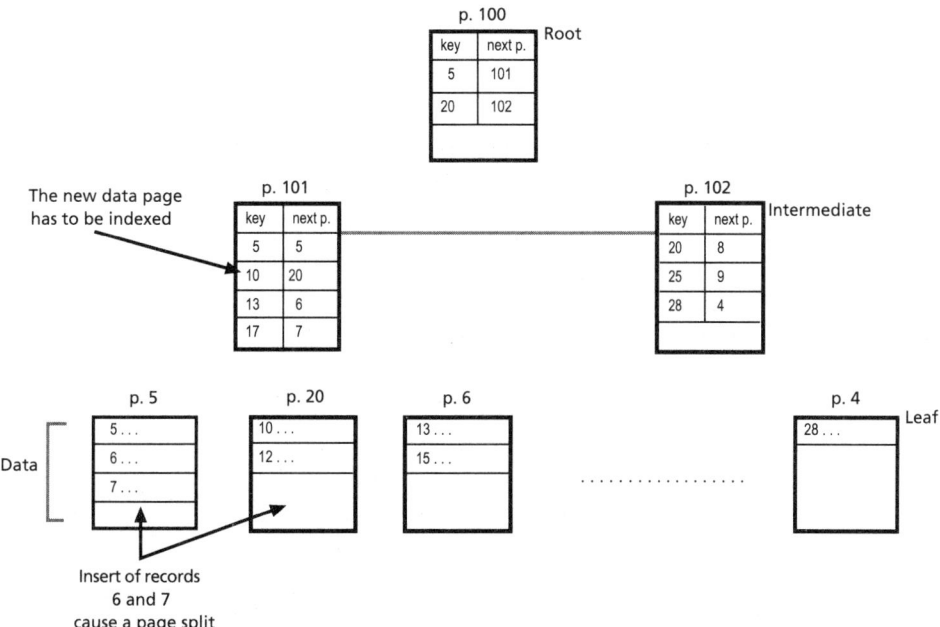

Figure 6.4 *Data page split*

Monotonic data page split

When the index key values of a clustered index are increasing—1, 2, 3, 4,... or Jan 1 1996, Feb 1 1996, Mar 1 1996... or 1, 3, 7, 10, 11, 12,—this is recognized and the page splits 100:0. This effectively does not split the page at all but allocates an empty page to continue horizontal growth. This is extremely efficient; a 50:50 split would leave half empty pages as new inserts are always to the end of the key sequence, i.e., to the last page of the table. This is shown in Figure 6.5.

Since there is no room for record 19 in the page, the page must split to accommodate it. If the page splits 50:50, the page left with records 13, 14, 15 would not be used for any further inserts. The next page would begin with record 16 and therefore no other records would be allocated to the page beginning with record 13. SQL Server recognizes this and splits 100:0 so that there is maximum space utilization when the data is growing monotonically. The server recognizes monotonic growth if the record is being inserted at the foot of the page and the last insert was also to the foot of the page. There is a status setting in the page header which indicates that the last row insert was at the free page offset, i.e., at the end of the data in the page. Occasionally, this will occur when not required but the incidence of unnecessary 100:0 splits is far outweighed by its usefulness. Even in Figure 6.5, if we add records 11 and 12 to the second page, record 12 does not fit into the page and causes a page split. This page split will be 100:0 as the last record added to the page was record 11. This is not a problem since we are using no more pages and, by leaving all the current records in the original page, we have less index updating to do than if the page split 50:50.

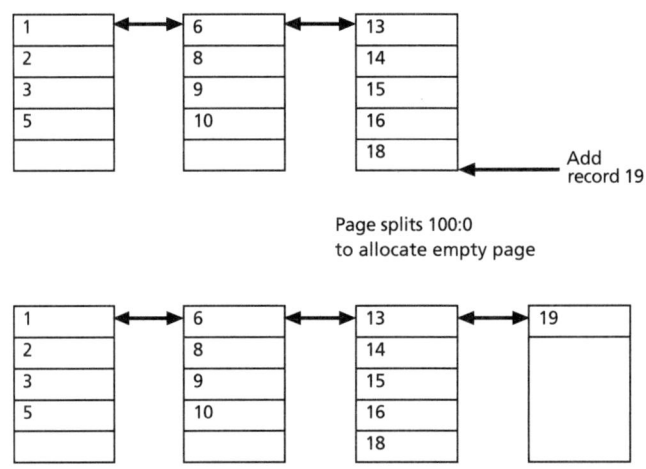

Figure 6.5 monotonic 100:0 page split

Duplicate data page split

When a page splits because of a duplicate key insertion, it splits 100:0. The difference with this empty page split is that the new page can be used only by records with the duplicate key value. This is shown in Figure 6.6.

Since there is no room for record E in the page it has to split. SQL Server recognizes this as a duplicate situation and splits 100:0 with the new record being allocated an empty page. The recognition of duplicate data is similar to monotonic: if the record is being inserted at the foot of the page and the previous insert was also to the foot of the page and for the same index key value, then the page splits 100:0. The significant difference in this case is that the new page is reserved for the record key value which caused the page split. This means that the new page in Figure 6.6 can be used only for records with a key value of E.

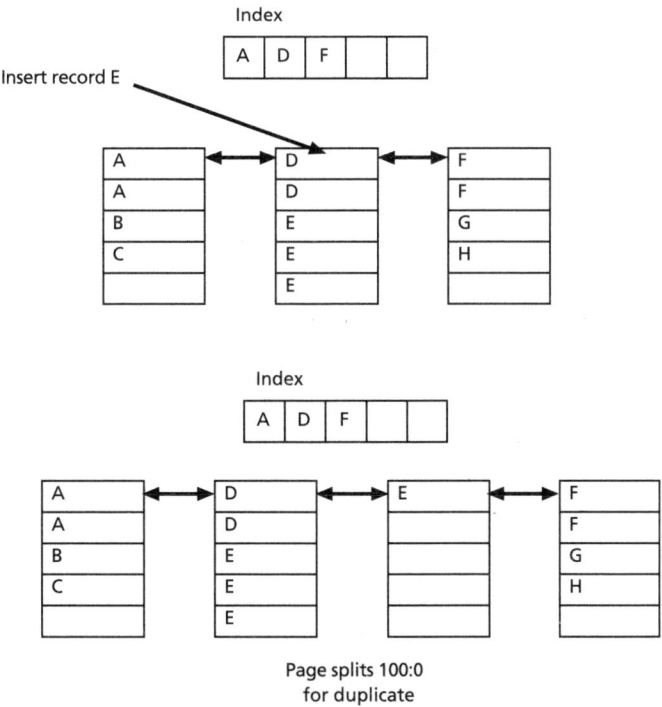

Figure 6.6 *Duplicate data 100:0 split*

This is actually an overflow of a record key value into a new page and you must be careful of the overhead when processing such an overflow. Although the overflow pages are part of the page chain, they do not have an entry in the index and so you need to start retrieval of any overflow record by starting at the first record for that value which is indexed. To insert another record E the initial page containing E is located via the index and then all other pages containing records with key value E are read until the end of the overflow chain when the new record is inserted. This is compounded in an update as the overflow pages need to be searched until the record is located and if the update is carried out as a deletion followed by an insertion then the overflow pages will need to be re-traversed to insert the new version of the record. In other words, retrieval is fast but insert/update/delete is significantly slower—depending on the extent of the duplication.

Forcing non-standard page splitting (ascending inserts)

The **dbcc tune** command can be used to force non-standard, i.e., other than 50:50 page splits.

```
dbcc tune(ascinserts, value, tab_name)

where           value   0: disable (default)
                        1: enable


dbcc tune(ascinserts, 1, trans_date_tab)
```

This forces the page to split at the offset where the row is being inserted instead of 50:50. This is not something to get excited about as it will eventually sort itself out but it will provide an advantage when the clustered index key is a composite key and the last column in the key increases monotonically. In this situation, an insert of a completely new key which would cause a page split could start to fragment the data in the pages. The 50% left in the original page might be unusable based on the index growth. This could also happen with the new page as it will grow monotonically but not at the end of the page. This will eventually result in true monotonic growth but you may get quite a high level of unusable space in the data pages depending on the type of index key allocation.

Delete

Deletion of a record from a clustered index has no index maintenance overhead unless the delete is of the first record or the last remaining record in a page.

Since the first record in a page is indexed, deleting this record requires an update of the intermediate level entry for that page.

Deleting the last remaining record in a page causes the empty page to be deallocated and removed from the page chain. This requires the adjacent data pages to be XLOCKed to update the page chain pointers and the index entry in the intermediate index level to be deleted.

Update

Direct in place and cheap updates have no effect on the clustered index as they do not change any of the index information. Even if the first record in the page is updated (because the record does not change its data page), there is no requirement to update the clustered index entries.

Expensive direct and deferred updates are executed as delete followed by insert and will cause index updates (as described above) if page splitting or shrinkage occurs or if the update is to the first record on the data page.

Summary

Indexes can be useful in reducing record retrieval times but they obviously are an overhead to maintenance commands. The actual overhead depends on the command and index type.

Nonclustered

All inserts must add a record to the leaf level. All deletes must remove a record from the leaf level. An update will affect the index only if the record moves to another data page.

Clustered

An insert adds a record to the index only if a new data page has to be created. A delete removes a record from the index only if the first or last remaining record in a data page is deleted. An update will affect the index only if the record moves to another data page and the deletion of the old record removes the first or last remaining record in the data page or if the insert of the new record creates a new data page.

The insert of a new record to the leaf level of either index type—the nonclustered leaf level or the clustered data level—may have additional overhead; it may cause the page to split into two because there is no room for the insert in the original page. The index key sequence must be preserved in the leaf level and this is achieved by linking a new page into the leaf level and splitting the records 50:50 between the original page and the new page. In the case of the clustered index, there is the additional overhead of having to update all nonclustered index records for the data records moved into the new page.

The delete of a record may also cause maintenance of the leaf level. If the delete of the leaf level entry empties the page, this page is no longer required and must be unlinked from the leaf level chain.

Updates in SQL Server cause additional overhead if they are carried out as deferred. This means that the update is not done until the transaction commit. The update is carried out in three stages: the first to write the record changes to the transaction log; the second to re-read the log and delete the records and the third to re-read the log and insert the updated records.

7

Index
Selection

Although you may believe that the indexes which you have defined are the best possible for the application SQL, the choice of index is made by the optimizer. You need to know how the optimizer works and especially why it will not choose your beautiful index. This chapter discusses the rules associated with index selection based on search arguments, index statistics, and index density. The various execution plan choices are then described for different types, of SQL commands.

How does the index get selected?

The SQL is analyzed by the optimizer which matches the columns in the where clauses with the columns in the indexes to see if there is an index which may be used. The optimizer then uses index distribution statistics to determine if the chosen index reduces the disk accesses below those required for a table scan.

The optimizer performs all decisions on the use of indexes. You may create what you consider are the best indexes in the world, but they may be ignored by the optimizer. The choice of indexes is determined by the optimizer based on the SQL. Optimum indexes cannot be created until the SQL has been written. Relational theory requires that the paths chosen through the data to execute a specific SQL command are not chosen or fixed by the application developer but are determined at run time by the database software. In other words, the application developer specifies what is required from the database and the optimizer determines how the command will be executed.

The objective of all optimization is to minimize the amount of disk I/O and CPU effort required to carry out an SQL command. Optimizers are continually being refined with each release of database software and the current (System 11) state of the SQL Server optimizer uses the following information to determine how the SQL is to be executed.

Index

The optimizer matches the *where* clause selection criteria with indexes built on the tables to determine if there is an index which can be used to reduce the disk I/Os required to retrieve the records.

Search argument

This is the form of the where clause which is recognized by the optimizer as being suitable for matching with any indexes.

Index statistics

Each index has statistics about data distribution to determine if using the index requires less disk I/Os than doing a table scan of all of the records in the table. In other words, an estimate of the number of records returned based on the input values of the where clause. The index statistics are used for individual table access.

Index density

Each index has a density figure which provides the level of replication in the data distribution. In other words, the average number of records retrieved for a single value of the index column. The density is used for join access between two tables.

In general, the optimizer takes the following decisions:

- Is the where clause in the form of a search argument?

- Is there an index for the where clause column?

- Is the index better than a table scan?

If the answer to each of these is "yes," the index is used. If any return the answer "no," then a table scan is done. There are refinements to these, especially in the slackening of the requirement to always have a where clause in the form of a search argument, but in general, the majority of the optimizer decisions are based on these three questions.

Search argument

The optimizer analyzes the SQL to match the columns in the where clauses with the available indexes. The where clauses must be of a specific format called a **search argument (sarg)** for the optimizer even to consider available indexes for the where clause. The index will not be used if the where clause is not in the search argument format unless the index covers the query. The command **select * from customer where upper(name) = "KIRKWOOD"** will table scan as there is no sarg but the command **select name from customer where upper(name) = "KIRKWOOD"** will scan an index on name as the index covers the command. This *sarg* format is:

```
column   operator   expression

Valid search arguments            price = 50
                                  name like 'Kir%'
                                  salary = 2000*12
                                  200 < qty
```

These will consider indexes on price, name, salary, and qty respectively.

```
Invalid search arguments          substring(name,1,3) = 'Kir'
                                  salary/12 = 2000
```

These will not consider any indexes on name and salary because they are not search arguments. Also note that the not equal operator (!= or <> or not) is not considered to be a search argument operator and will always cause a table scan.

Although it is not always possible, you should try to avoid the following non-search argument situations.

Table 7.1

NOT Search Argument	Equivalent Search Argument
150 = price * 12	150 /12 = price
upper(name) = 'KIRKWOOD'	No equivalent: be careful with upper and lower case. If possible, you can improve performance by converting on input.
qty + 10 > 200	qty > 200 - 10
firstname + ' ' + lastname = 'john kirkwood'	firstname = 'john' and lastname = 'kirkwood'
ltrim(name) = 'kirkwood'	No equivalent: be careful with leading spaces. Always worth removing any possible leading spaces on input.

Once a valid search argument has been found to match with an index column the optimizer checks the index statistics to estimate how many accesses are required to retrieve the records. The index statistics are column value distribution information which the optimizer looks up using the column values in the where clause to estimate the number of disk I/Os required to retrieve the data. The worst case disk access scenario for a table is a complete read of all data in the table. The optimizer executes this as a table scan by starting at the first page and reading each page in turn until the last page. This requires one I/O per page in the table. Therefore, the optimizer will not use an index if the estimated number of I/Os is going to be greater than a table scan, i.e., more than the number of pages in the table.

Index statistics

Each index has a **distribution** page which contains the distribution statistics for the index key values. These are allocated by sampling the data in ascending key sequence at a regular interval and recording the key value read at each sample. This defines a number of steps, each identified by a key value with each step representing a fixed number of records. This is illustrated in Figure 7.1.

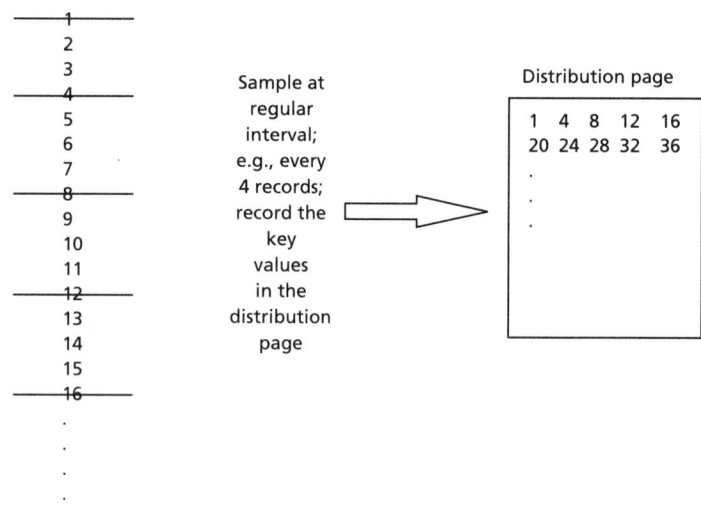

Figure 7.1 Creation of index statistics

The sampling interval is based on the number of entries which can be made in the distribution page, up to 256—the maximum number of records in a page. The 256 maximum is imposed because the statistics record has the same format as a data record with a 1 byte row number (see Chapter 8). This depends on the size of the key value which is recorded in the distribution page.

```
number of samples = distribution page size (2016) / size of index key
```

For example, an *int* key plus record overhead is 6 bytes which will be able to make 2016/6, i.e., 336 samples of the data, which then reduces to the maximum 256 records per page. There is no row offset table in a distribution page so the fixed row overhead is only 2 bytes. Each entry in the distribution page then represents a sample step containing a fixed number of records. The sample step size is determined by the number of samples as:

```
sample step size = number of records in table / number of samples
```

The optimizer now knows as much as possible about the index value distribution. It uses the value in the where clause to look up statistics and estimate the number of records which will be retrieved for the index values. In our example in Figure 7.1, a range request for records between 10 and 20 will include steps 8, 12, 16, 20 and will estimate 4 steps of 4 records, i.e., 16 records.

Clearly, the index statistics are estimates whose accuracy depends on the number of samples of the data. The more samples which can be made, the more accurate the index statistics. As the statistics are restricted to one page, the number of samples is determined by the size of the index key value; so keep your index key sizes as small as you can. Because of this, the index statistics are collected only on the first column of a composite index. So an index on (male_female, name) would create statistics based on male_female only. These two values only would not reflect the true, almost unique, nature of the index key values. Always try to place the most selective column first in a composite index to allow the index statistics to be most representative of the key values distribution.

Another important "feature" of the index statistics is that the optimizer accesses them as a lookup only. This means that the optimizer does no datatype conversion when accessing the statistics; therefore the datatypes must agree between the index key column and the column, variable or literal, used to access the statistics. Be careful of this as columns declared as null are held as variable datatypes and numeric literals with decimal places are held as numeric datatypes. Any mismatch in datatype means that the optimizer cannot use the statistics and has to revert to the search argument density (see below). Specific exceptions to this problem are *int null* and *int not null* which still use the statistics and variables defined with the *declare* statement. Although they are initialized to null, they still use the statistics when matched with a not null column. Examples of this are given in Chapter 20.

Index density

In addition to the value distribution statistics, the index distribution page also holds density figures which are a measure of the amount of duplication in the key values. The density is the average percentage of duplicate keys for the index. The smaller this is, the more unique the data. A density of 100% means that all keys have the same value. If we have a 1,000 row table with 25% density, we expect to get back, on average, 250 rows per index value. The best density is 100/n% where n is the number of records in the table, meaning we expect one record per key value.

The density is used in the join strategy to estimate the number of records per join. The average records per join is obtained by multiplying the number of records in the table by the join density.

```
average records per join = records in table * join density
```

If the index is a composite one, join densities are held for all valid combinations of the columns: An index on:

```
(a, b, c)
```

will have densities for:

```
(a, b, c)
(a, b)
(a)
```

This allows joins on less than the full index columns to correctly reflect the number of records per join.

The above density figures are used in joins but there is also a search argument density which can be used for sarg where clauses if the distribution statistics cannot be used. The *sarg* density differs from the join density in that it does not include duplicate values which span more than one cell in the statistics. Illustrating with an extreme example, consider the values:

```
# Rows    Value
   500      A
     1      B
     1      C
     1      D
     1      E
     1      F
     1      G
     1      H
     1      I
     1      J
     1      K
```

The density is evaluated as the sum of the number of occurrences to the power 2 divided by the total number of rows to the power 2.

```
density = Σ (n(i)**2) / (r**2)
```

```
where   n(i) = number of occurrences of each index key value
        r = total number of occurrences
```

The join density includes every occurrence:

```
join density = (500*500) + (1*1) + . . . . . + (1*1) / (501*501)
```

The sarg density eliminates duplicates which span more than one cell. If this included the A values we would have:

```
sarg density = (1*1) + (1*1) + . . . . . + (1*1) / (501*501)
```

Obviously, this is a very unbalanced example but it shows how the sarg density will normally be more optimistic in choosing the index.

How do I choose columns for an index?

Choose the index columns based on the columns used in where clauses in the SQL commands.

Although primary key and foreign key are obvious choices, the complete index choices for a table must be based on the actual SQL written to access the table. Remember, of course, that an index will be created automatically if you define the **primary key** constraint when you create the table. You cannot index for performance before the SQL is written since you do not know which columns will be used in the where clauses. There is no harm in creating initial indexes simply on primary and foreign key to assist during development, but you must throw these away when moving to production and recreate all indexes based on the application SQL.

How do I index for AND clauses?

Aim for a compound index on the columns in the AND clauses and cluster or non-cluster according to the above rules on number of records returned.

An important rule to consider is that SQL Server will use only one index to execute a single SQL command. The exception to this is when the command contains OR clauses as described later. If the command has many AND clauses, there is no point in creating a separate index for each AND clause column; the optimizer will use only one of them and the others will be ignored.

```
select * from order_item
     where price between 10 and 100
     and discount = 0
     and delivery_month = datepart(mm, getdate())
```

Creating three separate indexes for this command, say clustered(price); non-clustered(discount); and nonclustered(delivery_month) is pointless, since only one would be used—most likely the clustered index on price. The optimum indexing for this command is an index on (price, discount, delivery_month) and, based on the between operator, it is likely to be better as clustered.
Note the simple difference of:

```
select price from order_item
     where price between 10 and 100
     and discount = 0
     and delivery_month = datepart(mm, getdate())
```

where the best index is now nonclustered on (price, discount, delivery_month) as this index covers the query. This emphasizes the need to minimize the use of "*" in SQL and to display only those columns that have to be output as it helps to define covered indexes.

How do I sequence the columns in a compound index?

Based on the operator used in the where clause, place the most restrictive where clause column as the first column in the index and so on, so that the number of rows is reduced as quickly as possible. In the absence of selectivity bias in the where clause operator, sequence the columns based on the inherent selectivity of the data.

The objective in sequencing the columns of a compound index is to ensure that the first column reduces the number of rows to be looked at as much as possible, and so on for each column in turn. This is based on the operators used in the where clauses with the general selectivity order of:

- Equality

- Closed interval such as like, between

- Open interval such as greater than

This is best explained by an example.

```
select * from order_item
       where prod_no = 30
       and price between 5 and 15
```

Figure 7.2 illustrates how the equality has enabled the search for records to stop sooner than the between. The (price, prod_no) index has to read records which do not conform to the second column criteria but the (prod_no, price) index only reads records which conform to the second column criteria. The (price, prod_no) index is only marginally better than the simple index on (price).

index on (prod_no, price)		index on (price, prod_no)	
prod_no	price	price	prod_no
10	5	5	10
10	15	5	30
20	15	5	40
30	5	15	10
30	15	15	20
30	20	15	30
40	5	15	50
50	15	20	30
50	25	25	50

Figure 7.2 Column sequence in a composite index

When the operators have the same weighting there is no real selectivity reason to favor one sequence over any other.

```
select * from customer
       where last_name = 'kirkwood'
       and first_name = 'john'
```

There are as many *kirkwoods* with first name *john* as there are *johns* with last name *kirkwood*.

However, there is another reason for column sequence in a composite index based on the data selectivity. The index statistics are collected on the first column of the index only. As the index statistics are used to estimate the number of rows returned for input values, it is important to get the most accurate result from these statistics. Therefore, it is important to place the column which has the most distinct values first in a compound index. An index on (male_female, name) will have statistics collected on male_female with a 50:50 distribution whereas the index on (name, male_female) will have statistics collected on name with an almost random distribution.

Finally, make sure that you always include the first column in the compound key in a where clause, otherwise the index will not be used.

```
select * from customer
       where first_name = 'john'
```

This will not be able to use an index on (last_name, first_name) as there is no start point for the search to commence. Because the last_name has not been supplied and the index entries are in sequence of last_name every index entry would have to be read to check the first names. When the query is not covered this is not an efficient execution plan and a table scan will be chosen. This "having a start point" also applies to single column indexes. The command **select * from customer where a name like "%ood"** will not use an index on name; every index entry would have to be read to check the name. If you do not supply a start point in a where clause the index will not be used.

How do I index for OR clauses?

The OR clause requires a separate access for each clause; you need to build separate indexes for each column. If the total number of accesses is greater than a table scan, the indexes will not be used and the optimizer will table scan.

The OR clause operates by accessing the table for each OR argument and merging the results to eliminate any duplicates.

```
select * from customer
       where name = 'kirkwood'
       or city = 'London'
```

If indexes are used, this makes two passes through the customer table: once on *name* to get all records for "kirkwood" and once on *city* to get all records for "London." The two result sets are merged to eliminate duplicates and the combined results displayed.

This OR strategy is called a **dynamic index** strategy. The table is accessed for each clause of the OR statement and the qualifying row ids written to a worktable. Once all row ids have been located, they are merged to remove duplicates and the records then accessed using the remaining row ids to display the results. This is illustrated in Figure 7.3.

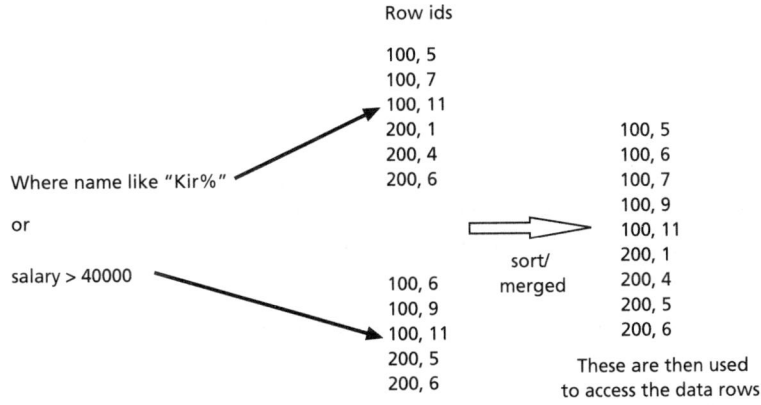

Figure 7.3 *Dynamic index strategy*

This ensures that a row is not displayed more than once even if it qualifies for more than one of the OR clauses.

The OR strategy always has the overhead of having to access the rows at least twice. It also suffers from retaining the SLOCKs on the data pages until the command is complete. Because the row ids of the records are being used in the worktable for subsequent read of the records, the command must ensure that the row id does not change or is deleted during the worktable processing. This is accomplished by retaining the SLOCKs on the data pages until the command completes. (In a normal select command, the SLOCKs would be set off as soon as all required records on the data page had been read.)

The OR is not an easy operator to index for as the sum of the I/Os is compared against the table scan. Even if one of the indexes is clustered, the other must be non-clustered and the sum may be greater than a table scan. In this case, the table scan is carried out. This applies even if the OR is issued on the same column:

```
select * from order_item
     where delivery_code in ('SE', 'SW', 'HC')
```

This does three separate accesses via an index on delivery_code; if the total number of I/Os is greater than a table scan, the table scan will be chosen—even if the index is clustered.

How do I index for join clauses?

Index based on the *join* keys as if they were normal *where* clauses.

There is no real difference here and you should simply treat the join key as another potential index key. This means that it has all of the problems of not being used when defined as nonclustered and returning more rows than pages in the table. Unfortunately, any table scanning has a significant overhead when it occurs during a join execution as it may be repeated for every record in the join.

The join is executed as **a nested iteration** by nesting the tables and iterating through the inner table for every qualifying row in the outer table.

```
select c.name, o.ord_no, o.ord_date
     from customer c, orders o
     where c.cust_no = o.cust_no
     and c.sales_area = 'SE'
```

If there are suitable indexes on the two tables—say customer(sales_area) and orders(cust_no) this will place *customer* as the outer table and *orders* as the inner table. For each qualify row from customer the orders table will be accessed via the cust_no index and the relevant rows displayed. If there are 50 customers in sales_area SE, the orders table will be accessed 50 times via the cust_no index.

The optimizer first puts the tables into sequence based on two rules:

• Number of qualifying rows expected from each table

• Size of each table

The emphasis is on (1) making the table which returns the fewest rows the outer table in the sequence and (2) making the smallest table the inner table in the sequence. Where there is a conflict between these criteria, the optimizer usually gives the most weight to the most selective—the outer table.

Having determined the table sequence, the optimizer then iterates through the tables from outer to inner. For each qualifying row in the outer, the next table is accessed and for each qualifying row in this table, the next table is accessed, and so on until all qualifying rows on all tables have been retrieved.

For the two table join:

```
select c.name, o.order_no
       from customer c, orders o
       where o.cust_no = c.cust_no
       and c.name = 'kirkwood'
```

The nested iteration is illustrated in Figure 7.4.

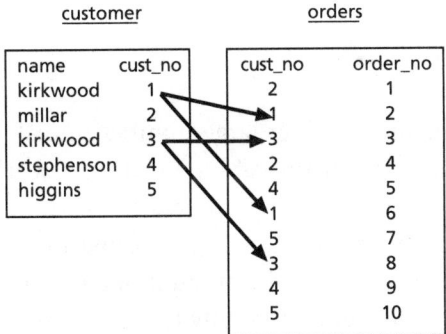

Figure 7.4 *Nested iteration join*

The customer is placed as the outer and accessed to retrieve all names of "kirkwood." The first one located is for customer number 1 which is then used to access the orders table and retrieve all orders rows for cust_no = 1. Once these have been located, the next row on customer is accessed and all orders rows for cust_no = 3 are retrieved.

Note that the cost of this join in terms of disk accessing is:

```
number of pages accessed in outer table +
(number of rows retrieved from outer table *
number of pages accessed in inner table for a qualifying outer row)
```

If there was no additional restrictive where clause:

```
select c.name, o.order_no, o.ord_date
       from customer c, orders o
       where c.cust_no = o.cust_no
```

The table nesting would be the same and the customer table would be table scanned with the orders table accessed once via the cust_no index for every record on customer. Joins can generate a large number of I/Os when there is little selectivity, so be careful.

When neither of the tables has suitable indexes, the join is evaluated with what is called a **reformatting** strategy. This is to be avoided since it is extremely expensive. In the reformatting strategy one of the tables is sorted to create an internal clustered index; then a nested iteration is carried out with the sorted table as the inner table. If a nested iteration strategy was adopted when there are no useful indexes, the I/O cost would be:

```
table scan of outer table +
(number of rows in outer table * table scan of inner table)
```

Clearly this will generate a rather large number of disk accesses; the optimizer tries to reduce this by taking one of the tables, creating a worktable with a clustered index on the join keys, and then doing a nested iteration with the worktable as the inner table. To further reduce the amount of work, the reformatting of the inner table is done as a projection and restriction to reduce the amount of data which has to be sorted into the join key sequence. The projection takes only those columns which are required and the restriction takes only those rows which are required into the worktable to keep it as small as possible.

Consider the join:

```
select c.name, c.required_date, d.delivery_date, d.delivery_qty
       from customer c, order_delivery d
       where c.required_date = d.delivery_date
       and c.postcode like 'RG%'
```

With no useful indexes on customer.postcode or order_delivery.delivery_date the join will be executed using a reformatting strategy. With a restriction on customer.postcode the optimizer place, the customer table as the inner table. It passes into the worktable only those rows and columns from the customer table which it needs to execute the command, i.e., rows for postcode beginning with RG and column name, required_date, and postcode. The worktable is then sorted into the sequence of the join column—required_date. This forms a clustered index on required_date; a nested iteration is performed by table scanning the order_delivery table and accessing the worktable on required date for every record in the order_delivery table.

This reduces the nested iteration disk accessing cost of formatting to:

```
table scan of the outer table +
(number of rows in outer table *
disk accesses on worktable required to retrieve rows for qualifying date)
```

You have to add the cost of the sort to create the worktable but, in general, this reformatting strategy is faster than a nested iteration when there are no qualifying indexes to access the rows.

It is rare for a reformatting not to benefit from indexing and every effort should be made to provide suitable indexes for joins. One point to bear in mind is that the reformatting passes the minimum amount of information to the internal clustered index creation. Therefore, only essential rows and columns are passed to the clustered index sort to make it as efficient as possible. Always try to display only those columns you are interested in when joining, especially if the reformatting strategy is used.

Do I need any special index considerations for outer joins?

No. Although the **outer join** produces additional results, the indexing and execution plan chosen is the same as a normal join. The optimization plan is the same as a natural join.

An outer join is a special form of join which includes rows from one table which have no joining rows on the other table. A problem with the normal join is that it is based on equality. So the join:

```
select c.name, o.order_no
    from customer c, orders o
    where c.cust_no = o.cust_no
```

returns only those rows from the customer and orders tables where there is a match on customer number. This means that we are unable to answer the question "show all customer rows with any matching order rows." With the above join any customer row which did not have order rows would not be displayed. However, the request is to show all of the customer rows plus any matching order rows. The outer join solves this by displaying all of the customer rows with null order information if there are no matching order rows. The syntax is:

```
select c.name, o.order_no
       from customer c, orders o
       where c.cust_no *= o.cust_no
```

where the *= operator indicates an outer join. This can also be written as =* but the operator is uni-directional and cannot be written as *=*.

If the table information was:

```
customer                       orders
cust no        name            order no        cust no
1              john            1               1
2              jill            2               1
3              fiona           3               2
4              craig           4               3
```

Then the normal equality join would output:

```
name           order no
john           1
john           2
jill           3
fiona          4
```

and the outer join would output:

```
name           order no
john           1
john           2
jill           3
fiona          4
craig          null
```

One aspect of the outer join that will give you SQL problems is the inability to join the outer join object table with any other table.

```
select c.name, o.ord_no, i.prod_no
     from customer c, orders o, items i
     where c.cust_no *= o.cust_no
     and o.ord_no = i.ord_no
```

This is NOT allowed and will give you a syntax error. You are not allowed to join orders with another table in the same command when it is the object of the outer join. In other words, the table from which nulls may be formed cannot be joined with another table when an outer join is defined. The subject of the outer, i.e., the table on the same side as the "*", can be joined with other tables but the table on the opposite side of the "*" cannot.

You need to use a two-stage evaluation using a temporary table to carry out the other join.

```
select cust_name=c.name, order_no = o.ord_no
     into #temp
     from customer c, orders o
     where c.cust_no *= o.cust_no

select t.cust_name, t.order_no, i.prod_no
     from #temp t, items i
     where t.ord_no *= i.ord_no
```

How do I index for nested commands?

Treat each nested command as a separate command to be indexed. Do not forget that the nesting is effectively a join and you should treat the nesting columns as join columns.

Nestings flattened to joins

SQL Server evaluates nestings as joins if the nesting can be flattened to a join.

```
select * from customer
     where cust_no in (select cust_no from orders
          where del_date = 'Feb 2, 1996')
```

This is evaluated as the join:

```
select customer.*
     from customer, orders
     where customer.cust_no = orders.cust_no
     and orders.del_date = 'Feb 2, 1996'
```

and should be indexed as if it was a join, i.e., orders(del_date) nonclustered; customer(cust_no) nonclustered and orders(cust_no) clustered. Note the date index as nonclustered instead of clustered. This is based on a date index which defaults the time to 12:00 A.M. as discussed in Chapter 2 normally having a large number of duplicates, i.e., records with the same date, and this usually adds a significant overhead to the clustered index maintenance. I have found a three times degradation on clustered index maintenance when there are a large number of duplicates per index value. The overhead is caused by the duplicate record overflow as all records for the same index value have to be read for inserts and an average of half of the records for updates and deletes. If you must cluster on such a key then overload the index to remove the duplication. In this example, overloading as (del_date, ord_no) would be most useful as the introduction of the primary key forces the index to be unique.

However, the results of these may be different as the nesting should not output a customer record more than once even if it has several orders on 2/2/96. Unfortunately, a join will output every match between the tables and will include one customer output for every occurrence on orders on 2/2/96. SQL Server uses a special EXISTENCE join when evaluating a nesting as a join so that it stops at the first occurrence of the join column. This makes the join execution faster but, in System 10, does require the nested table to be fixed as the inner table in the nested iteration join execution. This is unlikely to be a problem as the inner table scan stops at the first match. It is worth some attention if you believe that the command is taking longer than necessary to execute. This fixed execution sequence has been removed in System 11. The 4.9.2 execution does not do an existence join and so will include the duplicate records. You need to override this with a distinct in the nested command. If you are upgrading from 4.9 to 10 or 11 you do not need to alter any of this SQL as the distinct keyword is ignored when it appears in this type of nested query.

Non-correlated nestings which cannot be flattened to a join

When the nesting cannot be flattened to a join and the inner command may be evaluated independently of the outer command, the inner command is evaluated completely and the result passed to the outer command which is then evaluated. This is called **materialization** in SQL Server. The commands should be indexed as if they are separate commands.

```
select ord_no from order_items
    where qty = (select max(qty) from order_items)
```

In this case, the inner select is evaluated first and the maximum quantity is passed into the outer select which is then evaluated. Notice that in practice a nonclustered index on (qty) would satisfy both select commands as it provides a covered index for the inner command and a useful index for the outer command. With a bit more thought we might try an index on (qty, ord_no) as it covers both queries. However, the nested query creates an unknown value situation—explained in detail in Chapter 20 on high performance SQL—as the value of the max(qty) function call is not known when the nested query is optimized. This means that the value of the *qty* equals clause is not known at optimization time and the statistics cannot be used. In the above case the *sarg* density value of the *qty* index would be used.

Nestings with additional selection clauses in the outer command

When there is an additional selection clause in the outer command this is evaluated first to avoid unnecessary executions of the nested command. This means that it is often possible to avoid executing the nested command. Sybase calls this **short circuiting** the sub query.

```
select * from orders
      where tot_orders > all
            (select tot_orders from customer
                  where area = 'SE')
      and ord_date = 'Jan 1 1996'
```

In this example, if the orders.ord_date is not equal to "Jan 1 1996" the row is discarded and the nested query is not evaluated. The sub query is not evaluated until the row does not meet any of the external where clause conditions.

Nestings which cannot be flattened, materialized, or short circuited

In this case, the queries are optimized one at a time with the innermost queries optimized first. A memory cache is used for each sub query results set, and this cache is used for any duplicate correlation values to avoid physical disk I/O. This cache usage is dynamic and the size is reduced depending on the cache hit rate; a low cache hit rate causes the use of sub query cache to be reduced as the command executes. Information on the cache hits and misses can be obtained with the **set statistics subquerycache on** command.

This type of nesting is called **correlated** as it contains a correlation or relationship across the nesting, usually in the form of a join but also because of some of the more unusual operators. For example:

```
select name from customer
       where tot_orders > all
       (select tot_orders from customer
               where area = 'SE')
```

is a correlated query which cannot be flattened or materialized. In the correlated nesting, the nested command is evaluated for each qualifying outer row in the statement. In the above example, the nested command is evaluated for every record on the customer table. Clearly, this can require a large number of I/Os and you should try to avoid correlated nesting if possible.

The subquery results cache holds a combination of the join columns and the subquery result values. These are checked first if a subquery result value is already in the cache before the table is accessed. The effectiveness of the subquery cache can be investigated using **set statistics subquerycache**; although there is nothing you can do about it if you do not like the results.

```
set statistics subquerycache on
go
select name from customer
       where tot_orders > all
       (select tot_orders from customer
               where area = 'SE')
.
.
.
Statement:  1  Subquery:  1  cache size:  120  hits:  30  misses:  150
```

The subquery cache was used and it contained 120 rows with 30 hits and 150 misses.

Is an index used the same way in a procedure?

Yes. The SQL in the procedure is optimized in the same way in a procedure as it is in a stand alone SQL command. However, the procedure SQL is optimized when it is first loaded into procedure cache and is not changed as long as the procedure remains in procedure cache. This can present some performance problems.

The performance gain of the procedure is based on its being optimized and compiled on its first execution as it is loaded into procedure cache. Subsequent executions of a procedure in cache bypass the optimization and compilation phases and use the cache version to simply execute. So the parse, optimize and compile stages of SQL processing are not carried out when the procedure being executed is already in cache. The existence of objects and permissions is still checked, but if all objects exist and the permissions are still valid, the procedure simply executes. This is explained in more detail in the next section.

Most of the time this does not cause a problem but there are occasions when the optimization plan being used by the cache version of the procedure does not suit the specific execution. If the procedure contains a range-based query on a nonclustered index with the values being supplied as parameters, then there is the possibility that an unsuitable execution plan will be retrieved from a cache version of the procedure.

The procedure:

```
create proc jk_prc (@name varchar(30) = null)
as
select * from customer
        where name like @name + "%"
go
```

with a nonclustered index on name will give different execution plans based on the supplied parameter value.

```
exec jk_prc @name = 'kirkwood'       will use the index
exec jk_prc                          will table scan
```

If the second execution actually uses the cache version created by the first execution, then the index will be used when a table scan should have been carried out. And vice versa.

Regardless of the actual plan generated, there may be multiple copies of the procedure in cache, each with different plans. In this case, a subsequent execution may use one of these plans although it does not suit: what should be an index access on a few records may use a table scan plan or—usually worse—what should be a table scan may access most of the table via the index.

This is easily checked by executing the procedure with recompile which forces the procedure to be loaded from sysprocedures and recompiled. If this returns the procedure to "normal" execution, you need to decide how to avoid the problem on a more permanent basis. There are three choices for recompilation:

exec proc_name with recompile

Forces recompilation for this single execution. This has the problem that the next execution cannot be guaranteed to get this plan again as it may pick up one of the other—not appropriate—plans in cache.

create proc_1 with recompile

Forces recompilation on every execution of the procedure. This does not leave the procedure in cache. This guarantees the correct execution plan every time by compiling every time. This clearly minimizes the performance savings of procedures but does not negate the access security advantages (see below).

sp_recompile table_name

Forces recompilation of all procedures which use the named table. This is a one-off recompilation. This technique is most often used after update statistics to ensure that the procedure execution picks up the new index statistics or after defining a new index to ensure that the optimization plan takes it into account. Execution of a procedure version from cache only checks for existence of objects in its current execution plan. If everything is there, the plan is not recreated; new objects such as new indexes or new index statistics are not taken into account by cache resident versions of a procedure. sp_recompile forces recompilation of all procedures which use the table to overcome this.

Note that the problem of using an existing inappropriate plan will not happen all of the time and is restricted to procedures which:

- Have input parameters used in where clauses with wide variations on records returned: pay particular attention to like, between, less than and greater than

- Nonclustered indexes on the columns matching with the input variables

This is not normally a problem on which you should spend effort trying to anticipate but it is one to adjust if it occurs.

So why should I use procedures?

Procedures are normally used for two reasons: performance and security.

Performance

The procedure assists performance by reducing the load on the CPU and the network.

Stored procedures are pre-parsed and pre-optimized so that repetitive executions of a stored procedure only need to check object permissions and then execute. This saves CPU effort and is recommended to put any SQL which is repeated into a stored procedure. The sequence of events for a procedure is:

- Procedure is parsed at creation time and stored on sysprocedures

- On first execution, the procedure is read from sysprocedures, optimized, compiled and loaded into procedure cache

- On subsequent executions, the presence and permissions of objects used by the procedure are checked and the cache version executed

The more often a command is executed, the greater the savings in parse, optimize, and compile times. Therefore, unless the command is ad-hoc SQL which is unlikely to be re-issued, stored procedures should be used for all SQL.

The level of optimization and compilation savings is determined by the size of procedure cache. If procedure cache is full when a procedure is loaded from sysprocedures, space is obtained by swapping out unused procedures in least recently used priority. This means that procedures do not remain indefinitely in cache and may require re-optimization and compilation if not used for a period of time. The incidence of this depends on the size of procedure cache and the number of copies of each procedure in cache. The version of the procedure in cache is not re-entrant and therefore it can be executed by one user at a time only. If two users need to execute the same procedure at the same time there will be two copies of the procedure in cache. This means that there may be several versions of a procedure in cache at one time.

Execution of a procedure follows the steps:

- If no copies in cache

    read from sysprocedures
    check permissions
    optimize and compile
    load into cache and execute

- If copies in cache, but all are being used

    read from sysprocedures as if no copies in cache

- If copies in cache and one not currently being used

    check permissions
    execute cache version

If you are issuing a large amount of SQL from the client to the server, it is advantageous to put this into a procedure so that you are making a procedure call across the network instead of sending large amounts of SQL. You need to be a little careful here as partially full packets are not sent immediately but suffer a small time-out delay until the network software decides to send the partially full packet. This may be overcome from the server to the client using the configuration parameter **tcp no delay** but this does not affect the client and you will need to get involved in ct-library programming to achieve it at the client. Although you need to be aware of this, it is not normally a problem from the client to the server even when using simple stored procedure calls.

Bearing in mind the above optimization problem of parameterized procedures, it is still advantageous to put most server based code in procedures. Some recent tests I did on SQL versus procedures showed that, on a very lightly loaded machine, the procedures ran two times faster than the raw SQL. Procedures are a proven SQL performance advantage; use them as often as you can.

Security

A stronger argument than any performance advantage is the ability to force all data maintenance to be done via application procedures and not allow any direct maintenance of the base tables. This is illustrated in Figure 7.5.

The privilege mechanism reduces overhead by not checking the access privileges of contained objects as long as the ownership of the containing and contained objects is the same. This means the ability to execute a procedure is checked, but any table access by the procedure is not checked as long as the procedure and table is owned by the same user. Figure 7.5 shows the full privilege hierarchy of procedures containing views which contain tables. This allows you to revoke all access to the tables and restrict select access via the views and maintenance access via the procedures. Unless you are using the view to limit the data seen by the users, restricting select access via a view is not common as ad-hoc SQL is usually required against the base tables by some users of the system. However, it is very common to not allow any SQL maintenance of the tables and force all update/delete/insert to the data to be made via application controlled procedures.

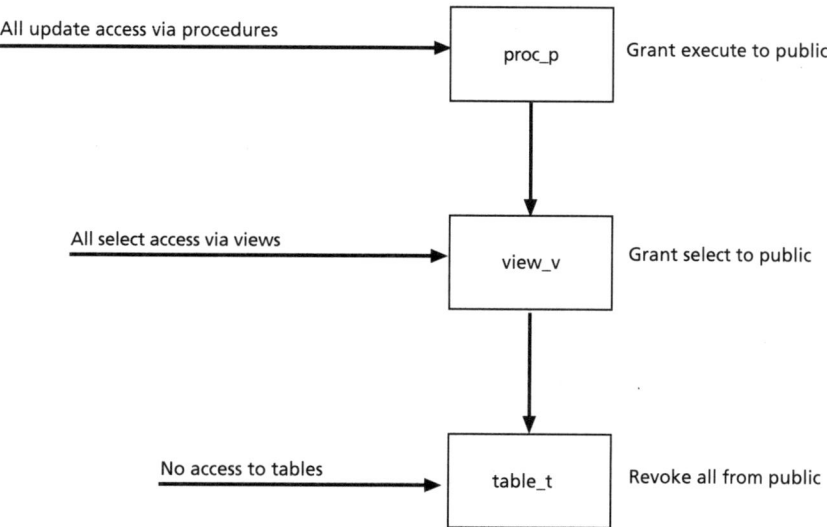

Figure 7.5 Restriction of table access via procedures

Summary

The decision on which, if any, index is used when taken by the optimizer based on the criteria:

- The where clause must be in the form of a search argument

- The column(s) of the where clause must be in an existing index

- The statistics of the index are used to estimate the number of records to be returned

If the number of logical I/Os estimated by the optimizer is less than a table scan, the index will be used. If not, the index is ignored and a table scan carried out. The statistics are not maintained dynamically and should be refreshed regularly with an update statistics. The statistics are also accessed as a look-up by the optimizer without any datatype conversion; it is important to ensure that both sides of the where clause are the same datatype: be especially careful with *char* versus *varchar* and the *numeric* datatype.

The statistics are made up of three components:

- Key value distribution: used in search arguments when there are no look-up conflicts

- Search argument density: used in place of the distribution values when there are look-up conflicts which mean that the distribution values may not be used

- Join density: used by join columns to estimate the number of records per join

Because of the one page size limitation on the distribution page, the index statistics are collected on the first column of a composite index only. This requires some care in the ordering of the columns of a composite index. Try to choose the most selective column as the first column in a composite, so the index statistics of the index look more selective, i.e., less records per index value. If there is no distinction between the columns, match the column sequence to the selectivity of the where clause operators, with the most selective operator, i.e., equality as the first index column.

Choosing indexes is based on the SQL and the rules of thumb are:

- Use composite indexes for AND clauses

- Use one index per OR clause

- Treat join columns as where clause columns

- Treat non-correlated nestings as joins if they can be flattened to joins by the optimizer

- Treat other non-correlated nestings as individual commands

- Treat correlated nestings as a combination of the other two

PART **III**

ADMINISTRATION INTERNALS

To get the best out of your database you need a detailed knowledge of how the software works. This is especially relevant to system troubleshooting, so I have given a low-level description of some SQL Server internals in this section. Having a detailed knowledge of how the various components of the server operate will allow you to react more comfortably to problems. It's not going to help you fix them—you still have to leave that to Sybase—but it will help you give Sybase a more detailed picture of the problem which might mean a faster fix.

This is especially true in the investigation of allocation and page errors. This chapter describes the allocation and management of data space; discussing allocation units, allocation pages, extents, OAM, GAM, and the data and index page and record layouts.

8

Storage

What is the unit of disk space?

All disk space is defined in units, called pages, of 2 Kb. This is the standard page size for all SQL Server implementations except for Stratus which has a page unit of 4 Kb. I have used 2 Kb throughout the material. If you are a Stratus user, you will have to make the appropriate adjustments.

SQL Server stores all information in 2 Kb pages which comprise a 32 byte header and a page body whose contents depend on the page type. The page types are:

- Data page: contains data records

- Log page: contains log records

- Index page: contains index records

- Allocation page: contains control information about groups of database pages

- Global allocation map (GAM) page: contains space usage information about allocation units

- Object allocation map (OAM) page: contains space usage information about objects

- Text/image page: contains text/image data

- Distribution page: contains information about index key value distribution

- Partition control page: contains pointers to the last page of a table partition and information on which device fragments the partition is using

These are explained in detail throughout this section.

How is disk space defined and managed?

Available disk space is defined to the server using the **disk init** command which allocates the disk space in 512 Kb allocation units. These allocation units are then allocated to a database via the create database command.

The **disk init** command informs the server where its available disk space is located on the physical disk drives. This disk space is allocated by the **disk init** command in units of 512 Kb each, composed of 32 extents of 8 pages per extent. These 8 page **extents** are the minimum units of space allocated to objects, as explained later. The first page in each allocation unit is called the **allocation page** and this controls the usage of the allocation unit by storing information about each extent in the allocation unit. This is illustrated in Figure 8.1. The **disk init** command does not initialize all of the pages in the allocation unit; only the allocation page in each allocation unit. The **create database** command initializes the allocation unit pages.

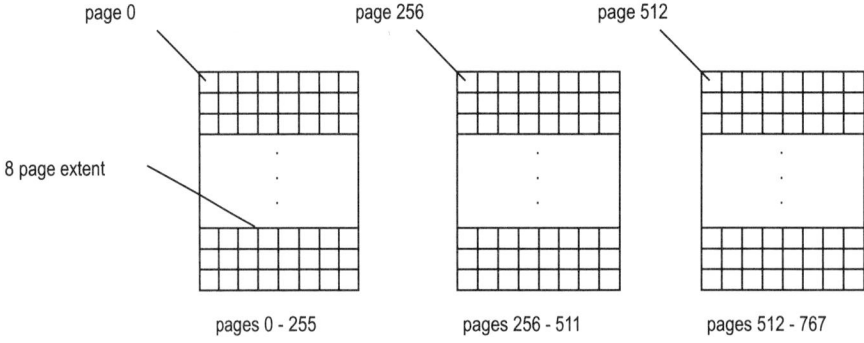

Figure 8.1 Allocation units

Figure 8.1 shows three allocation units, the first containing logical pages 0-255, the second 256-511, etc. Note that the allocation pages are always multiples of 256 and that the first extent in an allocation unit has only 7 usable pages, since the first page is used by the allocation page. The database create statement:

```
create database jk on data_0 = 10 log on log_0 = 2
```

will create the **sysusages** entries:

dbid	segmap	vstart	size	lstart
12	3	33554432	5120	0
12	4	50331648	2048	5120

which indicate a data allocation of 10Mb composed of 20 allocation units starting at logical page 0 and ending at 5199, followed by a log allocation of 2 Mb composed of 4 allocation units starting at logical page 5120 and ending at 7167.

The allocation page of each allocation unit contains an entry for each extent in the allocation unit indicating the object to which it belongs and the page numbers currently used by the object. This is illustrated in Figure 8.2.

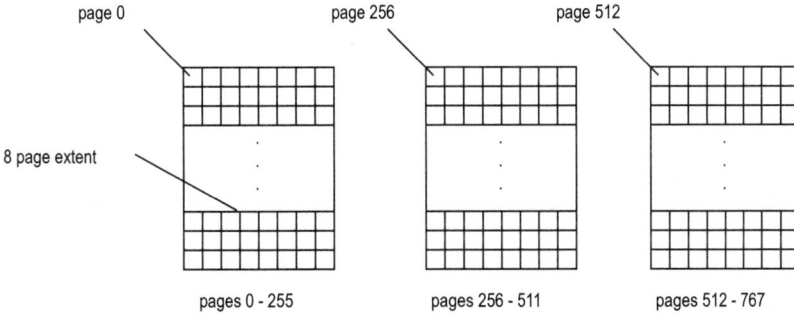

Figure 8.2 *Allocation page showing used page bit map for extent 408*

The two 4 byte unused fields in the extent structure were used for next and previous extent in the extent chain. The extents are no longer chained. This chaining was used to locate free pages in extents when a new page was required. This was replaced by the OAM from release 4.8. Figure 8.2 shows an allocation page containing extent 408 which has 5 pages used and 3 unused. This must be allocation page 256 as it contains extent 408. The allocation bit map for extent 408 shows that 5 pages are currently used and 3 unused. The unused pages remain allocated to the object as long as the extent is allocated to the object, i.e., until all of the pages are unused, at which time the extent is deallocated from the object. The dealloc bit map indicates extent pages which will be deallocated at the end of the current command. These cannot be deallocated while the command is running in case the command is rolled back. When the command commits, the dealloc bits are set off and the alloc (used page) bit map is updated.

The allocation page header contains:

- Logical page number

- Segment mapping for the allocation unit

- Object id of 99 (allocation pages are always object id 99)

- Database id using this allocation unit

The segment mapping and database id are used by **disk refit** to rebuild **sysdatabases** and **sysusages** during a recovery of master (see Recovery Chapter 10 for more detail on this).

The last 32 bytes of the allocation page are used by **dbcc checkalloc**. The first thing checkalloc does is set these bytes to zero. As each page in the object chain is read, a bit is set on in this area. After processing the page chains, checkalloc compares the allocation bit maps in the extent structures with the bit map. It reports on pages referenced in the page chain but not allocated in the extent structures and vice versa. The dbcc checkalloc and other storage structure dbcc commands are discussed in Storage and Troubleshooting, Chapter 15.

What is the system table relationship for storage allocations?

There are three system tables: **sysdevices, sysdatabases,** and **sysusages** which provide device, database and space allocation information.

The information about disk and database space allocations is held in three system tables:

Table 8.1

Table	Creation Command	Description
sysdevices	disk init	Physical disk space available to the server
sysdatabases	create database	Header information about a database
sysusages	create database	Space allocation information about a database

These are related as shown in Figure 8.3.

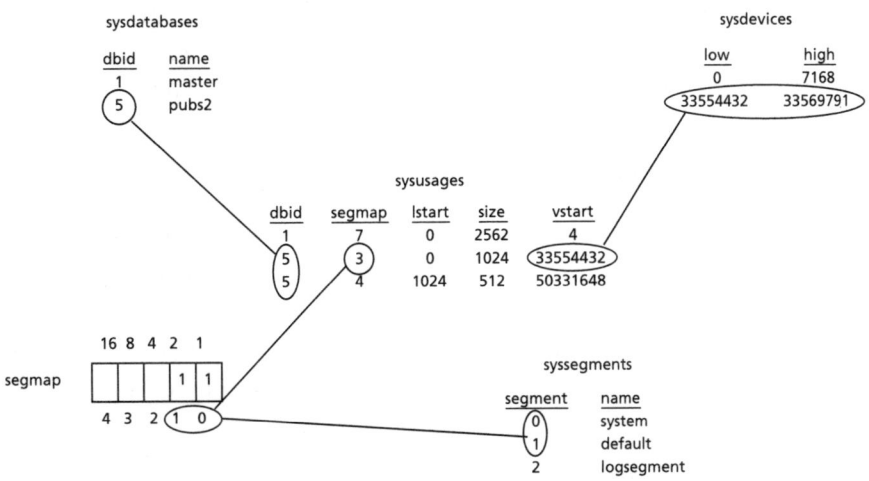

Figure 8.3 *System table space allocation relationships*

Sysdevices contains the low and high virtual page numbers for the allocation of space on disk. This relates to the **sysusages** table which contains the individual fragments of disk space which have been allocated to a database. **Sysusages** also contains the size of the fragment in 2Kb pages and the logical start page number. The dbid on **sysusages** joins to **sysdatabases** to obtain the name of the database. The segmap column on **sysusages** indicates the type of space allocation: 3—system and default, i.e., data; 4—logsegment only; 7—all three, i.e., data and log. So the above illustrates the pubs2 database having two space fragments, one for data and one for log, each on a different device (the log device is not shown on this example).

How is table and index space controlled?

Objects in a database have space allocated in units of extents, i.e., 8 pages. The used and free pages in these extents are controlled by the Object Allocation Map (OAM) and the Global Allocation Map (GAM).

Space is allocated to a table and index (but I shall use table as the example) as it is required. A request by an object for more space is satisfied by allocating an extent from an allocation unit belonging to the database. Therefore, a table with one row has 8 pages allocated to it. As records are deleted from pages and become empty, the page is not released to free space but remains allocated to the table but currently unused. Pages are returned to free space only when the extent is fully empty, in which case the extent is deallocated from the object and becomes available for reuse. Therefore, space is allocated and deallocated to and from objects in extents.

When a table requires a new page, an empty page in the current extent is used. When the extent is full the server tries to allocate an empty page from another of the existing extents allocated to the object. To avoid searching the object's extents serially, the object has one or more OAM pages which define the number of used and unused pages in each allocation unit. This indicates whether the current extents in the allocation unit are fully used or have unused pages in them, giving direct access to an allocation unit with free pages in the extents used by the object. The OAM page is illustrated in Figure 8.4.

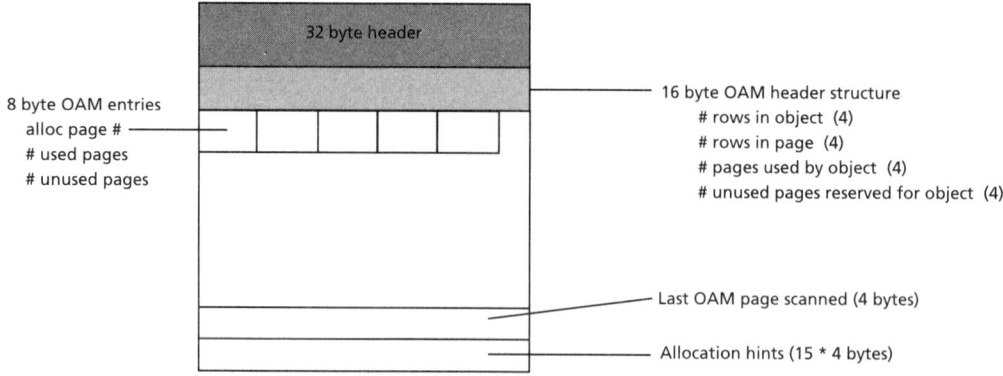

Figure 8.4 OAM page layout

When there are no free pages in existing extents, the server allocates a new extent from the allocation units belonging to the database. The server initially tries to allocate the new extent from an allocation unit already used by the object. To avoid searching all of the allocation units, the GAM holds a bit mapping of the allocation units indicating which have free extents. The GAM is illustrated in Figure 8.5.

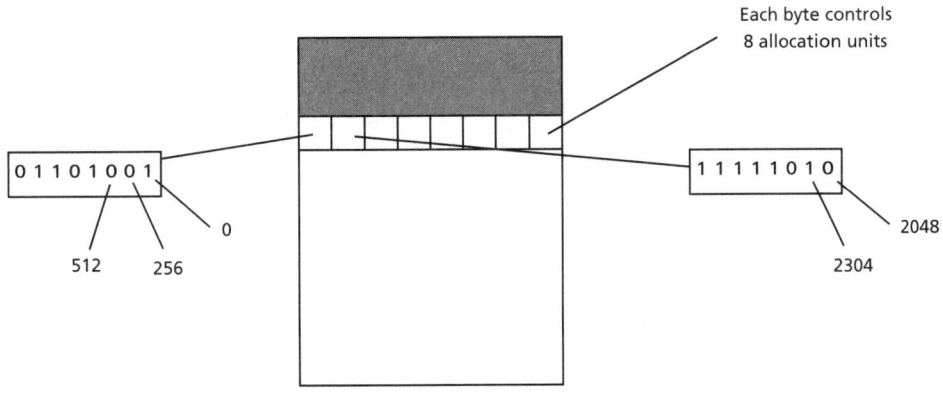

Figure 8.5 GAM page layout

As with all objects (see data page discussion later), the OAM pages are linked by next and previous page pointers in the header. An interesting aspect of the OAM page chain is that it is a circular chain, so be careful if you run a **dbcc pglinkage** on the OAM pages: it might not stop.

The available space for OAM entries is 2048-(32+16) = 2000 bytes which allows 250 entries. These calculations are slightly inaccurate as the 16 byte OAM structure, the last page scanned and the allocation hints are present in the first OAM page only. This means that an OAM page can store allocation information for 250*8 to 250*255 pages of data, i.e., from about 4 Mb to about 125 Mb of data. Each OAM entry contains page usage information for one allocation unit. The minimum number of pages which can be allocated to an object in an allocation unit is an extent, i.e., 8. The maximum is all of the pages less the allocation page, i.e., 255. Unfortunately, the OAM information can be displayed only with a dbcc command:

```
dbcc listoam(pubs2, 208003772,0)


objid:  208003772      indid:  0
OAM pg cnt:  1         Entry cnt:   2
rows:  346             rows per page:   14
used pgs:  24          unused pgs:  0
OAM status bits set:   PG_OAMPG, PG_OAMSORT
ALLOCATION HINTS:
          0         0         0         0
          0         0         0         0
          0         0         0         0
          0         0         0
OAM pg#: 264 has the following entries (allocpg: used/unused)

          256: 16/0
          768: 8/0
```

This shows table (indid=0) 208003772 as having 346 rows at 14 per page using 24 pages in 2 allocation units with no unused pages.

The OAM pages are stored on the extents allocated to the object. The first OAM page number is held in the sysindexes columns *doampg* and *ioampg* for data and index respectively. The tables **syslogs** and **sysgams** do not have OAM pages. The first OAM page contains 15 allocation hints, which are allocation page numbers where free space is most likely. The last OAM page scanned allows the next search for space to start at this point on the basis that the OAM pages before this one have just been scanned and found not to contain free pages.

The GAM header uses only the logical page number, next and previous pointers and the object id (14). Each byte in the GAM controls 8 allocation units, i.e., 4 Mb of data so 1 GAM page controls up to about 8 Gb of data. If the allocation unit has free extents, the GAM bit is set to 0 otherwise it is set to 1. On initial database creation, all GAM bits are set to zero and then adjusted as the space is allocated to objects. The above GAM in Figure 8.5 shows free space in allocation units 256, 512, 1024, 1792, 2048 etc.

The GAM is held in the system table **sysgams** but it is not available to you via SQL. The only information you can see is the header via **dbcc page**.

So how does the server allocate more space to an object?

Space is allocated to an object as:

- Use empty page in current extent
- Use empty page in another existing extent
- Allocate new extent from allocation units used by object
- Allocate new extent from beginning of database allocation chain

When an object requires a new page for expansion, it is allocated in order of the following steps.

1. If the OAM indicates that there is an empty page in the current extent, this is used.

2. If there is no space in the current extent, the OAM is used to find an existing allocation unit with unused pages in the allocated extents. The allocation page is accessed and the extent structures searched for a free page in one of the extents used by the object.

3. If there are no unused pages in existing extents, a new extent must be obtained. The OAM is used to first check the allocation units already used by the object. The GAM is accessed for these allocation units to see if there are free extents. If there are, the allocation page is accessed and the extent allocated to the object.

4. If there are no free extents in the allocation units used by the object, the GAM is searched from the beginning to find the first allocation unit with free space and an extent is allocated from this.

How is the data page itself laid out?

The data page is a 2Kb page with a 32 byte header and contains an integral number of rows. A row cannot span more than one page and must be fully contained in one page.

The data page layout is shown in Figure 8.6.

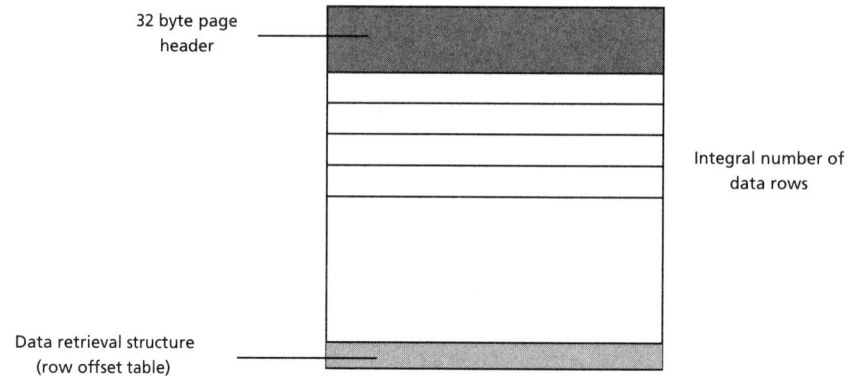

Figure 8.6 Data page layout

The page header contains the following information. All types of pages (OAM, GAM etc.) have this header structure although they do not use all of the columns.

```
fields                   bytes          description
pageno                   4              logical page number
nextpg                   4              next page in chain
prevpg                   4              previous page in chain
objid                    4              object id to which page belongs
timestamp (low)          4              low order bytes of page timestamp
nextrno                  2              next row number on page
level                    1              index level (0 for data)
indid                    1              index id
timestamp (high)         2              high order bytes of page timestamp
freeoff                  2              offset of available space on page
status                   2              system information
minlen                   2              length of fixed portion of data row
```

The pages are linked together with a two-way pointer chain in the nextpg and pre-vpg columns. The timestamp columns are used in recovery as detailed in Transaction Log and Recovery, Chapter 9. All free space in the page is held after the last record. The free-off column contains the offset for this space from the beginning of the page. If a record is deleted, the records are shuffled up to reclaim the space. If a record is inserted, it is insert-ed at the foot of the page identified by the free space offset or it is inserted in key sequence for a clustered index if necessary and the records are shuffled down to make room.

The row offset table at the foot of the page is the means of locating records in the page. Each offset table entry contains a 2 byte offset of the record from the beginning of the page. The record is identified by the combination of the logical page number and the offset number. This is illustrated in Figure 8.7.

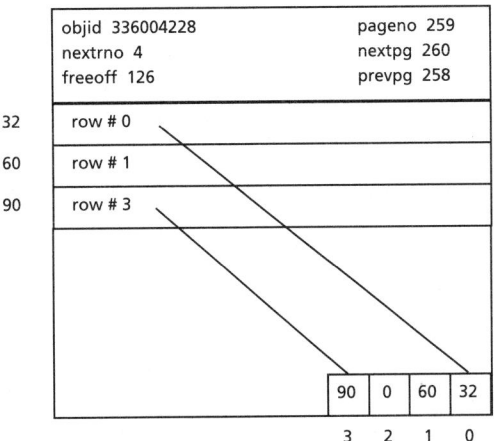

Figure 8.7 Record location by row offset table

The page (259) contains three records at offsets 32, 60, and 90. These records have record_ids of 259:0, 259:1, and 259:3 respectively. Because the record_id is a combination of the logical page number and the offset entry number, the record can move up and down in the page without changing its record_id. The position of the record in the page may change but this changes the contents of the offset entry, not the offset number. As long as the record stays in the same page it does not change its record_id. This is important in record updates since no index entries need to be updated if the record_id of the record does not change.

The offset entry 2 has been zeroed to indicate that this record has been deleted. When a new record is inserted to this page, it uses the first available offset entry; in this case offset 2. Therefore, there is no guarantee that the records are held in the page in record_id sequence as offset entries are reused to reduce the amount of space taken up by the offset table. Notice also that this reuse of offset entry numbers can cause a record_id to change even if the record stays on the same page. The above page layout would result in a change of record_id for row 259:3 if it was updated as a delete followed by an insert, i.e., as a direct expensive or deferred update (see Chapter 6 on Update Strategies for a detailed explanation of these terms). This is illustrated in Figure 8.8 where row 259, 3 is updated as a delete followed by an insert which changes the row_id to 258, 2.

When the update of row 259, 3 is executed as a delete followed by an insert, the insert uses the first zero offset entry and the inserted record is given the new record_id of 259:2.

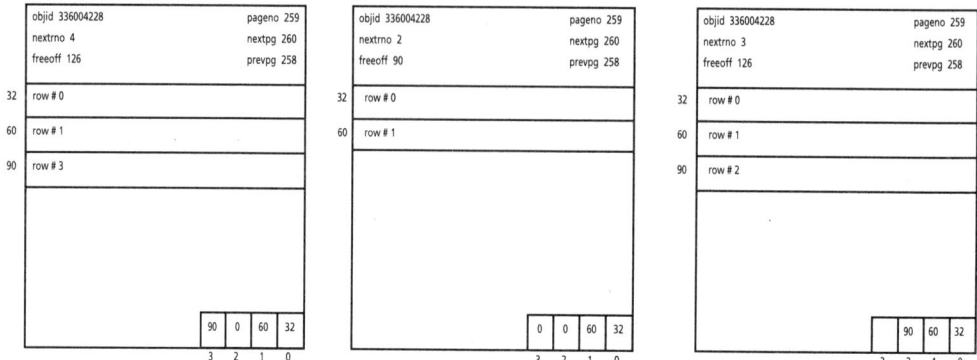

Figure 8.8 Record update causing new record_id

The maximum space available for records is 2048–32, i.e., 2016 bytes. This is obviously reduced by the offset table. The maximum record size is 1960 bytes which is caused by the requirement to write log records. The transaction log has to contain its records in a 2Kb page and so the log record has to be restricted to the available 2016 bytes of free space in a page. The transaction log record has additional columns such as transaction_id and operation code (see Transaction Log and Recovery Chapter 9) which have to be catered for and these reduce the maximum available data record size. There is no minimum row size but the maximum number of records per page is 256 caused by a 1 byte row number in the data record (see below).

How is the index page laid out?

The basic structure is the same with a 32-byte header and an integral number of rows. The index page does not contain an offset table.

The index page contains the index rows in sequence of the index key. This means that the index records may be located by key value in the page, so the offset table is not required. Once the page which contains the index record is located (see Types of Index, Chapter 5 for a detailed description of how this is done), a binary search is carried out on the index key values to locate the required record. This is actually similar to how records are located in a clustered index. The index entry in the clustered index points only to the page which contains the record; record_ids are not stored in the index. This means that the offset entry in the data page cannot be used to locate the clustered index record and so a binary search on the key value is carried out.

How is the data record laid out?

All the fixed length columns are located at the start of the record followed by all of the variable length columns. Both the fixed and variable length portions have system overheads as explained below.

The table:

```
create table jk_tab (
        col_a           int,
        col_b           varchar(30),
        col_c           float,
        col_d           varchar(20))
```

has the columns stored on the record in the sequence col_a, col_c, col_b, col_d. In other words, the table definition fixes the sequence of the columns within the fixed and variable groupings.

The data record layout with overheads is shown in Figure 8.9

Some of the documentation states that the fixed length overhead is 4 bytes. This is made up of the 2 bytes on every record and the 2 bytes in the offset table at the foot of the page. Even if the record has no variable length columns, the number of variable length columns is still present and is set to zero. The start positions of the fixed length columns are held in the **syscolumns.offset** column. If the record contains fixed length columns only, the record finishes after the fixed length columns and does not contain the record length. This can be obtained from the header minimum record length.

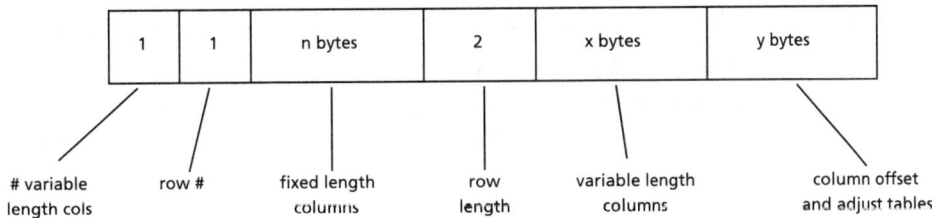

Figure 8.9 Data record layout

The variable columns offset table at the end of the record contains a one byte offset for each variable column. The first byte is the number of offset entries (i.e., the number of variable columns + 1), the second byte is the offset of the end of the variable columns and then one byte for each column containing the offset of the column from the beginning of the record. The record layout for the above create table statement is given in Figure 8.10 with col_b having 5 characters and col_d having 10 characters.

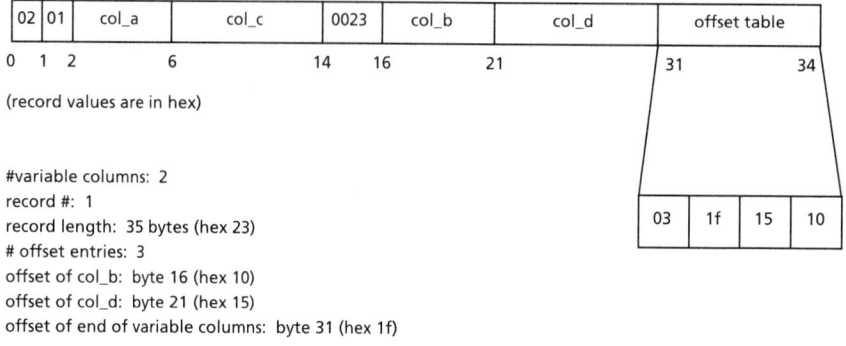

(record values are in hex)

#variable columns: 2
record #: 1
record length: 35 bytes (hex 23)
offset entries: 3
offset of col_b: byte 16 (hex 10)
offset of col_d: byte 21 (hex 15)
offset of end of variable columns: byte 31 (hex 1f)

Figure 8.10 *Example record layout*

For the variable length columns, the **syscolumns.offset** column holds the offset number as a negative number. For the variable columns above, col_b has **syscolumns.offset** equal to -1 and col_d equal to -2. The position of the variable column is obtained from the corresponding offset entry and the length of the variable column is the difference between this and the next offset entry. Columns which are defined as allowing nulls in the create table are held on the record as variable length columns. Columns with a null value are identified by not having a length when the offset entries are interpreted. Null values at the end of the record are not held on the record.

A problem with the offset table is that the offset value is only one byte which means that it cannot represent values above 255. This clearly causes problems as the maximum record length is 1960 bytes. When variable columns are located on the record above 255 bytes the offset table has additional entries indicating the first column number above each 256 byte breakpoint. The offset entries then hold the byte position of the column from the beginning of each 256 byte portion of the record. This is illustrated in Figure 8.11.

The record in Figure 8.11 has 3 variable columns, the first at offset 18 (0x12). The second is at offset 9 (0x09) which is not possible since it is less than the position of the first variable column. So the second variable column is the first column past the 256 byte breakpoint, confirmed by entry 02 in first column number past byte 256. The entries which specify the first column number past each 256 breakpoint are called the adjust table. Therefore, column 2 starts at offset 256+9, i.e., 265. The third column is at offset 242 (0xf2) and therefore starts at offset 256+242, i.e., 498. As there are no more entries in the adjust table, any variable columns after column 2 cannot start after another 256 byte breakpoint. The end of data is at offset 5 (0x05) which again is not possible since it is less than the offset of column 3. Therefore, the end of data offset is past the next breakpoint, i.e., the 512 byte breakpoint. Again, we know it must be the next breakpoint as the adjust table has only the one entry.

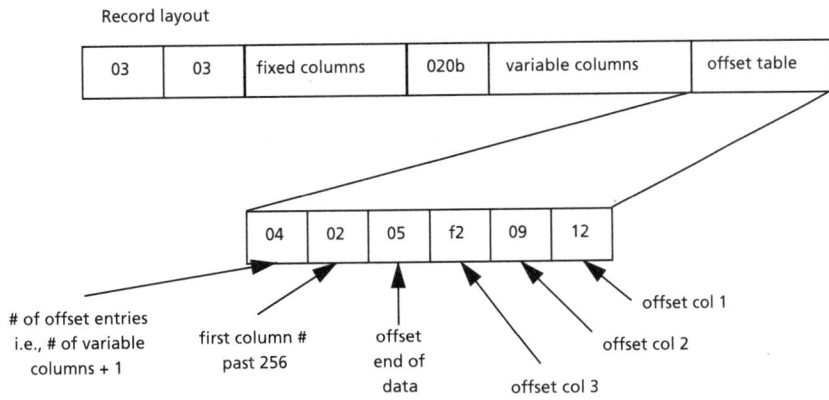

Figure 8.11 Offset entries for variable columns after byte 255

How is the index record laid out?

The index record is laid out the same as a data record except that there is no row number and the index record contains a record_id and/or a page number pointer. The row number in the data record is the same as the offset table entry at the foot of the data page. As the index record does not have an offset table, there is no need for a row number in the record.

The basic index record layout is shown in Figure 8.12.

The clustered index record has only a page pointer (4 bytes); the nonclustered leaf index record has only a record_id pointer (6 bytes) and the nonclustered non-leaf index record has both a page and a record_id pointer (10 bytes). The indexes are described in detail in the Types of Index, Chapter 5. Apart from there being no row number and the additional pointers, the layout of the index record is the same as a data record. Fixed columns are first, a row length if variable columns are present, followed by the variable columns and the offset table for the variable columns. As with the data record, the record finishes after the pointers if there are no variable length columns.

Index record layout

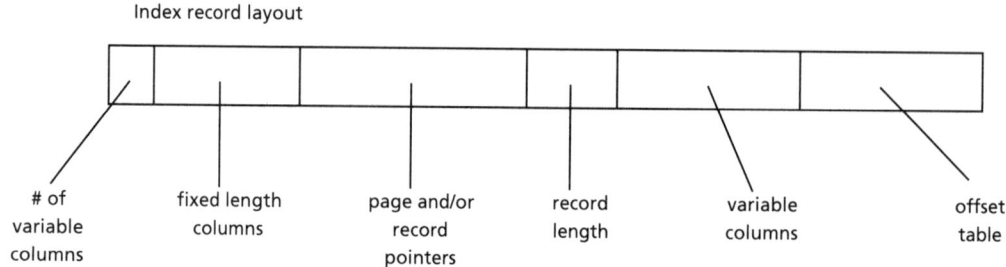

Figure 8.12 Index record layout

How are the text/image pages held?

The text/image datatype is held as a separate chain of pages containing the text/image data.

The text/image datatype is not held on the record but as a separate object in a separate page chain with a maximum size of 2 Gb. The page chain is linked forwards and backwards as with all page chains and is linked to the record with a 16-byte pointer in the data record. This is illustrated in Figure 8.13.

Data record

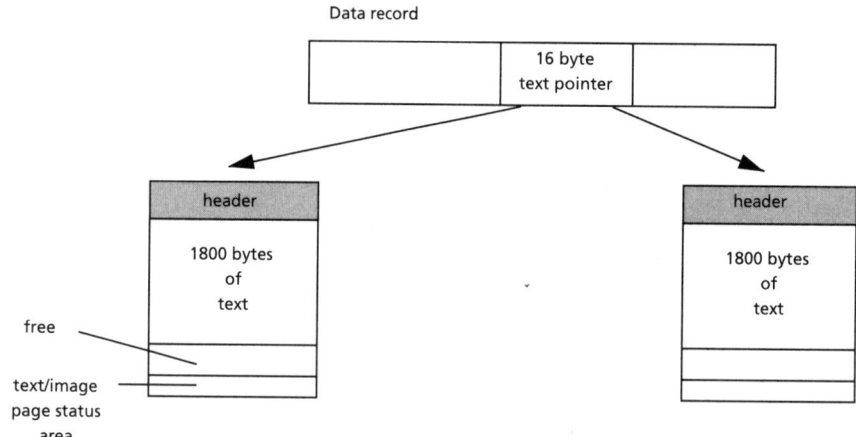

Figure 8.13 Text/image pages

The text/image status area (TIPSA) is 64 bytes but I have no further information. I'm not sure about the 1800 byte page limit but I assume that it is mainly caused by the need to log the text. Note that text/image data is not logged by default. Interestingly, if you have multiple text/image columns on one record they are able to share the same extents for space allocation. Each separate column has its own page chain and 16 byte pointer on the data record, but the text pages may share extents.

The first page of the text for a specific column may be located with the command:

```
select convert(int, textptr(col_name))
       from table
       where pkey = value
```

How is the distribution page laid out?

The index statistics distribution page is no different from any other page with a 32 byte header and an integral number of records describing the index key values distribution. There is no offset table at the foot of the page as the records are held in sequence of the index key values.

The method of determining the index distribution is described in detail in Index Selection, Chapter 7. The distribution page holds a number of records containing the key values from the record sampling and densities representing the level of duplication in the key values. The index key values are held in rows identical in format to a data row as shown in Figure 8.14.

1 byte	1 byte	fixed columns	2 bytes	variable columns	offset table

Figure 8.14 *Index distribution record layout*

As the statistics are collected on only one column even for a multi-column composite index, this layout seems a little daft and it would have been better to save space and get more records in the distribution page, but that's how it's done. The density figures are held at the foot of the page but are not displayed, even with a **dbcc page**, so I have no information on them. The location of the distribution page for each index is held in the column **sysindexes.distribution**. Note that the unnecessary use of a row number in the record restricts the number of records in a distribution page to 256.

Partition control page

The partition control page is a standard page with a 32 byte header.

The partition control page contains a pointer to the last page of the heap table partition. It is held in the initial extent allocated to the partition of the table and contains one record with the columns:

- Last page of the partition

- The partition number

- The number of pages allocated in the partition

- The number of entries in the device affinity table

- The logical page number in the device affinity table

- The size in pages for the entry in the device affinity table

Although the mapping of the partitioned table to the device is held in the control page it is not permanent as device mapping can change with a database load.

The partition control page numbers are displayed at the end of sp_help:

```
sp_help jk4_tab

.
.

.
.
Object does not have any indexes.
No defined keys for this object.

partitionid   firstpage     controlpage
-----------   -----------   -------------
          1          993             994
          2         1000            1001
```

and the page information may be seen using a dbcc page command with a print option of 3.

```
dbcc page(8, 1001, 3)
```

```
BUFFER:
Buffer header for buffer 0xe5ece800
    page=0xe5ecf000 bdnew=0x0 bdold=0x0 bhash=0x0 bmass_next=0x0
      bmass_prev=0x0 bvirtpg=0 bdbid=0 bkeep=0
          bmass_stat=0x0800 bbuf_stat=0x0000 bpageno=1001
          bxls_pin = 0x00000000 bxls_next = 0x00000000b
          bxls_flushseq 0 bxls_pinseq 0

PAGE HEADER:
Page header for page 0xe5ecf000
pageno=1001 nextpg=0 prevpg=0 objid=1458104235 timestamp=0001 0af1b751
nextrno=0 level=0 indid=0   freeoff=32 minlen=60
page status bits: 0x1,

Control Page Data:
lastpage=1011
slicenum=2
alloccount=11
 device affinity map count=1
lstart=0
size=102400
DBCC execution completed. If DBCC printed error messages, contact a user with
System Administrator (SA) role.
```

Summary

The basic unit of storage is a 2Kb page which contains an integral number of records. The pages are grouped together into 8 page extents which is the minimum amount of new space allocated to an object. The extents are grouped together into 32 extent allocation units which is the minimum amount of space allocated to a database. The first page of each allocation unit is the allocation page which manages the 32 extent structures in the allocation unit. When an object requires a new page, it uses an empty page in the current extent. If all of these are used it tries to use an empty page in one of its other extents. If there are no unused pages a new extent is allocated to the object.

The page consists of a 32 byte header, an integral number of records and an offset table at the foot of the page which holds the offset of the record from the beginning of the page. The record is identified by the combination of page number and offset entry number.

The data record is held as all fixed length columns followed by all variable length columns. All records have a 2 byte overhead at the beginning of the record which comprises a 1 byte column for the number of variable columns and a 1 byte column for the row number. The row number equates to the offset entry number. Note that the 1 byte row number limits the number of records in a page to 256. If there are variable length columns the total row length is held in a 2 byte column immediately after the fixed length columns. The length of each variable length column is held as a 1 byte off-set from the start of the page in an offset table at the end of the record.

Index records do not have a row number or an offset table at the foot of the page. Index records are always held in sequence of the key and do not need to be located by record id but can be located by a sliding binary search of the records in the page.

## 9

Transaction Log and Recovery

The transaction log is probably the most important system table in your database and a detailed knowledge of how it is organized, what is written to it and how to display the information is essential. This chapter describes the layout and usage of the transaction log and how it is used to provide automatic recovery using roll forward and rollback.

What is the transaction log?

The transaction log is the system table **syslogs** which contains log records for all changes to the database.

Each database has a system table **syslogs** which contains a record of all changes to the database. This is a heap table with no indexes, meaning that all inserts are written to the last page of the table. The **syslogs** table has no OAM page, allocation of new pages to the transaction log does not go through the same algorithm as all other tables. I have no information on how space is allocated to **syslogs** but I would imagine that giving the log its own segment with the **log on** clause of the **create database** statement would speed up new page allocation. In this case, the log would only have to locate the next page/extent in the allocation unit as all allocation units belong to the log instead of contending with the data and system segments for the next free extent.

However, the heap nature of the transaction log causes a "hot-spot" on the last page of the log as all transactions are trying to write their changes to this page. This is alleviated in System 11 by User Log Caches (ULCs), where each connection has its own ULC which it uses to write the transaction changes until the transaction completes. At this point the ULC is flushed to the central database transaction log. There are other reasons for the ULC being flushed, such as it becoming full. These are covered in detail in Chapter 13 This reduces the amount of I/O activity on the transaction log and reduces the contention for the last page. The ULC may be flushed more often than at transaction completion and this should be monitored as it can increase log contention. Simply for ease of presentation, I shall treat the ULCs and syslogs as one logical object throughout this section and discuss everything in relation to the transaction log. Where necessary I shall refer to the specific object. This is dealt with in detail in the monitoring sections.

When does information get written to the log?

The transaction changes are written to the log when the transaction completes or at a checkpoint.

The transaction log has to be viewed as three objects: ULC, cache log and disk log. While the transaction is executing, the changes are written to the ULC and the cache version. When the transaction completes, changes in cache are flushed to the disk copy of the log. Once the changes have been flushed to disk the transaction is fully recoverable and may be recovered from any error (except complete destruction of all versions of the log). Each ULC is a limited size—default 2 Kb—and therefore a large transaction may cause it to fill up before the transaction completes. When this happens the ULC is flushed to the central cache log to allow more log records to be accumulated in the ULC. This means that the cache version of the log is a mixture of multiple transaction changes and each record on the log must have an identifier which allows it to be grouped with its other transaction changes. This is a transaction identifier held in the log record header (see below). When a transaction completes, its ULC is flushed to the cache version and the cache version of the log is force written to disk. This force write ensures that every completed transaction has all of its changes written to the log so it may be recovered. This means that a transaction which runs for some time may be flushed to disk several times before it completes. This type of activity is illustrated in Figure 9.1.

The **checkpoint** fires based on the configuration variable recovery interval. This defines the maximum number of minutes which the system should take to run a recovery. The checkpoint routine regularly interrogates the log and determines how much recovery needs to be done. If it exceeds the recovery interval, a checkpoint is taken. The checkpoint routine decides how much work is required by recovery by multiplying the number of records on the log since the last checkpoint by 10 ms per record. System 11 has another server process called the **housekeeper** which flushes dirty pages during server idle cycles. If the housekeeper task flushes all dirty pages to disk it wakes up the checkpoint task to write a checkpoint to the transaction log. Although the housekeeper is using free writes, i.e., writes done during server idle cycles, it can still overload a device with the extra disk writes. The increase in database writes can be configured with **housekeeper free write percent** if this becomes a problem. Also, the maximum number of writes which the house-keeper can issue to a device in an I/O batch can be configured with **dbcc tune**.

```
dbcc tune(deviochar, vdevno, value)
```

where

vdevno	the virtual device number
	-1 to affect all devices
value	maximum number of writes in one I/O batch
	1 - 255 default 3

The Sybase documentation recommends that you consider increasing this for RAID devices based on the number of spindles, but I have no information on recommended values.

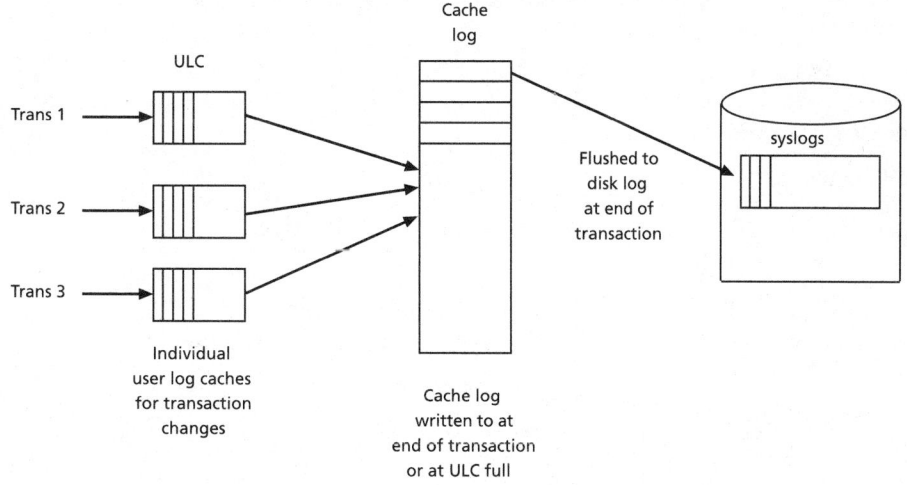

Figure 9.1 *Flushing of ULC and transaction log to disk*

What is the layout of the log page and the log record?

The log uses a standard 2 Kb page; the log record contains a log header and the changes to the page.

The transaction log records are held in a standard 2 Kb page with no overlapping of the page boundary and a row offset table as for normal data records. The log record has a 16 byte header followed by the data changes made by the command being logged. This is illustrated in Figure 9.2.

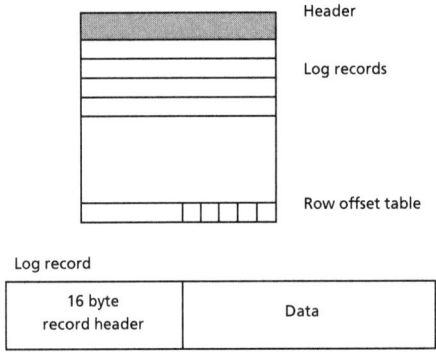

Figure 9.2 *Transaction log page and record layout*

The 16 byte log record header contains:

Table 9.1

Field Name	# of Bytes	Description
attcnt	1	0 if header only; 1 if data
rno	1	row #
op	1	operation code
padlen	1	# of pad bytes to align record
xactid	8	transaction id
len	2	length of row
stat	2	log status

This is the minimum log record header information which is present for all log records. The data portion of the log record contains additional log header information specific to the type of log record. For example, the modification log records—insert, delete, update—have the additional header information of:

- OAM page number

- Page number changed

- Row offset of row changed

- Status field

- Page timestamp before modification

- Page timestamp after modification

The principal operation codes are:

Table 9.2

Operation Code	Record Type	Description
0	BEGINXACT	begin tran
4	INSERT	data record insert
5	DELETE	data record delete
6	INSIND	second phase of deferred insert/update
7	IINSERT	index record insert
8	IDELETE	index record delete
9	MODIFY	direct record update
11	INOOP	first phase of deferred insert/update
12	DNOOP	first phase of deferred delete/update
16	SPLIT	data page split
17	CHECKPOINT	checkpoint
30	ENDXACT	end tran

The transaction id is the row_id of the begin transaction record logged for the transaction. This means that every log record for a transaction has the same transaction id which allows them to be identified together for recovery purposes.

What gets logged for the maintenance commands?

The transaction log is a changes log which means that only the changes to the pages get logged based on their offset from the beginning of the page.

The simplest way to visualize this is to consider that the recovery must be able to repeat (roll forward) or reverse (rollback) the effect of the command. Therefore, the changes recorded in the log must supply enough information to do both of these. The information logged is:

Table 9.3

Command	Data Logged
insert	complete record
delete	complete record
direct in-place and cheap update	changed bytes
direct expensive and deferred update	complete record for delete
	complete record for insert

All changes made during the transaction must be logged, so there may also be index records; OAM records and allocation pages logged if any of these are changed. Examples of what gets logged for a specific action are:

Table 9.4

Command	Log Records	Comments
begin tran	BEGINXACT	establishes transaction id
end tran	ENDXACT	
insert "direct"	INSERT	data
	IINSERT	index
delete "direct"	DELETE	data
	IDELETE	index
deferred insert/delete	INSERT/DELETE	
	IINSERT/IDELETE	
	DNOOP	page/row# of row to delete
	INOOP	new data row
	INSIND	pointer to INOOP which contains new data row

Table 9.4 (continued)

Command	Log Records	Comments
create new object allocation	DBNEXTID	next object id for creation (op code 14)page
	ALLOC	page allocation (op code 13)
	SALLOC	page split allocation (op code 24)
page deallocation	DEALLOC	op code 21
checkpoint	CHECKPOINT	
insert new entry in OAM	OAMINSERT	op code 39
delete entry from OAM	OAMDELETE	op code 40

The timestamps which are logged are very important and are used by recovery to decide what to do with the log record. Each database has a global timestamp which is stored in the DBTABLE structure. The DBTABLE structure is effectively a runtime copy of the DBINFO structure which is itself a copy of the **sysdatabases** entry for the database. The DBINFO structure stores system restart information and is used by recovery, dump and load and replication server. In addition to the **sysdatabases** information, DBINFO also contains the row_id of the most recent checkpoint log record and the next value for the server to hash to calculate the next object id. In addition to the DBINFO information DBTABLE also contains the current timestamp for the database. The DBTABLE structure is written to DBINFO at a checkpoint. The DBINFO structure is always held in page 24 of the database.

When a page is changed, the change is logged with the old and new page timestamps; the new timestamp is written to the page and the global timestamp is incremented. The recovery routines then check the page and log record timestamps to determine what action to take. This is discussed in detail later in this section.

Do multiple single maintenance commands in one transaction

If you are doing several update/insert/delete commands in one batch you should consider placing these in an explicit transaction.

SQL Server treats each maintenance command as a single transaction and commits the work before starting the next command. Therefore:

```
update tab_1 ....
update tab_1 ....
update tab_1 ....
```

are three separate transactions each of which is committed independently. Each commit requires a flush of the ULC (user log cache) to the cache version of the log. If the current log page is not full, this causes the task to be put to sleep until the log page is flushed to disk or the task migrates to the top of the runnable queue again. This is an obvious delay in the execution of the command batch, which can be removed by grouping the multiple commands into one explicit transaction.

```
begin tran
update tab_1 ....
update tab_1 ....
update tab_1 ....
commit tran
```

This requires only the one flush of the ULC with the possibility of the task being put to sleep only once. Clearly there are locking and contention considerations as the pages XLOCKed by the maintenance commands are now held for a longer time. Also, the ULC will be flushed when it is full and you may have to balance the ULC size with the amount of logging done by the multiple commands.

This is not an easy one and the increase in contention can make it not applicable. However, if you are doing overnight batch maintenance processing where the length of the locks is not important, you are strongly advised to consider transaction batching to reduce the commit time activity of the complete process. And, make sure that the transaction log is big enough to support the amount of logging caused by the long-running transaction.

How do I see the log records?

Standard SQL will show only the transaction id and op code from the log header. You need to use the **dbcc log** command to view the log records. Do not run **dbcc log** if the database has the **trunc. log on chkpt** option set. This can seriously corrupt your database. Always set this database option off before you start to use **dbcc log**.

Standard SQL will allow you to count the log records and display the transaction id and op code of each record. So you can be quite sophisticated even with this limited ability. The SQL will give quantitative information such as how many records are processed for each transaction/op code; when a BEGINXACT has an ENDXACT; and how many log records exist. Sizing information may be obtained with **sp_helpsegment logsegment**. To display all of the information on the log records use **dbcc log**:

```
dbcc log (dbid, objid, pageno, rowno, rowno, nrecords, type [,printopt])
```

objid	pageno	rowno	action
<0			pageno and rowno are start point in log
<0	-3		objid is a spid
<0	>0		all records for page number displayed
>0	>0		pageno and rowno represent transaction id
>0	0	0	all records for objectid displayed

nrecords	>0	display from beginning of log
	<0	display from end of log
printopt	0	header and data (default)
	1	header only

This displays all (not recommended as it can be rather a large output) or a number of records in the log and may display only those records for an object, page, spid or transaction id. The records may be displayed from the beginning (oldest) or end (most recent) of the log with data included or excluded as required. In other words, a full range of options which allow you to examine all or a selected portion of the transaction log. A sample output of the **begin tran** and an **index delete** is shown in Figure 9.3.

```
BEGINXACT       (1286, 4)
attcnt=1  rno=4  op=0  padlen=0  xactid=(1286, 4)  len=60
status=0x0009
masterid=(0, 0)  lastrec=(0, 0)  xstat=XBEG_ENDXACT,
spid=1  suid=3  uid=1  masterdbid=0  mastersite=0  endstat=3
name=del  time=Apr 27 1995 5:15PM


IDELETE (1286, 7)
attcnt=1  rno=7  op=8  xactif=(1286, 4)  len=68
status=0x0000
oampg=912  pageno=1008  offset=32  status=0x00
old ts=0x0001  0x000019f2  new ts=0x0001  0x000019f3
xrow
008cf990:  01000003  98000000  1748656c  6c6f2074  .........Hi
```

Figure 9.3 Sample dbcc log output

How does recovery decide which records to roll forward and which to rollback?

The decision on roll forward/rollback is based on whether the transaction committed or not and when the checkpoint occurred.

If a transaction completes successfully, it is committed, which causes the log records to be force written to the disk. This means that every committed transaction on the disk version of the log has been completed successfully and, in theory, does not need to be repeated in a recovery situation. However, because the data pages are not written to the disk at the commit point, there is no guarantee about the actual state of the data pages on disk. The cache management of the data cache is based on doing as little physical disk I/O as possible, and may cause a data page to remain in cache for a long period of time. Therefore if a failure occurs which causes cache to be lost and the recovery routine ignores all committed transactions on the log, some of the committed updates will not have been written to disk and the database will be left in an inconsistent state.

This could be overcome by replaying every transaction on the log, but this could obviously take too long and would repeat many transactions unnecessarily. Therefore, a routine called the checkpoint is executed frequently to flush all "dirty" pages from data cache to disk. This enables the recovery to ignore any transactions which completed before the **checkpoint**. The checkpoint guarantees that the data page updates have been flushed to disk.

In Figure 9.4, transaction A has completed before the checkpoint, so the recovery takes no action. Transactions B, C, and E have completed after the checkpoint, so they are rolled forward. Transaction D both started and completed after the checkpoint, so it is treated as a completion after the checkpoint and rolled forward. Transaction F did not complete after the checkpoint, so it is rolled back.

The checkpoint writes a record to the transaction log to indicate that it has fired. It records in this log record the row_id of the oldest active transaction when the checkpoint fired. This allows the recovery routine to determine the active and inactive portion of the transaction log (see later in this section). The checkpoint routine also updates the DBINFO structure with the row_id of the checkpoint record on the transaction log. The log page has an offset table which allows individual records to be located based on row_id (page number, offset number). This means the recovery can access the latest checkpoint record directly from the DBINFO structure and then the oldest active transaction directly from the checkpoint record.

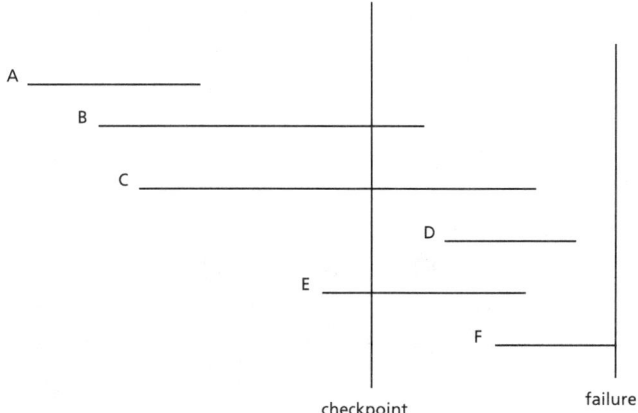

A _____

B _____

C _____

D _____

E _____

F _____

checkpoint   failure

Figure 9.4 *Checkpoint and rollback/roll forward relationship*

How does recovery work?

Recovery has three "layers," a **front end** layer, a **recovery** layer and a **do** layer. The front end layer does all communication with the commands driving the recovery such as **load database** and **load tran** and controls the automatic recovery at boot time. The front end layer calls the recovery layer with appropriate parameters from the invoking routines. The recovery layer scans the log and determines which transactions to pass to the do layer which does the rollback and roll forward.

Front End Layer

The front end layer is responsible for communicating with the invoking routines and passing the appropriate parameters to the recovery layer. When invoked at a server start the front end layer is responsible for ensuring that the server databases are recovered in the correct sequence. This sequence is master, sybsecurity, model, sybsystemprocs, and then the user databases in order of dbid. Note that tempdb is not recovered but is recreated as a copy of model. This sequence means that if a failure occurs before sybsystemprocs is recovered the system procedures will not be available. If you experience a failure during startserver which recovers master but not sybsystemprocs, you will not have any system procedures available; this can make some simple tasks such as sp_configure, and sp_addumpdevice quite difficult. It is recommended that you copy some system procedures into master in case this happens or be prepared to have to reinstall sybsystemprocs—which is no big deal, of course. Obvious candidates are **sp_configure**, **sp_addumpdevice**, **sp_volchanged** and some of the help procedures such as **sp_helpdevice** and **sp_helpdb**.

Recovery Layer

The recovery layer is called by the front end layer or directly by load database and load transaction to determine the log boundaries and build a list of transactions which have to be passed to the do layer for rollback or roll forward.

The log boundaries are defined as active and inactive portions, as shown in Figure 9.5.

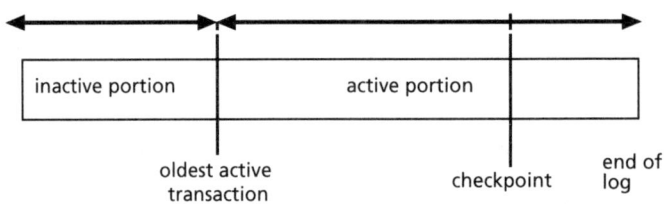

Figure 9.5 Log boundaries for recovery

The DBINFO structure contains the record id of the latest checkpoint record, which contains the transaction id of the oldest active transaction. As the transaction id is the row_id of the BEGINXACT for the transaction, this points directly to the start of the oldest active transaction. Anything before the oldest active transaction is considered to be inactive and transactions in this portion are not passed to the do layer. A list of transactions is then built from the active portion in two phases: phase 1 processes from the oldest active transaction to the latest checkpoint, and phase 2 from the latest checkpoint to the end of the log. All changes during phase 1 have been written to disk as they are before a checkpoint. This phase detects any transactions which have not completed before the checkpoint so that they may be recovered. Any transactions which completed before the checkpoint are not recovered. In phase 1, the log is scanned from the oldest active transaction to the latest checkpoint; each BEGINXACT adds the transaction id to a list and each ENDXACT also adds the transaction id to the list and deletes the corresponding BEGINXACT. At the end of phase 1, all ENDXACT transactions may be ignored by recovery as they have already been written to disk by the checkpoint. All outstanding BEGINXACT transactions must remain on the list for subsequent processing. Phase 2 of the recovery layer then scans the log from the latest checkpoint record to the end of the log. The end of the log is determined by reading a null next page pointer or the timestamp of the current page that is less than the timestamp of the previous page. In the timestamp situation, the previous page is the end of the log. Again, in phase 2 any BEGINXACT records are written to the transaction list and any ENDXACT records are written to the list and the corresponding BEGINXACT deleted from the list. At the end of this phase, transactions with an ENDXACT on the transaction list are passed to the do layer for roll forward and transactions with a BEGINXACT are passed to the do layer for rollback. In practice, ENDXACT transactions are rolled forward as they are encountered and the transaction list at end of the phase 2 scan contains only those transactions which have to be rolled back. This is illustrated in Figure 9.6.

Transactions 1 and 2 have completed before the latest checkpoint, so they are guaranteed to be on disk and need not be recovered. Transactions 3 and 5 were incomplete at the end of the log, so are rolled back; transaction 4 completed after the latest checkpoint, so is rolled forward. More correctly, transaction 4 is repeated as it is the ENDXACT log record which determines whether the transaction committed, in which case it is rolled forward. If it rolled back, it is rolled back again.

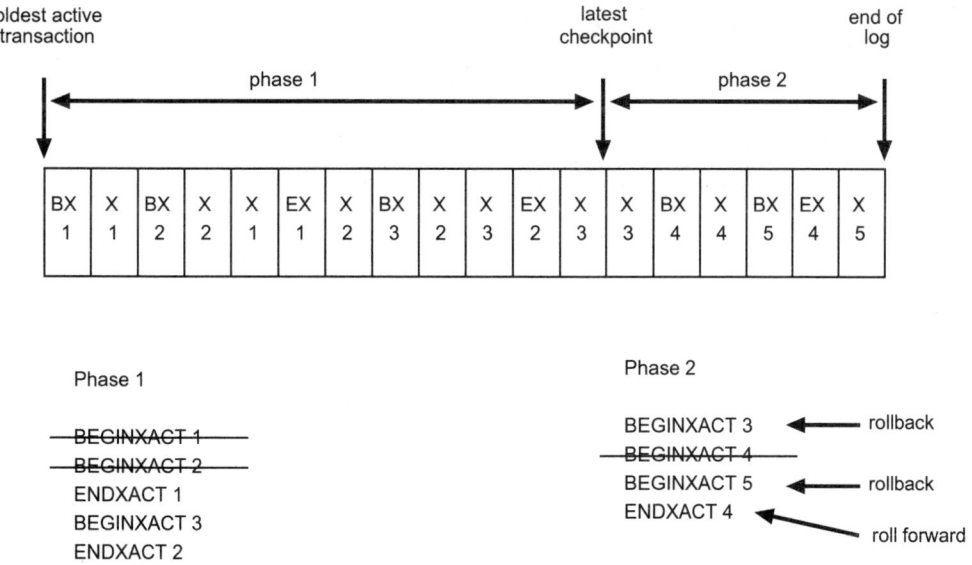

Figure 9.6 *Transaction log scans during recovery layer*

Do layer

The do layer is called by the recovery layer and rolls the transactions forward or backward as requested.

In a roll forward, the transaction is scanned in a forward manner and the timestamps of the log records and the corresponding data page are compared to decide what action to carry out. This is illustrated in Figure 9.7.

Each log record has an old and new timestamp for the change to the page. This is compared with the current timestamp in the header of the page. In Figure 9.7, the first two records for the transaction have the new timestamp less than or equal to the timestamp on the page. This means that these have already been written to disk and do not need to be recovered. The new timestamp of the third and fourth log records for the transaction is greater than the current timestamp of the page and so these log records have to be applied to the page.

In a roll back, the log records for the transaction are scanned in reverse direction and again the timestamps are compared with the disk page to determine if the changes need to be applied. This is illustrated in Figure 9.8.

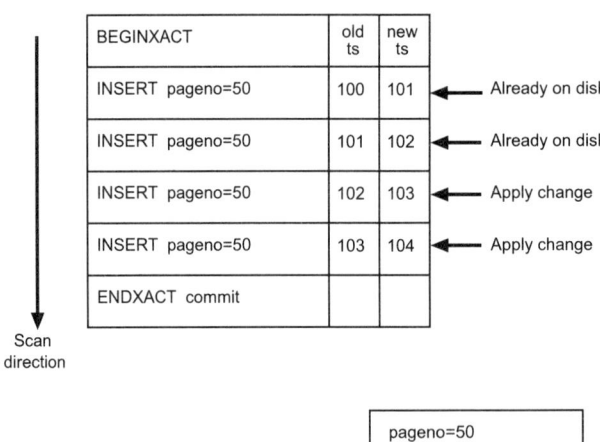

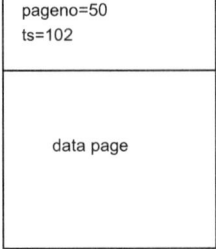

Figure 9.7 *Transaction roll forward*

In this situation, the new timestamp of the first and second log records for the transaction are less than or equal to the current timestamp of the page. This means that these changes have been applied to the page and must be rolled back.

Once the do layer has redone or undone the necessary transactions, the recovery routine initializes the database timestamp in the DBTABLE structure, writes a checkpoint record to the transaction log and updates the DBINFO structure to point to this checkpoint record. The checkpoint record is not written if the recovery was called from a load transaction.

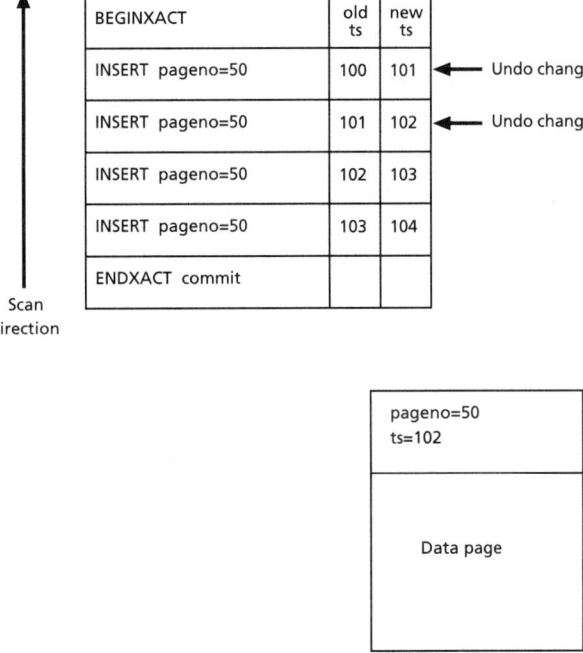

Figure 9.8 *Transaction roll back*

Summary

The system table syslogs is a heap table with no indexes which is the transaction log for the database. The transaction log holds all changes for the maintenance commands so that a transaction may be recovered to its before or after state with a roll back or a roll forward. When the transaction completes, the page changes are written to the disk version of the log which guarantees that the transaction changes can be recovered in the event of a system failure. For each change made to a page, a log record is written containing the change and the offset of the change from the beginning of the page. For an update both the version of the data before and after the update are recorded to allow both roll back and roll forward. The log record also contains an operation code to signify the type of command executed and a timestamp to record when the change occurred.

A separate checkpoint routine is run by the server at a regular interval to flush the dirty cache pages to disk. This establishes a point when all page changes have been written to disk. It creates a record on the log before which all changes must be on disk and after which there is no guarantee that any change has been written to disk. The recovery can safely ignore any completed transaction before the checkpoint record and recovers only those transactions which completed after the checkpoint.

During the actual recovery of the transactions, the timestamp on the log record is compared with the current timestamp of the relevant page. For a roll back, only those log records with a timestamp less than the page timestamp are applied and for a roll forward, only those log records with a timestamp later than the page timestamp are applied.

10

Database Recovery

Not only must we be able to recover from a system or application failure which requires a roll forward or rollback of current transactions, but we must also be able to recover from a complete failure of disk devices which cause the current database to be damaged and unusable. This applies to both the user databases and the system databases. This chapter describes the database dumping and how to recover from lost user and system databases.

How does the dump database work?

The dump database has three phases:

- Phase 1:   Starts at the beginning of the database and dumps all used pages—data and log. Called the DBPAGES phase.

- Phase 2:   Dumps any pages which were changed during Phase 1 but the change was not logged. Called the FLUSHPAGES phase.

- Phase 3:   Dumps the active portion of the transaction log. Called the SCANLOGPAGES phase.

Phase 1 simply dumps each used page without checking for any possible updates to the pages; the other phases ensure that all changes since the start of phase 1 are also recorded.

Database and transaction log dumping is done through the backup server which is a separate open server process which handles all dumping and loading of databases and transaction logs. The **dump** and **load** commands are input to the SQL Server which then passes the necessary information via rpcs to the backup server which takes control of the dump/load.

Dump Phase 1 (DBPAGES)

The dump database command is input to the server. It makes multiple rpcs to the backup server to inform it about the database sysusages mappings and the dump device information. The backup server then dumps the allocated pages of the database. While the backup server is dumping the allocated database pages, users which generate non-logged updates write the page numbers to a **flush list**. These non-logged activities are caused by the commands **bcp**, **select into**, **truncate** and **create index** and for any index splits or non-logged text manipulation. If the flush list becomes full during this phase, the server sends the flush list page numbers to the backup server which then dumps these pages. The flush list contents may be deleted and used again.

Dump Phase 2 (FLUSHPAGES)

When all allocated database pages have been dumped the server sends the contents of the current flush list to the backup server which then dumps these pages. The server then suspends the processes which are writing flush pages and sends any remaining flush pages to the backup server which dumps them. We now have the situation of all pages dumped and no processes running which do not write to the transaction log.

Dump Phase 3 (SCANLOGPAGES)

SQL Server chooses this point as the dump instant, i.e., the point to which the database will be recovered by a load, turns off the flush list and awakens the flush processes. The server then sends the log page numbers which have to be dumped to the backup server. If the log is on a separate segment to the data, only the active portion of the log has to be dumped; if data and log are mixed then all log pages have to be dumped. Once the backup server has dumped these log pages, the dump is complete and the backup server deallocates the dump resources.

What does the load database do?

The **load database** effectively reverses the dump process, writing all dumped pages back to the database. Any pages which are not written from the dump are initialized by the load process.

The load writes all dumped pages back to the database and initializes any pages which were not restored. Always remember that the database load will take longer than the database dump—by a factor of 2 to 3. The most up-to-date figures that I have for dump speed in system 11 is 2G per 10 minutes. Remember, the dump is writing out only the allocated pages, so the load has to ensure that any new page allocations made after the dump are removed. Once all dumped pages (including flush list pages) have been loaded, a recovery is initiated to process the transaction log pages dumped in phase 3 of the dump. This gives us a database restored to its state at the dump instant, which is effectively at the end of the dump. So, if your database dump started at 16:00 hours and completed at 20:00 hours, the dump reflects the database at 20:00 hours.

How do I recover from a lost database?

The obvious assumption is that you have a recent database dump with associated transaction log dumps. The minimum requirement is a recent database dump, which means that you will be able to recover to this point. The addition of transaction log dumps will enable you to recover the changes made since then, up to the last committed transaction.

You can recover from a database failure only if you have previously dumped the database using the **dump database** command. This allows you to reload the database using the **load database** command. The reloaded database will reflect the status of the data as at the end of the database dump. Clearly, this may have been some time in the past and you will need to recover all of the transactions made against the database since the dump. This is possible only if you have been taking regular dumps of the transaction log with the **dump transaction** command, which allows you to roll forward all of the transactions using the **load transaction** command. The sequence of events is to dump the database at regular intervals with regular transaction log dumps between the database dumps. For example you might dump the database once a week and the transaction log every day or the database every day and the transaction log every hour. The frequency of these is based on how long each takes and the amount of space required.

If the database dump takes 5 minutes, you might ignore any transaction log dumping and simply dump the database every hour. Of course, this will leave you with a maximum of one hour of data which can not be recovered if the database failure occurs immediately before a dump. If this is a problem, you may still want to dump the transaction log between database dumps. If the database dump takes 24 hours, you will not want to run it too often; regular transaction log dumps are more practical.

The transaction log dump frequency is based on how much space you can allocate to the log and how much data you might lose if you lose the current transaction log. You can recover only from a transaction log which has been dumped. When a media failure, occurs you will have a current transaction log which has not been dumped. The **dump tran** command has an option **with no_truncate** which allows you to dump the current transaction log in a failure scenario. The normal **dump tran** command requires the database to be present and in a usable state. This may not be the case if a media failure has occurred. If you cannot dump the current transaction log, you will lose all of its transactions. There is no guarantee since you are in a failure situation, but the **with no_truncate** option does not require the database to be available and does as little as possible to try to dump the current log. However, you should compensate for not being able to dump the current log and should set the dump frequency to a value which leaves you comfortable with the potential number of lost transactions. There is no problem with a very short time between transaction log dumps. I have worked in situations with a 15 minute transaction log dump frequency. You simply have to ensure that the operating system files which the dump devices are defined on are not overwritten by subsequent dump commands.

The sequence of dump and load command events when a failure occurs is shown in Figure 10.1.

The most common problem you will experience with a database recovery is load the inability to load the database dump since the database is so damaged that it is unusable. The load needs to be able to recognize the database and after a failure it may not be able to do so. In this case you need to drop and recreate the damaged database. If you are lucky, you will be able to drop the database with a **drop database** command but, more often than not, this does not work since the database has been marked as "suspect" and you need to drop it using **dbcc dbrepair**.

```
dbcc dbrepair(db_name, dropdb)
```

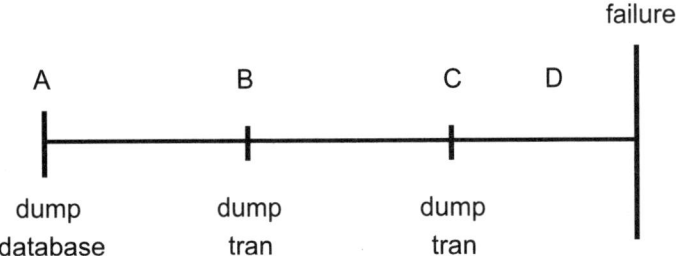

1. dump tran ... with no_truncate (D)
2. load database ...   (recovers to state at A)
3. load tran B .....   (recovers to state at B)
4. load tran C .....   (recovers to state at C)
5. load tran D .....   (recovers to last committed transaction)

Figure 10.1 Dump and load sequence to recover from database failure

Once you have dropped a database, you need to recreate it. You have to be careful to recreate it in the same space allocation fragments that it had before you dropped it. Of course you will have an operating system script file which has the necessary **create** and **alter database** commands to do this. (You always keep your script files up-to-date for all objects...don't you?) If you do not have the most recent script file information or you are not sure, take a look at **sysusages** for the database. This will display the allocation information (see the storage section for detail of this) and you can reconstruct the create and alter database commands.

For example:

```
select segmap, size from sysusages
    where dbid = db_id('database_name')

segmap size    lstart
    3  10240        0
    4   5120    10240
    3   5120    15360
```

This shows two data allocations (segmap=3) of 20 Mb and 10 Mb and a log allocation (segmap=4) of 10 Mb. The lstart column indicates the sequence of creation and so this database was created in two steps: the first a **create database** for 20 Mb data and 10 Mb log and the second an **alter database** for 10M of data. The easiest way to determine the device names is to try **sp_helpdb**. If this does not work, you will have to join to **sysdevices** to get the device name.

```
select dev.name, u.size
       from sysdevices dev, sysusages u, sysdatabases d
       where d.dbid = db_id("database_name")
       and d.dbid = dev.dbid
       and u.vstart between dev.low and dev.high
```

This allows you to recreate the database allocations exactly as they were:

```
create database "name" on dev_1 = 20
       log on log_dev1 = 10
       for load
go
alter database "name" on dev_2 = 10 for load
go
```

Note the use of the "for load" clause to prevent the create/alter commands initializing pages as the load will load in the used pages from the dump and initialize all unused pages. If you do not recreate the database and log allocations as they were, the load may not map the logical page numbers properly and mix log and data pages on the same segment. This will generate Error 2558 when you run a **dbcc checkalloc**. There are two types of 2558 problems: "data on log" and "log on data." Neither of these is a disastrous situation: "data on log" is usually solved by a clustered index rebuild which remaps the data (and any nonclustered indexes) into the data segment; "log on data" will eventually disappear as the log is dumped and truncated, freeing the space. However, the "log on data" does have the more serious aspect that the transaction log may be unusable for recovery until it has migrated totally onto the logsegment. Do not let this remapping happen during recovery. It takes time to resolve and then you really should dump the database after resolution.

How do I recover the system databases?

The only problem here is the **master** database. The other system databases—**sybsystemprocs, model, sybsecurity**—should be dumped and loaded as for a user database. The **tempdb** database is reinitialized from model during startserver and you need not worry about it.

Model

The system database model should be dumped immediately after installation and after any changes. You can ignore the transaction log for this database as it is not large and a **dump database** only takes minutes. You can then treat model as a user database for recovery purposes and issue the appropriate **load database** command.

If you never change model, you can simply recreate it by running buildmaster with the -x option.

```
buildmaster -dmaster_dev_name -x
```

This restores the original model database as at installation time. You then need to run the install script **installmodel** to set the permissions on the database.

```
cd $SYBASE/scripts
isql -Usa -Pwhatever <installmodel
```

Sybsystemprocs

The system database sybsystemprocs should be dumped immediately after installation and after any changes. You can ignore the transaction log for this database since it is not large, and a **dump database** takes only minutes. You can then treat sybsystemprocs as a user database for recovery purposes and issue the appropriate **load database** command.

You need to be careful if you are reloading sybsystemprocs from tape, since you may have to issue sp_volchanged. As this is a system procedure, it will not be available until sybsystemprocs is available. Limit the sybsystemprocs dump to one tape or copy **sp_volchanged** to master to avoid this "Catch 22."

Because sybsystemprocs does not normally reside on the **master** device, but on its own separate device, you will have to find out if this device is available using the SQL described in the user database section above, and possibly recreate it, and then recreate sybsystemprocs as it was before the failure. Not normally difficult, as it should be on one device only.

Similarly to model, if you do not make any changes to sybsystemprocs you can rebuild it from the install script **installmaster**.

```
cd $SYBASE/scripts
isql -Usa -Pwhatever <installmaster
```

Be a little careful here; the installmaster script will install the system procedures on master if sybsystemprocs does not exist.

Tempdb

You never need to consider dumping tempdb, as it is never restored but always re-initialized as a copy of model during startserver. Tempdb is a truly temporary storage area and is completely re-initialized every time you start the server.

Sybsecurity

The system database sybsecurity should be treated as a user database for dump and load purposes and included with the regular user database dumps. It is not normal to worry about the transaction log for sybsecurity although you may need to persuade the system auditors that this is the case.

Master

The assumption of this section is that you do not have any user databases on the **master** device. If you do, they are loaded as for any user database after the system databases have been recovered. Having user databases on the master device is not a good idea as it simply slows down recovery of the master device.

The master database is the most awkward one to recover as it contains all of the server wide system tables and you need it to be present to run the commands. But you cannot run **create database** as the master database is not available. The first thing you must do is to run buildmaster to rebuild the master database. In practice you may have to recreate the master device first. Then you can reload your dump or, if you do not have an up-to-date dump, you can run two special commands—**disk reinit** and **disk refit**. Because of the special nature of the **master** database, we need to recover it as follows:

- Rebuild it to the state after installation using **buildmaster**

- Reload an up-to-date dump to recover it to the state before failure, using **load database**

- If no dump, or the dump is not up-to-date, run the special routines **disk reinit** and **disk refit** to rebuild the system tables **sysdevices**, **sysdatabases**, and **sysusages** to reflect the current state of the server

The important point to remember is that only the master has crashed and the rest of the server is perfectly fine. However, if there is no up-to-date dump of master the rebuilt system tables do not reflect what the rest of the server looks like. If we can get these system tables up-to-date without destroying the data devices and databases we will returned got back to the current state of the server. This is why an up-to-date dump of master is so important. We can get back to the current state of the server in two easy steps—buildmaster and load database—instead of complicating things with **disk reinit** and **disk refit**.

As well as having an up-to-date dump of master it is strongly advised that you keep a separate copy of the information on **sysdevices**, **sysusages**, **sysdatabases**, and **syslogins**. In my opinion, this is best done as a hard copy using select commands:

```
select * from sysdevices
       order by cntrltype, low

select * from sysusages
       order by vstart

select * from sysdatabases
       order by dbid

select name, suid, dbname from syslogins
       order by suid
```

since you can define a useful order by sequence. The system procedures show all of the information and they are sometimes easier to interpret. But it is important—especially with **sysusages**—to get the records in an order which makes them easy to understand and rebuild. If you feel happier, do both, but at least make sure that you have a hard copy of the information on these tables. When the master crashes, you do not want to be guessing what the disk layout and database allocations looked like; have an up-to-date dump and a hard copy of the system tables just in case.

Recreate master database

The first thing we have to do is to recreate the master database as it was immediately after installation, using buildmaster.

```
buildmaster -d master_device_name -s database_size_in_pages -m
```

where the -m option rebuilds only the master database. If you are rebuilding all the system databases on the master device, omit this option. Make sure the server has stopped running before you issue **buildmaster**, otherwise the master dump load will fail. The state of the server might not be obvious, since you cannot log into it. It is worthwhile checking that the operating system process is not present. If it is, kill it. Make the master database size as big as you originally did in the installation (your copy of **sysusages** will help you here), since subsequent loads may run out of space if you do not have enough space in the first space allocation for master. In practice, you can make it bigger, since the subsequent loads will cope with that.

```
buildmaster -d/dev/rsd2f -s2048 -m
```

will recreate master as a 4 Mb database on the stated master device. You can run **buildmaster** without parameters and it will prompt you for the relevant information. When you are asked for the disk controller, always enter 0.

Now we have a master database to log into. We need to login as *sa* with a null password. The master setup is as if it has just been installed, and none of the normal user logins exist. Remember to change the password. If you have created sa_role logins and locked sa, make sure that you recreate the sa_role logins before you lock sa again. It can be embarrassing not to be able to login into the server. If you do this—or forget the sa password—you have option -l on the dataserver command which will start the server with a one-time password for sa. We need to start the server before we can login. Use startserver with the -m option in this recovery situation.

```
startserver -f runserver_name -m
```

The -m option starts the server in master-recovery mode which means that only the sa may login and allow updates on the system tables is automatically enabled.

Load master from a dump

We are now ready to load the last dump of master, but before we do this we need to check the sysusages allocation of space to master. Remember, we must load a database into the same allocations as when it was dumped. Again let me stress how important it is to have the backup of hard copy which is at the same allocation structure as the most recent dump of master. In this case the hard copy of sysusages is essential as you need to use this to see what the space allocations were. If there is only one entry, there has been no size change and you can reload the dump. If there is more than one entry for master, you need to reconstruct sysusages exactly as it was.

There are two situations: only master has been expanded or several system databases on the master device have been expanded. If only master has been expanded, you can simply reissue the alter database commands to recreate the sysusages entries.

```
select dbid, segmap, lstart, size, vstart
       from sysusages
       order by vstart
```

dbid	segmap	lstart	size	vstart
1	7	0	1536	4
3	7	0	1024	1540
2	7	0	1024	2564
1	7	1536	2048	3588
.				
.				
.				

This shows four space allocations of the system tables (you determine that these are on the master device by the **vstart** falling within the **low** and **high** range on **sysdevices**). The first three entries are created by the **buildmaster**, i.e., 3 Mb for master, 2 Mb for model and 2 Mb for tempdb. The fourth entry is an additional allocation for master of 4 Mb. You recreate this with a simple **alter database**:

```
alter database master on default = 4
```

If several system databases have been expanded, you need to repeat the original sequence of database size alteration to get exactly the same space allocations.

```
sysusage
```

dbid	segmap	lstart	size	vstart
1	7	0	1536	4
3	7	0	1024	1540
2	7	0	1024	2564
2	7	1024	2048	4612
1	7	1536	2048	6660
.				
.				
.				

This now shows the original three allocations from **buildmaster**, with an extra 4 Mb allocated to tempdb and 4 Mb to master. The important point is that the tempdb expansion has been made before the master expansion and you **must** recreate in this sequence.

```
alter database tempdb on default = 4
go
alter database master on default = 4
go
```

Check them against the hard copy to make sure that you got it right. Note that you do not have to worry about any **sysusages** entries after the last dbid = 1 (master) entry as these will be restored by the **load database**. Only the master database entries have to be right; so you must define everything up to the last master database entry on **sysusages**.

Now we are in a position to reload the last dump of master.

```
load database master from "/dev/dump_0/master.dmp"
```

Note the use of the full path name instead of the device name. You have just rebuilt master to its installation state and may not have the appropriate device available on **sysdevices**. You could easily create it but it's just as easy to use the file name capability of **load database**. The server will automatically shutdown after master has been loaded; you should check the errorlog to see if there were any errors during the **load** and the shutdown.

If the dump was up-to-date you are ready to go again. It is worth briefly restarting the server in single user mode to check that everything is OK.

Rebuild current state of sysdevices, sysdatabases, and sysusages

If the dump was not up-to-date, restart the server in single user mode (-m option). The **disk refit** command updates the system tables and requires **allow updates** on. We need the hard copy of **sysdevices** again to allow us to recreate the entries for the existing disk devices. The devices exist and have user databases on them. The incomplete recovery of **master** does not have the correct **sysdevices** entries for them. If we reissue **disk init** commands for the devices, the allocation pages will be initialized and we will lose the data currently resident in the allocation units. We need to run **disk reinit** which takes the exact same parameters as the original **disk init** commands but simply updates the **sysdevices** table. Make sure that you get these **disk reinit** commands absolutely correct or you will not be able to recreate the databases from an incorrect device specification. If you get a size wrong, the mappings to **sysusages** will not be correct and **disk refit** will fail. The exception to this is the vdevno which may be different; you could take this opportunity to reorganize the device numbers. This used to be mildly useful as the server serviced the disk requests in device number order. So a very high device number for tempdb could be altered in this situation. This is no longer the case in System 11 and there is no disk access advantage to low device numbers.

```
disk reinit
      name = "tempdb_dev1",
      physname = "/usr/data/tempdb.dat",
      vdevno = 6,
      size = 102400
```

Similarly to **disk init**, we cannot issue **create database** commands as these will reinitialize existing good data. We need to run **disk refit**, which reads the existing allocation units and rebuilds the **sysusages** and **sysdatabases** entries. The server needs to have been started in -m mode to execute this command.

```
disk refit
```

Again, have a good check of the recreated **sysusages** and **sysdatabases** with your hard copy to make sure that this rebuild worked. There is no reason why it should not rebuild these system tables correctly—but make sure. If there is still a difference, you will need to call Sybase Technical Support.

To summarize:

- Rebuild the master database (and other system databases on master) using **buildmaster**

- Start the server in -m mode and **load database master**

- If the dump is not up-to-date

    - Run **disk reinit** for each device
    - Run **disk refit**

Rebuild syslogins and sysservers

If the dump was not up-to-date, we are not finished since we have to recover the **sysservers** and **syslogins** tables. Hopefully, you have hard copy or scripts for these. If you don't you have not the **sysservers** table is little trouble as you can simply re-add the remote servers. The remote logins may be more of a problem but essentially you are redefining from scratch and so it is only effort that you are wasting.

The logins are more troublesome as you have to recreate these in the same sequence as before the dump to ensure that the **suids** are created as before. Mismatches on **suid** may cause permission errors when the users login and try to access the objects. Your permission scenario might avoid this but, if not, you will have to make sure that you re-add these in the same sequence as they were defined on **syslogins** before the failure. The simple way is to rerun your login script; the long way is to reinput every login from your hard copy of syslogins; the tedious, although still easy, way to do this is to compare the suid and name in each database on the server with the **suids** on **syslogins**.

```
select suid, name from master..sysusers
union
select suid, name from db1..sysusers
union
.
.
.
```

If you find any gaps in the **suids** in the range which you are recovering you will have to create dummy logins so that these numbers are allocated and then drop them when you are finished. This is one good reason to lock logins which you no longer require instead of dropping them.

The **master** database is now fully recovered. If the dump was out of date, make sure that you take a current dump before you restart the server for normal use.

Summary

Recovery from a media failure which has lost data or made the database unusable requires a copy of the database at a point in time and copies of all subsequent transaction logs from the database dump. These copies are made with the dump database and dump transaction commands and allow any database to be reconstituted by loading the database dump and the transaction dumps in sequence. A transaction log cannot be restored against a reloaded database dump unless it has itself been dumped with the dump transaction command. This will restore the database to its state as at the end of the last reloaded transaction log dump. If you have managed to dump the log immediately prior to the failure than you will have recovered the database to the last completed transaction.

The only thing that needs careful attention is that the dump has to be restored to the same space allocation structure that was in place when the dump was taken. If you need to recreate the database to allow the load database to take place, you must ensure that you recreate the space fragments as they were when the dump was taken. If you do not, the load database will load data pages on log space and/or log pages on data space. This is not a good idea.

The system database master requires a little extra attention as you may have to redefine system table information such as devices, databases, and logins which have been altered since the last dump of master. This requires use of the special commands disk reinit and disk refit and is not really recommended. The master database is very small and you should ensure that you always have an up-to-date dump by dumping it every time you change it.

11

Locking

Locking contention is one of the most serious problems in database processing; an unusually slow response time is often the result of a lock contention between processes. Delays in waiting for resources to be free are transient and often difficult to detect, which makes it important to understand how locking works and how to minimize it. This chapter describes the types of locks supported by SQL Server and how they are used to ensure data consistency. The chapter concludes with suggestions on how to minimize the performance overheads caused by locking.

What locking is available?

SQL Server uses three locks to ensure data integrity:

- SLOCK: a shared multi-reader, no writer lock
- XLOCK: an exclusive single writer, no reader lock
- ULOCK: a temporary intent to update lock which allows readers

Locking is the mechanism used to ensure that a transaction cannot use data which is currently being changed by another transaction. Data being changed is reserved solely for that transaction and cannot be read or changed by any other. This is achieved by the use of two locks—a shared read lock called an SLOCK and an exclusive lock called an XLOCK. The SLOCK is a multiple reader lock which allows concurrent transactions to read data but does not allow update to the data. The XLOCK is a single writer lock which allows only one update transaction at a time and no transactions. Multiple

SLOCKs may be performed concurrently on an object but only one XLOCK. SQL Server uses a third lock called an update lock—ULOCK. It is set by update commands with the intent to update before the XLOCK is placed on those pages. The ULOCK increases concurrency by allowing other transactions to read the data before it is the subject of the XLOCK. For example the command:

```
update tab_1 set col_3 = 20
where col_1 = 5 and col_2 in (10, 12)

(with an index on col_1 only)
```

may have to read more records than are updated to check the second where clause. In this case, ULOCKs are set on all of the pages read while the command is determining which records are to be updated, but XLOCKs are set only on the updated pages. Until the ULOCKs are escalated to XLOCKs, the pages may be read by other transactions. This is illustrated in Figure 11.1 for the above command.

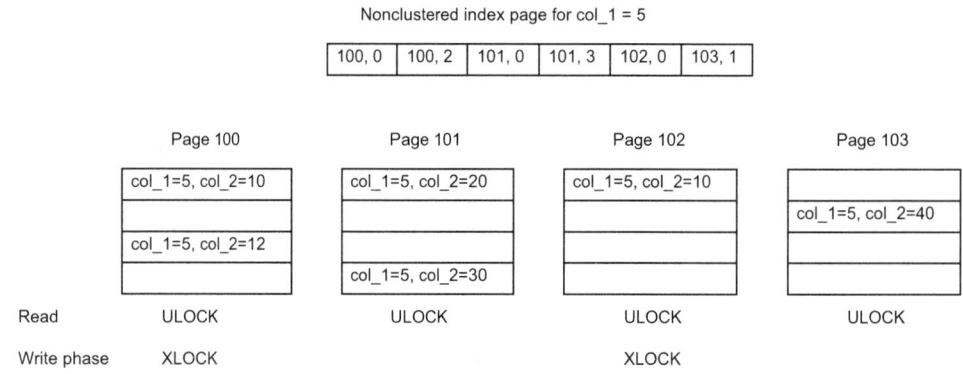

Figure 11.1 ULOCK and XLOCK phases of update command

The initial read to determine which records have to be updated requires all records with col_1 = 5 to be read; places ULOCKs on pages 100, 101, 102, and 103. While this is occurring, other transactions may still read data in these pages. When all records have been identified, the XLOCKs are placed only on the qualifying pages for col_2 in (10, 12), i.e., pages 100 and 103.

The ULOCK does not exist outside of the update commands and is not relevant to the subsequent discussions in this section. It is used extensively in cursor locking as described later.

How are the SLOCK and XLOCK used to ensure data consistency?

The shared and exclusive locks are applied based on standard isolation levels. The SQL Server default isolation level does not conform to ANSI standards as it does not enforce read consistency or prevent phantom records.

There are four levels of locking required to overcome the problems of concurrent transactions using these SLOCKs and XLOCKs. These are called isolation levels and are defined as in the following table which also illustrates how the isolation level is implemented in SQL Server.

Table 11.1

Isolation Level	What It Means	How It Is Implemented in SQL Server
0	There is no locking for reads	No locking on reads is implemeneted using the set command
	Transactions are allowed to read data even when it is XLOCKed	**set transaction isolation level 0**
	The XLOCK lasts only during the update command	Limited XLOCKING is not implemented: XLOCKS always last until the transaction is completed
1	Only one transaction may update data at a time and any changes must not be visible until the transaction is complete	This is the default SQL Server locking mode
	Uses the SLOCK and XLOCK as described above	
	The SLOCK is released as soon as the data has been read	
	The XLOCK is retained until the end of the transaction	

Table 11.1 *(continued)*

2	Data read during a transaction must not change until the end of the transaction The SLOCK is retained until the end of the transaction or until escalated to an XLOCK	Use **holdlock** in the select command OR Use the set command **set transaction isolation level 3**
3	The data set to be read by the transaction must remain as at the start of the transaction until the transaction is complete	Use the **holdlock** in a select command which locks at the table level OR Use the set command **set transation isolation level 3**

SQL Server does not independently support isolation level 2 but incorporates it into isolation level 3. SQL Server may eventually escalate multiple page locks on an object to the table level at isolation level 2, but this does not guarantee isolation level 3. A table lock must be taken at the start of the command to enforce isolation level 3. System 11 also has configuration level settings to control lock escalation. Isolation level 1 is the default isolation level for SQL Server. The SQL Server locking mechanism uses SLOCKs and XLOCKs as described above and does not retain the SLOCK any longer than it takes to read the data. Isolation level 2 is the ANSI isolation level where all locks are retained until the end of the transaction. In practice, the isolation levels layer on top of each other: level 1 is level 0 plus additional locking control, level 2 is level 1 plus additional locking control, and so on.

The choice of which isolation level to use in a specific situation depends on the application requirements. The higher the isolation level, the longer the locks are retained and therefore the lower the level of concurrency for transactions.

- If you are not interested in the immediate 100% accuracy of the data and require only a snapshot, isolation level 0 will suffice for reads.

- If you want 100% accuracy of the data as you read it, isolation level 1 is the choice.

- If you want the data you are reading or about to read to remain unchanged for the duration of your transaction, isolation level 3 is the choice (isolation level 2 is not available in SQL Server).

Are there any problems using the default SQL Server locking?

Yes. The optimistic approach of SQL Server means there may be a difference between the version of the record you read and the version of the record you are about to update. This requires you to make a check of the record status when you are updating it to ensure that you do not corrupt data.

The optimistic locking approach of SQL Server means that shared locks are not retained any longer than is necessary to read the data page. Two processes are able to read the same record, process the data, and independently update the record without deadlock because the shared lock is no longer active on the page. This allows the second update to corrupt the first update as illustrated in Figure 11.2.

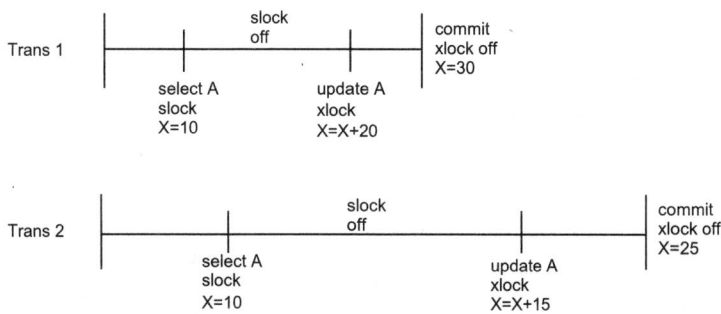

Figure 11.2 *Corruption of data with optimistic locking*

When using optimistic locking, you need to make an additional check on the update to make sure that the record has not changed since you read it. This is illustrated in Figure 11.3.

For optimistic locking, every table must have a common column which is updated by every update command. If you simply update the record without previously reading it, there is no problem and no other transaction could have obtained control of the record during your update. However, if your transaction profile is to read the record, display to the user, accept the new values and update the record, you must make this additional check. The select stores the value of the common column from the record—such as a timestamp, transaction id or user id—and then rechecks this in the update to see if it has changed. If the value on the record is still the same as the value read initially, the update succeeds. In addition to changing the data supplied by the user, the update command must also update this value. The second update command also checks the value on the record with the value read initially, but this time it has been changed by the first update, so the second update fails. Note that the failure of the update may not be caused by the timestamp column but instead for another reason. You will have to resolve the reason for failure in the application. For example, the command: **update employee set salary = salary * 1.1 where emp_id = value and time-stamp = @ts** may fail because the record identified is no longer present or because the timestamp column has been changed. In both cases, someone has processed the record since you read it, but the subsequent action may be different and you may need to differentiate between them. The application must take some action to correct the problem. This will depend on the application, but may be simply to tell the user that it has happened and request if new values should be displayed. Or, it could check which values have changed to see if it is important, or simply abort and request the user to reinput the update.

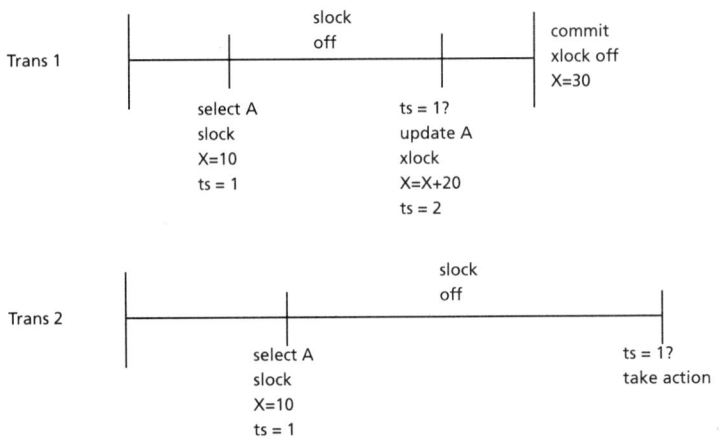

Figure 11.3 Rechecking for record changes on update

The column that you use to make the check and the action taken on failure to update are not important. However, it is essential to take this extra action in SQL Server as a failure to do so may cause data corruption.

What locking granularity is supported?

SQL Server locks at the page level as the lowest level of locking granularity. Table level locks may also be acquired. Page locking may escalate to table level locking if a specific number of locks are exceeded.

The final criteria of a locking mechanism is the granularity of the locks on an individual object. This varies through the levels of record, page, and table. There is no reason why the lowest level should not be at the column level but this is not currently implemented by any of the relational database software. The general argument against this is that the amount of lock checking to be done with column granularity is too high to justify the increase in concurrency. The lower the granularity the less chance of concurrent transactions being blocked by locks placed by other transactions. However, the lower the granularity, the greater the amount of work which has to be done to check the locks already set when a transaction requests a lock on an object.

SQL Server's lowest level of granularity is the page level. This means that a single record lock will also lock all other records on the same page. This can be a serious throughput bottleneck when there are many records per page. SQL Server may escalate the page locks to a table lock after a specified number of locks on the table are exceeded. This figure is pre-set at 200 locks per table in System 10 but may be configured in System 11. The System 11 configuration parameters **high water mark**, **low water mark** and **lock promotion percent** define an upper level above which lock escalation will always be attempted; a lower level below which escalation will never be attempted, and between these extremes a percentage of the total data records at which escalation will be attempted.

It is important to recognize that escalation is not automatic and the server only attempts to acquire the table level lock. If this is unsuccessful because of a conflicting lock on a page of the table, the attempt will not succeed and page level locking will continue. The attempt is repeated when the number of locks is exceeded again and so it will be unusual for escalation not to be successful. Also, the escalation is based on the number of locks per scan of the table. During a multi-table command such as a join, a table may be accessed several times. Each of these accesses is called a scan, and lock escalation occurs only if the number of locks per scan exceeds the limit. Although a normal select does not retain the SLOCKs, this is best illustrated by a nested iteration join which has a holdlock on the inner table.

```
select c.name, orders.ord_no, orders.ord_date
       from customer c, orders holdlock
       where c.cust_no = orders.cust_no
```

If this is evaluated as a nested iteration with the orders table as the inner table then the orders table will be scanned once for every record on the customer table. If one of these scans exceeds the locking high water mark then the join will attempt to escalate to a table lock on orders. However, if every scan is one lock less than the high water mark no escalation will be attempted and the total number of locks for the join will be the product of the number of customer records and the number of orders pages.

How do I see what locks have been acquired?

The normal way to view the locks is with the **sp_lock** system procedure. If you need to go to a lower level or to see some lock types not shown by sp_lock you can use **dbcc lock**.

Locks may be viewed using the system procedure sp_lock.

```
spid   locktype     table_id      page   dbname        class
1      Ex_intent    1589580701       0   STS_AM_INT    Non Cursor Lock
1      Ex_page      1589580701   41448   STS_AM_INT    Non Cursor Lock
1      Ex_page       589580701   41480   STS_AM_INT    Non Cursor Lock
1      Sh_intent     448004627       0   master        Non Cursor Lock
```

If this does not help you may get some additional information from dbcc lock.

```
        dbcc lock

LOCKS:
TABLE LOCKS

e3b711d0 Objid 1784231890, dbid 6, (bucket 5)
e3b700b0     swstatus=(), swskipped=0, swsemaphore=0xe3b711d0
e3b74330         lrspid=1, lrtype=ex_int, lrsemawait=0xe3b700b0,
lrstatus=(granted ), lrsuffclass=0
 .
 .
 .
PAGE LOCKS

e3b732b0 Page 41448, objid 1589580701, dbid 8, (bucket 200)
e3b6f490     swstatus=(), swskipped=0, swsemaphore=0xe3b732b0
e3b6da90         lrspid=1, lrtype=ex_page, lrsemawait=0xe3b6f490,
```

```
lrstatus=(granted ), lrsuffclass=0
.
.
.
```

This does not normally provide much more useful information than sp_lock although it does show you the address and semaphore locks which may be blocking a process. Address locks are exclusive locks which control memory addresses and are used for:

- OAM pages

- Allocation pages

- Updating disk maps in the DBTABLE structure

- Updating values for descriptors and site buffers

Blocked processes being blocked is a serious problem since it is not resolved automatically by the server and a process may sit forever idle because it is blocked by another process. The only approach is to look at the sp_who output to see if a process is being blocked:

```
sp_who
```

spid	status	loginame	hostname	blk	dbname	cmd
.						
.						
10	runnable	sts_cw_int_dbo	gd-dba5	0	STS_CW_INT	AWAITING COMMAND
11	runnable	sts_cw_int_dbo		0	STS_CW_INT	AWAITING COMMAND
12	lock sleep	sts_am_int_dbo		13	STS_AM_INT	UPDATE
13	runnable	sts_am_int_dbo		0	STS_AM_INT	AWAITING COMMAND
14	runnable	sts_am_int_dbo		0	STS_AM_INT	AWAITING COMMAND
15	recv sleep	sts_tm_int_dbo		0	STS_TM_INT	AWAITING COMMAND
16	lock sleep	sts_tm_int_dbo		17	STS_TM_INT	UPDATE
17	runnable	sts_tm_int_dbo		0	STS_TM_INT	AWAITING COMMAND

and then to look at the sp_lock output to see what the problem is.

```
sp_lock
```

spid	locktype	table_id	page	dbname	class
.					
.					
16	Ex_intent	1380002684	0	STS_AM_INT	Non Cursor Lock
16	Ex_page	1380002684	10024	STS_AM_INT	Non Cursor Lock

```
16      Ex_page         1380002684      10028   STS_AM_INT      Non Cursor Lock
16      Sh_intent       448004627           0   master          Non Cursor Lock
17      Ex_table        3001386624          0   STS_AM_INT      Non Cursor Lock
17      Ex_page-blk     1123002358      40032   STS_AM_INT      Non Cursor Lock
```

You then know who is causing the block and can contact them to commit their transaction or you can kill the process to allow the blocked process to continue.

What locks are set by a cursor?

The locks set by a cursor are no different than a set based command—shared, update, and exclusive—but the timing of the intent locks is different and can cause problems. The intent locks are set on by the open cursor command and are not released until the close cursor command. This means they last longer than you might expect and you should be careful to close the cursor as soon as possible. Any update commands do not take exclusive locks on the pages but rely on the update lock of the read phase. This means that the page is not locked until the end of the cursor but only for the duration of reading the page.

The sequence of cursor commands and the timing of the locks is shown in Figure 11.4.

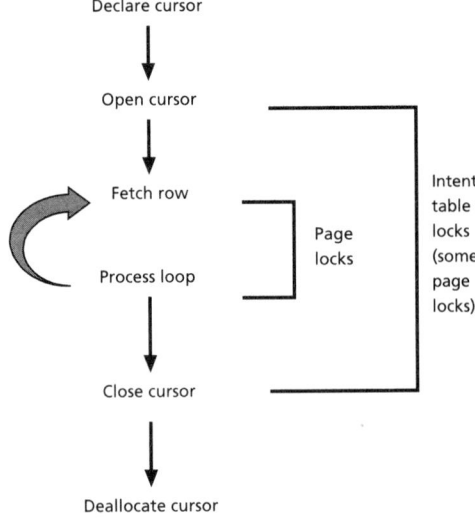

Figure 11.4 Cursor lock timings

The page locks taken by the fetch are what you would expect: SLOCKs when the cursor is read-only and ULOCKs when the cursor is for update. The pages remain locked until the cursor fetches move the cursor position onto the next page. This will be longer than an equivalent set based command as the cursor is processing row by row and taking time to read and process all rows in a page. Note that the **update ... where current of cursor_name** does not set an XLOCK on the page but relies on the update lock of the read phase; it does not allow any other update transactions into the page. However, it does mean that the changed data is not locked until the end of the cursor, but is available to other transactions when the cursor position moves off the page and the update lock is removed.

If an explicit transaction is used to update any records, an XLOCK is taken on the page and remains on until the transaction is closed, even if the cursor is closed and deallocated.

```
declare c1 cursor for select a, b from jk1_tab for update
go
open c1          ----------     sh_intent lock on jk1_tab
go
begin tran
go
fetch c1         ----------     update lock on page
go
update jk1_tab set b = 'new'          ----------     ex_intent on jk1_tab and
      where current of c1                             exclusive lock on page
go
close c1         ----------     removes update lock on page and
go                              sh_intent lock on jk1_tab
deallocate cursor c1
go
commit tran      ----------     removes exclusive lock on page and
go                              ex_intent lock on jk1_tab
```

The open command places a shared intent lock on all of the tables in the cursor declare command. This intent lock does not get turned off until the close command, which means that other exclusive table locking requirements will be blocked. Do not delay in closing a cursor in SQL Server, as it increases the possibility of blocking updates which require an exclusive table lock.

Transaction isolation levels have the expected effect on the cursor locking: isolation level 0 forces a read-only cursor with no locking; isolation level 3 forces all locks to be retained until the end of the transaction.

Why do I get so many deadlocks?

SQL Server is rather prone to deadlocks, and the major cause of this occurs when an update process deadlocks with an inquiry process, because both use a different index to access the data.

SQL Server adopts an optimistic approach to locking, which reduces contention and allows many processes to be active on an object. Because of this, SQL Server is less prone to deadlocks than ANSI standard locking systems. The traditional deadlock situation is illustrated in Figure 11.5.

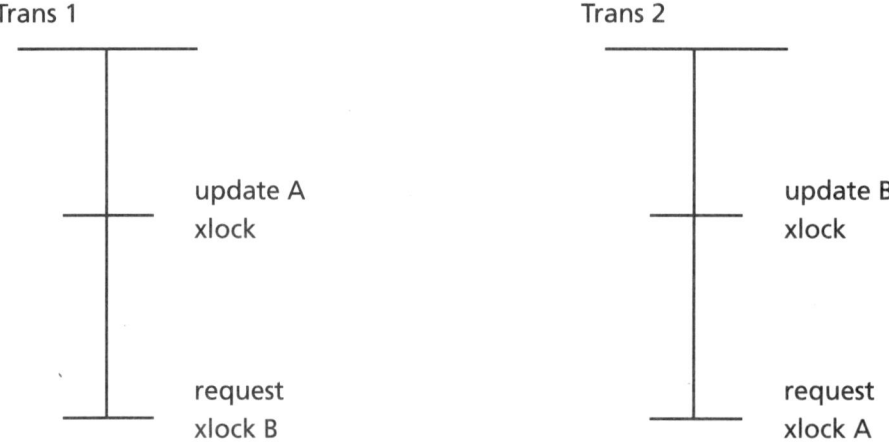

Figure 11.5 *Traditional deadlock*

Transaction 1 has a lock on Object A and requests a lock on Object B. However, Transaction 2 already has a lock on Object B which prevents transaction 1 from obtaining its lock on A. If this was all that happened, Transaction 1 would be blocked until Transaction 2 completed and released the lock on B. However, Transaction 2 now requests a lock on Object A, which is blocked because of the existing Transaction 1 lock on A. Both transactions are now blocked by each other, i.e., they are deadlocked. This deadlock will continue forever unless the server recognizes it and takes some action. After a transaction has been blocked waiting for a lock for 500 msecs, the server checks to see if there is a deadlock situation. If a deadlock exists, the server rolls back one of the deadlocking transactions based on which process has accumulated the least CPU time. Unfortunately you have no control over which transaction is rolled back. The time interval before the deadlock is checked may be configured with the **deadlock checking period** configuration variable. Prior to System 11 there was no deadlock checking period and the deadlock was checked immediately when a lock request blocked.

Note that in Figure 11.5 the locks are all XLOCKs. In SQL Server, the SLOCKs are not held on the data pages any longer than necessary to read the record. This means that deadlock between two updating processes is unusual in SQL Server because the SLOCKs are not normally held long enough to cause a blocking situation. In an ANSI standard environment where SLOCKs are retained until escalated to an XLOCK or until the transaction is complete, this deadlocking may occur between two processes reading with the intent to update.

However, SQL Server will still deadlock between read processes and update processes. This is caused by the read process accessing the data via a different index than the update process. This is illustrated in Figure 11.6.

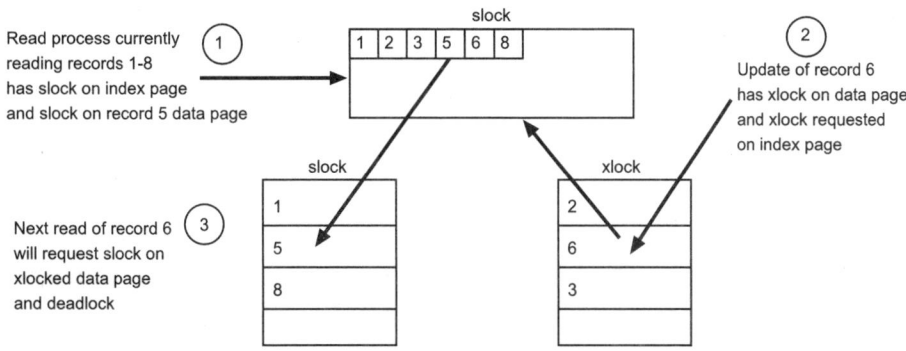

Figure 11.6 *Deadlock between read and update process*

The read process has an SLOCK on the index page which it is using to access the records. Because the index page has many records in it, the SLOCK is not set off until all of the data records pointed to by the index records have been read. In Figure 11.6 the SLOCK on the index page will not be set off until records 1, 2, 3, 5, 6, and 8 have been read. If an update process tries to update the data via the same index it may be blocked before it reaches the data records because of the read process SLOCKs on the index. But if it locates the data via another index, it will be allowed to update the record. This is fine if only the data record is updated, but if the update causes a change to the index being used by the read process, the update on the SLOCKed index page will be blocked. If the read process now moves on to another data record, it may try to access the data page which is XLOCKed by the update process. Unfortunately, when this deadlock occurs it may be the update process which is rolled back. Deadlock is a run-time error (1205) and simply tells you that you are a deadlock victim. This is no help in resolving why the deadlock occurred, and you need to set the configuration parameter **print deadlock information**. However, to get really useful information you still need to use the 1204 trace flag.

```
sp_configure "print deadlock information", 1
```

This writes an error message to the error log indicating which processes were deadlocking to help resolve the problem. But, the 1204 trace flog tells you more useful information about the locks.

```
Deadlock detected. Two processes were involved in the deadlock.
Process 12 belongs to user 'jkirkwood'.
Process 12 was executing a SELECT command at line 1.
Process 24 belongs to user 'mjackson'.
Process 24 was executing an INSERT at line 1.
Process 24 was waiting for an exclusive page lock on page 3467 of the orders
table in database 8 but process 12 already held a shared lock on it.
Process 12 was waiting for an exclusive page lock on page 1608 of the orders
table in database 8 but process 24 already held a exclusive lock on it.
Process 24 was chosen as the deadlock victim. End of deadlock information.
```

There are occasions when a deadlock occurs outside of the server's control and is not detected. This is most obvious when the client process deadlocks because a client resource is blocked. The block is dependent on a server resource blocked by previous client action. In this case, the server is aware only of the server side block and cannot see any deadlock. Therefore, the server is unable to resolve the situation and the client will remain inactive until you intervene and kill one of the processes. This is illustrated in Figure 11.7.

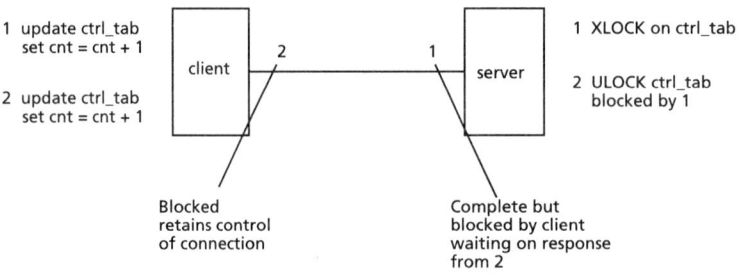

Figure 11.7 Client deadlock

In Figure 11.7, the client submits an asynchronous update to the server. It replies that everything is OK, so both client and server continue: the server with the update and the client with more work until the server completes the update and calls back to the client. However, the client then submits another update on the same connection. This blocks at the server as it is unable to obtain an XLOCK for the update. This block does not release the connection, so the first update is unable to notify the client that it has completed. The XLOCK stays on until the server can make this notification. The result is that the client deadlocks itself on the connection. This is a rather naive example but it does illustrate that you should not do too much work over the same connection when working asynchronously at the client. However, even with multiple connections there may still be client operating system semaphores that will cause this type of deadlock.

If you find that processes are blocking indefinitely, it is probably a client deadlock. Identify the blocking processes at the server and translate these to client processes. Then get the client to close the transaction if it is not a deadlock, or kill the client process and identify which client resource is causing the block at the client. Only by removing this client block will you eliminate this type of deadlock.

How do I reduce the locking contention?

There are several approaches to this:

- Reduce the number of records locked by a single lock
- Reduce the number of records locked in a transaction
- Reduce hot-spot activity on objects
- Reduce deadlocking by sequencing table access

Number of records locked by single lock

This is caused mainly by the SQL Server's lowest level of locking granularity being at the page level. This means that a single page lock will lock every record in the page. If this is causing blocking, you need to reduce the number of records in each page by setting max-rows_per_page or padding the row to the necessary size. In System 11, the max_rows_per_page is the obvious solution.

This solution is most common when record level locking is required in SQL Server. Sybase are finally recognizing the need for record level locking and it is being developed. Information at the time of writing this was that it would be included in a late 1997 release. However, reducing the number of records per page will be most beneficial for updates and will have little effect on inserts (or deletes). Although you have reduced the contention on the data pages for the inserts, you will probably simply transfer the blocking to a nonclustered index as each insert must update the indexes. Since you were contending on the data pages(based on the primary key) being inserted to the data page, you will now be contending on the index pages for the same key values. If you do not have any nonclustered indexes on the table, the max_rows_per_page will benefit inserts and deletes.

   If you can limit your updates to direct updates which do not change the indexes, reducing the number of records in each page will certainly reduce the contention for updates. You could also set a max_rows_per_page on the index but this may increase the level of index page splitting and not give you any advantage.

If you are locking at the table level, you need to look at the processing to determine why it is table level locking. Then alter the transaction or adjust the indexing to eliminate the table scan.

Number of records locked in a transaction

Keep your transactions as short as possible so that they lock the pages for as short a time as possible.

   If you do not explicitly define a transaction in SQL Server, each command is an implicit transaction. Therefore, multiple stand-alone commands in SQL Server are committed separately and are recovered independently. To ensure that multiple commands are treated as a single recoverable unit you must enclose them in a transaction block. So:

```
update tab_1
delete tab_2
insert tab_3
go
```

are three separate stand-alone commands. If a problem happens during the delete which requires a rollback, only the delete is rolled back. The update remains committed and the insert will be actioned once the rollback of the delete has completed. The locks taken by each command are set off when the command commits, so the locks taken by the update are set off when the update completes, i.e., before the delete starts. However:

```
begin tran
update tab_1
delete tab_2
insert tab_3
commit tran
go
```

now treats the three commands as a complete logical unit and a rollback in the delete will also cause the update to be rolled back. The insert will still be actioned once the rollback has completed. The locks taken by each command are not set off until the command commits, so all locks are held until the commit tran statement.

Holding the locks until the commit is essential to prevent other transactions seeing uncommitted data. You should ensure that all XLOCKing statements take place as close to the commit as possible to ensure that the XLOCKs are held for as short a time as possible. A standard transaction structure of:

```
begin tran
read all data
process all data
update all data
commit all data
```

ensures that the records are XLOCKed for as short a time as possible.

Be careful of the ability in SQL Server to nest transactions. The nested transactions do not function as real transactions and all committing and release of locks is controlled by the outer transaction.

```
begin tran
update tab_1
        begin tran
        exec proc_1........................  proc_1
                                             begin tran
                                                     delete tab_2
                                             commit tran
        insert tab_3
        commit tran
commit tran
```

The above example is only one transaction and the delete in the procedure is not committed until the final commit tran of the outer tran. The XLOCKs taken by all commands are not released until the outer commit tran.

Hot-spot activity on objects

Several transactions accessing the same page of a table or index will block each other and cause serial processing through this resource. When this happens, you should consider overnormalizing the object into one independent piece per transaction. The simple situation shown in Figure 11.8 shows three transactions contending for a single resource, but with each of them accessing an independent portion of the resource.

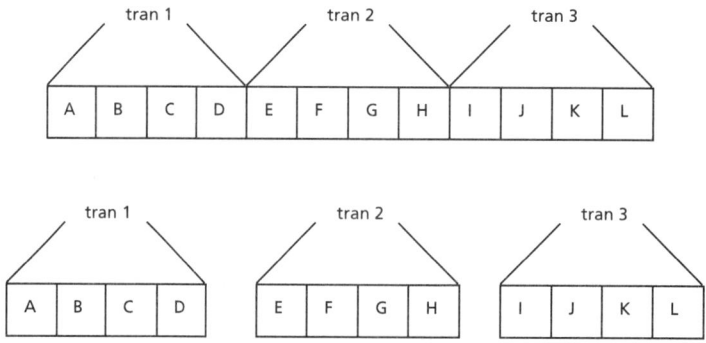

Figure 11.8 Overnormalizing to reduce contention

By segmenting the resource into one partition per transaction, you can eliminate contention on the resource. Approaches to overnormalization have been detailed in Chapters 3 and 4.

However, you should also consider indexing and partitioning of the data to reduce contention. Partitioning is most obvious when a heap table subject to multiple insert transactions benefits from segmenting into multiple partitions to effectively create multiple last pages. This is illustrated in Figure 11.9.

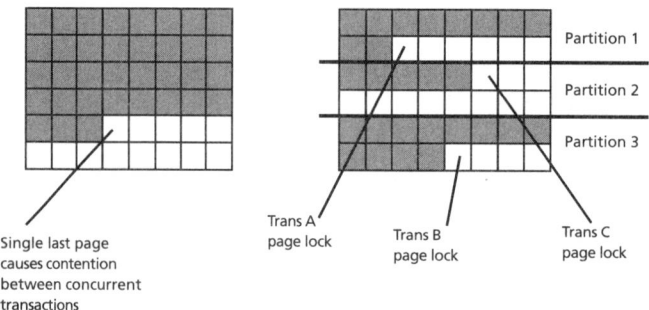

Figure 11.9 Table partitioning

This clearly assists inserts but has little effect on updates and deletes. Be careful here, since you may simply shift the contention to any nonclustered index defined on the heap table. If the index key values inserted are growing serially, although you have removed the data page contention you will now have index page contention. A possible approach to this, depending on the index key distribution, is to create a clustered index which spreads the inserts throughout the data pages. It is likely you will still require a nonclustered index on the serially growing key which will give index page contention. In this situation, you really need to consider segmenting the table into several tables based on a non-indexed column value, and control the assignment of data to each table at the application level.

Sequencing table access

Deadlocking between objects can be significantly reduced if you always access the objects in the same sequence. This is easiest to control at the table level. Most database relationships are of a hierarchical nature as indicated in Figure 11.10.

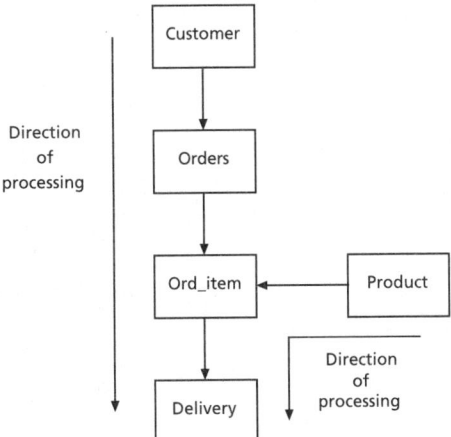

Figure 11.10 Top to bottom sequence of processing to reduce deadlock

If you always access these tables from top to bottom, you will never deadlock between the tables. You will deadlock within the tables especially between index pages, but you will eliminate inter-table deadlock. It requires an exercise at the logical model level to ensure that all processing accesses the entities in the same manner, i.e., top to bottom. There will obviously be some processes which cannot do this, but they will be surprisingly few, and early identification will allow you to take some application based action to prevent a processing clash.

Summary

SQL Server supports three types of lock:

- SLOCK: a shared multi-reader, no writer lock

- XLOCK: an exclusive single writer, no reader lock

- ULOCK: a temporary intent to update lock which allows readers

The ULOCK is unique to SQL Server. It is used during update processing to place a single-writer, many-readers lock prior to the XLOCK being taken. During some update processing, more pages may be read than are updated; the update lock allows other transactions to read the pages while the update command is determining which pages to place XLOCKs on.

SQL Server's lowest level of locking granularity is the page level. This means that a single lock can lock multiple records. The other locking granularity level is at the table level. If an update or delete command executes as a table scan, an initial table lock will be acquired. Inserts always take page locks and if these accumulate to more than a configurable number of page locks on a table then the command will attempt to escalate to a table lock. Select commands do not escalate as the SLOCKs are not retained longer than it takes to read the page. Unless holdlock is used when the SLOCKs will be retained and escalation is possible.

SQL Server does not support ANSI level locking but adopts a more optimistic approach of not retaining shared locks any longer than is necessary to read the data on the page. This normally means that the shared lock will have been set off on the page before the exclusive lock is requested. Although this reduces the length of time for which shared locks are held and consequently reduces the incidence of deadlock between updating transactions it does mean that you need to check that another transaction has not changed the data since you read it.

Although SQL Server's optimistic style of locking reduces contention, locking is one of the most serious problems in high performance systems. It can easily cause serious contention problems and effectively reduce the throughput to a single processing stream. It is important to minimize the time for which locks are held and to reduce the number of records which are held by a single lock. This is normally achieved by paying close attention to the following areas.

Number of records locked by a single lock

Try to always lock at the lowest level and if there is still a problem reduce the number of records per page.

Length of time the record is locked in a transaction

Try to issue the exclusive lock as close to the end of the transaction as possible and keep all transaction, as short as possible.

Hot-spot activity on a resource

If forcing record level locking with one record per page does not solve this, segment the resource into several objects to introduce parallelism into the maintenance processing so that transactions are not contending for the one large resource, and can lock separate smaller resources in parallel.

## PART IV

SYSTEM MONITORING

Monitoring the system allows you to take a proactive approach to the most common problems. If you can see trends occurring, you may be able to take corrective action before a trend requires an immediate reaction. Problems will always occur without warning, but with advanced notice, you will be able to resolve most of them without a big impact on the users.

Even when you are firefighting, it is advantageous to approach each problem in a uniform manner, looking for the obvious before delving into the gory details. Always make sure that you view the system as a unit at the macro level before you try to pinpoint the specific detail that is causing the problem.

This section presents a high level methodology for analyzing, diagnosing, and solving a problem, and then discusses the output of the sp_sysmon monitoring tool.

12

Methodology

This chapter illustrates how to analyze the symptoms of a problem, how to diagnose the problem from the available symptoms and how to formulate a solution to the problem. The intent is to provide a set of regular system monitoring approaches for the overall configuration and a set of problem analysis, diagnosis, and solution approaches to the most common day-to-day problems.

Generic problem analysis

A standard approach to performance problems is important since it ensures finding a solution as fast as possible. A series of steps refining a problem until a solution is possible is the most common approach. The general idea is to approach each problem in the same way. Eliminate reasons for problems in a fashion that gradually narrows down the options until the reason for the problem is identified. Practice means you will be able to hit the correct solution almost immediately most of the time, but keep the full approach in reserve for the more "interesting" ones.

Identify which resource is bottlenecking

This may be obvious if the user process has failed with an error message or there is a message in the error log. Ask the user for any error messages and check the error log. Such "hints" as stack overflow, no more locks, no free procedure space, and threshold firing are the first things you should look for. Check to see if one of the principal resources—CPU, disk, network—has reached a limit. Be careful to measure both the

SQL Server and the overall machine utilization; high SQL Server activity may not be a problem symptom, only a temporary high usage of a specific resource. If there is no obvious major bottleneck, the specific processes will need to be analyzed to determine the problem area.

Identify what is causing the problem

Having identified which, if any, resource is bottlenecking or where a specific transaction is being delayed, it is necessary to look closer at the resource to determine why the problem has occurred. At the macro level, this involves a breakdown of the resource usage to see if any process is showing an abnormally high usage. At the transaction level a check should be made that the transaction is still running and is not blocked by another process.

If there is an obvious problem, the problem process may need to be stopped or the resource increased to allow the system to get back to normal. Then the reason why the problem occurred may be investigated in detail.

Isolate the problem

When the overall resources are sufficient to cope with the day-to-day processing of the system, the majority of the performance problems will reduce to investigating a single transaction or process to see why it is using so much of a resource. To do this, the problem process should be isolated and investigated without any external influences which can alter the findings. This is particularly so with network investigations, where other users can significantly alter the readings you are measuring. Of course, where the problem is due to concurrency of several processes there is every likelihood that the individual process will function quite efficiently in isolation. This is not a negative result as it highlights that the problem is one of concurrent transactions and you can take relevant action.

Establish metrics

To diagnose a problem it is important to know what the baseline performance characteristics are: from the CPU, I/O, network loading to the individual amount of logical I/O required to table scan the tables in the system. Having these metrics makes it easier and faster to recognize when a problem has arisen or even to anticipate it, and much easier to make a specific diagnosis.

When the problem is at a macro level and involves one of the major resources—CPU, disk, network—it can be useful to repeat the problem to analyze its characteristics. This is often very difficult as such overall resource problems are often transient and not repeatable. However trends will occur (such as a high CPU usage) when a specific application profile is running. Generating the same profile under controlled testing can prove conclusively that a specific application is at fault. Having done so, isolate the application and start to investigate its execution profiles without the interference of the other applications.

Regular system monitoring

Prevention is better than a cure and the most important dba activity is regular monitoring of the system to spot when resources are being used up, and proactively preventing problems which reduce the service to the users. There are various monitoring tools available, both third party and Sybase proprietary tools such as SQL Monitor and sp_sysmon which can be used to show the overall trends in CPU, I/O, network and cache. Unfortunately, monitoring tools use a reasonable amount of resource, often showing themselves as the highest usage process while the system is not doing much, so it is seldom appropriate to keep them running constantly. Usually a flexible monitoring schedule has to be devised, the optimum timings and their alterations becoming clear from the monitoring exercise itself. As always, the best times to run a monitoring analysis are when the system is already heavily loaded, but be aware that the monitoring tool itself will affect the overall readings. It will become clear that a few resources are regularly being stretched and regular monitoring can concentrate on these to minimize the system overhead.

Chapter 13 provides a detailed analysis of the output from the System 11 sp_sysmon system procedure. This has been chosen because it is generally available as part of the System 11 server. It uses the same internal counters as SQL Server Monitor, and it provides a detailed analysis of server utilization.

Trigger levels

Pro-active response to a high monitor value is much better than reacting to a plea for better performance from an exasperated user. It is useful to do regular monitoring to highlight any usage trends which may be causing trouble. The principal problem is determining what constitutes a "high" usage; there are no definitive times when a specific usage figure can be diagnosed as a problem. However, some rules of thumb will save time in analyzing the monitoring output.

The trigger levels depend on local knowledge of the current usage and the application profiles. A 100% I/O activity on one device may cause alarm signals at most sites, but if it happens during a clustered index build or a massive bcp, it may not be cause for concern. Therefore, be careful of generalizations as there are always exceptions which will be valid and acceptable based on the application profile.

As a general comment, there are usage levels which, in normal operation, are worth further investigation. For example, running sp_sysmon at specific high usage times of the day, passing the output to a file and reporting only on trigger values above certain levels, will save you time and not lose any important information. The following section discusses detailed trigger levels for sp_sysmon values.

Disk space

This is no longer a problem from a user service aspect, since the thresholds will alert you to impending problems. The location of these on the segments will depend on growth rates of the data, we suggest that you give yourself a week's worth of warning from a data segment threshold.

Disk usage

More important than thresholds firing is any imbalance in disk usage. The aim is to share disk activity across the available drives. As mentioned above, a single high activity is not necessarily a problem but a longer period of imbalance needs to be addressed. We suggest that disk activity be analyzed on a weekly basis and any trends of imbalance be investigated. Again, local configuration is important. A disk balance of:

```
tempdb_dev:        80%
log_dev:           80%
data_dev1:         20%
data_dev2:         30%
```

is probably just what you have been aiming for, although it would be advisable to have the tempdb_dev and log_dev on separate controllers if possible. But two data disks balanced 80% : 10% requires investigation to even out the disk activity.

CPU usage

This needs regular daily monitoring. When activity is close to 100%, an investigation can determine what the application mix was, to see if one application was causing the problem. Of course, high CPU activity is not necessarily a problem; a general trend of increasing CPU usage is more of a problem. You will know when high CPU activity is going to occur—early in the working day; after lunch; or during the overnight batch job—so do not set alarms on these, but look for unexplained levels of high CPU activity. More interesting may be the multi-engine scenario where CPU loading is unbalanced and most work is being done by one CPU. It might be network I/O of course but you might be able to balance the machine by assigning the server to a single CPU and letting other processes use another CPU.

Network usage

Again, daily monitoring is best for 80–90% of usage trends, investigating a transaction mix to determine if one application is causing a problem. The obvious high usage processes—bcp—are not the problems. The simple transactions which suddenly hit the network with very high usage are the ones to look at. And unfortunately, you are often going to need to see what is actually being sent across the network by the client. A network "sniffer" process becomes mandatory, especially when dealing with third party software whose SQL is not immediately available to you.

Cache usage

A ratio of logical-to-physical is the trigger here, with a logical percentage lower than 80% being a cause for concern. Again, exercise judgment, since a large table scan can trash the data cache and cause a high physical I/O rate for some time as the cache settles down again. Regular high physical I/O rates over several weeks are an obvious sign that the cache is too small. While this may not be a significant problem, it will be impacting response time and a larger cache should be considered. Monitoring of logical to physical I/O should not be confined only to the server, but close attention should be given to the operating system page swapping rate. Any page swapping is serious since it will cause the executing process to stop until the necessary pages are available, and so it should be minimized. Swapping out of the server is particularly serious as it causes all server processes to stop (the server is one process to Unix) until the server is completely swapped in again.

Summary

Regular system monitoring is important to allow proactive problem identification and resolution. Each problem should be analyzed in the same way with a top-down approach that quickly narrows the search and allows fast resolution of the problem. Each problem should be tackled in the steps:

- Identify the resource which is bottlenecking

- Identify the cause of the problem

- Isolate the problem

- Establish metrics

- Monitor the solution against the metrics

The actual metrics values which you define will depend on the specific implementation but you should address the areas:

- Disk space

- CPU usage

- Network usage

- Cache usage

13

System Monitoring with sp_sysmom

Introduction

There are several third party and Sybase products which provide system monitoring. The newest and probably the most comprehensive is the System 11 procedure, sp_sysmon. Although some of the other monitoring software has a more pleasant output display, and SQL Server Monitor uses the same internal counters, I personally think that nothing surpasses the detail of sp_sysmon. I have used the output to discuss an approach to performance monitoring and what to look for in the output values.

The syntax is:

```
sp_sysmon [interval_in_minutes]
```

where

interval_in_minutes is between 1 and 10 with a default of 1.

Many of the counters used by sp_sysmon were added in System 11.0, so sp_sysmon will not produce accurate results on pre-11.0 servers. sp_sysmon has an overhead of 5-7% on a single CPU which increases with the number of CPUs, although I do not have a figure for this. As with most monitoring software, it does contribute to the CPU usage and you should not run it constantly on a heavily-utilized system, but only for specific problem and change analysis.

When you execute sp_sysmon, it clears the internal counters and enters a wait-for for the specified time interval. During this time, the counters are incremented by the server processes and at the end of the time interval, sp_sysmon reads the counters and outputs the results.

The output from sp_sysmon is broken down into the topics:

- Kernel utilization

- Task management

- Transaction profile

- Transaction management

- Index management

- Lock management

- Data cache management

- Procedure cache management

- Memory management

- Recovery management

- Disk I/O management

- Network I/O management

The column data in each section represents the following:

```
per sec       Average number per second
per xact      Average number per committed transaction
count         Total number
% of total    This depends on the results being displayed
```

```
For example:
Task management              Per sec    Per xact     Count   % of total
-------------------------    --------   --------   --------   --------
Task Context Switches by Engine
     Engine 0                   37.4        3.8      24322      32.0%
     Engine 1                   79.3        8.1      51611      68.0%
-------------------------    --------   --------   --------   --------
Total Task Switches            116.6       11.9      75933
```

Of the total task switches, 32% were done by engine 0 at 37.4 per second and 68% by engine 1 at 79.3 per second.

The following sections describe the output for each topic and indicate how you may adjust the configuration to improve performance. A fuller discussion of sp_sysmon value troubleshooting is given in Chapter 18.

Kernel Utilization

This reports on the server engines with percentage busy, CPU yields and number of network and disk I/O checks. These are real system figures but are a mixture of two different systems so I could get most output results displayed; don't try to establish any relationship between the separate sections.

```
Kernel Utilization
--------------------
Engine Busy Utilization:
       Engine 0                    63.2%
       Engine 1                    96.3%
---------------         --------------------      ---------------------
Summary:            Total:    159.5%     Average:      79.7%

CPU Yields by Engine              per sec  per xact     count  % of total
----------------------            --------  --------  --------    --------
                                      0.0       0.0         0         n/a

Network Checks
       Non-Blocking               8513.9     866.5   5543183       97.3%
       Blocking                    233.5      23.8    152020        2.7%
----------------------            --------  --------  --------    --------
Total Network I/O Checks          8747.4     890.3   5695203
Avg Net I/Os per Check              n/a       n/a    0.00436         n/a

Disk I/O Checks
       Total Disk I/O Checks      8778.8     893.5   5715665         n/a
       Checks Returning I/O       2078.8     211.6   1353482       23.7%
       Avg Disk I/Os Returned       n/a       n/a    0.01701         n/a
```

Engine Busy Utilization

This reports the percentage of time the server kernel is busy executing tasks on each engine. Note that this does not include the time spent looking for tasks and therefore will generally report a different value than the CPU usage from an operating system monitoring tool. When the server has no tasks to process, it loops looking for network I/O, completed disk I/O, and run queue tasks. This activity looks like server activity to the operating system but is considered idle time by sp_sysmon. If you have a large discrepancy between the server and operating system values, but have a low throughput, you need to look elsewhere than the CPU for a resource which is causing the bottleneck. If these values are consistently over 90%, you should consider an additional engine if you have a spare CPU.

CPU Yields by Engine

This is the number of times that each engine yielded to the operating system. If engine busy utilization is low and CPU yields are high, the CPU is truly inactive. Low utilization and low yields indicate the server is being starved of CPU time by other processes and you should consider removing some of these other processes and dedicating the machine to SQL Server.

Network Checks

SQL Server performs two types of check for network I/O:

Non-blocking   An active engine checks the network for I/O and then continues to process whether or not it found any I/O.

Blocking   When the engine has yielded to the operating system, it awakens each clock tick to check for network I/O. If I/O is found, the operating system blocks the engine from any other processing until the network I/O completes.

If you have a high number of blocking I/Os, it means the engine has yielded often to the operating system. In this situation there may be a delay of up to one clock tick—not a lot—between a network packet arriving and the engine recognizing that it has arrived and processes it. The number of blocking I/Os may be reduced by increasing the **runnable process search count** configuration parameter as this will cause the engine to yield less often to the operating system when it has no tasks to process. Increasing the **runnable process search count** causes an inactive server to spend more time looping, looking for I/O before it yields to the operating system.

Disk I/O Checks

When a task requests disk I/O, the engine issues the I/O request and puts the task on a sleep queue to wait for the I/O completing. The engine uses a schedule loop to check for completed I/O and, when it finds some, it moves the task to the run queue. The disk I/O checks figure gives a comparison of the number of times a completed I/O is found compared with the number of checks made. If you find that this figure is too low and that many checks are being made with no returns, you can alter the checking frequency using the **i/o polling process count** configuration parameter. Be careful here; a low figure does not necessarily indicate a problem, since the I/O itself may not be uniform. Also consider the **ave I/Os returned per check** before making any decision on this one. However, it is an overhead; if you feel it is too high—as you have many large CPU tasks—you can reduce the polling interval.

Task Management

This section provides information on connections opened and task context switches.

Task Management	per sec	per xact	count	% of total
Connections Opened	0.0	0.0	1	n/a
Task Context Switches by Engine				
Engine 0	37.4	3.8	24344	32.0%
Engine 1	79.3	8.1	51611	68.0%
Total Task Switches	116.6	11.9	75933	
Task Context Switches Due To:				
Voluntary Yields	17.5	1.8	11425	15.0%
Cache Search Misses	0.1	0.0	97	0.1%
System Disk Writes	1.7	0.2	1107	1.5%
I/O Pacing	6.1	0.6	3983	5.2%
Logical Lock Contention	0.3	0.0	199	0.3%
Address Lock Contention	0.1	0.0	69	0.1%
Log Semaphore Contention	0.1	0.0	44	0.1%
Group Commit Sleeps	0.7	0.1	450	0.6%
Last Log Page Writes	11.4	1.2	7421	9.8%
Modify Conflicts	2.0	0.2	1282	1.7%
I/O Device Contention	0.2	0.0	142	0.2%
Network Packet Received	9.6	1.0	6255	8.2%
Network Packet Sent	28.5	2.9	18584	24.5%
SYSINDEXES Lookup	0.0	0.0	4	0.0%
Other Causes	38.2	3.9	24871	32.8%

Connections Opened

The number of connections opened during the sample interval. If this one is regularly high, you probably need to address the application code to reduce the number of times the clients open and close connections. Repeated opening and closing of connections is not a good performance idea.

Task Context Switches

The number of times and the reasons why each engine switched from one task to another.

Voluntary Yields

A yield by a task after it has completed or executed for its allowed timeslice. A high value here indicates that there is little task contention for the CPU; you might consider increasing the timeslice configuration parameter to give each task more execution time.

Cache Search Misses

A yield caused by the data or index page not being in cache when physical I/O is required. The task is switched out while the physical I/O is performed. A high value here may indicate a need for more data cache or—less likely—a need to configure some objects to their own named cache to avoid them being washed to disk as often.

System Disk Writes

A yield caused by a disk write or access to a page being written by a system task such as the housekeeper or the checkpoint processes. Normal disk writes occur asynchronously and the task continues processing. However, a write during a system process including a page split, recovery or OAM page write causes the task to be put to sleep. If this figure is high and page splits is also high you may need to consider your indexing strategy to reduce page splitting; otherwise you cannot affect this one as it is caused by system processes.

I/O pacing

A yield caused by the batching of large amounts of I/O. When a task performs large amounts of I/O—such as a checkpoint—the server controls the number of disk requests sent to the disk I/O system to prevent it from being overloaded. The I/O is batched and the task put to sleep between each batch. There is nothing that you can do about this one.

Logical Lock Contention

A yield caused by contention for page and table locks. If this is high, consider the design and length of your transactions or the concurrency of certain transactions in the system. If you are also doing a large number of deferred and direct expensive updates, this can increase the number of index locks acquired by a transaction.

Address Lock Contention

A yield caused by contention for memory address locks. These locks occur on index, OAM and allocation pages and on data pages when a page split occurs. Check for high deferred and direct expensive updates, and high page splits as before; otherwise you cannot affect this figure.

Log Semaphore Contention

A yield caused by contention for the transaction log semaphore in an SMP environment. If you have a high value here you may have too small a user log cache which is causing more flushes to the log. You may try to reduce the log writes by increasing the size of the user log cache. ULC flushes occur for other reasons and you should check your transactions for too many accesses to other databases. Or they may simply be too large and need to be split into multiple smaller transactions. These latter two reasons may be unavoidable and you may have to suffer this bottleneck.

Also, if the queue for the transaction log disk is high you may be blocking log writes. If you have other files on the physical log disk, consider dedicating a disk to the transaction log device. Finally, the more engines you have the more contention there will be for the log. If the CPU utilization is low and the user is getting a fast response time you may consider reducing the number of engines. This is a last resort, since the number of engines may be for another design reason entirely—such as concurrent processing of update and select.

Group Commit Sleeps

A yield caused by a transaction commit with the committing task put to sleep until the log is written to disk. When a task commits, the user log cache is flushed to the current page of the transaction log in cache. If this is not full, the task is switched out and placed on the end of the run queue. The task wakes up either when the log page is filled by another task and is flushed to disk or when the task reaches the head of the run queue. A high percentage of group commit sleeps is not a problem, but you can reduce the commit time by reducing the size of the log I/O buffer pool—if greater than 2 Kb— or reducing any log disk queue to speed up the write to disk. Not one to worry about.

Last Log Page Writes

A yield caused by the task being put to sleep because it wrote the last page of the log. This is in direct contrast to the group commit sleep when the task is waiting for another task to write the last log page. If this value is high and the ave number of writes per log page is also high, the engine is repeatedly writing the same last page to the log. Again, reducing the log I/O size—if greater than 2 Kb—may reduce the number of last log page writes.

Modify Conflicts

A yield caused by a modify conflict which is a special light weight mechanism to gain exclusive access to a page. This is less of an overhead than an exclusive lock but still prevents concurrent access. In general this type of access is used by tasks which do not modify the page contents but still require exclusive access. It is used most often when accessing system tables and by the dirty read process. You have no control over this one.

I/O Device Contention

A yield caused by the task being put to sleep while waiting for the semaphore of a disk device. When a task requests physical I/O, the engine completes a block I/O structure and links it to the I/O queue for the device. A request from another engine for the same device will sleep until the semaphore is available. If you are getting significant contention here you will have to reconsider the object placement on the disks to even out the disk access. Separating nonclustered indexes and data or segmenting a high activity table across multiple devices are examples of object placements which can help.

Network Packets Received

A yield caused by the task waiting for the next packet from the client. This occurs when the task has completed a command and is waiting for another command from the client or when the task is waiting for the next packet in a multi-packet TDS batch. If this figure is high, consider increasing the network packet size. Or, perhaps you are sending too much SQL and should be making procedure calls.

Network Packet Sent

A yield caused by a task waiting for the network to send a TDS packet. Each connection can have only one outstanding TDS packet at a time, which causes the task to sleep after each packet is sent. If this is high, consider increasing the network packet size.

SYSINDEXES Lookup

A yield caused by a task waiting for another task to release control of a page in sysindexes. You have no control over this one.

Other Causes

Any yield not covered by the above categories. Sybase says that this value will rise as you tune the server to reduce the other reasons for context switching. (So you don't get rid of the bottlenecks, you only move them somewhere else. Isn't tuning fun!)

Transaction Profile

This reports on the various types of modification transactions.

```
Transaction Profile
--------------------
Transaction Summary           per sec  per xact     count  % of total
--------------------          -------- --------  --------  ---------
      Committed Xacts              9.8      n/a      6397         n/a

Transaction Detail            per sec  per xact     count  % of total
--------------------          -------- --------  --------  ---------
Inserts
     Heap Table                 130.5     13.3     84949       75.1%
     Clustered Table             43.4      4.4     28225       24.9%
--------------------          -------- --------  --------  ---------
Total Rows Inserted             173.8     17.7    113174       80.8%

Updates
     Deferred                     4.5      0.5      2899       31.2%
     Direct In-place              6.7      0.7      4367       47.1%
     Direct Cheap                 2.9      0.3      1859       20.0%
     Direct Expensive             0.2      0.0       153        1.6%
--------------------          -------- --------  --------  ---------
```

Total Rows Updated	14.3	1.5	9278	6.6%
Deletes				
Deferred	24.5	2.5	15943	90.8%
Direct	2.5	0.3	1615	9.2%
Total Rows Deleted	27.0	2.7	17558	12.5%

Transaction Summary

This section reports on the number of transactions committed and rolled back and the number of multiple database transactions. A transaction is counted if it completes during the sample interval even if it started before the interval. For multi-database transactions each, separate database modification is counted as a separate transaction. So a transaction which inserts to two databases is counted as two transactions.

Transaction Detail

A breakdown of the transactions by command type.

Inserts

Inserts are broken down into inserts on heap and inserts on clustered tables. Inserts on heap includes inserts to unpartitioned and partitioned heap tables; select into and slow bulk copy. It does not include fast bulk copy. If this value is high and **last page locks on heap** is also high, you may have a contention problem on the last page of a heap table. You should consider partitioning it or creating a clustered index which spreads the inserts throughout the data pages.

   If the **inserts to clustered table** is high and **page splits** or **RID updates from clustered split** are also high, you should consider dropping or altering the clustered index. Page splits are an overhead which you should try to avoid. Of course, you may need the clustered index for retrieval purposes—try covering—and will have to suffer the insert overhead. If it is a batch insert problem, try dropping the clustered index for the duration of the insert batch and rebuilding it later; this will also help reclaim any fragmented space.

Updates

Updates are separated into deferred, direct in-place, direct cheap, and direct expensive. The optimum is to have all updates direct in-place. A practical target is no deferred and a minimum of direct expensive. Direct updates significantly reduce overhead because they limit the number of log scans, reduce I/O, (they do not have to refetch pages) and reduce locking contention. Try to make all your updates direct.

Deletes

The aim is identical to updates and you should try to eliminate deferred deletes.

Transaction Management

This section reports on transaction log activity.

```
Transaction Management
----------------------
ULC Flushes to Xact Log       per sec   per xact    count   % of total
----------------------        -------   --------   --------  --------
      by Full ULC               0.2       0.0         156      0.3%
      by End Transaction        8.0       0.8        5189      8.4%
      by Change of Database     15.2      1.5        9866     16.0%
      by System Log Record      68.0      6.9       44248     72.0%
      by Other                  3.1       0.3        2036      3.3%
----------------------        -------   --------   --------  --------
Total ULC Flushes               94.5      9.6       61495

ULC Log Records                139.0     14.2       90542      n/a
Max ULC Size                    n/a       n/a        2048      n/a

ULC Semaphore Requests
      Granted                 324.3      33.0      211115    100.0%
      Waited                    0.0       0.0           0      0.0%
----------------------        -------   --------   --------  --------
Total ULC Semaphore Req       324.3      33.0      211115

Log Semaphore Requests
      Granted                 101.4      10.3       65991     99.9%
      Waited                    0.1       0.0          44      0.1%
----------------------        -------   --------   --------  --------
Total Log Semaphore Req       101.4      10.3       66035

Transaction Log Writes         18.4       1.9       11959      n/a
Transaction Log Alloc           6.8       0.7        4409      n/a
Avg # Writes per Log Page       n/a       n/a     2.71241      n/a
```

ULC Flushes to Xact Log

This is the number of times a user log cache (ULC) was flushed to the transaction log in cache. Each connection has a ULC which is used to buffer the transaction log records to reduce log I/O and contention for the last page of the log. The transaction log is a heap table (syslogs) and therefore suffers insert contention for the last page as for any heap table. The problem can be severe with syslogs as there may be many concurrent tasks trying to write to the log. The ULC is an attempt to reduce the amount of activity on the cache version of the log. On one of the events described below, the server copies all records in the ULC to the transaction log in cache.

By Full ULC

The ULC is flushed when it becomes full. A high value here indicates that the ULC is being flushed more than once per transaction. You may consider increasing the ULC size using the configuration parameter **user log cache size**, or you may shorten the length of your transactions. Sybase recommends to increase the ULC size if the percentage of total is greater than 20%. But be careful here; this will increase the amount of memory used by each connection and subsequently reduce data cache. And it may be an inherent transaction length problem anyway.

By End Transaction

This should be the norm as it is caused by the end of the transaction and indicates the incidence of short transactions which are always good for performance. A high value here using the default ULC size is a good idea.

By Change of Database

A transaction which accesses another database causes the ULC to be flushed to disk. This is a design issue and you will probably not be able to avoid it, but try not to make it too high.

By System Log Record

The ULC is flushed when a system transaction—such as an OAM page write—occurs in a user transaction. Sybase recommends to reduce the ULC size—if greater than 2 Kb—if this value is higher than 20%.

By Other

Any other reason for a ULC flush. Again, recommended to reduce the ULC size if this value is greater than 20%.

ULC Log Records

The average number of log records written to the ULC per transaction. For example, a deferred update may write several modification records for a single data modification transaction. If this value is high, you should consider reducing the incidence of deferred updates or the number of rows updated in one command.

Maximum ULC Size

The maximum number of bytes used in any of the ULCs. If this is much less than the ULC size, and the ULC size is greater than the default of 2 Kb you should consider reducing it. If this equals the ULC size and **flushes by full** ULC is also high you should consider increasing the ULC size.

ULC Semaphore Requests

The number of times a task was granted or refused a ULC semaphore. The server protects the ULC—and other resources—with semaphores so that only one task can access the data structure currently in use. This prevents more than one task accessing the ULC at the same time.

Log Semaphores Requests

The number of times a task was granted or refused a log semaphore. If the contention is high, the ULCs are being flushed frequently to the log record. You should consider redesigning your transactions to be longer, so there are less commits, and to contain less multi-database access, since both cause a flush of the ULC. If flushes by full ULC are also high, consider increasing the ULC size.

Transaction Log Writes

The number of times the server wrote a transaction log page to disk. Log pages are written to disk on transaction commit or when the current log page becomes full.

Transaction Log Allocation

The number of times additional pages were allocated to the log.

Avg # Writes per Log Page

The average number of times each log page was written to disk. As the log page is written to disk for each transaction commit, it is possible to write the same log page multiple times. If there is little queueing on the log disk this is not really a problem but a high figure with queueing on the log disk is worth investigating to try to reduce the number of commits or the I/O on the log disk.

Index Management

This section reports on nonclustered index maintenance with information on page splits and page shrinks.

```
Index Management
--------------------
Nonclustered Maintenance        per sec  per xact      count  % of total
--------------------            -------  --------   --------  --------
    Ins/Upd Requiring Maint         6.0       0.6       3897         n/a
       # of NC Ndx Maint            6.0       0.6       3907         n/a
       Avg NC Ndx Maint / Op        n/a       n/a    1.00257         n/a

    Deletes Requiring Maint         2.3       0.2       1475         n/a
       # of NC Ndx Maint            2.3       0.2       1485         n/a
       Avg NC Ndx Maint / Op        n/a       n/a    1.00678         n/a

    RID Upd From Clust Split        0.6       0.1        395         n/a
       # of NC Ndx Maint            4.2       0.4       2739         n/a
       Avg NC Ndx Maint / Op        n/a       n/a    6.93418         n/a

Page Splits                         0.1       0.0         48         n/a
    Retries                         0.0       0.0          0        0.0%
    Deadlocks                       0.0       0.0          0        0.0%
    Empty Page Flushes              0.0       0.0          0        0.0%
    Add index level                 0.0       0.0          1        2.1%

Page Shrinks                        0.0       0.0          5         n/a
```

Nonclustered Maintenance

This reports on the number of maintenance (insert/update/delete) operations which updated nonclustered indexes. If a table has a nonclustered index, all inserts, deletes, page splits and some updates must update the index. The figures show the number of operations which were potential index updates and the number which actually updated the indexes. These figures should be compared with the number of inserts/updates/deletes to see if the index configuration is placing a high overhead on the maintenance commands. You may not be able to do much about it, although an index review may allow you to get rid of some obsolete indexes. At least you can get a measure of the impact of the indexes on the maintenance commands. In really severe situations, it can assist a decision to replicate the database for decision support purposes to split the on-line and inquiry processing.

Page Splits

The number of times a data or index page was split because there was no room for the new data. Page splitting incurs overhead because of the need to update page pointers and nonclustered index entries, and because of the increased lock contention of the several locked pages. If this value is high, you should consider reducing the fillfactor on the objects which are causing the problem. If you have set max_rows_per_page on a table you may need to remove it as it can be a prime cause of page splitting.

Retries

The number of times the server attempted to lock a page for a split but was prevented because another task had a lock on the page or on an adjacent page in the page chain. A page split must lock the page to be split and the next and previous pages in the page chain as the chain is being updated. When blocked for a page split lock the server always restarts the index access from the root page on the retry. Keep this figure as low as possible by using a suitable fillfactor.

Deadlocks

The number of page splits which resulted in deadlock.

Add Index Level

The number of times a new index level was added to cope with the pointer to the new page created in the page split. Non-zero values should not be common here with the most common occurrence being for large inserts (especially to small tables).

Page Shrinks

The number of times a deletion caused the index to shrink off a page. Removing a page from the index is a high contention overhead as the next and previous pages in the chain have to be locked to update the page pointers. A high value here indicates many index pages with few index rows in them and an index rebuild should be considered to reclaim the fragmented space.

Lock Management

This section reports on summary and detail information on all locks granted and blocked.

```
Lock Management
--------------------
Lock Management            per sec  per xact     count  % of total
--------------------       --------  --------  --------  ---------

Total Lock Requests         17232.2    1753.9  11219393         N/A
Avg Lock Contention             0.4       0.0       268        0.0%
Deadlock Contention             0.0       0.0         0        0.0%

Lock Summary               per sec  per xact     count  % of total
--------------------       --------  --------  --------  ---------

Exclusive Table
    Granted                    19.9       2.0     12954      100.0%
    Waited                      0.0       0.0         0        0.0%
--------------------       --------  --------  --------  ---------
Total EX-Table Requests        19.9       2.0     12954        0.1%
/*   Then an identical format output for the following locks    */

Shared Table
Exclusive Intent
Shared Intent
Exclusive Page
Update Page
Shared Page
```

```
Exclusive Address
Shared Address
Last Page Locks on Heaps

Deadlocks by Lock Type        per sec  per xact    count  % of total
--------------------          -------- --------  --------  ---------
                                0.0      0.0         0      n/a

Deadlock Detection
    Deadlock Searches           0.4      0.0       269      n/a
    Searches Skipped            0.0      0.0         0      0.0%
    Avg Deadlocks per Search    n/a      n/a   0.00000      n/a

Lock Promotions                 0.0      0.0         0      n/a
```

The waited figures are obvious sources of contention and should be addressed. How to address them is never easy and often requires redesign of the application. Such approaches as accessing the tables in the same sequence in all code, keeping transactions short and retaining locks for as short a time as possible are all discussed in the design section.

Headings to note in the lock management data are:

Average Lock Contention

The average number of times lock contention was detected. This should be kept as low as possible.

Contention

The total deadlock contention percentage. Keep this as low as possible.

Last Page Locks on Heap

A high contention for the last page of a heap table indicates that some heap tables would benefit from partitioning or from a clustered index which spreads the insert activity throughout the data pages.

Deadlock Searches

The number of times the server initiated a deadlock search. If this is high compared with the **avg deadlocks per search**, you should consider increasing the time delay before a deadlock search is initiated. Do this using the configuration parameter **deadlock checking period**.

Searches Skipped

The number of times a deadlock search was initiated but was stopped because one was already in progress. If this is high and the **avg deadlocks per search** is low you should increase the **deadlock checking period**.

Avg Deadlocks per Search

The number of deadlocks found per search. Comparing this with the total number of searches can indicate if you need to adjust the deadlock checking period.

Lock Promotions

The number of times that page locks were escalated to table locks. If both lock contention and lock promotion are often regularly high, you should consider changing the lock promotion thresholds.

Data Cache Management

This provides summary information for all caches and detailed statistics for each named cache.

```
Data Cache Management
---------------------

Cache Statistics Summary (All Caches)
-------------------------------------

Cache Search Summary
    Total Cache Hits          14642.6    1490.3    9533428      99.1%
    Total Cache Misses          129.6      13.2      84369       0.9%
---------------------         --------  --------  --------    ---------
Total Cache Searches          14772.2    1503.5    9617797

Cache Turnover
    Buffers Grabbed               0.2       0.0       1031        n/a
    Buffers Grabbed Dirty         0.0       0.0          0       0.0%

Cache Strategy Summary
```

```
           Cached (LRU) Buffers       19131.5     1947.2  12456011      100.0%
           Discarded (MRU) Buffers        0.0        0.0         0        0.0%

Large I/O Usage
      Large I/Os Performed              31.3      352.7     20106       95.0%
      Large I/Os Denied                  1.6       18.4      1050        5.0%
---------------------                --------   --------  --------   ---------
Total large I/O Requests               33.0      371.2     21156

Large I/O Effectiveness
      Pages by Lrg I/O Cached           65.5      737.4     42032         n/a
      Pages by Lrg I/O Used             57.1      642.9     36647       87.2%

Dirty Read Behavior
      Page Requests                      0.0        0.0         0         n/a
------------------------------------------------------------------------------

default data cache

                                    per sec   per xact     count   % of total
---------------------                --------   --------  --------   ---------

Spinlock Contention                      n/a        n/a       n/a        6.7%
Utilization                              n/a        n/a       n/a       29.8%

Cache Searches
      Cache Hits                       817.3     9202.6    524551       96.1%
          Found in Wash                 63.2      711.6     40564        7.7%
      Cache Misses                      33.1      372.5     21231        3.9%
---------------------                --------   --------  --------   ---------
Total Cache Searches                  850.4     9575.1    545782

Pool Turnover
      2 Kb Pool
          LRU Buffer Grab                0.3        3.8       215        1.0%
             Grabbed Dirty               0.0        0.0         0        0.0%

      4 Kb Pool
          LRU Buffer Grab               32.7      368.7     21016       99.0%
             Grabbed Dirty               0.0        0.0         0        0.0%

---------------------                --------   --------  --------   ---------
Total Cache Turnover                   33.1      372.5     21231

Buffer Wash Behavior
      Buffers Passed Clean              30.8      346.5     19750       81.0%
      Buffers Already in I/O             0.0        0.0         0        0.0%
      Buffers Washed Dirty               7.2       81.1      4622       19.0%

Cache Strategy
      Cached (LRU) Buffers             985.8    11099.6    632676      100.0%
      Discarded (MRU) Buffers            0.0        0.0         0        0.0%
```

```
Large I/O Usage
     Large I/Os Performed        31.3    352.7    20106        95.0%
     Large I/Os Denied            1.6     18.4     1050         5.0%
---------------------          --------  --------  --------  ---------
Total large I/O Requests        33.0    371.2    21156

Large I/O Detail
   4 Kb Pool
        Pages Cached            65.5    737.4    42032          n/a
        Pages Used              57.1    642.9    36647        87.2%

Dirty Read Behavior
     Page Requests               0.0      0.0        0         0.0%
-------------------------------------------------------------------------
```

(The above output for the default data cache is then repeated for each named cache.)

Cache Search Summary

This shows the total cache hits and misses where a hit is a logical I/O which found the required page in cache and a miss is a physical I/O which had to go to disk for the required page. If misses is high, do not think immediately of more memory, since you need to look at the individual named cache statistics. At the extreme, a 10 Mb tempdb cache with most of your applications using tempdb heavily will significantly increase the physical I/O since you have not given tempdb enough cache.

Cache Turnover

A measure of the number of buffers moved from the wash area to be used by a database page from disk. This figure is not incremented when the cache page starts empty, such as after starting the server or after unbinding and rebinding an object to a named cache. The **LRU buffer grab** shows the normal replacement of a buffer page by another page read in from disk. If the cache page has reached the end of the buffer pool cache but has not yet been written to disk, this is shown in the **grabbed dirty** figure.

If the **LRU buffer grab** figure is high you should consider increasing the size of the buffer pool, since this will be affecting the cache hit rate and the I/O rate.

If the **grabbed dirty** figure is non-zero, the page cannot be read from disk until the cache page has been written to disk. This is obviously a serious overhead, and you should aim to keep this figure at zero. A non-zero grabbed dirty figure indicates that the wash area is too small for the buffer pool throughput; you should consider increasing the size of the wash area and/or increasing the size of the buffer pool. If you are at your cache limit, you need to address the level of physical I/O of the SQL, especially those doing table scans, and try to reduce it by indexing. Also, you could try increasing the housekeeper free write percent to flush more pages before they reach the wash marker. The latter may increase throughput as less physical I/O is waiting for a clean page. Check the buffer wash behavior to see if the wash rate is comparable with the disk I/O rate and that you are not simply swamping the disk.

Cache Strategy Summary

This indicates the number of times the LRU or MRU buffer replacement strategy was used. LRU is the common strategy which cycles pages to the mru end of the cache so that they remain in cache as long as possible. MRU is the fetch and discard strategy which replaces pages at the wash marker so that they are reused almost immediately. In general, MRU will be low. If your SQL makes use of large worktables, you will see higher MRU activity. The optimizer assumes that the worktable is required only for this command and automatically uses MRU replacement strategy. If you feel that some of your table scans are trashing useful cache pages, you can force the optimizer to use MRU replacement strategy for specific commands.

Large I/O Usage

This reports on the number of large I/Os performed and denied. If the denied frequency is high, you need to look at the individual cache statistics to find out why. A large I/O may be denied if:

- A page in the buffer pool currently resides in another pool

- There are no buffers available in the large I/O pool

- The extent contains the allocation page, since this is always in the 2 Kb pool

As each allocation unit has 32 extents, this means that you may see 1:32 requests denied for no other reason than the allocation page is in the extent. This will be most obvious for large table scans. A high denied figure means that the large I/O pool is not being used effectively, and it may be simpler to remove it. Be careful here, as a denied request does not use the next available I/O size but immediately defaults to the 2 Kb pool. Do not immediately discard a large I/O pool but try allocating its buffers to the next highest pool size to see if this makes any difference.

Large I/O Effectiveness

This compares the number of large I/O pages read into cache against the number actually used. An I/O using a 16 Kb buffer will always read in 8 pages. If the commands using the large I/O buffers only require 4 of these pages, you are wasting cache and need to adjust the large I/O figure. Investigate the named cache information to determine which cache is causing the problem.

Dirty Read Behavior

The number of pages requested at isolation level 0 and the number of times a restart was required. When a page is read at isolation level 0 and another process causes the page to be reallocated, the isolation level 0 scan has to be restarted from the beginning of the scan. This is an obvious overhead but there is nothing you can do about it— except to stop using isolation level 0 reads.

Individual Cache Management

Descriptions for some of these individual figures have already been covered in the cache summary section.

Spinlock Contention

The percentage of spinlock requests which met with contention for the spinlock and had to wait. If this is high, consider dividing the default cache into several named caches to provide parallel access to several spinlocks. A spinlock is a semaphore system which tasks must obtain before accessing cache. With a single engine, there is no contention as only one task has control of the engine at any one time. In an SMP environment with multiple engines this prevents more than one task from changing cache at the same time. These are very short locks but can still have an effect on performance, so keep an eye on this figure.

Utilization

The usage of this cache compared to all other caches. If you go for multiple named caches, this will help you get the sizes correct, it indicates how much each cache is being used.

Cache Searches

The hits and misses for the cache. In general, aim to keep the misses low so that most I/O is logical. This will depend on what you are using the named cache for, but a high misses rate is not normally a good thing. The **found in wash** figure indicates the number of hits where the page was in the wash area. If this is high, consider reducing the size of the wash area. As a dirty page passes the wash marker it is written to disk. If the wash area is too large, this page cleaning can generate more writes to disk than is necessary.

Pool Turnover

Same as for cache turnover.

Buffer Wash Behavior

This reports on the state of the buffer pages as they cross the wash marker. Three states are possible:

- Clean: the page did not need to be written to disk
- Already in I/O: the page was currently being written to disk as it crossed the wash marker caused by the checkpoint or the housekeeper process
- Dirty: the page needed to be written to disk. This figure can help if the grabbed dirty figure is non-zero. If the rate that pages are crossing the wash marker is faster than the disk system can handle, some of them will reach the end of cache still dirty.

Cache Strategy

Same as for cache strategy summary.

Large I/O Usage

Same as for the summary figures large I/O usage and effectiveness.

Large I/O Detail

This provides usage information for each configured pool, reporting on the pages read into cache and the pages used. An 8 Kb request will read in 4 pages, but if only a single data page is read the pages used is 1 page. Clearly, a low pages used figure means that the large I/O is not being used effectively and that space in cache is not being fully utilized. In this case, consider reducing or removing the large I/O cache.

Dirty Page Read Requests

Same as for dirty read behavior.

Procedure Cache Management

This section reports on the stored procedure and trigger requests. The requests are of two types: when an idle copy of the procedure is used (it is already in procedure cache) and when the procedure has to be read from disk (there is no idle copy of the procedure in cache). A procedure is read from disk when there is no copy in cache or all cache versions are currently being executed.

The **procedure writes to disk** reports on the number of procedures created in the sample interval and **procedure removals** is the number of procedures dropped in the sample interval.

Procedure Cache Management	per sec	per xact	count	% of total
Procedure Requests	76.6	7.8	49871	N/A
Procedure Reads from Disk	0.0	0.0	0	0.0%
Procedure Writes to Disk	0.0	0.0	0	0.0%
Procedure Removals	0.0	0.0	0	0.0%

If you have a high read from disk, you should consider increasing the size of the procedure cache. If a zero read from disk, you may be able to reduce the procedure cache to free up more cache for the data; but do not reduce it so far that you begin to read from disk. Note that System 11 needs more cache for procedures and so this is one figure you should verify with sp_sysmon after an upgrade.

Memory Management

This section reports on the number of database pages allocated and deallocated during the sample interval.

Memory Management	per sec	per xact	count	% of total
Pages Allocated	0.0	0.0	12	N/A
Pages Released	0.0	0.0	10	N/A

Not a lot that you can do about this one; if you see a high activity here it may be an indication of high extent fragmentation in your page allocation. If pages are frequently deallocated and allocated the contiguous use of pages in extents can become fragmented with the page chains jumping between extents and allocation units.

This can reduce the effectiveness of large I/O and you should consider rebuilding clustered indexes to refresh the page allocation structure of the tables.

Recovery Management

This section reports on the number of and the time taken by checkpoints.

```
Recovery Management
--------------------
```

Checkpoints	per sec	per xact	count	% of total
# of Normal Checkpoints	0.0	0.0	12	100.0%
# of Free Checkpoints	0.0	0.0	0	0.0%
Total Checkpoints	0.0	0.0	12	N/A

Avg. Time per Normal Chkpt   4.33333   seconds

Two types of checkpoint occur: a "normal" checkpoint initiated by the checkpoint process and a "free" checkpoint initiated by the housekeeper process. When the server has no user tasks to run, the housekeeper uses this "idle" time to flush dirty pages to disk. If the housekeeper manages to write all dirty pages to disk it checks the transaction log. If there are more than 100 log records on the transaction log since the last checkpoint, the housekeeper task issues a checkpoint. This causes a free checkpoint since there is little overhead.

If the normal checkpoints is high and the time taken is also high, you should consider reducing the **checkpoint interval** configuration parameter. If the number of free checkpoints is high, you should consider increasing the checkpoint interval.

Disk I/O Management

This section reports on the disk activity for the server and for each individual device.

```
Disk I/O Management
--------------------
```

Max Outstanding I/Os	per sec	per xact	count	% of total
Server	n/a	n/a	31	n/a
Engine 0	n/a	n/a	20	n/a
Engine 1	n/a	n/a	31	n/a
I/Os Delayed by				
Disk I/O Structures	n/a	n/a	0	n/a
Server Config Limit	n/a	n/a	0	n/a
Engine Config Limit	n/a	n/a	0	n/a
Operating System Limit	n/a	n/a	0	n/a
Total Requested Disk I/Os	32.4	3.3	21088	N/A
Completed Disk I/Os				
Engine 0	12.9	1.3	8375	36.4%
Engine 1	22.5	2.3	14654	63.6%
Total Completed I/Os	35.4	3.6	23029	

```
Device Activity Detail
--------------------------
```

```
/dev/DATA_0
```

	per sec	per xact	count	% of total
Reads	0.1	0.0	78	1.2%
Writes	9.8	1.0	6352	98.8%
Total I/Os	9.9	1.0	6430	19.8%
Device Semaphore Granted	14.9	1.5	9683	98.8%
Device Semaphore Waited	0.2	0.0	115	1.2%

Max Outstanding I/Os

The maximum number of I/Os pending for each engine. If these values are high, you need to look for the reason in the **I/O delayed** information to determine why the I/O is blocked.

Disk I/O Structures

An I/O delay caused by reaching the limit on disk I/O structures. Each task initiating a disk I/O has to get control of a disk I/O structure control block. If all I/O control blocks are being used, the task blocks waiting on one being freed. The number of disk I/O control blocks may be altered using the **disk i/o structures** configuration parameter.

Server Config Level

A delay caused by the server exceeding its limit for the maximum number of outstanding asynchronous disk I/O requests. This may be altered using the **max async i/os per server** configuration parameter.

Engine Config Limit

Same as for the Server Config Level on a per engine basis.

Operating System Limit

A delay caused by exceeding an operating system limit on the maximum number of outstanding asynchronous disk I/Os. The operating system will have both a per-process and a per-system limit on disk I/O, you will need to check its configuration.

Requested and Completed Disk I/Os

There will naturally be some differences between these figures, since some I/Os will start before the sample interval and some will complete afterward. Neither of these types of "orphan" will be included in the figures. However, much fewer completions than requests indicates that there is a disk I/O bottleneck; you need to look at the individual device figures to see if any are being overloaded. If this is the case, redistribute the data across the available disks. If disk activity is evenly spread, check than if an I/O limit has been exceeded.

If there is no obvious bottleneck, you may simply be swamping the disk I/O system and need to reconsider your disk activity by eliminating large table scans or moving activity to another machine.

Device Activity Detail

The reads and writes to each device owned by the server. This is useful in determining if the disk activity is evenly spread across the available disks.

Device Semaphores Granted and Waited

In SMP environments, a semaphore controls concurrent access to the disk I/O control blocks by the multiple engines. A high waited figure indicates that there is high contention for a particular device and redistribution of the data should be considered.

Network I/O Management

This section reports on network I/O requests and delays and on the number and size of TDS packets.

```
Network I/O Management
----------------------
```

	per sec	per xact	count	% of total
Total Network I/O Requests	38.2	3.9	24902	n/a
Network I/Os Delayed	0.0	0.0	0	0.0%
Total TDS Packets Received	per sec	per xact	count	% of total
Engine 0	0.3	0.0	211	3.4%
Engine 1	9.3	0.9	6044	96.6%
Total TDS Packets Rec'd	9.6	1.0	6255	
Total Bytes Received	per sec	per xact	count	% of total
Engine 0	73.8	7.5	48055	5.3%
Engine 1	1330.5	135.4	866222	94.7%
Total Bytes Rec'd	1404.3	142.9	914277	
Avg Bytes Rec'd per Packet	n/a	n/a	146	n/a

Total TDS Packets Sent	per sec	per xact	count	% of total
Engine 0	5.3	0.5	3454	18.6%
Engine 1	23.2	2.4	15131	81.4%
Total TDS Packets Sent	28.5	2.9	18585	

Total Bytes Sent	per sec	per xact	count	% of total
Engine 0	918.9	93.5	598244	11.2%
Engine 1	7263.5	739.3	4729065	88.8%
Total Bytes Sent	8182.4	832.8	5327309	
Avg Bytes Sent per Packet	n/a	n/a	286	n/a

Transaction Log Alloc	6.8	0.7	4409	n/a

If the network is bottlenecking, look at the application use of the network. Areas to consider are; use of procedures, use of batches, reducing the number of select commands in a batch—these are covered in Chapter 19.

If the **ave bytes per packet** is close to the packet size, you may have occasions when multiple packets are required for each command. An input/output which spans more than one packet has to wait between each packet. If you cannot reduce the data flow, you should consider increasing the packet size for specific application connections.

Summary

There are several methods of monitoring these usage levels, both proprietary and third party. The most recent proprietary method is the System 11 procedure sp_sysmon which provides detailed statistics on:

- Kernel utilization
- Task management
- Transaction profile
- Transaction management

- Index management

- Lock management

- Data cache management

- Procedure cache management

- Memory management

- Recovery management

- Disk I/O management

- Network I/O management

## PART V

TROUBLESHOOTING

When something goes wrong, or not quite right, you need to have some idea of what is happening and how to approach a problem so you can solve and fix it. Most problems are common ones and will recur frequently. This makes it easier to analyze them in a uniform manner and apply the necessary changes.

This section categorizes the problems into broad groupings of index, storage, space, and network and then presents drill-down analysis and diagnosis of the problems to provide the optimum solution.

The sp_sysmon monitoring tool is discussed to show how the various outputs should be interpreted and what the effects are of making alterations to the related configuration parameters. The section then closes with a discussion of writing high-performance SQL.

14

Index Troubleshooting

The best index strategy does not always produce expected results, so we need to find out why. Sometimes the answer will be quite simple, at other times you will need to revert to detailed analysis of the execution plans to discover why the indexes are not being used. This chapter discusses index solutions. The optimizer trace flags are detailed to show how to investigate optimization problems and the techniques used to force specific optimizer behavior are also described.

I have created an index but it is not being used

You are not supplying a search argument; or,

The column range or the index values themselves are returning too many records; or,

You are not providing a start point for the search to commence.

Not providing a search argument

The best index will not be used if you have not specified the where clause as a search argument. The exception to this is a covered index where the index is always used if it covers the query, even when there is no search argument on the indexed column. A search argument is mandatory before the index will even be considered by the optimizer.

```
valid search arguments          invalid search arguments
name like 'KIR%'                    substring(name, 1, 3) = 'KIR'
salary = 2000*12                    salary/12 = 2000
```

This has been discussed earlier; you should try to avoid the following non-search argument situations.

Table 14.1

NOT Search Argument	Equivalent Search Argument
150 = price * 12	150 /12 = price
substring(name, 1, 3) = 'kir'	name like 'kir%'
upper(name) = 'KIRKWOOD'	No equivalent: be careful with upper and lower case. If possible, improve performance by converting on input.
qty + 10 > 200	qty > 200 - 10
firstname + ' ' + lastname = 'john kirkwood'	firstname = 'john' and lastname = 'kirkwood'
ltrim(name) = 'kirkwood'	No equivalent: be careful with leading spaces. Always worth removing any possible leading spaces on input.

Too many records being accessed

Even when you have a valid search argument, the number of records accessed may be too high. When the index is nonclustered, the number of I/Os to retrieve the records may be more than the number of I/Os to table scan. When the number of records accessed via the index is more than the number of pages in the table, the optimizer will not use the index but will table scan. When the index is nonclustered, there is one index entry for each record and so each record access requires at least one logical I/O. It is obviously greater than this since each record access requires a read of the leaf level and a read of the record. However, as the leaf level is being scanned in sequence of the index key, the overhead of doing this is normally ignored and the number of record I/Os taken as the overriding factor. This is only an estimate, so do not rely on it when the values are close. For a clustered index, the leaf level is the data pages themselves; a clustered index scan is equivalent to a table scan and the problem of too many record accesses is not relevant.

There is obviously a break point when the nonclustered index access will switch to a table scan. This depends on the number of records per page, i.e., the record size.

If we consider a 1,000,000 record table, then differing numbers of records per page give the following breakpoints.

Table 14.2

Number of Records Per Page	Number of Pages	Breakpoint
1	1,000,000	none
2	500,000	50%
4	250,000	25%
8	125,000	12.5%
10	100,000	10%
20	50,000	5%
50	20,000	2%

There is a mathematical solution to this but, it is clear that the breakpoint is inversely proportional to the number of records per page, i.e., the breakpoint is the reciprocal of the number of records per page.

No start point in the index

A third common problem is that the where clause is not providing a start point for the search of the index. You do not have to tell the optimizer where to finish the search but you must provide a start point. If you don't, all of the records have to be read and the optimizer will choose a table scan. There are two simple examples of this:

single index on name
      where name like "%oo"'   In this case every index record has to be read to see if the name ends in "ood."

compound index on (order_no, product_no)
      where product_no = 10   In this case the index is not appropriate as it is sequenced on order_no. Every index record will have to be read to see if the product_no equals 10.

The latter is an important aspect of compound indexes: if you do not provide a where clause on the first column of the compound index, the index cannot be used by the optimizer. Again, the proviso is that when the index covers the command, an index scan will be carried out in preference to a table scan.

It's a perfect index but still not being used

If you are confident that everything is in place for the index, but the optimizer still table-scans, you should ensure that the index statistics are current and that they are being used.

The index statistics are not maintained dynamically but are created by the **create index** command and may be refreshed by the **update statistics** command. Therefore, it is possible for them to get out of step with the actual data distribution unless you keep them up-to-date with regular update statistics. Unfortunately, there is no timestamp on the index statistics that will indicate when the last update statistics were run. In general, if you cannot explain the non-use of the index, run the update statistics and try again.

Be careful of the index statistics on table creation. The sequence:

- Create table

- Create index

- Insert data

will have created the index on an empty table and no index statistics will be initialized. You can find out which indexes have no statistics by looking at sysindexes. The column **distribution** on sysindexes holds the page number of the statistics page. If this is 0, there are no statistics for the index.

```
select object_name(id), name, indid, distribution
       from sysindexes
       where distribution = 0
```

The indid column indicates the type of object: 0—a table without a clustered index, 1—the clustered index, 2-249—the nonclustered indexes. Indid 0 and 1 cannot exist at the same time and the nonclustered indids are allocated in sequence of creation. When there are no statistics for the index, the optimizer defaults to fixed percentages for the where clause based on the operator used.

Equality	10%
Closed interval (like, between)	25%
Open interval (less than, greater than)	33%

These percentages can provide high estimates and force the optimizer to think that a table scan is better than an index access. Consider a 100 byte record with 100,000 records. There are 20 records per page and 5000 pages. If there are no statistics on the primary_key_col index the command:

```
update tab_1 set col_1 = 30
      where primary_key_col = 100
```

will table scan as 10% of 100,000 is 10,000 records. This is twice the number of pages so the optimizer will table scan. Although we know that the update is being done to 1 record on primary key, the lack of statistics has caused a 5000-page table scan.

I have updated the statistics and it still table scans

In this case, you have to look at the SQL. There are two principal reasons: non-matching datatypes and unknown values in the SQL command.

Non-matching datatypes

Optimizer access to the statistics is a look-up with no conversion of datatype being done. This can cause problems when using variables or numeric literals. If you do not use the same datatype for the variable/literal as the index column, the statistics cannot be used. However, the optimizer knows the statistics exist and it uses the sarg density of the index column held in the statistics. This usually gives a sufficiently accurate estimate for the index to be considered useful but there will be occasions when even this is not sufficient and the index will not be used.

One problem in SQL Server is that null and not null column definitions are held as different datatypes. A column which allows nulls is held by SQL Server as a variable datatype which requires conversion to be tested against the fixed not null datatype. Accessing the index statistics does no conversion and therefore the index statistics will not be used if the datatypes or the null/not null status is different. The only exception to this is the datatype, which is treated the same regardless of null status.

Be especially careful of the numeric datatype, since conversion will occur unless the precision and scale match. So, although most numeric datatypes use the statistics even when different, the numeric datatype will use the statistics only when the precision and scale match exactly.

```
column          expression      showplan
int             a < 20          index
int             a < 20.0        index
int             a < 2e+1        index
float           a < 2e+1        index
float           a < 20          index
float           a < 20.0        index
numeric(4, 1)   a < 20          table scan
numeric(4, 1)   a < 20.0        index
numeric(4, 1)   a < 2e+1        index
numeric(4, 1)   a < 20.12       table scan
numeric(4, 1)   a < 2e+2        table scan
```

Unknown values

Another problem in using the statistics occurs when the SQL generates an unknown value to the optimizer. The simplest example of this is arithmetic in the where clause.

```
select * from tab_1
       where col_1 = 2*2
```

When the command is optimized, the expression 2*2 has not been evaluated, so the optimizer does not know what value to use to match against the statistics. Therefore, the statistics cannot be used and again the optimizer uses the sarg density of the column held in the statistics page.

Other normal occasions of the optimizer meeting an unknown value occur when the value in the where clause is contained in a variable or generated by a nested select command. Because the density is being used, you will often get the correct use of the index. But when you do not, the table scan can be avoided by using stored procedures.

```
Unknown variable values              Unknown nested select value

declare @var1 int                    select * from tab_1
select @var1 = 50                           where col_1 = (select max(col_2)
select * from tab_1                                             from tab_2)
       where col_1 = @var1
```

```
replace with                      replace with

create proc proc_1 (@par1 int)    create proc proc_2 (@par1 float)
as                                as
select * from tab_1               select * from tab_1
      where col_1 = @par1               where col_1 = @par1
go                                go
declare @var1 int                 declare @var1 float
select @var1 = 50                 select @var1 = max(col_2) from tab_2
exec proc_1 @par1 = @var1          exec proc_1 @par1 = @var1
```

When the procedure is executed, it is optimized with the input value of the parameter. The value in the where clause is known at optimization time and the statistics can be used.

How do I see the index choices for my SQL?

Use the **showplan** option of the **set** command: **set showplan on**. This is usually used with the **noexec** option which does not execute the command: **set noexec on**

The SQL Server optimizer is a statistical optimizer which means that it uses distribution statistics about each index to decide on an execution plan. This means that you need a very representative sample of the data—in practice a full copy of the production system is best—to allow the optimizer to make the best choice. If you do not have the resource to keep a full copy of production, you will find it advantageous when trying to solve a production problem to take a copy of the relevant tables into development. I know that it might take a little time to bcp out and in and then recreate the indexes, but you really do need data volumes which are representative of production. To do this, you will tend to be executing against a large amount of data when you are checking optimization plans and it is usually advantageous to combine the set showplan with the set noexec to see the optimization plan but not to execute the command.

```
set showplan on
go
set noexec on
go
```

You should still do a full execution of the command—preferably with **set statistics io on** to see the actual disk accesses. This ensures that the index choices are as good as the optimizer thinks they are. This is not always necessary as an index plan for equality on a unique index is rather obvious. However, if you are checking a five table join with multiple selection criteria, you will often have a choice of indexed solutions and the only way to check which is best is to run them with **set statistics io on** to check the actual logical disk accesses. Set showplan off before you execute any system stored procedures as the showplans from these are extensive (assuming that you have remembered to set noexec off in the first place).

How do I see more detail on the optimizer index choices?

Run the showplan with two trace flags on: 302 and 310.

Optimizer trace flag 302 displays detailed information on the decisions made in evaluating where clauses; 310 trace flag displays detailed information on the decisions made in evaluating join clauses. These trace flags are set on and off using the **dbcc traceon** and **dbcc traceoff** commands. By default, the output of these trace flags is written to the error log and you need to redirect it to the terminal with the 3604 trace flag. So to see detailed information on optimizer index choices, you need to set up as:

```
dbcc traceon(3604)
go
dbcc traceon(302, 310)
go
set showplan on
go
set noexec on
go
select ......
```

Trace flag 302 output

The 302 trace flag outputs detailed information on where clause selection. Each where clause that is a search argument or a join clause has an output describing the **q_score_index()** which contains the following information:

- The table has nnnn rows and nnnn pages

  The size of the table in rows and pages from sysindexes. The number of pages here is the table scan limit, which is the maximum number of logical I/Os that the optimizer will perform to execute the command. Any index which is no better than this is not used.

- Scoring the SEARCH CLAUSE

- Scoring the JOIN CLAUSE

  This identifies the clause which is being evaluated. All search clauses are evaluated before the join clauses. An index may be considered for both a search clause and a join clause.

- Base cost

  This displays the cost of a table scan displaying:

      the indid (0)
      rows in the table
      pages in the table
      prefetch strategy
      I/O size
      data cache id
      cache replacement strategy

- Statistics page information

  If statistics are available, it displays how they are being evaluated:

      the statistics page number
      the number of statistics steps
      the search value to access the statistics
      if a match was found and how many statistics pages qualify

  The type of statistics matching which occurs is:
      match found on statistics page
          an exact match of the search value was found
      no steps for search value—qualpage for LT search value finds value between step K, K+1, K=2—use betweenSC
          no exact match was found—indicates the steps that the value falls between.

SARG is a subbed VAR or expr result or local variable (constat=40)—
use magicSC or densitySC

> indicates the search argument is a subquery, expression or local
> variable, i.e., the actual value is unknown and the density will
> be used

- Cost estimate

This displays the final cost estimate for the index displaying:

> the indid
> the selectivity: fraction of rows expected to qualify rows and pages

Once each index has been examined, the cheapest is displayed as:

```
Cheapest index is index 2, costing 2 pages and generating 3 rows per scan, using no
data prefetch (size 2) on dcacheid 0 with LRU replacement strategy.
```

The prefetch and replacement strategies are explained later in the chapter.

An example of the 310 output is:

Trace flag 310 output

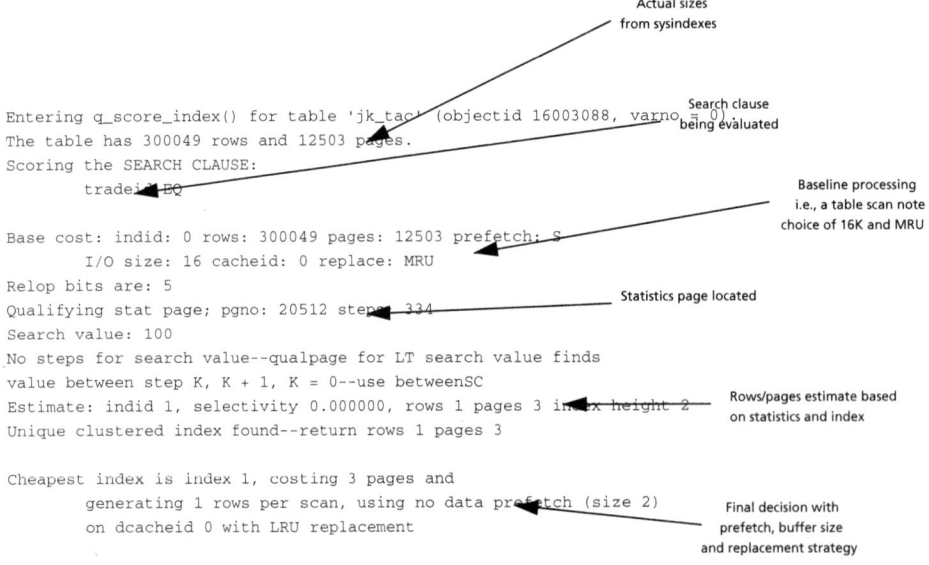

Figure 14.1

The 310 optimizer trace flag displays detailed information on table sequencing in join statements.

All table join sequences are evaluated for all possible index accesses and a cost calculated for each of them. A table sequence is not considered if there is no join clause between the tables. For example:

```
select .....
       from titles t, titleauthors ta, authors a
       where t.title_id = ta.title_id
       and ta.au_id = a.au_id
```

will evaluate (numbering from left to right in the from clause):

```
0 - 1 - 2
2 - 1 - 0
```

but will not evaluate:

```
0 - 2 - 1
```

as this does not have a valid join clause between titles and authors. It can, of course evaluate it as two joins 2-0 and 2-1. I have not included this here, although I have seen it happen.

The following is displayed for each join sequence and each possible access path on the tables:

total cost

The estimated total cost of each iteration sequence.

for each table in the join sequence

table number (starting at 0 from the left as above)
table name
index id and name
access information
rows
pages
selectivity
prefetch
i/o size
cache strategy

The final plan is displayed with cache information on cache id used and the buffer pool size used.

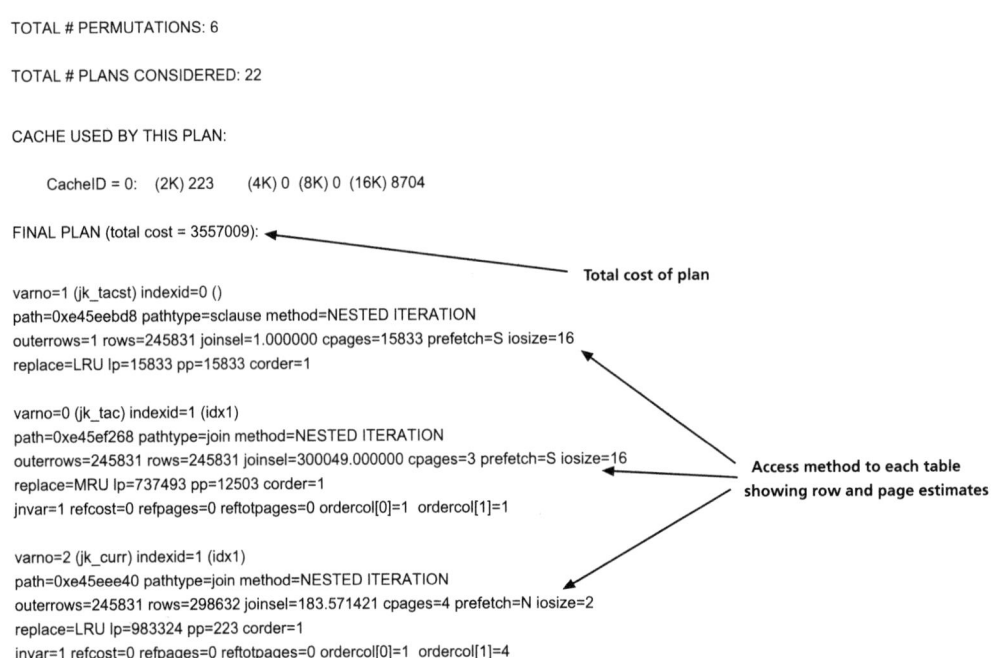

TOTAL # PERMUTATIONS: 6

TOTAL # PLANS CONSIDERED: 22

CACHE USED BY THIS PLAN:

   CacheID = 0:   (2K) 223   (4K) 0 (8K) 0 (16K) 8704

FINAL PLAN (total cost = 3557009):   ◄─────────────────────────── **Total cost of plan**

varno=1 (jk_tacst) indexid=0 ()
path=0xe45eebd8 pathtype=sclause method=NESTED ITERATION
outerrows=1 rows=245831 joinsel=1.000000 cpages=15833 prefetch=S iosize=16
replace=LRU lp=15833 pp=15833 corder=1

varno=0 (jk_tac) indexid=1 (idx1)
path=0xe45ef268 pathtype=join method=NESTED ITERATION
outerrows=245831 rows=245831 joinsel=300049.000000 cpages=3 prefetch=S iosize=16   ◄───── **Access method to each table**
replace=MRU lp=737493 pp=12503 corder=1   **showing row and page estimates**
jnvar=1 refcost=0 refpages=0 reftotpages=0 ordercol[0]=1 ordercol[1]=1

varno=2 (jk_curr) indexid=1 (idx1)
path=0xe45eee40 pathtype=join method=NESTED ITERATION
outerrows=245831 rows=298632 joinsel=183.571421 cpages=4 prefetch=N iosize=2
replace=LRU lp=983324 pp=223 corder=1
jnvar=1 refcost=0 refpages=0 reftotpages=0 ordercol[0]=1 ordercol[1]=4

Figure 14.2

The meaning of the output variables is:

Table 14-3

Variable	Description
varno	Table number starting at 0 and numbering from the left
indexid	Index id being considered (0: table scan, 1: clustered, 2-249: nonclustered
pathtype	Type of clause being evaluated (sclause; join; orstruct)
method	Evaluation method being considered (NESTED ITERATION; REFORMATTING; OR OPTIMIZATION)
outerrows	Number of outer rows (the number of iterations on the inner table)

Table 14.3 *(continued)*

Variable	Description
rows	Number of matching rows
joinsel	Join selectivity
cpages	Number of page I/Os per look-up
prefetch	Use of prefetch (N, S=Yes(sequential))
iosize	I/O buffer size used (2, 4, 8, 16)
replace	Buffer replacement strategy (LRU; MRU)
lp	Number of logical page accesses costed at 2 ms
pp	Number of physical page accesses costed at 18 ms
corder	Most significant sort column
refcost	I/O cost of reformatting
refpages	Number of pages per look-up using the temporary clustered index in reformatting
reftotpages	Number of pages accessed when reformatting used

Can I force an index to be used?

Yes. You can specify the index name with the table name in the FROM clause.

There will be occasions when the optimizer does not make the correct decision or you want to check the actual disk accesses with a different index choice. If you are satisfied that everything is as it should be—search arguments, up-to-date statistics, no unknown values, no datatype mismatches etc.—you can specify the index to be used for a table by including the name of the index immediately after the table name in the FROM clause.

```
select * from order_item (index price_idx)
      where price > 50.0
      and qty < 100
      and ord_date between '1/1/96' and '12/31/96'
```

This is not something you should be using often, as the optimizer will always use this index regardless of any changes you make to the indexing or the SQL. If your manual choice is better than the optimizer's choice you should be concentrating on why the optimizer is making the "wrong" choice. The most common reason is that the optimizer is seeing the index value distribution differently than you know it should be. Remember that the index statistics are collected in one 2 Kb page and therefore are only an estimate of the distribution. Unfortunately, there is little you can do about it: try reducing the index column size with a different datatype; if it is a composite index with a low selectivity first column, try a denormalized concatenated column for the index; deliberately force it not to use the statistics but to use the density or the default percentages. You never know...you might get lucky. But even these deceptions are forced optimizations and make sure that you have documented them or someone will change them in the future because they are not using the most obvious index!

You can force a table scan by using the table name in the index clause:

```
select * from customer (index customer)
     where name like 'S%'
```

If you are using pre-System 11 software, force index is still available but you need to use the indid after the table name.

```
select * from customer(2)
     where town like 'Woking%'
```

This will force use of the nonclustered index 2 to execute the command. Be careful, since the indids of a table scan (0) and the clustered index (1) remain constant, but a nonclustered index may change indid because of an index rebuild. The nonclustered indexes are numbered in sequence of creation, so be careful that you do not accidentally change them or you will be using the wrong index to execute a query.

Is there any optimum sequence to the where clauses?

No.

SQL Server never takes the position of the where clauses into account when evaluating the execution plan of any command. The only situation where you can influence the index chosen, is when two (or more) indexes look exactly the same to the optimizer. In this case, the optimizer will use the first index it meets when evaluating the where clauses. If we have two unique indexes on a table:

```
customer(cust_no, name, address)

unique indexes on (cust_no) and (name)
```

Then the command:

```
select * from customer
       where cust_no = 1
       and name = 'john kirkwood'
```

would use the index on cust_no. The command:

```
select * from customer
       where name = 'john kirkwood'
       and cust_no = 1
```

would use the index on name.

As both indexes are identical to the optimizer there is no reason to replace the first one with the second as it is no better. In general, this is trivial but it may allow you to drop an index if it is used only in the above situation. Of more relevance here is when the indexes are different but, because the first column in the index is the same, they look identical to the optimizer. Consider the indexes:

```
customer(name, first_name)
customer(name, postcode)
```

Because the statistics are collected on the first column only, both of these indexes appear the same to the optimizer. As the indexes are checked in indid sequence, the index created last will never be used. So there is the distinct possibility that:

```
select * from customer
       where name like 'kir%'
       and postcode like 'RG%'
```

will always use the index on (name, first_name) which is clearly less efficient than the (name, postcode) index.

This is unfortunate in SQL Server. The options are to suffer the retrieval over-head and drop one of the indexes; restructure the unused index to have the other column first (e.g., postcode, name) or to force the use of the required index.

Is there any optimum sequence to the tables in the from clause?

No.

SQL Server never takes the position of the table in the from clause into account when evaluating the execution plan of any command.

You need to be aware of how joins of more than four tables are evaluated. In evaluating join sequence, the optimizer only considers the tables four at a time. So the join:

```
select ...
        from A, B, C, D, E
        ...
```

will consider all 4 table join sequences:

```
ABCD
ABCE
ABDE
ACDE
BCDE
BACD
etc.
```

but will not consider any five table join sequences.

When the from clause has more than four tables, all four table join sequences are considered to determine the best outer table; then the remaining tables are considered for all four table join sequences to determine the next table in the nested iteration, and so on until only four tables are left to consider.

Can I alter the number of tables considered in the join sequence?

Yes. Use the **set table count** command.

In System 11, you can alter the number of tables considered in sequencing tables in a multi-table join using the set table count command.

```
set table count number
```

where

number is between 0 and 8.

In general, altering this number makes little difference to the execution plan and a value of 4 usually generates the best join sequence. In practice, I have found that there are more problems with the index choices than with the join sequences and forcing an index choice is more common than increasing the number of tables considered in join sequences. Also be aware that increasing this number can significantly increase the number of combinations considered by the optimizer. As the SQL Server optimizer does not have a maximum time limit on the optimization phase, this can effect the command response time and the overall throughput of the system.

Can I force the table evaluation sequence in a join command?

Yes. Use the **set forceplan** command.

You can force the optimizer to consider the tables in the fixed sequence of left to right as defined in the from clause by using the set forceplan command.

```
set forceplan on
```

This will cause all join commands to be evaluated left to right as defined in the from clause.

```
set forceplan on
go
select ...
        from A, B, C, D
        ...
```

will evaluate as A outer; B next; C next and D inner. This is independent of the join clauses or any other optimization on search arguments.

Are there any other ways I can affect the optimizer decisions?

Yes. You can specify the I/O buffer size to be used for the table in the from clause. You can specify the cache strategy to be used for the table in the from clause.

These are all System 11 options. In conjunction with the index name clause, you can specify the size of the buffer pool and the cache replacement strategy for an individual table or index.

Buffer pool I/O size (prefetch)

Each cache may be split into four I/O pool sizes—2 Kb, 4 Kb, 8 Kb, 16 Kb. The optimizer will choose the best available buffer pool size for each command, but you can override this using the prefetch option of the index name clause.

```
select * from order_item (index price_idx prefetch 16)
        where price > 50.0
        and qty < 100
        and ord_date between '1/1/96' and '12/31/96'
```

This forces the optimizer to use the 16 Kb buffer pool for the order_item table. If there is no 16 Kb buffer pool or there are insufficient free pages in the 16 Kb buffer pool, the optimizer reverts to choosing the best available buffer size. The efficiency of this forced plan can be compromised when existing pages of the table are already in cache in a different buffer pool size. In this case, the existing buffer pool size is used for all pages of the extent to which the page(s) in cache belong.

The object name used in the index clause, i.e., index object_name prefetch 16, determines which part of the table or index uses the specified buffer pool size.

Table 14.4

object_name	Object which uses prefetch size
Nonclustered index	Index leaf pages
Clustered index	Data pages (i.e., leaf pages)
Table	Data pages

For example:

```
select * from orders (index orders prefetch 4)
```

will force the optimizer to use 4 Kb I/O buffers for the table scan of the orders table.

Cache strategy

SQL Server has two cache strategies: MRU and LRU (most recently used and least recently used). MRU is also called **fetch and discard**. The MRU replacement strategy tries to reuse the pages which have just been used and the LRU replacement strategy tries to use a new page every time. This is illustrated in Figure 14.3.

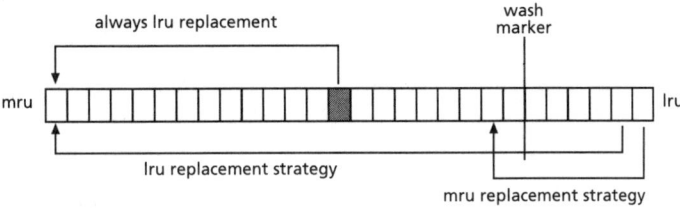

Figure 14.3 *Cache replacement strategies*

Figure 14.3 depicts the cache as a chain of pages from the most recently used to the least recently used, i.e., from the page just accessed to the page which has not been used for the longest time. In this representation, pages migrate from the mru end to the lru end and when they pass the **wash marker** they are written to disk to create 'clean' cache pages which can be used to hold pages from disk.

When a page has to be read from disk, one of the "washed" pages in cache is used and placed into the 'dirty' portion of the cache chain depending on the cache replacement strategy. If LRU replacement strategy is used, the page is placed on the mru end of the cache chain so that it is not subject to immediate reuse. This means that the page will remain in cache for the longest possible time to make optimum use of logical

I/Os. If MRU replacement strategy is used, the page is placed just before the wash marker so that it will be one of the first pages to be re-used for physical I/O from disk. The MRU replacement strategy destroys as little of the cache as possible with maximum re-use of pages that are not expected to be needed again in the short term. Therefore, a large table scan using MRU should use the same pages in cache repetitively so that the most active cache pages are left untouched. A worktable used in an SQL command, e.g., in a join, will normally use MRU as it will not be required again outside of the join.

You specify the cache strategy in the index clause as LRU or MRU.

```
select * from order_item (index price_idx prefetch 8 MRU)
       where price > 50.0
       and qty < 100
       and ord_date between '1/1/96' and '12/31/96'
```

How can I tell if the statistics have been created?

The column **distribution** in the system table **sysindexes** is non-zero.

The column **sysindexes.distribution** contains the page number of the statistics page. If this is zero, the statistics have not been created. You can easily display this as:

```
select object_name(id), name, indid, data_pgs(id, doampg)
       from sysindexes
       where distribution = 0
```

The data_pgs(id, doampg) is not essential, but since tables with three or less pages are guaranteed to table scan regardless of the indexing, you can ignore them. Regular distribution = 0 should not be ignored, even on these small tables as it may indicate a need to implement a regular **update statistics** process.

How can I tell if the statistics are up-to-date?

Sorry, there is no way to do this.

SQL Server does not have a date/time update for the statistics page. You cannot tell when it was last updated. If you are having an optimization problem and suspect the statistics, the simplest approach is to run **update statistics** and then retry the problem. The statistics are not updated dynamically and require regular update statistics. In practice, if you have any optimization problems, it is worthwhile to eliminate any possible doubt about the statistics by immediately running update statistics before you analyze the optimization plans. It might save you some wasted effort.

Can I see the expected number of I/Os in the optimizer plan?

Not in the basic plan, but you can set a trace flag—311.

The optimizer trace flag 311 displays the estimated logical and physical I/O which the optimizer expects to make to execute the command. As with most trace flag settings, this requires trace flag 3604 to redirect the output to the terminal. Undocumented trace flags normally send their output to the error log. You need to set 3604 to redirect this to the terminal. You can set multiple flags in the one command: dbcc traceon (3604, 311).

```
dbcc traceon(3604)
go
dbcc traceon(311)
go
```

Table: jk_tacst scan count 1, logical reads: 19370, physical reads: 19370
Table: jk_tac scan count 300000, logical reads: 900000, physical reads: 12503
Table: jk_curr scan count 300000, logical reads: 1200000, physical reads: 223

QUERY PLAN FOR STATEMENT 1 (at line 1).

STEP 1
The type of query is SELECT.

FROM TABLE
jk_tacst
Nested iteration.
Table Scan.
Ascending scan.
Positioning at start of table.
Using I/O Size 16 Kbytes.
With LRU Buffer Replacement Strategy.

.
.
.
.

This displays the estimated logical and physical I/O identically to the **set statistics io on** command.

Note that this is no substitute for actually running the command with set statistics io on, since the I/O figures displayed by the 311 trace flag are the optimizer estimates based on the statistics or density figures of the indexes. They will often be different from what you expect or what you get in practice. Interestingly, a large difference in estimated and actual logical I/O can indicate a simple need to update the statistics.

How long does it take to create an index?

It obviously depends on how big the table is and what type of index you are creating, but there are some formulae you could apply to get an estimate of the index creation time.

Clustered

The formula supplied by Sybase in their training material is:

```
(2 * (ceiling(log8(# data pages / 50))) + 1) * # data pages
```

The 50 is the current of an internal sort in SQL Server.

A more "from first principles" approach is to calculate the number of merge sorts, the number of merge runs, the number of I/Os per data page and the total number of I/Os.

Number of merge sorts

```
# merge sorts = # data pages / 50     (again where 50 is the size of an
                                       internal sort)
```

Number of merge runs

Divide the number of merge sorts progressively by 8 until the result is equal to 1. This is the number of merge runs. For example, if the number of merge sorts was 1200, the number of merge runs is calculated as:

```
# merge runs = 1200/8 = 150/8 = 19/8 = 3/8 = 1     i.e., 4 merge runs
```

Number of I/Os per data page

```
# I/Os per data page = # merge runs * 2
```

Each merge run requires 2 I/Os on the data page: one to read and one to write.

Total number of I/Os

```
total I/Os = # data pages * # I/Os per data page
```

For example, with 20,000 records in 770 pages the calculation gives:

```
# merge sorts = 770 / 50 = 16

# merge runs = 16/8 = 2/8 = 1          i.e., 2 merge runs

# I/Os per data page = 2 * 2 = 4

total number of I/Os = 770 * 4 = 3080
```

Nonclustered

The formula supplied by Sybase is:

```
# data pages
+
2 * (ceiling(log8(# data pages/50))) + 1
*
# data pages * (index_row_size/data_row_size)
```

The "from first principles" approach is the same as the clustered index: number of merge sorts; number of merge runs; I/Os per page and total I/Os. However, the non-clustered index creation is more dependent on the number of rows in the table which requires you to calculate the number of pages in each merge run.

Number of pages per merge sort

```
# pages per merge sort = # rows / # index rows per index page
```

Number of merge sorts

```
# merge sorts = # data pages / 50
```

Number of merge runs

Divide the number of merge sorts progressively by 8 until the result is equal to 1. This is the number of merge runs. For example, if the number of merge sorts was 1200, the number of merge runs is calculated as:

```
# merge runs = 1200/8 = 150/8 = 19/8 = 3/8 = 1      i.e., 4 merge runs
```

Number of I/Os per merge run

```
# I/Os per merge run = (# merge levels * I/Os per level) - 1
```

In the nonclustered, case the number of I/Os per level is still 2 (one read and one write) but we need to subtract one for the first read on the data pages.

Total number of I/Os

```
total I/Os = (# I/Os per merge run * # pages per merge sort)
             + # data pages
```

I used the 20000 record, 770 page table.
          The calculation gives:

```
# pages per merge sort = 20000 / 15 = 1334  (using an overhead of 7 for
                                             the index row)

# merge sorts = 770 / 50 = 16

# merge runs = 16 /8 = 2/8 = 1      i.e., 2 merge runs

# I/Os per merge run = (2 * 2) - 1 = 3

total I/O = (3 * 1334) + 770 = 4772
```

When create index takes a long time: Can I speed it up?

Sometimes. If you are building a clustered index and the input is in the sequence of the index key, you can use the **with sorted_data** clause of **create index**. Try increasing the number of extent buffers used in the create index by altering the **number of extent i/o buffers** configuration parameter.

A clustered index build involves the steps:

- Read existing data records

- Sort to the index key sequence

- Write the sorted output records to new data pages

- Delete the old data pages

You can bypass the sort by telling the create index command that the data is already in key sequence using the with sorted_data clause.

```
create unique clustered index jk_idx1 on tab_1(col_1)
     with sorted_data
```

This can be a significant index build time saving for a large index. If you are simply rebuilding an existing index, e.g., to defragment space, use the with sorted_data clause.

The create index uses the normal 2 Kb page I/O when building the index. You can increase this to use extent I/O by using a configuration parameter.

```
sp_configure 'number of extent i/o buffers', 50
```

This really does speed up a large index build. If you have some large index builds you will find that increasing the extent i/o buffers from the default of 0 will speed up the index build. For each allocated extent I/O buffer, the server allocates 1 extent, i.e., 8 pages from the server memory, effectively reducing the data and procedure cache. So the above setting of 50 is allocating 800 Kb which is coming from existing data and procedure cache. Sybase recommends that you do not set this value above 100, since this has a detrimental effect on creation time. I have been informed by several dbas that settings between 40 and 60 seem to give optimal index creation performance. Finally, if you run multiple index creates at the same time, only the first one uses the large extent I/O; the others revert to 2 Kb page I/O.

I have created the index but it has no statistics

This is possible only if you created the index on an empty table.

The create index command initializes the index statistics. If there is no data in the table when you issue the create index, there will be no statistics created. The sequence:

- Create table
- Create index
- Load data

does not initialize the statistics as there is no data to create any statistics. If you must create in this sequence, make sure you issue an update statistics after you have loaded the data.

My procedure has started going slowly

There are two reasons for this: an unsuitable execution plan from an existing version of the procedure in cache or the procedure needs to be recompiled to use updated index statistics or new indexes.

Unsuitable execution plan

A procedure execution first checks to see if a free version of the procedure is in cache. If one is available, this version is used. In some cases this may have an unsuitable execution plan and the procedure may not perform efficiently. The simplest example of this is a query reading a variable number of records from a nonclustered index when the number of records is controlled by input parameter values. In this case, the execution plan will vary between a table scan and an index access depending on the number of records estimated by the optimizer for the input parameter values. If the execution you need is an index access but you use a table scan version from procedure cache, the response time will not be what you expected.

This is easily checked by executing the procedure with recompile. This forces the procedure to be loaded from sysprocedures and recompiled. If this returns the procedure to "normal" execution, you then need to decide how to avoid the problem on a more permanent basis. There are three choices for recompilation:

exec proc_name with recompile

Forces recompilation for this single execution. This has a problem since the next execution cannot be guaranteed to get this plan again as it may pick up one of the other—not appropriate—plans in cache.

create proc_1 with recompile

Forces recompilation on every execution of the procedure. This does not leave the procedure in cache. This guarantees the correct execution plan every time by compiling every time. This clearly minimizes the performance savings of procedures but does not negate the access security advantages.

sp_recompile table_name

Forces recompilation of all procedures which use the named table. This is a one-off recompilation. This technique is most often used after update statistics to ensure that the procedure execution picks up the new index statistics, or after defining a new index to ensure that the optimization plan takes it into account. Execution of a procedure version from cache only checks for existence of objects in its current execution plan. If everything is there, the plan is not recreated so new objects such as indexes or index statistics are not taken into account by cache resident versions of a procedure. sp_recompile forces recompilation of all procedures which use the table to overcome this.

Note that the problem of using an existing, inappropriate plan will not happen all of the time and is restricted to procedures which:

- Have input parameters used in where clauses with wide variations on records returned: pay particular attention to like, between, less than and greater than

- Nonclustered indexes on the columns matching with the input variables

This is not normally a problem which you should spend effort trying to anticipate, but it is one to adjust if it occurs.

Not using up-to-date statistics or indexes

If a free copy of the procedure is in cache, the only checks made are that the required objects are still available and the permissions are still valid. If everything used by the execution plan is available, no compilation takes place and any changes to existing objects will not get taken into account. This is particularly relevant with new indexes and updated statistics for existing indexes. If you suspect that this is the case, recompile the procedure by dropping and recreating it or—more easily—by issuing sp_recompile.

```
sp_recompile  table_name
```

This recompiles all procedures which use the table at the next execution.

The bottom line with poor performing procedures is to exec them with recompile to see if the problem goes away. If it does, make sure that you understand why—wrong plan, new stats, etc.—and that you take steps to ensure that it does not happen again.

Summary

Even the best index strategy is sometimes ignored by the optimizer. You may not be able to do much about it, but it is always useful to know what may be going wrong. There are several reasons to address when an index is not being used.

- No search argument
- Too many records returned from a nonclustered index
- Not providing a start point in the index
- Index statistics not created or not up-to-date
- Index statistics not being used
  - Mismatching datatypes
  - Unknown values

When you are really stuck and cannot work out what is going on, you can get more information using the optimizer trace flags 302, 310, 311. The 302 and 310 flags provide more detail on why an index has or has not been used and the 311 shows the I/O estimates associated with the final execution plan.

If all index and SQL manipulation fails, there are some index forces that you can use to make the optimizer choose a specific index or a specific execution sequence. These are:

- Forcing a specific index to be used by naming the index with the table in the from clause

- Forcing the join sequence as left to right in the from clause by issuing **set forceplan on**

- Alter the number of tables considered in the evaluation of join sequence by using **set table count number**

- Specify the I/O buffer size and/or the buffer replacement strategy in the index name clause of the from clause

Procedure executions can also use poor execution plans because existing unused cache versions of the procedure will be chosen instead of recompiling the procedure. This means that a parameterized selection on a nonclustered index may pick up a non-optimal execution plan from procedure cache. If this happens, recompile the procedure for this or every execution. It will be forced to create the optimal execution plan for the specific parameter values being supplied. Also, if an existing procedure cache version is used, it will not be recompiled if all objects still exist. This means that any updates to these objects, specifically refreshed statistics or new indexes are not picked up. If this causes a problem, recompile the procedure or force recompilation for all procedures which use the table by using **sp_recompile**.

15

Storage Troubleshooting

Storage errors such as 605s will probably be the most common type of error that you will have to deal with. There are not that many of them that you can fix without the assistance of Sybase, but there are several **dbcc** commands which will help you analyze the problem and, hopefully, assist in solving it. This chapter describes the **dbcc** commands associated with monitoring and troubleshooting the database space allocation. It then discusses the approach for identifying why allocation, OAM, data, and index errors have occurred.

How do I check the space allocations and object structures?

The allocation structures are checked with **dbcc checkalloc, dbcc tablealloc, dbcc indexalloc;** and the page linkage and pointers are checked with **dbcc checkdb** and **dbcc checktable**.

The above commands are the documented and supported means of checking the consistency of database space allocations and page pointers. Of course, you do not want the database to get into such a mess that there are allocation, extent and/or page pointer problems. Usually, when these types of problems occur, the reason is beyond your control. You have the means of checking for such errors with these dbcc commands and you should take the opportunity to run them regularly. The principal question is how often to run them. There is no definitive answer; it normally depends on how long it takes to run the dbcc checks and how much time you have to run them. Each major release of SQL Server increases the speed of the dbcc commands and maybe soon we will get the ability to run them against a dump of the database. Sybase will always recommend to run them before a dump of the database, since dumping rubbish is not a good idea. If you get the time to do this, then by all means do it and run **dbcc checkdb**, **dbcc checkcatalog**, and **dbcc checkalloc** prior to each database dump. If you do not have the time to run these before each dump, make sure that you run them before you lose the appropriate version of the dump. If you are keeping multiple generations of database dumps, run **dbcc checkdb** and **dbcc checkalloc** before you lose the last generation since the previous dbcc checks. If either of the dbcc commands shows a serious problem with the current database, one of the dump generations must be valid since it was dumped after the last successful dbcc checks.

So what do these dbcc commands check for and display?

```
checkalloc

dbcc  checkalloc [(database_name [,fix|nofix])]

where          fix            fixes allocation errors
               nofix          does not correct allocation errors (default)
```

This checks the consistency of the data and index pages with the corresponding extent structure.

```
dbcc checkalloc(fred)

Checking fred.
Database "fred" is not in single user mode—may find spurious allocation
problems due to transactions in progress.


***************************************************************

TABLE:  jk_tab     OBJID:  1838629593
INDID=1            FIRST=2736  ROOT=2760      SORT=1
       Data level: 1.          5 data pages in 2 extents.
       Indid: 1.               2 index pages in 2 extents
INDID=2            FIRST=2768  ROOT=2768      SORT=0
       Indid: 2.               2 index pages in 2 extents.
TOTAL # of extents = 6
***************************************************************
TABLE:  jk2_tab    OBJID:  1616008788
INDID=0 FIRST=817  ROOT=821      SORT=0
       Data level: 0.          5 data pages in 1 extents.
```

```
INDID=2              FIRST=1016  ROOT=1016      SORT=1
                     Indid: 0.                  2 index pages in 2 extents.
TOTAL # of extents = 3
*****************************************************************
Processed 32 entries in the Sysindexes for dbid 6.
Alloc page 0           (# of extent= 32  used pages = 98    ref pages = 98)
Alloc page 256         (# of extent= 32  used pages = 119   ref pages = 111)
Alloc page 512         (# of extent= 32  used pages = 159   ref pages = 143)
Alloc page 768         (# of extent= 29  used pages = 206   ref pages = 86)
Alloc page 1024        (# of extent= 9   used pages = 17    ref pages = 17)
Alloc page 1280        (# of extent= 1   used pages = 1     ref pages = 1)
Total (# of extent = 135  used pages = 600  ref pages  = 456) in this database.
DBCC Execution completed. If DBCC printed error messages, contact a user
with System Administrator (SA) role.
```

The initial warning of "single user mode" is worth paying attention to as check-alloc can take some time and often page linkage errors are displayed. These are caused by updates taking place while checkalloc is checking the page allocations. So run in "single user mode." When using the fix mode you must be in single user mode. The fix option replaces the dbcc fix_al command which was available in 4.9.

```
use master
go
sp_dboption fred, "single user", true
go
use fred
go
checkpoint
go
```

If you have problems running a database in single user mode, such as 24 hour availability, you can use the dbcc 2512 trace flag. This stops checkalloc from checking the transaction log, which is the source of the spurious allocation errors. You may then use **dbcc tablealloc** to check syslogs.

```
dbcc traceon(2512)
go
dbcc checkalloc(fred)
go
dbcc traceoff(2512)
go
dbcc tablealloc(syslogs)
go
```

Checkalloc does the following consistency checks:

- Checks the extent is for the correct table/index: object_id and index_id in the extent is the same as object_id and index_id in sysindexes, i.e. all pages are correctly allocated

- An extent occurs only once in the extent chain

- Checks the allocation bit map settings with the pages linked into the object page chain: pages marked as USED in the extent allocation bit map match those REFERENCED in the page chain, i.e., all used pages are allocated and all allocated pages are used

Individual tables and/or indexes may also be checked using **tablealloc** and **indexalloc**.

```
dbcc tablealloc({table_name|table_id}
                    [,{full|optimized|fast}][, {fix|nofix}]])
where
full            Reports all allocation errors.
optimized       Default mode which reports only on the allocation pages in the
                object allocation map (OAM). Does not check unreferenced alloca-
                tion extents which are not in the OAM pages. If the OAM pages are
                not accurate, you may miss some errors (2540s).
fast            Reports only on the pages referenced but not allocated in the
                extent. Does not check the allocations.
fix             Fixes allocation errors; the default for user tables. To fix sys-
                tem tables, you need to put the database in single user mode using
                sp_dboption.
nofix           Does not fix allocation errors, the default for system tables.

dbcc tablealloc(jk_tab)


The default report option of OPTIMIZED is used for this run.
The default fix option of FIX is used for this run.
********************************************************
TABLE: jk_tab                  OBJ_ID: 1838629593
INDID=1       FIRST=2736       ROOT=2760     SORT=1
        Data level: 1     5 data pages in 2 extents
          Indid: 1        2 index pages in 2 extents
INDID=2       FIRST=2768       ROOT=2768     SORT=1
          Indid: 2     2 index pages in 2 extents
TOTAL # of extents = 6


Alloc page 2560 (#of extents=2 used pages=3 ref pages=3)
Alloc page 2560 (#of extents=2 used pages=6 ref pages=6)
Alloc page 2560 (#of extents=2 used pages=3 ref pages=3)
Total (#of extents=6 used pages=12 ref pages=12) in this database.
Statistical information for this run follows:
Total # of pages read = 12
Total number of pages found in cache = 5
```

```
Total # of physical reads = 2
Total # of saved I/O = 5

dbcc indexalloc({table_name|table_id}, index_id
                    [, {full|optimized|fast} [, {fix|nofix}]])
```

This provides the same checks on the indexes as tablealloc does on the data.

```
dbcc indexalloc(jk_tab, 1)
```

```
The default report option of OPTIMIZED is used for this run.
The default fix option of FIX is used for this run.
*******************************************************
TABLE: jk_tab                          OBJ_ID: 1838629593
INDID=1             FIRST=2736   ROOT=2760      SORT=1
                    Data level: 1              5 data pages in 2 extents
                    Indid: 1    2 index pages in 2 extents

TOTAL # of extents=4

Alloc page 2560 (#of extents=2 used pages=3 ref pages=3)
Alloc page 2560 (#of extents=2 used pages=6 ref pages=6)
Total (#of extents=4 used pages=9 ref pages=9) in this database

Statistical information for this run follows:
Total # of pages read = 8
Total number of pages found in cache = 5
Total # of physical reads = 2
Total # of saved I/O = 1
```

```
dbcc indexalloc(jk_tab, 2)
```

```
The default report option of OPTIMIZED is used for this run.
The default fix option of FIX is used for this run.
*******************************************************
TABLE: jk_tab                          OBJ_ID: 1838629593
INDID=2     FIRST=2768   ROOT=2768   SORT=1
            Indid: 2    2 index pages in 2 extents

TOTAL # of extents=2

Alloc page 2560 (#of extents=2 used pages=3 ref pages=3)
Total (#of extents=2 used pages=3 ref pages=3) in this database

Statistical information for this run follows:
Total # of pages read = 2
Total number of pages found in cache = 2
Total # of physical reads = 2
Total # of saved I/O = 0
```

checkdb

```
dbcc  checkdb [(database_name [, skip_ncindex])]
```

where

skip_ncindex	skips the checking of the non-clustered indexes

This checks every table in the database carrying out the following integrity checks:

- The page pointer chain is intact: each page points back to the page that pointed to it.

- The page offset table is consistent: each data row has an entry in the page matching its offset in the page offset table.

- Index rows are located in the index pages in ascending key sequence.

- The nonclustered leaf index keys match the column(s) in the data row pointed to.

```
dbcc checkdb(fred)

. . .
. . .
. . .
Checking 1742629251
The total number of data pages in this table is 5.
Table has 5 data rows.
Checking syslogs
The total number of data pages in this table is 2.
        Space used in the log segment is 0.40 M bytes, 10%
        Space free in the log segment is 3.60 M bytes, 90%
DBCC Execution completed. If DBCC printed error messages, contact a user
with System Administrator (SA) role.
```

If syslogs is on a separate device, you get a report on used and free space during checkdb.

Individual tables may be checked using **dbcc checktable**.

```
dbcc checktable (table_name|table_id [, skip_ncindex])
```

There is no difference in the functionality of a **checkdb** and a **checktable**, the difference is in the timing of the table locks. The **checktable** takes a lock on the table specified in the command, therefore you can control the sequence of table locking by executing individual **checktable** commands. The **checkdb** also takes table locks but you have no control over the sequence of tables it is locking. If you have a specific concurrency problem with **checkdb** you might be able to minimize it by issuing the object based **checktable** in a specific sequence.

In addition, you might want to run **dbcc checkcatalog** which checks the consistency of the system tables in a database.

```
checkcatalog
dbcc  checkcatalog [(database_name)]

dbcc checkcatalog(fred)

Checking fred.
The following segments have been defined for database 20 (database name fred).
virtual_start_addr    size    segments
4100                  1536    0
                      1       2
DBCC Execution completed. If DBCC printed error messages, contact a user
with System Administrator (SA) role.
```

Some of the principal checks are:

- Every row in syscolumns has an entry in systypes and sysobjects

- Every row in sysobjects has an entry in syscolumns or sysprocedures

- Every row in sysindexes has an entry in sysobjects and syssegments

- Bit settings in sysusages.segmap for the database reference an entry in syssegments

- The last checkpoint in syslogs is valid

These dbcc commands may be summarized as:

Table 15.1

Command	When to Run	Scope	Locking	Speed
checkdb	Before dump	Checks all tables	Table locks	Slow
checkalloc	Before dump	Checks all object allocations	Table locks	Slow
checkcatalog	Before dump	Checks system tables	Page locks	Fast
checktable	For suspect table	Checks table	Table lock	Slow
tablealloc	For suspect table	Checks table allocations	Table lock	Slow
indexalloc	For suspect index	Checks index allocations	Table lock	Slow

Table 15.1 (continued)

Command	When to run	Sope	Locking	Speed
checkdb checktable skip_ncindex		Ignores nonclustered indexes	Table lock	Medium
tablealloc indexalloc fast		Checks OAM pages only	Table lock	Fast

Is there more detailed information on space allocation?

Yes. There is a series of unsupported dbcc commands which display further information on allocation units and extents. These are:

- allocdump   Extent information for an allocation page

- extentcheck   Extents in a database used by an object

- extentdump   Extent structure for a page

- findnotfullextents Extents for an object which have unused pages

- listoam   OAM page information for an object

- rebuildextents   Rebuilds extents and OAM pages for an object

- usedextents   Extents that are in use for a database or log device

These dbcc commands are not supported; you must take the warning that an incorrect execution could stack trace and/or crash your server. These should not be run regularly (as for the normal dbcc commands in the previous section) but only when you have specific problems which you cannot solve by any other means. Quoting an incorrect value in any of these commands, e.g., a page number which does not belong to the database, can crash your connection and may also crash the server. So, do not get carried away with these; they are very useful to learn about the storage allocation of the server, and can expose problems which are only reported upon by the regular commands, but they are dangerous and not to be used lightly. Make sure that you double check the syntax and the values that you are supplying before you execute the command.

If you have any doubt about the syntax you can get minimal help on some, but not all of the dbcc commands, using the **dbcc help** command. This shows the syntax but without any explanation of what each option does.

```
dbcc help(page)

page (dbid|dbname, pagenum [, printopt={0|1|2} [, cache={0|1}
      [, logical={1|0} [, cachename | -1 ]]]] )
```

None of these commands can be run with the normal **sa_role** privileges; you need to set the **sybase_ts_role** administration role.

```
sp_role 'grant', sybase_ts_role, sa
go
```

You need to logout and login again before this is active or you can run the **set role** command to modify your current session after you have granted the role.

```
set role 'sybase_ts_role', on
go
```

And finally, you need to redirect the output to the terminal with the 3604 trace flag when you are running one of these dbcc commands.

```
dbcc traceon(3604)
go

allocdump
```

This displays the extent information for a given allocation page number, showing the object id to which each extent is allocated and the allocation bitmap information.

```
dbcc allocdump(database_name|dbid, page#)

dbcc allocdump(12, 256)
```

EXTID: 256	objid 9	indid 0	alloc 7	dealloc 0	status 1
EXTID: 392	objid 336004228	indid 2	alloc ff	dealloc 0	status 1
EXTID: 504	objid 208003772	indid 0	alloc f3	dealloc 0	status 0

The highlighted allocation bit maps indicate that:

- Extent 392 is allocated to object 336004228; nonclustered index id 2 has no free pages since the bit map is 0xff, i.e., binary 11111111. All pages (392 - 399) are used.

- Extent 504 is allocated to the data of object 208003772; it has 2 unused pages as the bit map is 0xf3, i.e., binary 11110011. Pages 504, 505, and 508 - 511 are used but 506 and 507 are currently unused.

extentcheck

This displays the same information as allocdump for all extents used by an object.

```
dbcc extentcheck(dbid, objid, indexid, sort)

dbcc extentcheck(12, 656005368, 0, 0)


EXTID: 584        objid 656005368    indid 0   alloc ff   dealloc0   status 1
 .                 .                  .         .          .          .
 .                 .                  .         .          .          .
 .                 .                  .         .          .          .
 .                 .                  .         .          .          .
EXTID: 632        objid 656005368    indid 0   alloc 3f   dealloc 0 status 1
Total extents 7
```

The sort parameter matches with the EX_SORT bit. This is set to 1 if the extent is being used in a sort or create index. Since this is impossible to forecast, you may have to run the **extentcheck** twice with different sort settings to display all extents for the object.

extentdump
This displays the extent information for a page number.

```
dbcc extentdump(dbid, page#)

dbcc extentdump(12, 434)

DISPLAY EXTENT FOR GIVEN PAGE REQUESTED
logical page 434
        Extent id 432 on allocation 256
        Object id is 336004228
        Index id is 0
```

```
        Allocation bit map: 0x3
        Deallocation bit map: 0x0
        Reference bit is off
```

findnotfullextents

This displays all of the extents that have unused pages.

```
dbcc findnotfullextents(dbid, objid, indid, sort)

dbcc findnotfullextents(12, 1838629573, 0, 0)

Id of extent not full = 12608
Total extents that are not full = 1
```

The sort parameter has the same meaning for extentcheck. You may need to run this twice for each sort bit setting. A large percentage of extents with unused pages indicates a high degree of extent fragmentation, and you should consider defragmenting the table with a clustered index rebuild or a bcp export and import.

listoam

This displays the OAM page information, both heading and detailed used:unused allocation page information.

```
dbcc listoam(dbname|dbid, objid, indid)

dbcc listoam(12, 208003772, 0)

objid: 208003772        indid: 0
OAM pg cnt: 1           Entry cnt: 2
rows: 346               rows per page: 14
used pgs: 24            unused pgs: 0
OAM status bits set: PG_OAMPG, PG_OAMSORT
OAM pg#: 254 has the following entires
            (alloc pg: used/unused)
        256: 16/0
        768: 8/0
```

The above shows the data for table 208003772 with 24 pages in two allocation units and no unused pages in either of the allocation units. Note the interesting rows per page figure; is not available anywhere else except doing it by yourself with a simple division of data_pgs(id, doampg) and rowcnt(doampg) from sysindexes.

```
rebuildextents
```

This rebuilds the extents and OAM pages for an object. Obviously, "emergency use only" for this one; you may be able to get out of some problems by rebuilding the OAM pages when there are errors reported for OAM page and allocation differences.

```
dbcc rebuildextents(dbid, objid, indid)
```

This walks the page chains to determine which pages and extents are used for the object, and then rebuilds the extent structures and OAM pages from the page chain information. The page chain must be intact for this command to succeed. The database must be in single user mode and the command does not work on text/image pages.

```
usedextents
```

This displays used extents for a database or a log device.

```
dbcc usedextents(database_name|dbid, printopt, display[, bypiece])
```

where

dbid	Database id
printopt	0: Both data and log
	1: Log only
	2: Data only
display	0: Display extents
	1: Count extents
bypiece	0: No disk information (default)
	1: Extent information on each disk piece

```
dbcc usedextents(8, 0, 1, 1)

Disk piece 0 (102400 pages), extents used = 337, free = 12463
Disk piece 102400 (25600 pages), extents used = 1, free = 3199
Total used extents = 338
Total free extents = 15662
```

Although not immediately obvious, this example shows one disk fragment for the data and one for the log. In practice, you would need to also run a log-only command to identify the log fragments.

```
dbcc usedextents(8, 1, 1, 1)
```

```
Disk piece 102400 (25600 pages), extents used = 1, free = 3199
Total used extents = 1
Total free extents = 3199
```

Is there any more detailed information on pages and page chains?

Yes. There is a series of unsupported dbcc commands which display further information on data and index pages and associated chains. These are:

- page   Display the contents of a page in a database
- pglinkage   Display the page chain validating its integrity
- prtipage   Display the page number pointed to by each row in an index page
- locateindexpgs   Display all references to a page within an index page

This displays the contents of a page; shows all three portions—header, data, and offset table, if present.

```
dbcc page(dbname|dbid, pageno, printopt, cache, logical, cachename)
```

where

dbid	Database id
pageno	Logical or virtual number
printopt	0: Print page/buffer header only (default)
	1: Print header information, data in row format and page offset table
	2: Print header information, unformatted data and page offset table
	3: Print control page data for a table partition using control-page column from syspartitions
cache	0: Fetch disk version of page
	1: Fetch cache version of page if possible (default)
logical	0: Pageno is virtual page number

cachename	1: Pageno is logical page number (default)
	-1: Search all caches
	null: Choose cache based on page number (default)
	name: Name of cache where page resides

```
dbcc page(12, 473, 2)

PAGE:
page not found in cache-read from disk.
BUFFER:
Buffer header for buffer  0x739dc8
        page=0xa6b800  bdnew=0x0  bdold=0x0  bhash=0x0  bmass_next=0x0
        bmass_prev+ 0x0  bvirtpg=0  bdid=12  bkeep=0
             bmass_stat=0x0800  bbuf_stat=0x0000  bpageno=473
             bxlas_pin=0x00000000 bxls_next=0x00000000

PAGE HEADER:
Page header for page 0xa6b800
pageno=473  nextpg=475  prevpg=0  objid=208003772
timestamp=0001 000009b8
nextrno=8  level=0  indid=0   freeoff=1201  minlen=23
page status bits: 0x10, 0x1
.
.
.
data content
.
.
.
OFFSET TABLE
Row-offset
4 (0x4) - 560 (0x230),    3 (0x3) - 428 (0x1ac)
2 (0x2) - 296 (0x128),    1 (0x1) - 164 (0xa4),
0 (0x0) - 32 (0x20)
```

Most of the "funny stuff," e.g., bdnew: address of next buffer in the chain, bhash: next hash buffer in chain, will always be 0x0; bmass_stat: status bits, will always be 0x800 i.e, BUF_NOTHASHED. Appendix B lists the page header status bits.

This is one of the more useful unsupported dbcc commands—it is explained in the Troubleshooting Guide. It allows you to see everything about the page when you are having problems. Useful information, even when there is no problem is the page linkage. You get information from the next and previous page, the type of page from index id and status in the header, the minimum record length, the free space and so on.

`pglinkage`

This displays the page numbers in a page chain, checking the integrity of the page pointers as it traverses the page chain.

`dbcc pglinkage(dbname|dbid, startpg#, #pages, printopt, targetpg#, asc)`

where

dbid	Database id
startpg#	Logical page number to start following the page chain
#_of_pages	Number of pages to scan before stopping
	0: Stops at end of page chain
printopt	0: Print count of pages only
	1: Print last 16 pages in scan
	2: Print each page number in scan
targetpg#	logical page number at which to stop scan
	0: Searches until end of chain
asc	0: Descending
	1: Ascending

```
dbcc pglinkage(12, 577, 0, 2, 0, 1)

Object ID for pages in this chain: 336004228

Page:  577
.         .
.         .
.        583
.        600
.         .
.         .
Page:  604
End of chain reached
12 pages scanned. Object id:336004228. Last page in scan: 604

Starting slice = 1. End Slice 2.
```

If you have a page chain problem, the simple approach is to start from the beginning, step forward until the problem is encountered, and then to repeat, starting from the end of the chain and stepping backward. In this fashion, you should be able to identify where a page breakage has occurred by studying where both the forward and the backward chains stop. The first page in a chain is given by **sysindexes.first** which points to the first data page for the table or clustered index or the first leaf index page for the nonclustered index. This applies to an unpartitioned table. With a partitioned table, you will get the appropriate pages from **syspartitions.firstpage** and **sysparti-tions.controlpage**. The last page in a chain is pointed to by **sysindexes.root** for a non-clustered data table. The clustered index data does not have a **sysindexes** pointer to the last data page but you have to use **prtipage** to step down from the root page.

Pglinkage understands partitioned tables and will move across partitions.

Be careful, when you do not specify a number of pages to search, since the command will loop if the page chain is circular (as for OAM pages).

```
prtipage
```

This displays the pages pointed to by each row in the specified page. The effect of this is to look down an index.

```
dbcc prtipage(dbid, objid, indid, page#)

dbcc prtipage(12, 208003772, 2, 472)

INDEX Level 0-PAGE #472

Leaf row at offset 32 points to data page 1560, row# 0
Leaf row at offset 43 oints to data page 1564, row# 8
Leaf row at offset 54 points to data page 1560, rows#5
```

The most common use of this is to walk down from the root page to the last page in the clustered index data. This is not pointed to directly but you need to step down from the root node by following the last index entry in each level. This is illustrated in Figure 15.1.

The root node is located from sysindexes.root and two executions of prtipage are required for the two levels in the index.

```
locateindexpgs
```

This displays the references in the next higher index level for the specified page number. The effect of this is to look up levels of an index.

```
dbcc locateindexpgs(dbid, objid, page#, indid, level)
```

```
dbcc locateindexpgs(12, 208003772, 1560, 0, 0)

INFO ON INDEX ROWS POINTING TO GIVEN PAGE:
INDEX ROW ON:
Index page #: 472
At offset: 32
Pointing to data row #: 0
INDEX ROW ON:
Index page #: 472
At offset: 54
Pointing to data row#: 5
```

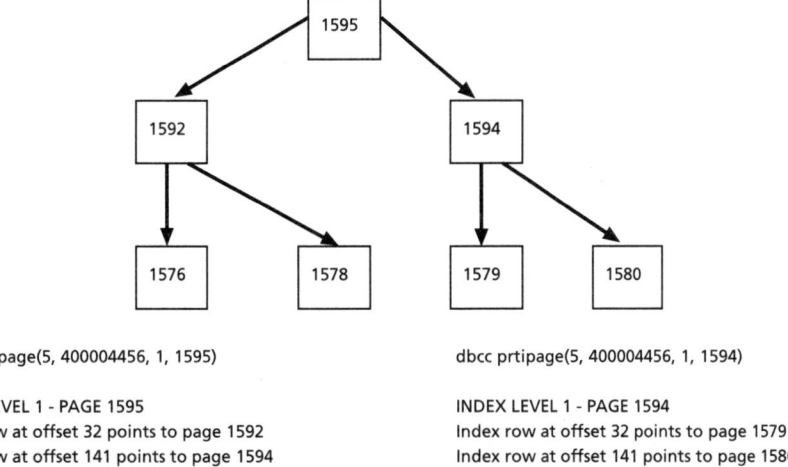

dbcc prtipage(5, 400004456, 1, 1595)   dbcc prtipage(5, 400004456, 1, 1594)

INDEX LEVEL 1 - PAGE 1595   INDEX LEVEL 1 - PAGE 1594
Index row at offset 32 points to page 1592   Index row at offset 32 points to page 1579
Index row at offset 141 points to page 1594   Index row at offset 141 points to page 1580

Figure 15.1 Locating the last data page in a clustered index

This is useful in conjunction with **pglinkage** to locate all index occurrences for a page which is the end of a broken page chain. The end of the broken chain can be found with a forward and backward pglinkage; this page is used to look up index references for the page. If the broken page linkage has to be fixed, you need to know the effect on indexes so that you can rebuild or fix them. This is illustrated in Figure 15.2.

Having located the first and last data page in the chain, **pglinkage** is used to see where the breakage has occurred; **dbcc page** can then be used to analyze both ends of the breakage to determine which page is in error to decide if the orphaned page should be relinked or unlinked. I am only showing you the display options of dbcc. There are a corresponding number of update commands which can be used to fix problems. Such fixing MUST be left to Sybase since they have to take the responsibility for such modifications to the database. However, knowing the exact detail of the problem allows you to tell technical support as much as possible and will assist them in fixing it. Let them know that you have analyzed the problem to this level of detail; it should speed up the resolution of the problem. The **locateindexpgs** command may then be used to see if any other indexes are pointed to by the orphaned page, since you may need to make some fixes to them.

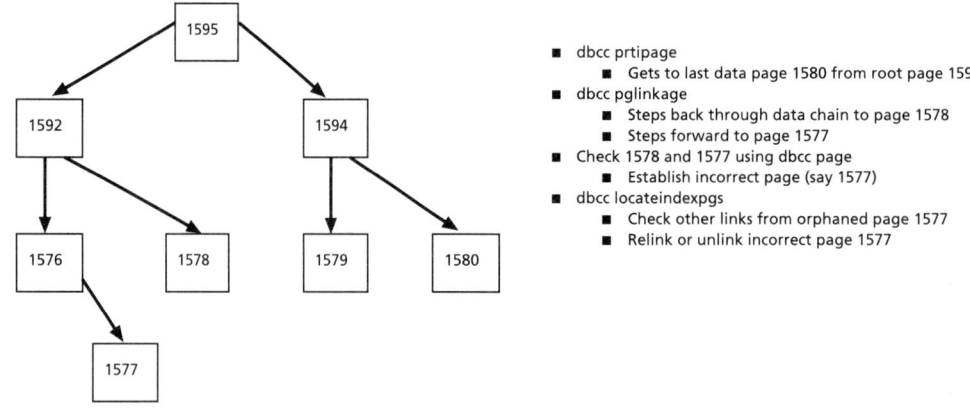

- dbcc prtipage
  - Gets to last data page 1580 from root page 1595
- dbcc pglinkage
  - Steps back through data chain to page 1578
  - Steps forward to page 1577
- Check 1578 and 1577 using dbcc page
  - Establish incorrect page (say 1577)
- dbcc locateindexpgs
  - Check other links from orphaned page 1577
  - Relink or unlink incorrect page 1577

Figure 15.2 Analyzing a broken page chain

A similar approach is taken to wrong object id problems in page chains (605 errors) as illustrated in Figure 15.3.

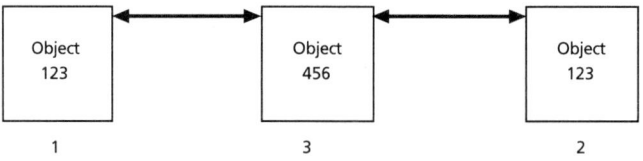

- dbcc pglinkage to check page chain and get to 1
- dbcc locateindexpgs to look up to clustered index page
- dbcc prtipage to look down to get to 2
- dbcc prtipage on 3 to see what other indexes involved

Figure 15.3 Analyzing a 605 error

The page chain is scanned forward using **pglinkage** to get to page 1 where the 605 has occurred. The **locateindexpgs** command is then used look up to the index page in the level immediately above. Then **prtipage** is used to look back down to page 2, i.e., the next valid page for the object in the page chain. **Locateindexpgs** should also be used on the incorrect page at 3 to determine which other indexes are involved.

ERROR HANDLING

How do I correct allocation and page errors?

These normally require a call to Sybase Technical Support. However, there are two options which you should try first; Sybase will always ask about the checkalloc anyway. These are the **dbcc checkalloc (tablealloc, indexalloc)** commands and you may also be able to repair extent problems with **dbcc rebuildextents**.

Your first choice to fix allocation errors is the standard dbcc commands—**dbcc checkalloc, tablealloc, indexalloc**. When run with the **fix** option—default on user tables—it will fix most of the allocation errors on the orphaned objects. You might lose some data here, so it is worthwhile doing a detailed analysis of the problem first and running with **no_fix** initially. Sybase will always ask you if you have run a checkalloc when you report an allocation error, and the output from it may be useful.

If you have an extent problem (or an OAM page problem) you may run **dbcc rebuildextents** which rebuilds the extent structures and OAM pages. This command scans the object page chain; you will need to ensure that the page chain is intact before running this one. It does not work on text/image data.

In the end, you may not be able to do anything about it and will need the assistance of Technical Support. Run the appropriate dbcc commands to determine exactly what the error is, and then place a call with all of the information. If you give them enough information, they might be willing to patch it for you.

So what errors will I get?

You name them—they occur. However, the errors tend to be grouped depending on the type of error and a number of errors can be analyzed and fixed in the same fashion. I have grouped these depending on the type of error and given one example of each. You should refer to the Error Messages and Troubleshooting Guide manuals for detailed descriptions of all server errors. Well, all the ones which Sybase has documented. I have summarized these and the Client Library errors in Appendix A.

Allocation errors

These are displayed by dbcc checkalloc and include such errors as 1108, 1120, 2521, 2525, 2540, 2541, 2543, 2544, and 2546.

Error 2525

This is a mismatch between the object id on the extent structure of the allocation page; the object id in sysindexes and the object id in the data/index page or the index distribution page. If the mismatch is in the index distribution page, this is not stated explicitly in the error message. it may also be caused by mismatched indids.

Figure 15-4 shows an example where the object id in the extent structure does not match the object id in the page or in sysindexes.

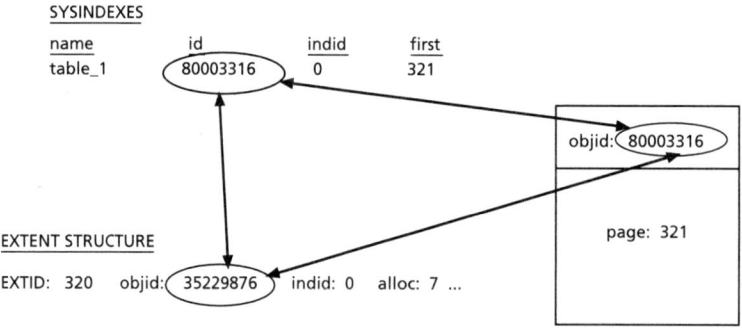

Figure 15.4 *Allocation error 2525 with extent structure object id mismatch*

This is normally reported by **dbcc checkalloc** although it could appear as a runtime 605 if it is sysindexes or when accessing the data page which has the incorrect object id.

Check the three objects using **dbcc allocdump** and **extentdump** for the extent structure; **dbcc page** and **pglinkage** for the page and a **select name, id, indid, first from sysindexes**.

If the page chain is corrupt, a **checkalloc** with the fix option may fix it. If the sysindexes or extent object id is incorrect, it you may be able to recover the data by copying it to another table. This is principally an extent allocation problem and you should be able to select the data since the extent is not used for a select. Use **select into** or **bcp** to take a copy of the data, then drop the original table.

Be careful here; if the mismatching object id is still an active table in the database, do not try to drop the object. The extent structure may be deallocated which will cause 1108 errors in the other object. In Figure 15.4, if we dropped object 80003316, the extent 320 might be deallocated, which would give errors for object 35229876. However, if the table 35229876 no longer exists (**select object_name(id)** does not return an object name) then there is no other table to worry about. You could drop the table, recreate it and reload the data from the previous copy. Or, you could simply recreate a clustered index on the table; this will deallocate existing extents and allocate new ones. If you cannot drop the table because the extent is used by an existing object, you need to call Sybase. If they cannot patch the problem, you will need to go back to a clean dump and roll forward.

If the 2525 error occurs but there is no object id mismatch on the error message, this means that the page pointer to the index distribution page is corrupt or the index id on the allocation page does not match the index id on the object page. If the index exists on sysindexes—**select ... from sysindexes where id = object_id and distribution = page_no**—then simply drop and recreate the index. If the index is no longer on sysindexes, you need to call Sybase.

If you have taken any corrective action, make sure that the problem has gone by rerunning **dbcc checkalloc** or **tablealloc**.

OAM errors

These are displayed by **dbcc checkalloc** but may also occur at run time and include such errors as 1129, 1133, 1142, 1143, 7939, 7940, and 7949.

There are three types of OAM error:

- **Sysindexes.doampg** or **sysindexes.ioampg** point to a page that is not an OAM page

- Sysindexes.doampg or sysindexes.ioampg point to a page that is an OAM page but the status bits on the page are not set properly

- The OAM entries are incorrect

Error 1142

This occurs when the pointer in sysindexes does not point to an OAM page.

The column **sysindexes.doampg** points to the data OAM page and the column **sysindexes.ioampg** points to the index OAM page. If this is not the OAM page or if the status bits in the header do not indicate that it is an OAM page (0x8000), an 1142 will occur. This error can occur by poor SQL which tries to use the **data_pgs, reserved_pgs, rowcnt** or **used_pgs** functions which access the OAM page. If these are used in a cross database command, an 1142 or 1133 error will occur. Obviously, an SQL occurrence is not serious and can be ignored since it has not corrupted the pages.

Use **dbcc page** to determine whether the error is on an index or a table. If on a nonclustered index, a simple rebuild of the index should remove the error. Sybase advises a rebuild of all nonclustered indexes on the table if an OAM error occurs. Non-fatal 7939 errors may be fixed with **dbcc rebuildextents**. If the error is on the data, run **dbcc tablealloc** with the fix option. If neither of these solves the problem, call Sybase.

Page errors

These are displayed by **dbcc checkdb** but may also occur at run time and include such errors as page header and pointer errors 605, 2502, 2503, 2509, 2513, 2514, 2529, 2596, and 7902 and data and offset table errors 614, 623, 624, 625, 631, 2506, 2507, 2524, 2544, and 2620.

Error 2503

This occurs when there is an inconsistency in the page pointers in the forward and backward chains in the page header.

This type of chain linkage problem frequently gives various errors such 605 at run time and 2525 via **dbcc checkalloc**, especially if the pointer corruption points to another object. The general problem is illustrated in Figure 15.5.

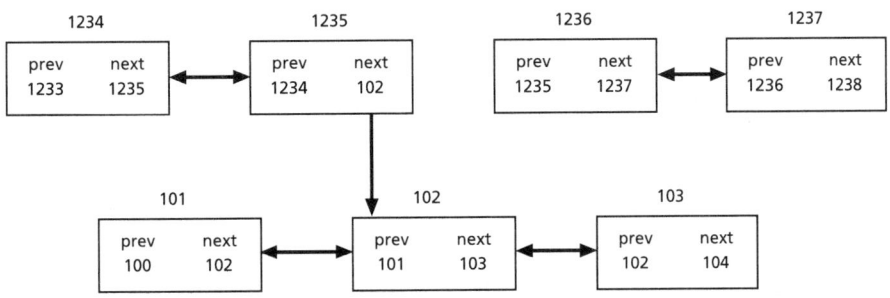

Figure 15.5 Page linkage error

Resolution of this is similar to all linkage problems using **dbcc page** on the pages which have incorrect pointers (1235, 102 and 1236 in figure 5); use **dbcc prti-page** and **pglinkage** to walk the forward and backward pointer chains to determine exactly what the problem is, and **dbcc locateindexpgs** from the problem pages (1235 and 102) to determine the extent of the problem in related indexes. In general, if the mispointing page belongs to an index, you will be able to rebuild the index. If the page is a data page and you have no other errors you may be able to read the data using **select into** or **bcp** and create a new table. Assuming in Figure 15.5 that 1234 - 1235 - 1236 - 1237 is the complete and correct page linkage, you will need to update the sysindexes pages and run two bcps. In the first case, set sysindexes.root to 1235 and run a bcp to export all data in pages 1234 and 1235. Then reset sysindexes.first to 1236 and sysindexes.root to 1237 and run a second bcp to export all data in pages 1236 and 1237.

In other circumstances, or if these do not fix the error, it's a call to Sybase and back to a clean dump.

Error 2509

This occurs when a row does not have a matching offset entry in the row offset table at the foot of the page.

You will need to call Sybase for this type of error. However, you may be able to see exactly what the problem is with a **dbcc page** and ask Sybase to patch the page. If you can recognize the data on the page in error, patching the page out of the page chain may be the simplest solution. But again, the only solution may be to go back to the clean dump.

This type of data row:offset table mismatch is often caused by some other error and will recur until you find out what is causing it. Client connections crashing and not cleaning up properly are a common source of this type of error. You need to be careful with how much freedom the client connections have to cancel out of an application as they may not be handling the clean-up properly. Ctrl-alt-del can cause havoc here—try to avoid it.

Index errors

These are displayed by **dbcc checkdb** but may also occur at run time and include such errors as 623, 624, 625, 629, 644, 2510, 2511, and 2610.

In general, these are pointer mismatches between the data and the index and the most obvious solution is to assume that the data is correct and rebuild the index. Of course you will always check this first with the dbcc commands **page, prtipage, locateind-expgs**, and **pglinkage**.

Error 624

This occurs when the row_id in the index has a higher offset table entry than the highest offset table in the page. This is illustrated in Figure 15.6.

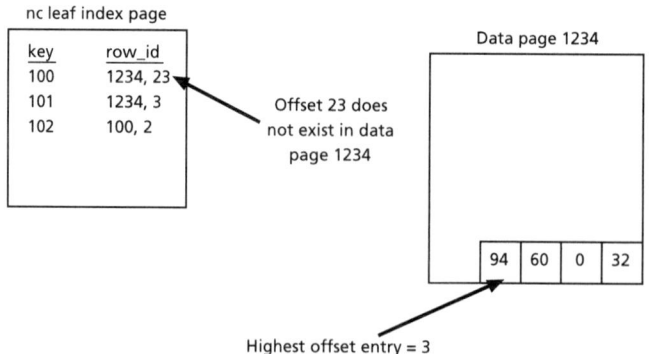

***Figure 15.6** Mismatching row_id and data page offset table*

The error message for this one only supplies the data page number, so you need to find out which index is causing the problem. Try **dbcc locateindexpgs**, but this may not find the incorrect index row_id. If you know which query caused the problem you can use the query showplan to see which index is being used and then you can rebuild the index. If you do not know the index, you will need to rebuild all indexes.

Summary

Errors will always happen and those which cause storage and page linkage problems are often very serious. You must run regular checkdb, checkalloc, and checkcatalog on your production databases to ensure that there are no potentially disastrous problems waiting for you. Fixing this type of error without any data loss normally requires a reload of a clean database dump and a recovery from the transaction logs: make sure that you have a clean dump of the database by regularly checking the database with these dbcc commands. You will also find it useful to know how to run and what the output means for page, pglinkage, locateindexpgs, and prtipage.

16

Space Problems

This chapter investigates database space problems, discussing diagnostic methods for specific problems and their associated solutions.

Threshold fires

Problem

A threshold firing is an indication that space is becoming short in one of the databases or logs. The action taken depends on whether a data or log device is running short of free space.

Data device

Diagnosis

A free space threshold procedure will execute when free space on a segment falls below a defined value. You need to create the threshold procedure yourself, so what happens when the threshold fires is entirely up to you. Least you will be warned that you are in danger of running out of space in the data segment. You can investigate the problem with **sp_spaceused** and **sp_estspace**.

sp_spaceused may indicate space fragmentation problems with the data. Indexes fragment very rarely since their records are smaller and their pages are empty less frequently. Fragmentation occurs when unused space becomes a significant percentage of the data. Data pages which have become empty by deletion are not returned immediately to free space but remain allocated as part of an 8 page extent until the full extent becomes empty. Tables with a high update/delete activity may be prone to this. Run sp_spaceused on each table to see how big they are. As an alternative to multiple sp_spaceused executions, you could look directly at the number of pages and rows from sysindexes; and select object_name(id), data_pgs(id, doampg), rowcnt(doampg) from sysindexes where indid in (0, 1). Then run sp_estspace with the number of rows from sp_spaceused to see how big they should be. Serious fragmentation should be removed by rebuilding clustered indexes.

Full page fragmentation is not the only problem, since SQL Server can exhibit a high degree of empty space in used pages. This is caused by a non-reuse of pages in heap tables and even in clustered indexed tables where the growth is not spread throughout the table. This is often a significant problem, since it increases the size of the table for a limited increase in the number of rows. A comparison of the sp_spaceused used space and the sp_estspace number of data pages will indicate a problem. This type of fragmentation should always be removed.

Solution

Growth is the obvious problem here; the simplest, and usually the only solution is to allocate more space to the data. If you find serious data fragmentation, a clustered index rebuild or a bcp out and in will reclaim the fragmented space. Reclaiming fragmented space will also give a reasonable performance improvement, since there are less pages to access for the same number of records. Be careful here. You are already short of space and a clustered index rebuild requires free space to rebuild the index. Although you are reclaiming space, it may be advantageous to allocate more space with alter database before you start. If you cannot allocate more space, rebuild the smaller indexes first. Rebuild with the sorted_data clause since it is faster.

The system may have archiving routines to remove out-of-date information. The frequency of these should be checked and possibly altered to free space more regularly. This is often a good time to have a regular clustered index rebuild or unload/reload, since the archive may delete large numbers of records, causing some fragmentation. At least you should run update statistics after bulk deletion, since the distribution of data will have changed.

If neither of these show any promise, you will have to increase the data space with an alter database.

Log device

Diagnosis

There are two situations here: a free space warning threshold or a last chance threshold. Every production system should have two thresholds on the log: the last chance threshold is set automatically and the warning threshold which you set to avoid the last chance threshold firing. When the last chance threshold fires, all current transactions are suspended and no new transactions can start. This is not a situation you wish to be in, so a warning threshold is advised or aborted if you have set the database option **abort tran on log full**.

Both thresholds should simply dump the transaction log to free space. The major problem here is when a long-running transaction has been open for some time; the dump tran only clears the log prior to the oldest open transaction. There is a danger that the used space in the log will continue to grow for as long as the long-running transaction is open, since the dump tran cannot clear any space from the log after the start of this transaction. **sp_helpsegment** can be used to see if the dump tran has cleared the log. If not, you can confirm the open transaction using:

```
select xactid from syslogs where xactid not in
     (select xactid from syslogs where op = 30)
```

which indicates all transaction ids that do not have a commit or rollback tran record. A large number of records for the same xactid will indicate that the cause is a long-running open transaction.

You can be a bit more precise with the use of a dbcc log:

Show the oldest active transactions (page# and row#) by displaying the latest checkpoint record

```
dbcc log(dbid, 0, 0, 0, -1, 17, 0)
```

Display the first and root page for syslogs; if this is the same as dbcc log then you cannot truncate the log

```
select first, root from sysindexes where id = 8
```

Find the end transaction (op=30); if none, have open active transaction

```
dbcc log(dbid, 1, active_xact_page#, active_xact_row#, 0, 30, 0)
```

Show the corresponding begin transaction; displays spid, suid, uid

```
dbcc log(dbid, 1, active_xact_page#, active_xact_row#, 0, 0, 0)
```

Of course, in System 11 you can take the easy way and display the syslogshold table which holds information on the oldest open transaction.

```
select * from syslogshold
```

<u>dbid</u>	<u>res'd</u>	<u>spid</u>	<u>page</u>	<u>xactid</u>	<u>masterxactid</u>	<u>starttime</u>	<u>name</u>
15	0	10	1113	0x00000459000d	0x000000000000	Dec 3 1996 9:19AM	$user_transaction

Solution

A threshold firing on the log may not be a problem situation; you have planned for it to happen so you can dump the transaction log which will normally clear the log. However, there are two monitoring aspects to be careful of. The first is based on the placement of the warning threshold. If the warning threshold is too close to the last chance threshold, the dump tran run by the warning threshold will not complete before the last chance threshold fires. This is not a good idea; the last chance threshold will suspend this dump tran and try to start another one with interesting recovery possibilities. If the warning threshold is too far away from the last chance threshold, it will fire too often and be an unnecessary overhead on the system. Regular monitoring of the free space on the log while the warning dump tran is running will indicate if there is a problem with the warning threshold placement.

Of course, simple maintenance activity growth will also cause the warning threshold to fire frequently and in this case the log will have to be increased. Note that the last chance threshold is automatically reset when you alter the log size, but you will have to recalculate the position of the warning threshold.

If the dump tran does not clear the log, you will have to identify the open transaction and determine what action to take. Having identified the process, you will need to force it to complete or roll it back before the last chance threshold fires. All processes will be suspended when this happens, and you will get into a loop of last chance threshold activations since the dump tran does not clear the log. Other possibilities are to alter the database settings with sp_dboption to abort the transactions when the last chance threshold fires, or to allow processing to continue using lct_admin which will either allow the long running transaction to complete or will cause the log to fill up.

Log full

This should not happen in System 11 as the last chance threshold on the log should prevent it. Only logs defined separately with the log on clause in create database have their own logsegment and have a last chance threshold, so make sure that all production systems are so defined. However, there are still circumstances when you may need to allow log full to occur. For the long-running transaction described above, when you cannot clear the log with a dump tran, you may disable the last chance threshold temporarily to allow the transaction to continue. In this case, the log may fill up which will cause the transaction to abort. Allowing log full to occur is not really a good idea and the last chance threshold should be used to prevent the log from filling up.

Solution

First priority is to get the database usable again by issuing:

```
dump tran db_name with no_log
```

This simply clears out the log, allowing the database to be used again. Unfortunately, the with no_log option does not write a dump tran message to the log. It cannot, since the log is full. This means that the transaction log dumps are now incomplete and the database cannot be rolled forward from them if there is a serious media failure which requires a roll forward from the last database dump. Therefore, it is mandatory to dump the database after a dump tran ... with no_log. You have no practical option here. If you use transaction log dumps for roll forward recovery, you must dump the database immediately after a dump tran ... with no_log.

Then you need to investigate why the log filled up. As an immediate fix, you can give the log more space with an alter database if you have the free disk space, but still try to determine why the problem arose. With the last chance threshold operating, it will normally be a conscious action on your part to allow a long-running transaction to complete. Try to reduce the size of this transaction to ensure that you do not get into a log-full situation again. But in the end, you may have to allocate more space.

Data full

Again, a free space threshold should warn you in time. If not, you should quickly investigate the possibility of running archive routines, and then possibly allocating more space.

Solution

More frequent archiving is often the optimum solution for a full data device, but you should also check for and reclaim fragmented space as described above in the data device section. However, simple growth can be catered for only by allocating more space with alter database. If you do allocate more space, remember to reposition the free space threshold. The log last chance threshold is repositioned automatically, but you need to redefine all other thresholds yourself.

tempdb full

Diagnosis

Don't panic on this one if it is a data full problem. Although it does not sound right, often the best action is no action. Often the reason for tempdb filling is a combination of circumstances which will not recur and the effort in determining what this combination is and how it occurred is not justified.

However, two occurrences in quick succession, or one occurrence at the wrong time, and you'll have to do something.

Check sysobjects to see how many temporary tables are current and how long they have been in existence from the creation date; this may indicate that they are not being dropped as often as they should. Temporary tables in procedures are not a problem, since they are automatically dropped when the procedure completes, but others remain until the session finishes or until explicitly dropped. A large number of temporary tables which have been in existence for some time, should be investigated to see if they are not being dropped immediately after use.

While checking sysobjects, note any user tables which do not begin with #, i.e., are "permanent" tables. These need to be explicitly deleted by the application as they are not dropped automatically when the session ends. If you are having a regular problem with tempdb, space the need for such tables in tempdb should be questioned at an application level. Remember, nothing is really permanent in tempdb, since it is rebuilt from model when the server starts.

Solution

If there are no obvious delays in deleting tables in tempdb, you will have to increase tempdb using alter database.

Tempdb size is often a trial and error situation by choosing a size and seeing if it gives any problems. The most obvious problem that you will see is tempdb running out of space which generates error messages for the specific connection.

The simplest approach may be to allocate a standard amount to tempdb, say 20%, and see how efficient it is. You could then adjust up or down depending on actual usage.

If you think that that is too naive or you cannot afford to get unnecessary production errors, you can get more detailed by analyzing the transaction SQL and sizing tempdb based on its usage. The processes for which you will need to allocate tempdb space are:

- Internal sorts; order by without an index

- Internal worktables: aggregates, group by, distincts, reformatting joins, OR clauses. You also need to determine the number of steps in strategies using worktables since this determines the number of temporary tables created.

- Temporary tables and any indexes on them

The worktable sizes can be determined by running the SQL with set statistics io on and seeing how many writes are made to the worktable. The same approach is also valid for the temporary tables, although you could try sp_spaceused while the table exists, if you can get to it before it is dropped.

Having determined the tempdb table sizes, you can sum these for the maximum number of concurrent connections which execute the SQL. Then add 25% to cover "undocumented" uses of tempdb and averages in the above sizes.

```
# connects * (((sort + worktable) * plan steps) + (temp table +index)) * 1.25
```

More accurately, you should use the appropriate number of connections per type of tempdb table instead of an overall number.

Summary

There are several database space problem events which require corrective action:

Table 16.1

Event	Action
Data threshold fires	Allocate more space
	Archive old data
	Reclaim fragmented space
Log threshold fires	Dump tran ...
	Allocate more space
Log full	Dump tran...with no_log
	Dump database...
	Reduce size of any long-running transactions
	Allocate more space
Tempdb full	Drop temporary tables sooner
	Reduce use of temporary/work tables
	Allocate more space

17

Response Time Problems

This chapter investigates response time problems, looking at diagnostic methods for specific problems and discussing the associated solutions. The chapter also provides a step-by-step approach to analyzing the SQL optimization plan to effect a "drill-down" method which will identify the most common problems first.

Process appears to "hang"

Problem

One user process gets no response but everyone else is working normally.

Diagnosis

In this case, the most common reason is that the process is being blocked by another process because of lock contention. This is easy enough to diagnose and to remedy, but not so simple to prevent a recurrence.

Issue an sp_who which will show if blocking is the reason with the blocking spid in the blk column.

```
sp_who
go
spid    status       loginame     blk   cmd
5       lock sleep   fred         6     SELECT
6       recv sleep   jill         0     AWAITING COMMAND
7       running      sa           0     SELECT
```

Issue an sp_lock to see who is doing the blocking and what object and page the lock is on.

```
sp_lock
go
spid    class          table id              page
6       Ex_page-blk    1838629593            2736
5       Sh_intent      1838629593               0
(there is more to these outputs but this shows the important information)
```

If necessary a dbcc page will show if it is a table page or an index page from the object_id and indid in the header information displayed by the dbcc page. If indid is greater than 1 and less than 250, the page belongs to an index of the object. The upper range is required to exclude text objects which have indid 255.

```
dbcc traceon(3604)
go
dbcc page(database_id, page_id)
go
. . . . .
. . . . .
dbcc traceoff(3604)
go
```

Solution

Contact the offending user to ask them to commit their transaction. If this cannot be achieved, you will need to kill the blocking process. Before you kill the blocking process it is always worthwhile to check the errorlog. It is unlikely to show anything out of the ordinary but always worth a look when an unresolved problem arises.

As simple as this diagnosis and solution is, the main work is in determining why the block occurred. It is unusual for these to be one-offs and thus recurrence is almost guaranteed, which makes the effort in finding out the cause well worth it. This is usually a client deadlock which the server cannot resolve because the server does not see any deadlock. This is detailed in Chapter 11. If a client deadlock is the problem, altering the application routine to process all results serially or using multiple connections should solve this problem.

If it does not, a change to the application design is necessary to prevent more than one connection from accessing the same resource at the same time. This may be done with a "softlock" or by segmenting the resource to allow parallel processing. The "softlock" can cause a significant degradation to the response time, since it forces serial access to the common resource. The segmentation approach can increase the problems of data concurrency. The decision will depend on the application but the segmentation approach may be introduced early in the design and can provide significant throughput improvements as a side effect.

Server appears to "hang"

Problem

In this case, no one is getting any response and you cannot login, but the server is still running.

Diagnosis

There is usually not much that you can do here except to stop the server from the operating system and restart. However, before you do so you should check the error log to see if there are any errors which indicate the reason for the problem. Usually there will be and a call should be made to Sybase.

A check should be made of the system activity. If the server is being swapped out, all processes using the server will be stopped. No process can run when part of the server has been swapped out. If this is the case, you will need to find more memory for the server or not run any other work on the same machine as the server. As a temporary measure the server may be configured in less memory to prevent it swapping out at the expense of more physical data I/O and less space for procedures.

Check if a last chance threshold has fired; all processes in that database may have been suspended until the transaction log has been dumped. These will be awakened when the dump is finished. You need to investigate how the last chance threshold fired when you have warning thresholds on the log. An **sp_who** will show processes with a status of LOG SUSPEND if the last chance threshold has fired.

Solution

If there is nothing obvious in the error log, you will need to stop the server from the operating system.

Slow transaction response time

Try to login to the server and execute a system procedure such as sp_who. If this takes much longer than usual, you have a server resource problem with all users getting a slow response time. If you get a normal response, you have an individual user getting a slow response time.

All processes go slowly

Diagnosis

Check the operating system first to see if another application process or the system is taking most of the CPU. If they are, the server is simply being starved of CPU and you need to dedicate the CPU to the server. If the operating system is the highest user of CPU, you probably have a swapping problem and you need to get the operating system experts involved. In the case of the system doing too much work, you should look at how much memory the server is taking. Server memory too close to the available machine memory may cause a lot of swapping. It is better in this case to reduce the server memory to reduce the server swapping. I do not have any easy figures here; trial and error is the normal approach, starting with a low(ish) server memory and gradually increasing until you locate the optimum position of most memory to the server without an increase in system swapping. The bottom line is that you should be dedicating your machine to the server but you should always leave a reasonable amount of memory for the operating system and any other processes which must run on the same machine. In practice I would leave about 20%–30% of available memory to the operating system and application processes as a first configuration.

Solution

You need to find out what is causing the problem here. Run your operating system monitoring tools to see which resource is most used and then run sp_sysmon to see how the server is working. If it is an operating system problem, you probably have to spend some money: more memory, faster CPU, additional CPUs.

However, even if some operating system figures are high, you still need to investigate the server to see if a server problem is causing the operating system bottleneck. The approach here is to get maximum benefit for the least effort, so you need to look at the figures in order of "most effect" so that you do not waste time. As important as ULC flushes information is, it is more realistic to take a look at CPU utilization and logical I/O first. If these are wrong, you are not going to get much improvement from adjusting the more detailed figures until you have fixed the "macro" problem.

One or more transactions go slowly

The approach to individual transactions depends on whether the transaction is a procedure or standalone SQL.

Procedure

Diagnosis

This is caused most commonly by a parameterized procedure executing with an unsuitable optimization plan or the procedure needing to be recompiled to pick up new index statistics.

Solution

Execute the procedure with recompile

```
exec proc_name with recompile
```

and if it reverts to the normal timings, you need to determine why.

A check of the SQL in the procedure will indicate if it could be using an unsuitable execution plan. You are looking for parameterized, range-based inquiries on non-clustered indexes. If this does not look likely, then the new execution must be using new index statistics or even a new index. Check when the index statistics are updated for the database indexes and insure that sp_recompile commands are run after the update statistics. New statistics are not picked up automatically; you must run sp_recompile after updating statistics on a table.

If the recompile does not work, you have an SQL problem within the procedure and you will have to investigate each SQL command as described below.

T-SQL statement

Diagnosis

The most common cause of this is that the index distribution has changed because of a large number of inserts and/or deletes but the statistics have not been updated. In this case, the command may still be doing an index access but is retrieving many more records than it used to and a table scan would be preferable. There is no way to check this, since the statistics are not dated; you need to try the solution to see if you have the problem.

Solution

Run update statistics on the tables in the command and rerun the command. If this does not help, a detailed review of the optimization plan is necessary.

Steps in reviewing an optimization plan

The approach of this section is to summarize the steps in reviewing an optimization plan from the most obvious reasons for poor performance to the more detailed ones. This provides a gradual "drill down" from simple to complicated on the basis that the simple diagnosis will find the problem most of the time and the more complicated diagnosis will be reserved for a few that are difficult to resolve. The detailed explanation of each cause is described in the index troubleshooting Chapter 17. In all of this discussion I say "may use the index." The only guarantee you have is that an index will not be used in specific circumstances. At other times it may be used, but the optimizer may decide not to for other reasons.

In general, the optimizer will not be using a plan that you expect it to when you have poor performance. What are the main reasons?

Index cannot be used

Check that one of the where clauses is on the first column of the index: if not, the index cannot be used.

```
index (a, b, c)     where b = 10          Will not use the index
                                          because 'a' is not
                                          present in a where clause
                    where a > 5 and b = 10  May use the index because 'a'
                                          is present in a where clause
```

This also occurs when you do not provide the first part of the index column in a wildcard:

```
select * from customer where name like "%ood"
```

This cannot use an index on name. There is no simple solution. If absolutely necessary to avoid a table scan, you will have to create a denormalized column on input which is the reverse of the query column, and then ask the query as:

```
select * from customer where rev_name like "doo%"
```

It's probably better to suffer the table scan or try covering the query when an index scan will be carried out.

Solution

Add a where clause for the first column of the index; or,

Create a new index for the current where clauses; or,

Alter the column positions in the existing index.

Not a search argument

Make sure that the where clause is a search argument or else the index cannot be used.

Solution

Rewrite the where clause to be a search argument; or,
Create a covered index for the query
The search argument format is:

```
column operator expression
```

Any operations on the columns such as arithmetic or functions means that the optimizer will not consider the index. Try to always write search arguments:

Table 17.1

NOT Search Argument	Equivalent Search Argument
150 = price * 12	150 /12 = price
upper(name) = 'KIRKWOOD'	No equivalent: be careful with upper and lower case. If possible, you can improve performance by converting on input.
qty + 10 > 200	qty > 200-10
firstname + ' ' + lastname = 'john kirkwood'	firstname = 'john' and lastname = 'kirkwood'
ltrim(name) = 'kirkwood'	No equivalent: be careful with leading spaces. Always worth removing any possible leading spaces on input.

An index which covers the query will allow the optimizer to consider the index even though the where clause is not a search argument. In this case, the complete index may have to be scanned, but this will still be faster than a table scan.

Consider:

```
select * from customer where substring(name, 1, 3) = 'kir'
```

This will table scan because the substring function is not a search argument. However:

```
select name from customer where substring(name, 1, 3) = 'kir'
```

will use the nonclustered index on name as the index covers the query.

(I know it is not good SQL and you should use the like operator to create a search argument; it is only an example of covering using the index.)

Statistics are not being used

Even if the index is considered by the optimizer, the index statistics may not be used. The reasons for this are mismatching datatypes or unknown values in the where clause

Mismatching datatypes

The statistics of each index are accessed on a look-up basis with no datatype conversion, so make sure that the column the statistics are collected on and the value being checked against are the same datatype. And be careful of columns which allow null, since SQL Server treats datatypes which allow null as variable—except for int. So char(6) not null and char(6) null are different datatypes—the latter is varchar(6)—and a conversion is necessary. The exception to this is local variables which are initialized to null but still access the statistics when compared with a not null column. Be especially careful with the numeric datatype when a mismatch on scale will require conversion.

When the statistics cannot be used, the optimizer uses the search argument density in the distribution page.

Solution

Ensure that the columns and variables being compared in the where clause are the same datatypes and have the same null status. Use of user defined datatypes can help here.

Unknown values in the where clause

If you do not supply a specific value in the where clause, the optimizer may not be able to determine the value at optimization time and will revert to the search argument density. This occurs quite simply if you do arithmetic in the command:

```
select * from employee
      where salary > 4000 * 12
```

but is more of a problem when you derive the value from a separate statement such as a variable assignment or a nested select.

```
declare @var_1 int
select @var_1=50
select * from tab_1 where pkey = @var_1
OR
select * from tab_1 where price = (select max(price) from tab_1)
```

The problem is based on the SQL batch being parsed and optimized before it is compiled and executed. This means that when the where clause is optimized the value has not been assigned to the variable as none of the SQL has been executed. Therefore, the optimizer does not have a value to use to access the index statistics and so the search argument density has to be used.

Solution

In these situations, rewrite the SQL with the arithmetic carried out, or run the command in a procedure with the value being supplied as a parameter. The procedure is optimized and compiled when it is executed at which point the value of the supplied parameter is known.

```
create proc jk_1 (@param_1 int) as
select * from tab_1 where pkey = @param_1
go

declare @var_1 int
select @var_1 = 50
exec jk_1 @param_1 = @var_1
```

This is also discussed in the high performance SQL Chapter 20.

Unknown table sizes

This is similar to the unknown values when the creation, population, and use of a table (usually a temporary table but it may be any table) in the same batch will not permit the optimizer to use the actual sizes as it does not know them at optimization time. Therefore, the optimizer uses default values of 10 pages and 100 records. These will often give poor performance when the actual values are much larger.

Solution

Create the table outside a procedure which uses it.

```
select * into #big_tab from tab_1
go

create proc jk_2 as
select * from tab_3, #big_tab .....
go

exec jk_2
go
```

This is discussed in detail in the High Performance SQL, Chapter 20.

Statistics are not available

In this situation, the statistics for the index have not been created. This is caused by creating the index without any data in the table. You can determine this by looking at the sysindexes.distribution column. This contains the page number containing the index statistics. If this is 0, there are no statistics.

```
select object_name(id), indid, distribution
       from sysindexes
```

If there are no index statistics, the optimizer uses the default "magic" percentages:

```
equality             10%
closed interval      25%
open interval        33%
```

Solution

Run update statistics on the table and retry the SQL. You should find a difference.

Optimizer trace flags

There are three useful optimizer traceflags which will help you in determining why a query is being optimized in a particular way. These are:

302: provides information on individual index selection

310: provides information on table sequencing in join statements

311: provides information on the estimated number of I/Os for a chosen plan

The outputs of the 302 and 310 have already been explained in the index troubleshooting section. The following is a summary of this from an actual output.

Trace flag 302 output

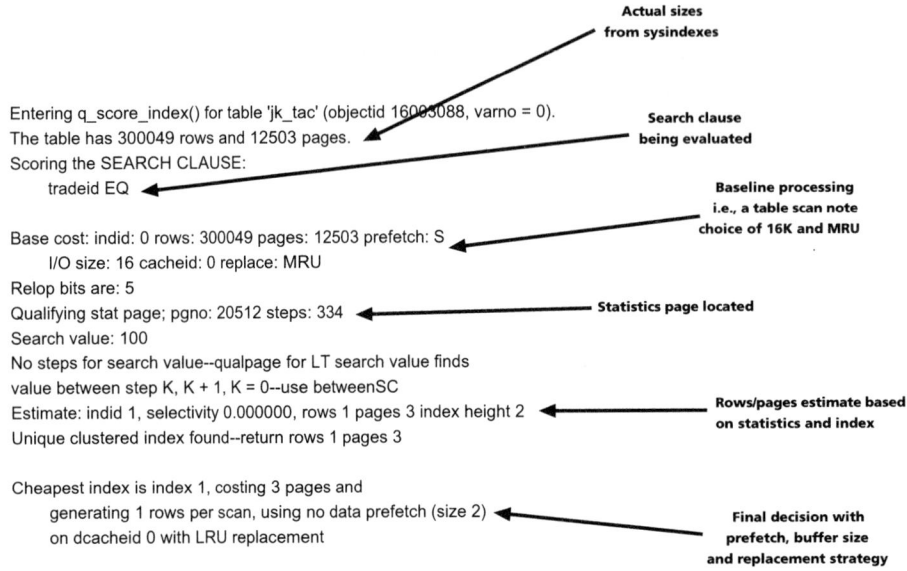

For each where clause, the 302 output compares useful indexes against the baseline table scan plan. The specific index information indicates the statistics page, how the statistics are being used (this will indicate if the "magic" percentages are being used) and the row/page estimates for the index. After each useful index for the where clause has been evaluated, the final "cheapest index" choice is displayed.

This trace flag output is invaluable when you cannot work out why a particular index is not being used. It may not solve the problem for you but at least you will know why the optimizer is not choosing the index.

The trace flag is invoked using dbcc (as are the 310 and 311 trace flags):

```
dbcc traceon(3604, 302)
go
set showplan on
go
set noexec on
go
select ......
go
```

Trace flag 310 output

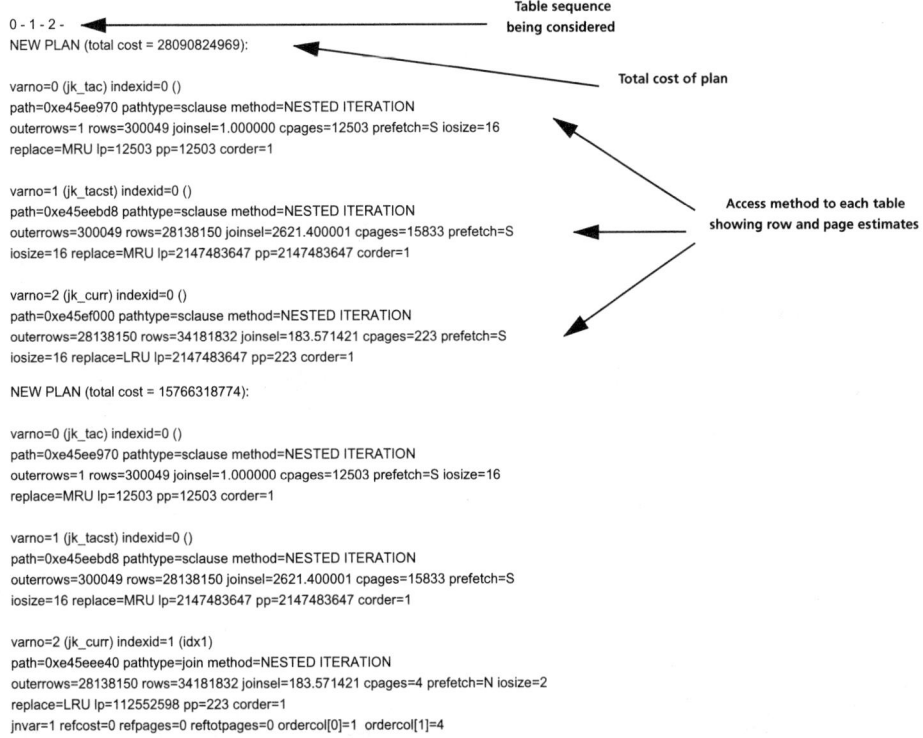

For each table sequence, the optimizer considers the possible join paths and calculates the cost of the path. The above shows two considerations for the table sequence 0-1-2; all three tables table-scanning and tables 0 and 1 table-scanning with table 2 (jk_curr) using the clustered index.

All of the possible considerations are displayed then the chosen (least cost) plan is shown.

TOTAL # PERMUTATIONS: 6

TOTAL # PLANS CONSIDERED: 22

CACHE USED BY THIS PLAN:

    CacheID = 0:   (2K) 223   (4K) 0 (8K) 0 (16K) 8704

FINAL PLAN (total cost = 3557009):

varno=1 (jk_tacst) indexid=0 ()
path=0xe45eebd8 pathtype=sclause method=NESTED ITERATION
outerrows=1 rows=245831 joinsel=1.000000 cpages=15833 prefetch=S iosize=16
replace=LRU lp=15833 pp=15833 corder=1

varno=0 (jk_tac) indexid=1 (idx1)
path=0xe45ef268 pathtype=join method=NESTED ITERATION
outerrows=245831 rows=245831 joinsel=300049.000000 cpages=3 prefetch=S iosize=16
replace=MRU lp=737493 pp=12503 corder=1
jnvar=1 refcost=0 refpages=0 reftotpages=0 ordercol[0]=1 ordercol[1]=1

varno=2 (jk_curr) indexid=1 (idx1)
path=0xe45eee40 pathtype=join method=NESTED ITERATION
outerrows=245831 rows=298632 joinsel=183.571421 cpages=4 prefetch=N iosize=2
replace=LRU lp=983324 pp=223 corder=1
jnvar=1 refcost=0 refpages=0 reftotpages=0 ordercol[0]=1 ordercol[1]=4

This shows the cache usage for the plan—in this case both 2 Kb and 16 Kb buffers will be used. The final execution plan is table 1 joining with table 0 on clustered index and table 1 joining with table 2 on clustered index. This is not obvious from the simple sequence of 1-0-2 and you need to know the actual SQL which is being optimized. There is no actual join in the sequence 1-0-2 but table 2 is a link table in a M:M relationship, and the join is actually two joins 1-0 and 1-2. This is identified from the 310 plan because the outerrows is the same for table 0 and table 2, and is the number of rows from table 1.

Trace flag 311 output

This trace displays a **set statistics io** style output before the showplan indicating the estimated number of I/Os to execute the chosen plan.

```
Table: jk_tacst scan count 1, logical reads: 19370, physical reads: 19370
Table: jk_tac scan count 300000, logical reads: 900000, physical reads:
12503
Table: jk_curr scan count 300000, logical reads: 1200000, physical reads: 223

QUERY PLAN FOR STATEMENT 1 (at line 1).

    STEP 1
      The type of query is SELECT.

      FROM TABLE
         jk_tacst
      Nested iteration.
      Table Scan.
      Ascending scan.
      Positioning at start of table.
      Using I/O Size 16 Kbytes.
      With LRU Buffer Replacement Strategy.

    .
    .
    .
    .
```

Although this output is extremely useful (and would be worth including in the standard showplan output, in my opinion), you have to treat it with care. It is the optimizer estimates of disk I/O based on the statistics for the index and will seldom be 100% accurate. If you have a choice between two similar optimizer plans, do not rely on these figures but always run the SQL in production with **set statistics io on** to see the actual disk activity. If you have a—quite justifiable—horror at running SQL in production simply to check the optimizer plan, especially if you are checking an update, then you will have to get the production data into your development system to check the execution times. I know that it is not easy, but when you have a complicated piece of SQL to check, you cannot assume from any of the optimizer output on test data that production will execute efficiently. I have seldom found an occasion when the estimates are the same or higher than the actuals.

With that proviso, I tend to run this trace flag as standard, since I like to see the expected number of I/Os for a command. There are a whole range of optimizer trace flags in the 3xx range. Try them by setting the appropriate flag on as shown for 302 and look at the output to see if you find them useful. Try to understand the output from 315; although not obvious you might find an occasional different plan from the 320 trace flag when joins are involved.

Summary

There are several response time events which require corrective action:

Table 17.2

Event	Action
Process "hangs"	Commit or kill any blocking transaction
	Determine reason for block, e.g., client dead lock
Server "hangs"	Check error for any reason
	Bounce server
All processes go slowly	Identify and remove any resource bottleneck
	Analyze transaction SQL for poor performance
Specific transactions go slowly	Isolate transaction for testing
	Analyze SQL optimization plan

In checking the optimization plan of the SQL, you need to address the areas:

- Valid SARG

- Where clause on the first index column

- Matching datatypes
- Statistics present
- Statistics up-to-date
- No unknown values in where clause
- No unknown table sizes in command

Troubleshooting with sp_sysmom

This chapter analyses the sp_sysmon output in a top-down approach to show how to get the most from the principal outputs and then what to look for in each output.

In my opinion, and in what I consider the order of importance, the sp_sysmon values to check first are:

- Engine busy utilization

- Total cache hits

- Total network i/o requests

- Avg lock contention

- Updates/deletes

- Page splits

- Avg bytes received per packet

- ULC flushes to xact log

- Network checks

- Procedure reads from disk

Then you can look for any resource bottlenecks, i.e., high-waited figures:

- ULC/log semaphore requests

- Buffers grabbed dirty

- I/Os delayed

- Device semaphores (especially the log device)

The rest are of interest. I'm sure that I have left out your favorite, such as connections opened, but they have less effect in general and often there is little that you can do about them anyway.

The following describes what action you should take if you believe that a value is causing a problem, and what else you might look at to confirm your diagnosis.

Engine busy utilization

This one will normally be high and this is where you want it to be. Do not worry about regular values above 90%. This is how hard the server is working to service the transactions and, if there is CPU time available, the server will use it. If you can still log in and execute a system procedure such as sp_who, sp_lock without having to wait, then there is no problem. If it is taking much longer than normal to log in and execute the system procedures, then the CPU is overloaded. This may be caused by other factors such as large table scans; you need to investigate the other values before making a decision.

If it is a CPU problem, you do not have many options and they usually involve spending money. You could consider:

- Configuring another engine in an SMP environment

- Dedicating the box to the server by moving application processing to another box

- Buying a more powerful box

Cache hits

If cache hits is low and misses is high, then you are doing a large amount of physical I/O to disk instead of logical I/O to data cache. Note that sp_sysmon reports higher figures here than equivalent **set statistics io on**. sp_sysmon is dealing with the cache, not the commands, and includes system use of the data cache such as log pages, OAM pages and system tables.

In general, a low figure for cache hits means that the cache is too small and most I/Os are having to hit disk to access the data. However, a specific sp_sysmon output has to be analyzed in terms of the applications running at the time. If regular, very large table scans were being mixed with high volume single-record access on other tables, you could see a high cache miss figure. It's not necessarily correct or desirable, but it is explainable.

In a single default cache situation, you should be operating with regular 90% and above cache hits. When you have defined one or more named caches then the overall cache hit rate may be acceptable at 70–80% because you have deliberately bound a large object to a small cache. Although this saves the rest of cache from being trashed by the large table scan, it will generate a high physical I/O rate for the named cache. When you have no named caches and you believe that you are in a stable state then cache hits below 80% indicate that you are short of memory. Before you buy more memory for the box, it is worthwhile to check the configuration to ensure that all of the memory-hungry values are set correctly. The important ones are:

- Memory: is it set to the correct value, and is there little to no swapping?

- Connections: are they all necessary; can you reduce them and free more memory for data cache?

- Procedure cache: is it larger than it needs to be? Reduce the percentage to provide more data cache. If the procedure **reads from disk** is zero, you could try reducing procedure cache to see if it has been set too high. If you do not like the trial and error approach, run a dbcc procbuf and see how much is actually being used. Be ready for a lot of output. If proc reads from disk is already high, it supports the requirement for more memory.

Other configuration variables which use memory are: number of locks; number of objects; and number of network listeners.

When you have configured named caches, you need to look at the individual cache hits and misses. A single named cache which is specifically designed for one or more objects will be doing physical I/O if the cache is deliberately smaller than the objects. You may be binding a very large table to a named cache to prevent it from trashing all of data cache when a table scan is done. In this situation, you will have a lower overall logical I/O because this cache is taking cache away from the rest of the system. If the remaining cache is still showing a high logical I/O, you are OK. This is illustrated in Figure 18.1.

Be careful here with named caches. Do not get carried away.

Named cache is designed to help in several situations but the principal one is to reduce spinlock contention in an SMP environment.

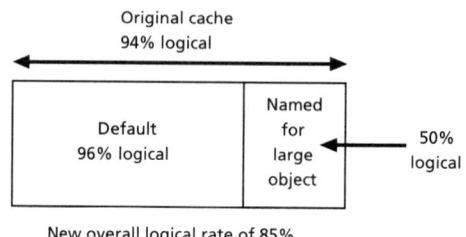

Figure 18.1 Named cache reducing overall cache hit rate

If you have a single engine, it is unlikely that creating named caches will make much difference. If the logical I/O is already greater than 90%, using a named cache will give no advantage and even for low logical I/O values the answer is usually more cache. The cache is already being used by all of the objects accessed. If they already fit into cache and you seldom get physical I/O when the system is stable, then splitting the cache up will probably just degrade the overall cache hit rate. For example, take the simple request to create a named cache for tempdb. Sounds like a good idea. It's in all of the manuals as one of the top uses of named caches. Let's say cache is 400 Mb and tempdb is 200 Mb. If we allocate less than 200 Mb cache to tempdb then we introduce the possibility of physical I/O on the tempdb cache when there is free cache in default. If we allocate 200 Mb to tempdb cache, we reduce the cache available to permanent objects when tempdb usage is less than 200 Mb. Leave it alone; let them share a larger default data cache.

However, in a multi-engine server the spinlock contention for a single cache will increase as the server utilization increases. The spinlock prevents more than one engine from changing cache at the same time. You need to treat this like any contention problem; and introduce parallelism by spreading the cache activity across more than one cache. This may not be possible if everyone is hitting the same object and data, but if the contention is on different objects in the same cache, you could reduce it by binding the objects to different caches.

Total requested network I/O

You need to compare this figure with the stated network capacity to see if you are overloading the network. If you are, you need to reduce the use of the network. Even if the network is not overloaded, you should review high figures and try to alter the application processing to make less use of the network. The normal approach is to make fewer requests from the client and do more work at the server for each network request.

Consider an example to update a record if it exists, and insert it if it does not exist, as illustrated in Figure 18.2.

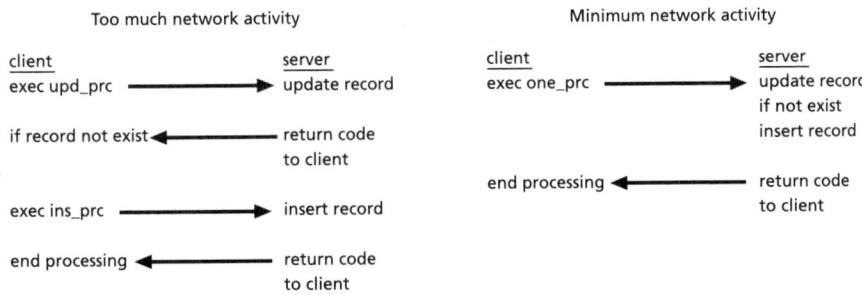

Figure 18.2 Comparison of client:server network activity

Even if the network is not overloaded, this reduction in network activity will always yield benefits. Be continually on the look out for these opportunities.

Note that the use of procedures in place of multiple SQL commands will automatically reduce the network traffic, since the procedure is one network request instead of one request per SQL command. You still need to check the returns from each command in the procedure but it does reduce the client:server requests. Chapter 19 describes some approaches to reducing the use of the network.

Avg lock contention

If this figure is high, you must try to reduce it. Lock contention is one of the biggest problems in relational databases, since it forces serial processing when you have a sophisticated multi-tasking parallel architecture available. Sybase's current adherence to page-level locking exacerbates the level of contention; you should take steps to reduce it. Chapter 11 describes SQL Server's lock management in detail and suggests approaches to reducing lock contention.

The problem with all of the current SQL Server monitoring tools is that they do not give you any indication of the SQL running when the contention occurred. The lock detail will help here, since it indicates the type of lock which suffered the highest contention. This will help you to narrow the search to the general type of processing but you will have to use other methods—third party software, a network sniffer, or System 11.1 SQL Monitor—to determine the tables/indexes which are causing the contention.

If you know roughly what is happening (not unreasonable as you are running sp_sysmon for a reason), you could simply run sp_lock to get object id and page number of the block.

Updates

Aim for a high **direct in place** and **direct cheap** and a **low deferred** and **direct expensive**. The direct in place and direct cheap do not change the record id of any record, so do not require any nonclustered indexes to be updated. The direct expensive and deferred updates are actioned as delete followed by insert and so the index entries for records being updated must also be deleted and inserted. Also, these updates may cause clustered index page splitting which increases the index update overhead.

The deferred update is particularly expensive, since it reprocesses the transaction log several times to action the updates at commit time instead of when the update is issued. Try to eliminate all deferred update processing. The principal reason for deferred occurring is when the update contains a join. This can be a simple join in the update statement or it may be concealed in a nesting which is executed as a join or in an update to a referential integrity column which requires a join to action the integrity.

Page splits/RID update from clustered split

Try to keep page splits as low as possible. Clustered index page splits are an overhead in the nonclustered index updates. These have to be done because the row id has changed. They are in locking contention as multiple pages have to be locked to maintain the page chain consistency. You need to identify which clustered index is causing the problem and then try to reduce the page-splitting using a fillfactor or by redefining the clustered index. It will be worth benchmarking the application with and without the clustered index which is causing the page splitting. Either replace it with a nonclustered index, or drop it altogether if the nonclustered is not efficient. Sacrificing inquiry response time for update/insert efficiency may well be beneficial. You cannot always prevent a table scan and you should check this.

If RID update is high, you have a real problem, since page splitting is cascading up the index. This should be zero most of the time; a few index page splits will create enough empty space in the index pages to prevent further splitting for some time. High activity here means that the index is growing as fast as the data and you need to review some of your index choices; at least one of them seems a bit large. Or perhaps you left an index on when running a large bcp and forgot to sort the data. Whatever... it is almost always a mistake.

Avg bytes per packet

This one will help you adjust the network packet size. The default size is 512 bytes. If you are well below this, less than 50%, you might want to consider allowing the packet to be sent immediately by altering the configuration parameter **tcp no delay**. Packets are sent automatically when they are full but delayed until a time-out if not full. Although setting tcp no delay will increase the network traffic (if the network requests are being continually delayed) you may still see an advantage.

If the ave packet size is close to or greater than the maximum, there are probably one or two connections which would benefit from a larger network packet size. You could take the sledgehammer approach and increase the configuration parameter **default network packet size** on a server-wide basis. This may have the opposite effect and delay too many packets since the packet is full less often.

Although it requires more investigation, you should identify which connections require the larger packet sizes—dbcc and bcp are the obvious processes—and you should set a run value for the specific connections.

ULC flushes

Try to keep the **by end tran** as high as possible. This means that the ULC is being flushed to the log at transaction commit time, which is exactly when you want it to occur. If the **flushes by full ULC** is high, the transactions are filling the ULC before they commit. Check the **max ULC size**; if it is equal to or close to the ULC size, you need to increase the size of the ULC using the configuration parameter user log cache size or reduce the length of your transactions.

High **by change of database** means that you should look at the incidence of multi-database access; but there's not really much to worry about. High **system log record** means that a system event occurred during the transaction which flushed the log. The most common of these is OAM page activity which may be an indication of extent fragmentation in the database. Clustered index rebuilds may reduce this figure.

Network checks

A high blocking figure means that the server is finding a lot of network I/O after it has yielded to the operating system. Once the server has yielded to the operating system, it checks for network I/O every clock tick. If there is network I/O, the operating system blocks the server from any other processing until the I/O completes. This synchronous activity means that there will be a delay between the network I/O being detected and the server waking up to process it. You should consider reducing this latency by increasing the configuration parameter **runnable process search count**. It defines the number of loops which the server executes waiting for network I/O before yielding to the operating system. If the **network checks** is low and the **CPU yields by engine** is high, the server may be yielding too often and not checking the network often enough. This combination would support an increase in **runnable process search count**.

Procedure reads from disk

If this is high, it usually indicates that the procedure cache is too small and you need to increase the procedure cache percentage or allocate more memory. All of the configuration checks which you applied to the data cache size are relevant to adjusting the procedure cache size. If you are getting frequent transaction failures because of insufficient space in procedure cache, then you definitely have a size problem.

Procedures can only be loaded into cache if there are sufficient free cache pages not currently being used. A procedure cache page is considered "dirty" if the procedure is currently being executed. If there are no free pages in procedure cache a request for a procedure not already in cache or a new version of a procedure being used in cache will fail; there is insufficient space to load the procedure.

You can still get a high read from disk but not have any cache space problems. This means that the procedure cache is being fully refreshed regularly but you are not swamping cache with a high degree of large, long-running procedures. Bear in mind that you are using procedures partially to avoid the optimize and compile overhead. A high read from disk cannot be a good idea and you should consider increasing the procedure cache to allow for unused procedures to remain longer in cache; there is a high chance of them still being in cache when you want to use them again.

ULC/log semaphore requests

High **waited** figures—especially for the log—indicate a high degree of contention for the log which will be creating a single thread bottleneck. Usually this should be compared with the ULC flushes to determine the action. If flushes are **by end tran** and **max ULC size** is the default of 2 Kb, there is not much you can do about it. You have a good transaction profile, but unfortunately a high contention on the log. Check the log disk activity. If this is also high then the problem may be at the disk level. If you have the log sharing the disk with other high activity objects it would be beneficial to move the log onto its own disk.

      If disk placement is not the problem, you need to introduce some parallelism into the log activity. As the ULC is not really helping here, you need to consider multiple logs, i.e., multiple databases. Not an easy solution to split the database so possibly a detailed look at the transaction profile and transaction mix is better, to try to alleviate the heavy concurrency on the log.

Buffers grabbed dirty

A non-zero value here means that a read from disk has been delayed because the page at the lru end of the buffer pool chain has not been written to disk. This means that the I/O activity has been unable to write the page to disk between the time it passed the wash marker and when it reached the end of the buffer pool chain. This is a significant hit on individual reads from disk and you should always try to reduce this to zero. There are several possible reasons which need to be checked:

- If the **buffers washed dirty** rate is higher than the disk I/O rate, you are simply overloading the disk capacity. You should increase the size of the wash area and possibly the buffer pool/cache to allow time for the pages to be written to disk before they reach the end of the buffer pool chain.

- Check the relevant disk activity to see if there is a device bottleneck on the disk that the page is being written to, since this will delay cleaning.

- If the buffer pool is small and there is a high turnover of pages, i.e., many requests from disk, you should consider increasing both the size of the buffer pool and the wash area.

- If the buffer pool is already large, increase the size of the wash area.

- If there are several high turnover objects using the pool, you may benefit from binding some of them to a named cache. This splits the page writes across more than one wash area.

I/Os delayed

If there are any I/Os being delayed, you should consider increasing one of the configuration parameters:

- **Disk i/o structures**: number of available disk I/O control blocks

- **Max async i/os per server**: maximum number of outstanding asynchronous disk requests for the server

- **Max async i/os per engine**: maximum number of outstanding asynchronous disk requests for an engine

Do not panic if some I/Os are delayed, it may well be transient and will not recur. Or, you may know that there has been an unusually high disk activity which will not be repeated. However, repetitive occurrences means that processes are running out of a resource; you will need to adjust these and possibly the operating system limit as well. There is no overhead in having the max async values as high as permitted by the operating system. You should not set them any higher than the **disk i/o structures**, since it is better for the server to delay an I/O request rather than having it block waiting on a disk I/O structure. So the one to pay most attention to is the **disk i/o structures** delays, as this will block the I/O request until a disk I/O structure is available.

Device semaphores

If the waited figure is high, I/Os are being delayed because of contention for the device. This normally indicates a hot-spot on one or a few objects and you will need to consider redistributing the data across more than one device. If the problem is a single object, you will need to partition the object first to allow parallel access to the data.

Total disk I/O checks

If the server does a lot of checks without returning much I/O, the checks which do not return I/O are overhead. You should consider reducing the number of disk I/O checks by increasing the configuration parameter **i/o polling process count** to check for disk I/O less often. Be a little careful here; make sure you know the pattern of the disk activity. An irregular pattern of disk activity such as infrequent large transfers will show a high number of checks returning no I/O. But there is little you can do about this because of the disk activity pattern. If you lengthen the time between disk I/O checks in this situation, you may simply delay the I/O when it does occur.

Large I/O usage

If you have configured large I/O buffer pools, the **large I/O denied** and the **large I/O effectiveness** will give you an idea of the usefulness of the large buffer pool. You need to look at the individual buffer pools for the details but these figures will indicate if the large I/O is usually granted and how much of the large buffers is being used.

The server cannot perform the large I/O if a page is in another buffer pool or no buffers are currently available in the pool. If the denied figure is high, you should try making the buffer pool larger. If this does not help, it is because of pages already in other buffer pools which you cannot do much about. It might be an indication of extent fragmentation and clustered index rebuild may recover the situation. If you have several large buffer pool sizes dropping the larger of them may increase use of the others. Failure to use a buffer pool automatically reverts the I/O to the 2 Kb pool. So when you drop the 16 Kb pool because it is frequently denied, you may revert to using the 8 Kb or 4 Kb pool.

If the large I/Os are being granted but the pages used figure is low, you are simply wasting cache space by not using all of the buffer size. Although you thought that 16 Kb was a good idea most of your I/O is being done in less pages. Reduce the size of the large buffer pool to a buffer pool size that fits the pages used.

Summary

When monitoring the system with sp_sysmon, the values to pay particular attention to are:

- Engine busy utilization
- Total cache hits
- Total network i/o requests
- Avg lock contention
- Updates/deletes
- Page splits
- Avg bytes received per packet
- ULC flushes to xact log
- Network checks
- Procedure reads from disk
- ULC/log semaphore requests
- Buffers grabbed dirty
- I/Os delayed
- Device semaphores (especially the log device)

## 19

Network Troubleshooting

This chapter is not so much about troubleshooting the network as it is about making optimum use of the network, mainly by reducing the use of the network. Although you may not see any bottleneck on the network it is quite possible for most of the performance overhead to be caused by overuse of the network. Keep a very close watch on the network usage figures from sp_sysmon; aim to reduce the number of packets and/or the number of bytes sent and received.

The general approach to this is to send as little as possible between the client and the server. Make the client send small pieces of SQL, such as procedures, which do the maximum amount of work and return only the essential information from the server. In a well-designed and configured system, the network overhead will be one of the most important areas to address.

Reduce opening and closing connections

Opening and closing a connection to the server takes a lot of effort and it is recommended to reduce the number of times a client opens and closes the "same" connection. A client application should open all connections that it requires and keep them open until it completes.

The client application may open as many connections as it needs, and the various modules within the client application routine may use the same connection or a low number of connections. It is always worthwhile for the initial routine in the application, such as the login or a main menu, to open all connections that the application is going to use and to keep them open until the client application ends. Each connection does require an amount of memory at the server but this is pre-allocated when the server starts based on the maximum number of connections and so there is no server overhead in the client keeping open all of the connections that it knows it will need. Clearly, if the client does not require a connection again it should be released, but if the connection is likely to be used again it should be kept open until the client application completes.

Use stored procedures

If the client frequently sends large batches of SQL, the load on the network may be reduced by writing the SQL batch as a procedure and sending a procedure execution across the network.

Using procedures instead of large batches of SQL reduces the number of packets sent across the network for client to server interaction. A little care is required here as the network software will not send partially full packets immediately. This will not be much of an overhead when the batch of SQL takes up many network packets but may start to have an effect when you are issuing small procedure executions. For the server to client interaction, it is recommended to set the **tcp no delay** configuration parameter to ensure immediate send of partially full packets. However, this does not affect the client to server interaction; you need to get down to the level of ct-library calls to set this at the client network layer. It is not normal to set this at the client side.

Minimize the client to server interactions

The above use of stored procedures is a specific example of the more general technique of reducing the amount of client to server interactions by doing as much processing at the server for each client call.

Consider the application which updates a record if it exists, otherwise the record is inserted. There are different ways of writing this:

Test existence and then insert or update

```
if exists (select * from table where pkey = value)
begin
exec upd_proc  /* with parameters */
```

```
end
else
begin
exec ins_proc /* with parameters */
end
```

<u>Update: if no records updated then insert</u>

```
declare @status int
exec @status=upd_proc /* with parameters */
if @status = 10 /* record not found  */
begin
exec ins_proc /* with parameters */
end
```

The latter is preferable as it eliminates the select in the if exists, and reduces the number of logical I/Os which the code carries out. We then write the second piece of code as one large procedure which does all of the work. We execute this procedure from the client so that we now have only one client/server interaction.

Return only the necessary data to the client

Reducing the amount of network traffic also applies to the server to client interaction and it is recommended to return only the data which the client requires.

Having reduced the amount of data sent from the client to the server, it is even more important to reduce the amount of data returned from the server to the client. This applies to the columns and the number of records returned. Wherever possible avoid the use of **select** *…and make it standard practice to request only those columns which you require in the client.

More importantly, try not to return unnecessary data by always including the appropriate where clauses in the SQL, which will filter the records at the server. Clearly sending all records in a table when the client requires only a few based on a specific selection criteria, is not making efficient use of the network. There will be occasions when the client requests large amounts of data for manipulation in client software, such as spreadsheets. These occasions should be limited and closely controlled based on execution time to reduce their impact on the other more interactive processes using the network. You should also consider altering the network packet size for these bulk transfer processes as described below.

Match the network packet size to the type of processing

In a mixed processing environment, it is appropriate to consider different network packet sizes for various types of work. The "per-packet" overhead of the network is one of the most important effects on network performance, so it is worthwhile trying to get this as low as possible.

SQL Server uses a 512 byte network packet size by default. This is normally sufficient for regular on-line interactive work, but may be causing far too many packet transfers when an application is sending/receiving large amounts of data. If there is sufficient data to justify a larger packet size, you will reduce the network overheads and increase physical throughput. Larger network packets should be considered for actions such as **bcp**, **text/image** and large selects. If you identify a need for larger packet sizes, you need to configure the memory for this using the configuration variables **additional network memory** and **max network packet size**. Make sure you allocate enough additional memory for the larger packets, since the connection will revert to the default size if there is not enough large packet memory for the connection to be made. Each connection requires three buffer areas—read, write, and read overflow—and you need to allocate:

```
(number of connections using large packet size) * (large packet size) * 3 * 2%
```

The 2% is for overhead and you round up to the nearest 2048 bytes.

The most common time for using large network packet sizes will be when loading large amounts of data using bcp. The large network packet size is specified with the -A option on the bcp command line.

```
bcp prod_db.dbo.sales_tab in salesdat.in -c -t"," -A2048
```

This specifies that a network packet of 2048 bytes will be used for this bcp input. You can also set this on isql.

```
isql -Ujkirkwood -Pwhatever -SSALESP1 -A2048
```

Match the SQL Server default packet size to the network packet size

The SQL Server 512 byte default may not match the underlying network packet size. Consider adjusting the default packet size in units of 512 so that you reduce wasted space.

When the network packet size is different than the SQL Server default, you will be doing more server reads and writes than necessary and may be suffering large amounts of wasted space in the packets. In this situation, you should consider adjusting the **default network packet size**. When you adjust this, you must also increase the **max network packet size** so that it is at least as large as the default size. If you set the maximum greater than the default you will also have to adjust the **additional network memory** as above.

The balance between the packet sizes has to consider the reduction in server reads and the amount of wasted space in the network packet. Both of these have an effect on throughput and you will have to check which one is more important in your configuration, usually by trial and error. Consider a network packet size of 1400 bytes:

```
SQL Server packet size     # server reads    wasted space
512                        2                  376 (27%)
1024                       1                  376 (27%)
1536                       2                 1264 (90%)
2048                       2                  753 (54%)
2560                       2                  240 (17%)
```

The 1024 SQL Server packet size reduces the number of server reads, but the 2560 packet size is the least wasted space. You will need to check the throughput of your application to decide between these. The calculations are explained in Figure 19.1 for 1024 and 2056 SQL Server packet sizes with the network packet size of 1400 bytes.

The 1024 byte SQL Server packet fits into a single network packet but leaves 376 bytes wasted space. The 2560 byte SQL Server packet is larger than the network packet and therefore requires two network packets, but it fills the space better, leaving only 240 unused bytes in the second network packet.

Isolate heavy network users

If the network is being heavily used and there is nothing else that you can do to improve it, you should consider introducing some parallelism into the network configuration by configuring multiple network listeners to a single server and/or using a separate network card for each server on the machine.

In a multiple CPU environment, it is not unusual for the machine to support more than one server. In this situation, the network may quickly become the single resource bottleneck and you should consider a separate network card for individual servers. This is a simple introduction of parallelism to a physical resource to alleviate bottlenecks. If you are using multiple servers per machine and multiple engines per server, there is no reason why you should not use multiple networks cards, each servicing a single server.

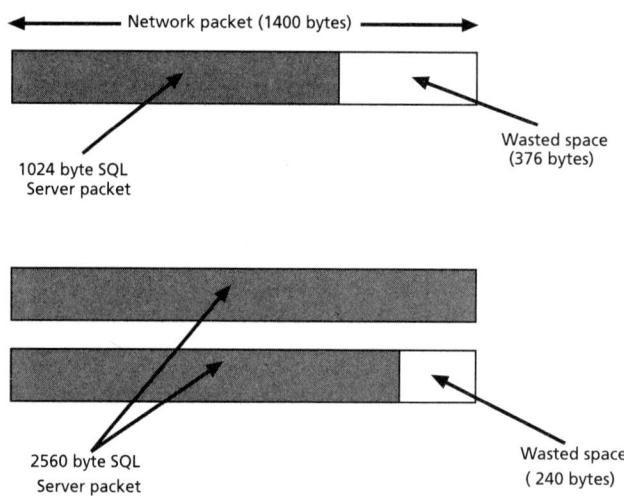

Figure 19.1 Matching SQL Server packet size and network packet size

This "network parallelism" is applicable to a single server by configuring multiple network listeners on the server. This allows clients to connect to a specific network handler and spread the network load. When the server starts, it spawns a network handler process for each "master" line in the interfaces file, i.e., for each DSLISTEN value. The clients can then connect to different DSQUERY names configured as separate entries in the interfaces file, or use different interfaces files with the appropriate network defined as the "query" entry.

Summary

In the environment of SMP boxes with lots of processing power and lots of memory, the network is becoming the principal large scale bottleneck in database systems. You should always be looking for ways to reduce the amount of network traffic:

- Reduce the opening and closing of connections
- Use stored procedures
- Minimize client to server interaction
- Return only the necessary data to the client
- Match the network packet size to the type of processing
- Match the SQL Server packet size to the network packet size
- Isolate heavy network users on separate network cards

20

High Performance SQL

This chapter describes the most common problems of SQL and how to avoid them with specific solutions given to indicate the relative performance merits of the solutions.

Avoid LIKE when no wildcard

Avoid the use of like when there is no wildcard in the expression:

```
where name like "kirkwood"
```

should be written with the equals operator:

```
where name = "kirkwood"
```

The like operator is always expanded into a range query as:

```
where column <= high_value
and column >= low_value
```

When the optimizer is evaluating this against index statistics, it can estimate more records than a simple equality because of the approximate nature of the step distribution of the statistics. Even worse, if the statistics have not been created, the optimizer will use the default 25% for a closed interval rather than the 10% for equality.

Avoid min and max in the same statement

The aggregate functions min and max cause a table or index scan if used in the same statement.

The aggregate functions **min** and **max** will use an index if available, except when they are both used in the same statement. In this case, they cause a table scan if the index being used is clustered, or an index scan if the index is nonclustered. The command:

```
select min(col), max(col) from table_1
```

will cause a table scan even if there is a clustered index on col. You should write these as two commands to access the index twice.

```
select min(col) from table_1
select max(col) from table_1
```

Of course, if the index is nonclustered, the command is covered by the index and an index scan will be done instead of a table scan. It is still more efficient to write these as two commands to do two index accesses.

If you must use one command, you can nest one of the aggregates, in which case the index is used in the separate statements for two index accesses.

```
select min(col), (select max(col) from table_1) from table_1
```

Be careful when mixing columns and aggregate functions

When you mix columns and aggregate functions in the select column list, always make sure that all of the columns appear in a group by clause.

```
select name, address, sum(credit)
      from customer
      group by name, address
```

SQL Server SQL is unusual in that it accepts the statement:

```
select name, address, sum(credit)
      from customer
      group by name
```

However, the results from this are not always what you might expect.

The aggregate function creates a worktable to evaluate the command which is composed of the group by column(s) and the aggregate values. So the above would create a worktable something like:

```
name        sum(credit)
andrews     145.78
beattie     267.56
kirkwood     34.20
logan       345.67
```

This worktable is then used to output the results. However, there is no address in the worktable, so the original customer table has to be used to retrieve the address. Unfortunately, there is no join clause between the worktable and the customer table. A cartesian product is done, matching every record in the worktable with every record in the customer table, producing an output something like:

```
name        address     sum(credit)
andrews     address1    145.78
andrews     address2    145.78
andrews     address3    145.78
.
.
.
logan       address1    345.67
logan       address2    345.67
logan       address3    345.67
.
.
.
```

This is not a good idea and you should always follow the rule: If you have a mixture of columns and aggregate functions in the select list, always have every column in the group by clause.

Do not mix the use of the where and having clauses

Use the where clause for selection on columns and the having clause for selection on aggregates.

SQL has two selection clauses—where and having. Although you cannot use the where clause on aggregates, you can use the having clause on columns. This is not a good idea. The SQL:

```
select name, address from customer
       where name like 'Kir%'
```

and

```
select name, address from customer
       having name like 'Kir%'
```

are identical in execution plan, response time and results.

However, the presence of the group by clause causes the having to be evaluated at a different place in the command execution. In the above simple command, with no group by clause, the where and the having are evaluated at the same time, as the records are read. However, when a group by is introduced, the where is still evaluated as the records are read but the having is evaluated against the worktable after all records have been read into the worktable. The SQL:

```
select name, sum(credit) from customer
       where name like 'Kir%'
       group by name
```

and

```
select name, sum(credit) from customer
       group by name
       having name like 'Kir%'
```

produce the same results but are evaluated differently. Both statements use a worktable to hold the group by information, however, the execution is very different. The where clause statement selects the records from the customer table and creates a worktable of only those records which conform to the where clause, i.e., whose names begin with Kir. The having clause statement selects all customer records into the worktable, and the having selects only those worktable records which conform to the selection criteria for display.

So the where clause can do an indexed access to the customer table and then a table scan of a small worktable, whereas the having has to do a table scan of the customer table and a table scan of a large worktable.

Avoid use of > operator when column has large number of duplicates

The where clause where date_col > "Dec 25 1996" should be written as where date_col >= "Dec 26 1996" to avoid scanning all of the records for Dec 25.

The query:

```
select * from transaction_tab where date_col > "Dec 25 1996"
```

is evaluated by scanning the index from the first record with date "Dec 25 1996". If there are many records with this value, you are doing an unnecessary number of index record accesses just to get to your start point of "Dec 26 1996". If you can, you should write this using the >= operator:

```
select * from transaction_tab where date_col >= "Dec 26 1996"
```

Make sure any where clause expressions and columns are the same datatype

SQL Server will not use the statistics if the datatype in the where clause expression is different from the datatype of the column the statistics were created on. When the datatypes are different, the optimizer uses the sarg density of the index.

SQL Server does not do any datatype conversion when accessing the index statistics. Therefore, if the datatypes do not match the index statistics are not used. The optimizer does know that the statistics are available for the index, so it uses the sarg density figure from the index distribution page. This is usually accurate enough to allow the index to be used, but you should be aware of the occasional time when mismatching datatypes will cause table scans when you are expecting index accesses.

The most common of these are when testing against variables and when testing against numeric literals.

Variables

The common situation here is the procedure parameter used in a where clause:

```
create proc name_prc (@name char(2))
as
select name, address, credit from customer
      where name like @name + %
```

Normally, the customer.name column is varchar and varchar:char are different datatypes which require conversion. This conversion will cause the statistics to be ignored. You also need to be careful with columns which allow null, since this automatically defines the datatype as variable. The only exception to this is the int datatype which does not require conversion whether or not it allows nulls. No, I do not know why! So **char_col char(10)** null is actually held as a varchar(10) column and will require conversion if tested against any char datatypes.

The one time when SQL Server gets this right is the declare statement. Any variable defined with the declare statement automatically allows and is initialized to null. However, this does not appear to alter the datatype and **declare @name char(10)** will still use index statistics when compared with a char(10) not null column.

Numeric literals

In theory, the problem that statistics are not used if datatype conversion is required should apply to the different numeric datatypes. Conversion is required between the integer, float and numeric types. However, I have found that the only conflict which causes trouble is when one of the datatypes is the numeric datatype. A complication here is that numeric datatypes with different scales require conversion and therefore do not use the statistics. The following table represents a test I ran when the index was used. If the index statistics were used and a table scan was required, the index density was used.

Column datatype	Expression	Showplan
int	a < 20	index
int	a < 20.0	index
int	a < 2e+1	index
float	a < 2e+1	index
float	a < 20	index
float	a < 20.0	index
numeric(4,1)	a < 20	table scan
numeric(4, 1)	a < 20.0	index

```
numeric(4, 1)          a < 2e+1     index
numeric(4, 1)          a < 20.12    table scan
numeric(4, 1)          a < 2e+2     table scan
```

The only occasion when the indexes were not used, was when the scale of the numeric column and the expression were different.

Joins and datatypes

When joining between two columns of different datatypes, one of the datatypes has to be converted. The optimizer cannot choose an index on the column that is being converted.

If the datatypes in a join clause are different, the lower one in the datatype hierarchy has to be converted. This internal conversion means that any index on the converted column cannot be used to effect the join.

```
select a.* from table_1 a, table_2 b
       where a.float_col = b.int_col
       and a.float_col = 12.34
```

This will not be able to use an index on table_2.int_col as this has to be converted to float.

Again, be very careful with the numeric datatype, since a difference in scale will render an index useless.

The initial version of System 11 exhibited this conversion behavior with char and varchar (char not null and char null). This has been removed in the later versions (11.0.2) and a mismatch on char to varchar datatype will still try to use the index.

Always write search arguments in the where clauses

Unless the command is covered by the index, the optimizer will not consider the index statistics if the where clause is not in the form of a search argument.

The optimizer is very strict in its where clause format and requires a search argument to consider the index statistics. The search argument format is:

```
column      operator      expression
```

and if this is not adhered to the index statistics will not even be considered and a table scan will be carried out.

<u>DO</u>	<u>NOT</u>
`name like 'kir%'`	`substring(name, 1, 3) = 'kir'`
`value = 40 * 1000`	`value / 1000 = 40`

`firstname = "john"`
`and`
`lastname = "kirkwood"`
	`firstname + " " + lastname = "john kirkwood"`

Avoid unknown values in statements

Any calculation in the where clause of a statement generates an unknown value to the optimizer and therefore the statistics cannot be used.Again, the optimizer still knows that there are statistics present for the index and will use the sarg density for the index.

The basic problem is that when the command is optimized, any calculations in the batch of commands have not been executed. The optimizer does not know the resulting value of the calculation and does not have a value which it can use to look up the statistics. The times when this occurs are:

- Arithmetic calculations
- Variable values
- Nested selects

However, do not anticipate problems here. The use of the sarg density will choose the index almost all of the time. Just be aware of the problem when the command table scans.

Unknown arithmetic values

The simple rule is to do your own arithmetic if possible.

```
select * from employee
       where salary = 1200 * 12
```

When the optimizer comes to this command the value 1200 * 12 has not been evaluated, so the optimizer does not have a value to use to look up the statistics.

If you have problems, write this as:

```
select * from employee
       where salary = 14400
```

Unknown variable values

In the batch of commands:

```
declare @var1 int
select @var1 = 14400
select * from employee
       where salary = @var1
go
```

the batch is optimized before it is executed. This means that, when the final select is optimized the value of the variable has not been evaluated, so the optimizer does not have a value to use to look up the statistics.

If a problem arises, this unknown value can be eliminated by using procedures and passing the variable value into a procedure parameter. First, create a procedure to execute the select command:

```
create proc emp_sal_prc (@par1 int)
as
select * from employee
       where salary = @par1
go
```

and then execute the procedure in the batch:

```
declare @var1 int
select @var1 = 14400
exec emp_sal_prc @par1 = @var1
```

When the procedure is executed, it is read from the system tables and optimized. However, this optimization knows the value being supplied to the parameter and so the select command is optimized with the supplied value and can look up the index statistics. There is no problem using existing execution plans, since the SQL command is strictly equality in the where clause.

Unknown nested select values

In the command:

```
select * from employee
       where salary = (select max(salary) from employee)
```

the result of the nested select is not known when the command is optimized. Again, if you experience a problem, this unknown value can be eliminated by using a procedure:

```
create proc emp_maxsal_prc (@par1 int)
as
select * from employee
       where salary = @par1
go
```

and executing the procedure as:

```
declare @var1 int
select @var1 = max(salary) from employee
exec emp_maxsal_prc @par1 = @var1
go
```

As before, the timing of the optimization of the procedure is at execution time and the value of the parameter is known to the optimizer.

Unknown table sizes

If you create and use a table in the same batch or procedure then the optimizer does not know the size of the table when it is used. In this case, the optimizer uses a default size of 10 pages and 100 rows.

This is an identical problem to the unknown values in where clause expressions. The optimization of the commands is done before the commands are executed, so the size of any table created in the batch or procedure cannot be known to the optimizer. However, this is more of a problem as 10 page temporary tables will not always reflect the actual sizes, and table scans of large temporary tables will occur. It is worth recognizing that this problem will occur and writing the SQL to avoid it.

In T-SQL batches, this can be solved by defining the table, and any index, in a separate batch to the one it is used in.

```
select * into #temp from employee
create unique index jk_idx1 on #temp(emp_id)
select * from #temp where emp_id = 20
go
```

This will table scan, since the optimizer has no knowledge of the size or index information on #temp and has to use the default values of 10 pages and 100 rows.

Writing this in two batches as:

```
select * into #temp from employee
create unique index jk_idx1 on #temp(emp_id)
go
select * from #temp where emp_id = 20
go
```

uses the index on #temp. The second batch is optimized after the first batch has been executed and the optimizer knows everything about the table #temp.

This problem is slightly more interesting in stored procedures, since the procedure cannot contain two batches. In the case of a table created within a procedure, you need to create another procedure to access the new table. This is slightly awkward, since the procedure which accesses the table has to know about the table it is accessing and if this is a temporary table, you will have to define it in the same batch that the second procedure is created.

```
create proc proc_1
as
select * into #temp from employee
create unique index jk_idx1 on #temp(emp_id)
select * from #temp where emp_id = 20
go
```

This has the same problem as a single batch, in that no information is available on the temporary table when the final select command is optimized. Two procedures are required:

```
create table #temp ( emp_id int, ...... )  /* same structure as employee table  */
go
create proc proc_2
as
select * from #temp where emp_id = 20
go
create proc proc_1
as
select * into #temp from employee
create unique index jk_idx1 on #temp(emp_id)
exec proc_2
go
```

Now the command:

```
exec proc_1
```

will create the table #temp and its index externally to the procedure proc_2. When proc_2 is executed, the optimizer will know all it has to know about #temp. This does have an overhead, since the execution of proc_2 has to rebind the columns of #temp because it is a different table from the one that it was created with. This column binding takes longer in System 10 and 11 than it did in 4.9.2. Be careful if you already adopt this technique when you upgrade, as you may suffer a performance degradation. The tests that I did indicated a 3 times degradation.

Do not test variable values in where clauses

It is very poor practice to test a variable value in a where clause. If the test is a logical OR, performance will also suffer.

If you write:

```
select * from employee
       where emp_id = 20
       and @var1 = 100
```

there is minimum overhead; the logical AND allows any index on emp_id to be used even though there is no suitable index for the variable testing clause.

However, if you write:

```
select * from employee
       where emp_id = 20
       or @var1 = 100
```

the OR requires each where clause to be evaluated independently, and the results of each to be merged into one output. If either of the clauses in the OR requires a table scan, the optimizer will use a table scan for the complete command. Unfortunately, the @var1 = 100 requires each record on the table to be tested even although @var1 does not correspond to a column on the table. Therefore, the variable test requires a table scan and the complete command does a table scan.

These should be rewritten as separate IF tests on the variables before the command is executed.

AND

```
if (@var1 = 100)
begin
        select * from employee
                where emp_id = 20
end
go
```

This is still marginally more efficient; the select is executed only when the variable equals 100.

OR

```
if (@var1 = 100)
goto lab1
else
begin
        if exists (select * from employee
                        where emp_id = 20)
                goto lab1
        else
                goto lab2
end
lab1: select * from employee
        where emp_id = 20
lab2:
```

No apologies for the goto. I'll debate such a simple and easily understood use of goto with the structured purists anytime.

Row by row processing

SQL is a set based language; you should try to avoid row by row processing. However, if you cannot avoid it, the optimum method is to use cursors.

I have done some tests on three approaches to row by row processing with the following results. Please do your own tests as everything in performance and benchmarking is best justified on your own data and results.

Table 20.1

Method	Time in Msecs
set rowcount 1	2000
min(pkey)	130
cursors	50

The SQL to support these is:

set rowcount

```
declare @cnt int
select * into #temp from employee
select @cnt = count(*) from #temp

while (@cnt > 0)
begin
        set rowcount 1
        select * from #temp
        set rowcount 0

        /*  process as necessary  */

        set rowcount 1
        delete #temp
        set rowcount 0
        select @cnt = @cnt - 1
end
```

min(pkey)

```
declare @min int, @cnt int
select @min = min(emp_id) from employee
select @cnt = count(*) from employee

while (@cnt > 0)
begin
        select * from employee where emp_id = @min

        /*  process as necessary  */
```

```
        select @min = min(pkey) from employee
                where emp_id > @min
        select @cnt = @cnt - 1
end
```

It was pointed out to me that you could use the property of the aggregate functions of returning null when no value is returned. Avoid the count to make this even faster. However, I used this SQL for the tests and so I reproduce it here. This requires a primary key on the data before it can be used.

cursors

```
declare cursor_1 cursor for
        select * from employee for read only
go

open cursor_1
declare @emp_id int
fetch cursor_1 into @emp_id
if (@@sqlstatus = 2)
begin
        /*  add   no records processing   */
close cursor_1
end
else
begin
        while (@@sqlstatus = 0)
        begin

                /*   process as necessary   */

                fetch cursor_1 into @emp_id
        end
        if (@@sqlstatus = 1)
        begin
                /*  error processing   */
        end
close cursor_1
end
deallocate cursor cursor_1
go
```

This looks much more complicated, but once you get the structure sorted out, it is quite easy to use. However, I stress that if you can do set based processing, then do so. Cursors are slow; it is just that they are the least slow method of doing row by row processing.

Avoid the use of not in (prior to System 11)

Any use of the not operator, in any of its guises (!=, <>, not), results in a poor performance command as the not equal is not considered as a search argument by the optimizer and therefore any index is not considered and a table scan is carried out. Prior to System 11, the nested construct using **not in** is very expensive and should be replaced with an outer join.

The *not in* nesting:

```
select * from employee
       where dept_no not in (select dept_no from department
       where ctry_code = 'UK')
```

is evaluated in three stages:

- Read the employee table and create a worktable of one row for each employee record containing the minimum data to execute the next two stages (in this case the emp_id, the dept_no and a flag column)

- Join the worktable with the department table and update the worktable flag column to indicate all records which join

- Join the worktable with the employee table to retrieve only those records which did not join in step 2

This involves a minimum of one table scan of the employee table and two joins of the unindexed worktable.

It is always faster to execute the not in as a two stage process using an outer join.

```
select emp_dept = e.dept_no, dept_dept = d.dept_no
       into #temp
       from employee e, department d
       where e.dept_no *= d.dept_no
       and d.ctry_code = 'UK'

select e.* from employee e, #temp t
       where e.dept_no = t.emp_dept
       and dept_dept is null
```

The first stage does an outer join which creates a temporary table containing all employee department numbers. Those which do not match with a department have a null in the second column of the temporary table. The second stage then joins the temporary table with the employee table, only for those temporary table records with a null second column, i.e., those which did not match with a department record. This approach effectively removes the first stage of the not in processing which scans the employee table.

In System 11, the optimization plan for the not in has been changed and a correlated nesting is carried out using the any aggregate and an existence join.

```
select * from employee
        where dept_no not in (select dept_no from department
                                        where ctry_code = 'UK')
QUERY PLAN FOR STATEMENT 1 (at line 1)

    STEP 1
            The type of query is SELECT

            FROM TABLE
                employee
            Nested Iteration
            Table Scan
            Ascending Scan
            Positioning at start of table

            Run subquery 1 (at nesting level 1)
            Using I/O Size 4 Kbytes
            With LRU Buffer Replacement Strategy

NESTING LEVEL 1 SUBQUERIES FOR STATEMENT 1

  QUERY PLAN FOR SUBQUERY 1 (at nesting level 1 and at line 1)

    Correlated Subquery
    Subquery under an IN predicate

    STEP 1
            The type of query is SELECT
            Evaluate ungrouped ANY AGGREGATE

            FROM TABLE
                department
            EXISTS TABLE: nested iteration
            Index: ctry_code_idx
            Ascending scan
            Positioning by key
```

```
Keys are:
        ctry_code
Using I/O Size 4 Kbytes
With LRU Buffer Replacement Strategy
END OF QUERY PLAN FOR SUBQUERY 1
```

This is now faster than an outer join and removes the major performance problem of writing not in nestings. The in nesting is still faster and you should still try to write the SQL in the positive, but the performance overhead of the negative not in has been reduced in System 11.

Exists versus not exists

Similar to the **in versus not in**, it was always advised to write a positive test for exists. This is no longer the case in System 11; **exists** and **not exists** give the same execution plans and the same logical I/O to execute the query.

Prior to System 11, it was always advised to write **not exists** as **exists** by altering the logical flow of the SQL.

```
if not exists ( select * ...) should be written as   if exists (select * ...)
begin                                                 begin
/* negative SQL  */                                   /*  positive SQL  */
end                                                   end
else                                                  else
begin                                                 begin
/*  positive SQL  */                                  /*  negative SQL  */
end                                                   end
```

This is no longer necessary; I have found in all the not exists I have run that the execution plan is identical and the number of logical I/Os is also identical.

Using characteristic functions

Characteristic functions were introduced to the SQL Server community by Rozenshtein, Abramovich and Birger and I strongly advise you pick up a copy of their book on the subject—Optimizing Transact-SQL: Advanced Programming Techniques (0-9649812-0-3). It's over 100 pages of detail that I cannot give you here and—although you must always check everything in performance tuning—will give you some quite significant performance improvements. From a performance viewpoint, characteristic functions are a means of replacing a where clause with a function call in the column list. When the where clause cannot be optimized, and causes multiple table scans, this can bring significant performance improvements.

I am not going into a detailed treatment of the characteristic functions—I refer you to the book mentioned in the footnote for this—but I shall introduce them and indicate where you might find performance benefits.

Processing in SQL often requires multiple passes of a table to store intermediate results in a temporary table. An example of this is where an amount has to be multiplied or divided by an exchange rate depending on the value of a code column. Consider the table:

```
rate_tab(pkey, mult_code, amount, exch_rate)

where   mult_code = "M" indicates to Multiply by exch_rate
        mult_code = "D" indicates to Divide by exch_rate
```

This is solved in most programming languages by a CASE statement, but as this is not available in SQL Server T-SQL, the normal approach is to create a temporary table from multiple passes of the source table. A request to output (pkey, calculated_amount) is most commonly achieved by two passes of the table into a temporary table:

```
insert into #temp
        select pkey, amount*exch_rate
                from rate_tab
                where mult_code = "M"
```

and

```
insert into #temp
        select pkey, amount*(1/exch_rate)
                from rate_tab
                where mult_code = "D"
```

and a table scan of the temporary table for output:

```
select * from #temp
```

Both passes of the source table (rate_tab) generally require a table scan as any index on 'mult_code' is usually not selective enough to be used.

The use of characteristic functions replaces the where clauses with function calls, and achieves the output in one pass of the source table without the need for a temporary table. In the above example, the function call would return exch_rate when mult_code = "M" and 1/exch_rate when mult_code = "D," allowing the SQL to be written as:

```
select pkey, calculated_amount = amount * function_call
     from rate_tab
```

The function calls are not the most intuitive constructs, and differ depending on the datatype. The above example requires the following:

```
isnull((exch_rate/charindex(mult_code, "M")), (1/exch_rate))
```

where

---

isnull returns the first argument if the first argument is not null and the second argument if the first argument is null

charindex returns the position of the string in the first argument and 0 if the string is not in the first argument

---

So:

```
if mult_code = "M"
        charindex(mult_code, "M") = 1
        isnull returns exch_rate

if mult_code = "D"
        charindex(mult_code, "M") = 0
        divide by 0 in T-SQL returns null
        isnull returns (1/exch_rate)
```

There are function calls for all possible where operator conditions and for all datatypes. I have not catered for null conditions; they get very long winded and complicated. If you must do so, please access the original material.

Numeric datatype

Consider the table:

```
amount_tab(pkey, current_amount, previous_amount, current_flag)
```

where

current_flag = 1 indicates that the current_amount should be used

current_flag = 0 indicates that the previous_amount should be used

and a requirement to output (pkey, current_flag, amount).

In this case we use the function call:

```
abs(sign(current_flag - 1))
```

where

sign returns +1 if the argument is >0

-1 if the argument is <0

0 if the argument is 0

abs returns the absolute value of the argument

If current_flag = 1

```
sign(current_flag - 1) = 0
abs(sign(current_flag - 1)) = 0
```

If current_flag = 0

```
sign(current_flag - 1) = -1
abs(sign(current_flag - 1)) = 1
```

and we can write

```
select pkey, current_flag,
       amount = current_amount * (1 - abs(sign(current_flag - 1))) +
                previous_amount * (abs(sign(current_flag - 1)))
       from amount_tab
```

Representing the function call as FC, the above becomes:

```
FC[current_flag = 1]
```

where

the function call FC returns 1 if current_flag = 1

and 0 if current_flag = 0

We can now represent all of the where clause operators as:

```
FC[A=B]              1 - abs(sign(A-B))
FC[A!=B]             abs(sign(A-B))
FC[A<B]              1 - sign(1 + sign(A-B))
FC[A<=B]             sign(1 - sign(A-B))
FC[A>B]              1 - sign(1 - sign(A-B))
FC[A>=B]             sign(1 + sign(A-B))
FC[A IS NULL]        isnull(0*A, 1)
FC[ A IS NOT NULL]   1 - isnull(0*A, 1)

FC[NOT expression]   1 - FC[expression]
FC[exp1 AND exp2]
     isnull(FC[exp1]*FC[exp2], 0/(1 - isnull(FC[exp1,1)*isnull(FC[exp2], 1)))
FC[exp1 OR exp2]
isnull(sign(FC[exp1]+FC[exp2]),1/(isnull(FC[exp1],0)+isnull(FC[exp2],0)))
```

Character datatypes

For the character datatype, the charindex function is used as described above.

```
charindex(column, value)
```

returns   1 (the start position of the value in the column)

                 0 otherwise

The single digit character datatype can be given special treatment using the ASCII function on the basis that the ASCII function will execute faster than the charindex function. The above:

```
charindex(mult_code, "M")
```

can be treated as:

```
1 - abs(sign(ascii(mult_code) - ascii("M")))
```

It's up to you on this one; I prefer to stick with one function for all character columns.

Datetime datatypes

For datetime datatypes we use the datediff function as we would the minus operator. Unfortunately, the date functions require a first argument which specifies the portion of the date for comparison—years, months, days etc.—and this often requires more than one datediff call. The best portion of the date to use would be millisecs:

```
datediff(ms, date_1, date_2)
```

but the datediff function returns an int datatype, so the range of this test is limited to 24 days and overflow errors are common. There are various solutions to this, but you may consider simply testing the day, month, year as:

```
datediff(yy, date_1, date_2) +
datediff(mm, date_1, date_2) +
datediff(dd, date_1, date_2)
```

If all three are 0, the result is 0. If one is non-zero, the result is non-zero. You can then treat it as before:

```
FC[date_1 = date_2]              1 - (abs(sign(datediff(yy, date_1, date_2) +
                                         datediff(mm, date_1, date_2) +
                                         datediff(dd, date_1, date_2)))))
```

It is not quite as easy this time, but you can construct all operator conditions.

Uses of the characteristic function calls

The following are some illustrations of the use of characteristic functions.

The principal performance reason for using characteristic functions is to reduce the number of passes through a table to carry out processing based on the value of a column. If this column is indexed and the index is used for the record accesses, the savings in disk I/O may be outweighed by the increase in CPU time to evaluate the functions. More generally, if the server you are using is CPU-bound, the use of characteristic functions is not advised. Characteristic functions swap disk I/O for CPU cycles; make sure that you verify the actual benefits.

More interesting is the fact that a characteristic function may save you the need for an index. You may be making several index passes on a table which can be replaced by one pass on another existing index. This allows you to remove an index which is no longer used. The fewer indexes you have on a table, the better for maintenance purposes, and the less chance you have of a deadlock between a maintenance command and a select command.

Representing row data as column data

Consider the table:

```
month_tab(name, month_no, amount)
```

with the requirement to display as:

```
(name, month_no, jan_amt, feb_amt, ... , dec_amt)
```

We can do this in a single pass of the table as:

```
select name, month_no,
       jan_amt = sum(amount * FC[month_no = 1]),
       feb_amt = sum(amount * FC[month_no = 2]),
          .
          .
          .
       dec_amt = sum(amount * FC[month_no = 12])
       from month_tab
```

Expanding the function call:

```
select name, month_no,
       jan_amt = sum(amount * (1 - abs(sign(month_no - 1)))),
       feb_amt = sum(amount * (1 - abs(sign(month_no - 2)))),
          .
          .
          .
       dec_amt = sum(amount * (1 - abs(sign(month_no - 12))))
       from month_tab
```

When the month_no is held as a character string - "Jan", "Feb", etc.

```
select name, month_char,
       jan_amt = sum(amount * charindex(month_char, "Jan")),
       feb_amt = sum(amount * charindex(month_char, "Feb")),
          .
          .
          .
       dec_amt = sum(amount * charindex(month_char, "Dec"))
       from month_tab
```

When the month is held as a datetime:

```
select name, month_char,
    jan_amt = sum(amount * (1 - abs(sign(datediff(mm, date_col, 1))))),
    feb_amt = sum(amount * (1 - abs(sign(datediff(mm, date_col, 2))))),
           .
           .
           .
    dec_amt = sum(amount * (1 - abs(sign(datediff(mm, date_col, 12))))),
    from month_tab
```

(Clearly the date function requires the dates to be for the current year. You can use the three tests on year, month, day discussed above to overcome this.)

Creating histograms

Consider the table:

```
employee(emp_id, salary)
```

and the requirement to output the histogram of number of employees in the bands less_10K, between_10_20K, over_20K. This is solved in one pass as:

```
select less_10K = sum(FC[salary < 10000]),
       between_10_20K = sum(FC[10000 <= salary < 20000]),
       over_20K = sum(FC[20000 <= salary])
from employee
```

I leave it to you to expand the function calls this time.

Use in group by clause

Consider the table:

```
calls(name, from_area, to_area, cost)
```

and the requirement to display:

```
call_totals( name, call_type, total_cost)
```

where call_type is "local" if the from_area and the to_area are the same, else the call_type is "long_dist."

Again, this is a conventional two-pass solution with a temporary table:

```
insert into #temp
select name, call_type = 'local', total_cost = sum(cost)
        from calls
        where from_area = to_area
        group by name, 'local'

insert into #temp
select name, call_type = 'long_dist', total_cost = sum(cost)
        from calls
        where from_area != to_area
        group by name, 'long_dist'
```

which can be written in one pass as:

```
insert into #temp
select name, call_type = substring("locallong_dist",
                                isnull(1/FC[from_area = to_area], 6),
                                isnull(5/FC[from_area = to_area], 9)),
        total_cost = sum(cost)
from calls
group by name, substring("locallong_dist",
                        isnull(1/FC[from_area = to_area], 6),
                        isnull(5/FC[from_area = to_area], 9))

If from_area = to_area
        the FC[from_area = to_area] returns 1
        the isnull functions return 1 and 5 respectively
        the substring returns 'local'

If from_area != to_area
        the FC[from_area = to_area] returns 0
        the isnull functions return 6 and 9 respectively
        the substring returns 'long_dist'
```

Summary

There are a number of SQL issues which you should pay attention to as they are good, high performance SQL practices.

- Avoid the like operator when there is no wildcard

- Avoid the min and max functions in the same statement

- Do not use the having clause with columns

- Replace > with >= when there are a large number of duplicate values
- Avoid datatype conversion in where clauses and join clauses
- Always write search arguments in where clauses
- Unknown values in where clauses may cause table scans
- Avoid unknown table sizes in SQL batches and procedures
- Do not test variable values in where clauses—especially with an OR operator
- If you have to do row by row processing use cursors
- Learn how to use characteristic functions to avoid multiple table scans

SQL Server Errors

This section itemizes and describes the server error messages with a brief explanation of what caused them. These are fully described in the Error Messages manuals and this is the most obvious source of material on the server errors. If only all of them were documented!!!

The server error messages are divided into severity levels from 1 to 24, of which 1-16 are mainly informational or SQL error messages. Some of them are important of course, e.g., for a 605 error, but in general these are self explanatory and I have not included them here. Levels 17-24 are generally serious enough to stop the task or even the server, and levels 19-24 are always reported in the error log. Always remember with SQL Server that you can get more than one error at a time and that one error may show up as a different error depending on which command is running. The most obvious is a run-time 605 which may appear as a different allocation error if you run **dbcc checkalloc**.

The general meanings of the 17-24 severity levels are as follows.

level 17   In general, the command has run out of a configurable resource such as number of objects, or number of locks. These do not normally get logged in the errorlog, and you will hear about them only if the user contacts you when they occur. The easiest solution is to adjust the relevant configuration variable, although you should do a little investigation to determine why it occurred and if it will recur.

level 18   These are normally internal software errors. However, they often do not cause the application to fail or the connection to be dropped. If the user informs you about them, they should be communicated to Sybase.

level 19 An internal non-configurable resource has been exceeded. The command will fail and the connection will be lost. Check the errorlog and get in touch with Sybase.

level 20 An internal software error has occurred. The command will fail and the connection will be lost. Check the errorlog and get in touch with Sybase.

level 21 A severe software error has occurred which causes all processes to fail and usually the server to crash. If the server is still running, you should stop and restart it.

level 22 A corruption in a database table or index has occurred which caused the server to fail. It is most likely that the current command has not actually caused the problem but simply been the victim of another process' corruption. Look for previous hardware failures. You may be lucky when you restart the server and find the physical data is OK and the error was confined to the cache version of the data only. (It's not very likely, but worth checking. And you might have won the lottery as well!)

level 23 A data corruption which is severe enough to affect the integrity of the database. Again, the cause is most likely with another process. The server will fail. Again, check to see if the corruption was confined to the cache version.

level 24 In general, this is a media failure and you will need to reload and recover the databases. If you are unlucky, it can be caused by a corrupt **sysusages**.

The following is a list of the severe errors with a brief description and possible solution. If the solution does not remove the error, you will need to contact Technical Support. Remember, SQL Server will often generate multiple errors; always check the error log when an error occurs. And if you do fix an error which is associated with indexes or data it is always advisable to run a **checkdb** and a **checkalloc** before you dump the fixed database.

Error number	Description/solution
601	systhresholds could not be opened because the descriptor cannot be located
	Check to see if systhresholds exists: if it does, restart the server; if not, or the restart does not clear the problem, run **checkalloc**, **checkdb**, **checkcatalog** and see if there are any other problems
603	You have run out of system session descriptors
	Break the SQL down into several steps to reduce the number of user tables, system tables and/or worktables involved
605	There is a page allocation/linkage corruption
	Run **checkdb**, **checkalloc**
	Run **pglinkage**, **page** etc. to determine extent of the problem; if not a transient problem a database restore will be necessary
614	A row is smaller than the minimum length in the header
	Run **page** to determine extent of the problem
	If it is an index page drop, and recreate the index
	If a data page, try to recover the data using bcp or select into
	Run **checkdb** and **checkalloc**
	Load and recover the database
623	A row_id does not point to a data page
	Check extent of problem with **checktable** and **page**
	If transient, restart the server
	Drop, load and recover the database
624	A row_id from an index points to an incorrect or non-existent row
	Run **page** and **locateindexpgs** to determine the extent of the problem
	Drop and recreate the index
625	A row_id points to an offset entry with a negative value
	Run **page** and **locateindexpgs** to determine the extent of the problem
	Drop and recreate the index
629	A clustered index entry could not be deleted because the index entry points to another page
	Use **page** to determine the extent of the problem
	Drop and recreate the index
631	A delete based on row_id failed because the expected offset or row length did not match the actual values

Use **page** to determine the extent of the problem

If an index page, drop and recreate the index

If a data page try to recover the data using bcp or select into

Run **checkdb** and **checkalloc**

632 The server generated more than 2048 bytes when creating result set data

Run **checkdb** to determine the extent of the problem

644 A delete for a nonclustered index row could not find the row

Run **page** and **locateindexpgs** to determine the extent of the problem

Drop and recreate the index

Run **checktable** and **tablealloc**

702 You have exceeded the number of search conditions (128) or the 1962 row width limit in a union

Rewrite the SQL

706 The memory manager tried to deallocate a procedure header which it no longer owned

Run **procbuf** and **pss** to determine the extent of the problem

Restart the server

707 The memory manager could not release memory for a process header

Run **procbuf** and **pss** to determine the extent of the problem

Restart the server

803 The server has run out of session descriptors or an attempt was made to allocate a buffer to a session descriptor when it was already allocated

Check the errorlog for any other errors

Restart the server

804 A buffer held in a session descriptor could not be located

Restart the server

806 A logical page number did not map to a virtual page number

This can happen with invalid parameters to **page**

Run **page**, **checkdb**, **checkalloc** to determine the extent of the problem

Restart the server

If the error is transient you may have to reset the database status

Load and recover the database

813	A page in cache is in use but not marked as allocated
	This is serious as data may be lost by another allocation of the page before the deallocation attempt succeeds
	Dump tran ... with no_log can cause this: use **with truncate_only** if you can
	Checkpoint the database
	Run **checkalloc** with the **fix** option
	Restart the server
	Load and recover the database
821	The hash buffer associated with the cache page cannot be located
	Again **dump tran ... with no_log** can cause this
	Check for other errors
	Run **checkalloc** and **checkdb** to determine the extent of the problem
	Restart the server
822	An I/O failed because the device or file was not available
	Check device is online and/or file permissions are OK
	This error marks the database as suspect which you should reset directly on **sysdatabases** if the error was simply a device off-line or wrong permissions
823	I/O error on a request to a device
	Check device is online and/or file permissions are OK
	This can occur for Sun if the operating system is not configured properly for asynchronous I/O
	Run **checkdb** and **checkalloc** after fixing the problem
840	Device unavailable during start-up
	Check device is online and/or file permissions are OK
	This error marks the database as suspect which you should reset directly on **sysdatabases** if the error was simply a device off-line or wrong permissions
903	**sysindexes** cannot be accessed
	Usually a corruption often caused by overlapping raw partitions
	Run **checkdb** and **checkalloc** to determine the extent of the problem
	Load and restore the database
905	You have run out of open database descriptors
	Increase the **open databases** configuration parameter

906	Static locations in the system tables, e.g., DBINFO have been corrupted
	Run **checktable** to determine the extent of the problem
	Usually caused by overlapping raw partitions
	Load and restore the database
913	The server cannot locate the dbid in **sysdatabases**
	Run **checktable** on **sysdatabases** to determine the extent of the problem
	Load and recover **master**
933	Timestamp at end of log is not consistent with the root page of **syslogs**
	Reset database suspect status
	Run **checkdb**, **checkalloc** and **checkcatalog** to determine the extent of the problem
	Restart the server
	Load and recover the database
945	The page number does not map to the database
	Sometimes a **sysusages** corruption
	Check **sysusages** is OK
	Restart the server
	Load and restore **master** and rebuild **sysusages** if possible
	If **sysusages** OK load and restore user database
1105	You have run out of space
	Allocate some more space
	Dump the log
	If occurs during a recovery of **master**, restart with trace flag 3607 and clear space in master
1108	Object id in extent being deallocated does not match object being deallocated
	Run **checkalloc** and **extentdump** to determine the extent of the problem
	Restart the server
	Load and recover the database
1120	Invalid allocation page number in the OAM
	Run **listoam**, **page**, **checkalloc** to determine the extent of the problem

	Try to recreate the index if OAM is for an index
	If a data page, try to recover the data using bcp or select into
	Load and recover the database
1129	Update to OAM entry will cause page count to go negative
	Run **listoam**, **page**, **checkalloc** to determine the extent of the problem
	Recreate index if OAM is for an index
	If a data page try to recover the data using bcp or select into
	Load and recover the database
1133	Page is not an OAM page
	Run **listoam**, **page**, **checkalloc** to determine the extent of the problem
	Recreate index if OAM is for an index
	If a data page try to recover the data using bcp or select into
	Load and recover the database
1134	Server fails to get address lock for OAM page
	Run **listoam**, **page** to determine the extent of the problem
	Call Technical Support
1142	Invalid OAM page
	This may be caused by SQL: using an OAM function (data_pgs, rowcnt etc.) across databases
	Run **listoam**, **page**, **checkalloc** to determine the extent of the problem
	Recreate index if OAM is for an index
	If a data page try to recover the data using bcp or select into
1143	OAM page status or object_id incorrect
	Run **listoam**, **page**, **checkalloc** to determine the extent of the problem
	Recreate index if OAM is for an index
	If a data page try to recover the data using bcp or select into
1203	Attempt to unlock an object which is not locked
	Run **lock** to determine the extent of the problem
1204	You have run out of locks
	Reconfigure **number of locks**
1265	Lock record structure is invalid

	Run **lock** to determine the extent of the problem
	Restart the server
1501	Sort failed in create index
	Reset **csortbufsize** and **csortpgcount** to 0
	Restart the server
1509	Row compared with itself in a sort
	Run **checktable** and **tablealloc** to determine the extent of the problem
	Try to copy the data with **bcp** or **select into**
1520	Create index sort failed, because space allocated from used pages count was incorrect
	Update count with **tablealloc**
1602	Unable to initialize network connection
	Interfaces file corrupt or not available
1605	You have run out of user connections or sockets
	This can occur with two different processes using the same network IP address
	Run **resource** to determine current configuration
1813	Cannot create new database because of uncleared buffers or corrupt **sysdatabases**
	Run **checkcatalog** to determine the extent of the problem
	Restart server
2502	Page chain linkage inconsistency
	Run **checkdb**, **checkalloc**, **pglinkage** and **page** to determine the extent of the problem
	If an index, drop and recreate
	Try to copy data using **bcp** or **select into**
2503	Page chain linkage inconsistency
	Run **pglinkage** and **page** to determine the extent of the problem
	If an index, drop and recreate
	Try to copy data using **bcp** or **select into**
2506	Inconsistent values in the column adjust table
	Run **page** to determine the extent of the problem
	If an index, drop and recreate

	Try to copy data using **bcp** or **select into**
2507	Inconsistent values in the row offset table
	Run **page** to determine the extent of the problem
	If an index page, drop and recreate the index
	Try to copy data using **bcp** or **select into**
2509	Row does not have offset table entry
	Run **page** to determine the extent of the problem
	If an index page, drop and recreate the index
	Try to copy data using **bcp** or **select into**
2510	Mismatch between index and data
	Run **page, prtipage** to determine the extent of the problem
	Drop and recreate the index
2511	Index records are not in correct sequence
	Run **page, prtipage** to determine the extent of the problem
	Drop and recreate the index
2513	Object exists in one system table but not in another
	Run **checkcatalog** to determine the extent of the problem
	Call Technical Support
2514	Mismatch between **syscolumns** and **systypes**
	Identify the rows in **syscolumns** which do not exist in **systypes**: this will show the existing type
	Update these rows to the correct type (requires **allow updates**)
2517	Mismatch between **sysprocedures** and **sysobjects**
	Remove the procedure from **sysprocedures**
	Recreate the procedure
2519	The last checkpoint on syslogs does not agree with the DBINFO structure
	This a transient error caused by running **checkcatalog** when not in single user mode
	Restart the server
2521	Page currently used but not allocated
	Run **page** to determine the extent of the problem
	Run **tablealloc** or **indexalloc** with the **fix** option
2524	Length of row does not match calculation using the offset entries

	Run **page** to determine the extent of the problem
	If an index drop and recreate the index
	Try to copy the data using **bcp** or **select into**
2525	Mismatching object_id between page, extent and sysindexes
	Use **page** to determine the extent of the problem
	Drop and recreate clustered index
	Try to copy the data using **bcp** or **select into**
2529	Mismatch between the page number in the page header and the location on disk
	Run **page, checkdb, checkalloc** to determine the extent of the problem
	Try to copy the data using **bcp** or **select into**
2540	Page is marked as allocated but not being used
	Run **page, checkdb, checkalloc, allocdump** to determine the extent of the problem
2541	Mismatch between the extent and sysindexes
	Run **page, checkdb, checkalloc, allocdump** to determine the extent of the problem
	If an index drop and recreate the index
	Try to copy the data using **bcp** or **select into**
2544	Extent allocated but not used
	Run **page, checkalloc, allocdump** to determine the extent of the problem
	If an index drop and recreate
	Try to copy the data using **bcp** or **select into**
2546	Extent has page allocated but page not being used
	This can happen if you do not use single user mode when running **checkalloc**
	Run **page, checkalloc, allocdump** to determine the extent of the problem
2559	Empty page in page chain
	Drop and recreate clustered index
	Or, copy the data using **bcp**
2596	Free byte offset in page header is incorrect
	Use **page** to determine the extent of the problem

	If an index, drop and recreate the index
	Try to copy the data using **bcp** or **select into**
2610	The server fails to update a nonclustered index after a page split
	Run **page, prtipage, locateindexpgs** to determine the extent of the problem
	Drop and recreate the index
2620	The actual offset and the offset table entry do not match
	Run **page, checkdb, checkalloc** to determine the extent of the problem
	If an index, drop and recreate
	Try to copy the data using **bcp** or **select into**
2824	Process tried to hold multiple process buffers for a view, rule or default
	This can occur when a view referenced by a procedure is dropped
	If the view exists, restart the server
3002	An unexpected page number found during a dump
	Can occur if defined two raw partitions on the same disk space
	Run **checkalloc** and **checkdb**
	Try to copy the data using **bcp** or **select into**
	Restart the server
3104	Dump found a higher page number than allowed in the database
	Can occur if define two raw partitions on the same disk space
	Run **checkalloc** and **checkdb**
	Try to copy the data using **bcp** or **select into**
	Can also occur if using Unix file system files for the database and you run out of space
3202	Received MULTARG is not for device expected
	The MULTARG is a memory structure used for dump device information
	Call Technical Support
3203	A remote procedure call error on the SQL Server side
	Check the connection as this is usually an I/O error
3225	An I/O failure when the load is clearing the unallocated database pages
3307	An attempt to release a lock but the page is not locked

	Use **sp_lock** and **lock** to determine the extent of the problem
	Restart the server
3404	A page was found on the log which has a different object_id in the header
	Use **page** to determine the extent of the problem
	Try to copy the object data using **bcp** or **select into**
	Load and recover the database
3418	Startserver could not recover a system database
	Call Technical Support
3425	Load could not find a BEGINXACT/ENDXACT pair
	Use **log** to determine the extent of the problem if you can
3626	The command ran out of stack space
	Split the SQL into several simpler commands
	Increase the stack size
3904	A rollback cannot undo a page split
	Use **page** to determine the extent of the problem
	If an index, recreate the index
	Load and recover the database
4204	A dump tran ran out of space in the log
	Extend the log segment
	Dump tran ... with no_log
4219	An attempt was made to deallocate the last page of the log
	Use **checktable, tablealloc, log** to determine the extent of the problem
	Use **tablealloc** with **fix** (need to be in single user mode)
6902	Recovery detected a page timestamp which does not agree with the log timestamps
	Can be caused by **shutdown with nowait** or **dump tran ... with no_log**
	Try to recover from a backup
7902	A mismatch between the expected length of a text column and its actual length
	Use **checkdb, page** to determine the extent of the problem
	Try to copy the data using **bcp**

	Run **checkalloc** with **fix**
7930	A mismatch between the index keys and the keys in the data pages
	Use **page, prtipage, locateindexpgs** to determine the extent of the problem
	Rebuild the clustered index
7939	Allocation pages belonging to an object are not recorded in the OAM
	Use **listoam, checkalloc** in single user mode to determine the extent of the problem
	Run **checkalloc** with **fix**
7940	The page count in the OAM is different from the number of pages in the page chain
	Use **listoam, checkalloc** in single user mode to determine the extent of the problem
	Run **checkalloc** with **fix**
7949	OAM number of allocated pages is different from number of pages in page chain
	Use **listoam, checkalloc** in single user mode to determine the extent of the problem
	Run **checkalloc** with **fix**
8201	Incorrect session descriptor count
	Restart the server
8203	Incorrect session descriptor state
	Restart the server
8204	Incorrect system catalog id when locating a session descriptor
	Call Technical Support
8207	You have run out of open object descriptors
	Reconfigure number of open objects
8211	An incorrect hash table or hashing id for a session descriptor
	Restart the server
8402	Expected row not found in **sysindexes**
	If an index recreate the index
8412	No object id supplied in a sysindexes manager call
	Call Technical Support
8704	An address lock could not be obtained
	Restart the server

Client-Library errors

It's a bit more difficult to get a list of Client-Library errors, so I have reproduced them in full based on a list I obtained courtesy of Sybase Maidenhead.

Client-Library message numbers are 4 bytes long.

byte 1: the layer that is reporting the message, decoded with CS_LAYER()

byte 2: the message origin, decoded with CS_ORIGIN()

byte 3: the message severity, decoded by CS_SEVERITY()

byte 4: the layer specific message number, decoded with CS_NUMBER()

Layer

Value	Meaning
1	user api layer
2	cslib user api layer
3	generic protocol layer
4	protocol specific layer
5	network packet layer

Origin

If Layer is 1,3,4 or 5 then the meaning of Origin is as follows:

Value of Layer	Value of Origin	Meaning
1, 3, 4, 5	1	External error
	2	Internal Client Library error
	3	Internal net library error
	4	Internal common library error
	5	Internal intl library error
	6	Internal async manager error
	7	Internal memory management error
2	1	External error

Value of Layer	Value of Origin	Meaning
	2	Internal CS-Library error
	4	Common library error
	5	Intl library error

Severity

Value	ct-library	Meaning
0	CS_SV_INFORM	No error has occurred. The message is informational.
1	CS_SV_API_FAIL	A Client-Library routine generated an error. Typically caused by a bad parameter or calling sequence.
2	CS_SV_RETRY_FAIL	An operation has failed, but the operation can be retried e.g., a network read that times out.
3	CS_SV_RESOURCE_FAIL	A resource error has occurred. Typically caused by a malloc failure or lack of file descriptors.
4	CS_SV_CONFIG_FAIL	A SYBASE configuration error has been detected e.g., missing interfaces or localization files, unknown server
5	CS_SV_COMM_FAIL	An unrecoverable error in the server communication channel has occurred. Server connection is not salvageable.
6	CS_SV_INTERNAL_FAIL	An internal Client-Library error has occurred.
7	CS_SV_FATAL	A serious error has occurred. All server connections are unusable.

Number

Value of layer	Value of Number	Meaning
1	0	State validation succeeded.
	1	The information being retrieved will not fit in a buffer of %1! bytes.
	2	Memory allocation failure.
	3	The parameter %1! cannot be NULL.
	4	When %1! is NULL the %2! parameter must be 0.

Value of layer	Value of Number	Meaning
	5	An illegal value of %1! given for parameter %2!.
	6	The maximum number of connections have already been opened.
	7	The server does not support the KEEP_CON capability.
	8	The %1! parameter must be NULL.
	9	The %1! parameter must be set to CS_UNUSED.
	10	Boolean values must be set to either CS_TRUE or CS_FALSE.
	11	A CS_SIGNAL_CB cannot be installed because the platform does not support interrupt-driven network I/O.
	12	A CS_COMPLETION_CB cannot be installed because the platform does not provide the interrupt or polling capabilities needed.
	13	This property cannot be set after a connection to a server has been established.
	14	This property/capability cannot be set.
	15	It is necessary to be connected to a server in order to get this property/capability.
	16	This routine cannot be called while results are pending for a command that has been sent to the server.
	17	The command structure already supports a declared cursor.
	18	A cursor must be declared before this command type can be initialized.
	19	This routine may be called only after a CS_SEND_DATA_CMD command has been initialized.
	20	A command must be initialized before this routine can be called.
	21	This routine cannot be used while a cursor is declared on the command structure.
	22	A cursor has already been declared on this command structure.
	23	The command cannot be initialized after the cursor has been opened.

Value of layer	Value of Number	Meaning
	24	The cursor on this command structure has already been opened.
	25	Cursor updates and cursor deletes are not allowed after ct_fetch() returns CS_END_DATA.
	26	A command has already been initialized on this command structure.
	27	The initialized command cannot have parameters.
	28	A command has already been initialized.
	29	This type of command cannot be batched with the command already initialized on the command structure.
	30	A row must be fetched before this routine may be used.
	31	A cursor rows command cannot be initialized after a cursor open command has been initialized.
	32	The connection's capabilities do not support this type of request.
	33	This routine cannot be called after ct_results() returns a result type of CS_CURSOR_RESULT.
	34	This routine cannot be called after ct_results() returns a result type of CS_CMD_DONE.
	35	This routine cannot be called after ct_results() returns a result type of CS_COMPUTE_RESULT.
	36	This routine cannot be called after ct_results() returns a result type of CS_COMPFMT_RESULT.
	37	This routine cannot be called after ct_results() returns a result type of CS_MSG_RESULT.
	38	This routine cannot be called after ct_results() returns a result type of CS_PARAM_RESULT.
	39	This routine cannot be called after ct_results() returns a result type of CS_ROWFMT_RESULT.
	40	This routine cannot be called after ct_results() returns a result type of CS_CMD_FAIL.
	41	This routine cannot be called after ct_results() returns a result type of CS_CMD_SUCCEED.
	42	This routine cannot be called after ct_results() returns a result type of CS_ROW_RESULT.

Value of layer	Value of Number	Meaning
	43	This routine cannot be called after ct_results() returns a result type of CS_STATUS_RESULT.
	44	This routine cannot be called since an asynchronous operation is currently pending.
	45	There is an internal error in the user api layer.
	46	An illegal value of %1! was placed in the %2! field of the CS_DATAFMT structure.
	47	When defining parameters, names must be supplied for either all of the parameters or none of the parameters.
	48	The server does not support parameters of type %1!.
	49	This routine cannot be called because another command structure has results pending.
	50	The connection has been marked dead.
	51	Exactly one of %1! and %2! must be non-NULL.
	52	In-line error handling must be initialized with the CS_INIT operation before any other ct_diag() action may be taken.
	53	There was not enough memory available to save messages. All previously stored messages have been cleared.
	54	In-line error handling has already been initialized for this connection structure.
	55	WARNING: Existing error and message handlers have been removed.
	56	The message limit cannot be set to a value less than the number of Client-Library or server messages which are currently saved.
	57	A result of type %1! cannot be bound to a program variable of type %2!
	58	The format field of the CS_DATAFMT structure must be CS_FMT_UNUSED if the datatype field is %1!.
	59	If the buffer parameter is NULL then the %1! parameter must also be NULL.
	60	There is a usage error. This routine has been called at an illegal time.
	61	Item of %1! is not greater than the largest item bound.
	62	Item %1! has already been read.

Value of layer	Value of Number	Meaning
	63	Read from the server has timed out.
	64	The option to specify debug files is not yet supported. All debug information will be sent to stdout.
	65	The requested type of trace information is not yet supported.
	66	A context structure must be supplied when setting/clearing this type of debug information.
	67	A connection structure must be supplied when setting/clearing this type of debug information.
	68	Descriptor not found.
	69	A descriptor of name %1! already exists on the connection
	70	The descriptor count of %1! is not possible because it exceeds the maximum count of %2!.
	72	The descriptor %1! has already been associated with a command structure.
	73	The %1! field of the CS_DATAFMT structure must be set to CS_UNUSED.
	74	When %1! is NULL the %2! field of the CS_DATAFMT structure must be set to 0.
	75	Inconsistent parameter settings were found for the dynamic descriptor when it was used as input parameters to a command All descriptor values must be set.
	76	Inconsistent parameter names were found for the dynamic descriptor when it was used as input parameters to a command. A parameter name must be supplied for all of the items or none of the items
	77	A dynamic descriptor is being used for input parameters; therefore ct_param() cannot be called.
	78	There are no rows affected.
	79	The bind of result set item %1! resulted in an overflow
	80	The bind of result set item %1! resulted in an underflow.
	81	The bind of result set item %1! failed because an illegal precision value was specified.

Value of layer	Value of Number	Meaning
	82	The bind of result set item %1! failed because an illegal scale value was specified.
	83	The bind of result set item %1! failed due to a syntax error in the source data.
	84	The bind of result set item %1! failed due to an illegal value in the format field of a CS_DATAFMT structure.
	85	The bind of result set item %1! failed because the source field value was not within the domain of legal values.
	86	The bind of result set item %1! failed because of an attempt to divide by zero.
	87	The bind of result set item %1! failed because Client-Library was unable to get a resource.
	88	The bind of result set item %1! failed. The cause of failure is unknown.
	89	The data for column %1! is NULL but no indicator was available.
	90	The data for column %1! was truncated but no indicator was available.
	91	The bind was missing for column %1!.
	92	A CS_IODESC structure must be set with ct_data_info() before ct_send_data() can be called.
	93	%1! bytes exceeds the amount of bytes specified for this send data operation. Only %2! more bytes can be sent.
	94	The number of bytes specified for this send data operation have not been sent. %1! more bytes need to be sent.
	95	The value %1! was truncated.
	96	No browse information exists.
	97	A CS_IODESC can only be retrieved for text or image columns. Column %1! is not a text or image column.
	98	A CS_IODESC cannot be retrieved for a column that has not been read. Column %1! has not been read.
	99	Capabilities cannot be set after a connection has been established.
	100	Request capabilities cannot be set.
	101	There was a failure initializing the Client-Library error cache.

Value of layer	Value of Number	Meaning
	102	This option is not supported by server.
	103	This routine can be called only if the CS_HIDDEN_KEYS property has been set to CS_TRUE.
	104	This message should not be seen.
	105	There was an unexpected failure while retrieving key data.
	106	Column %1! is not a key column.
	107	Column %1! is not nullable. The key data for a column can be set to NULL only if the column accepts NULL values.
	108	The key data supplied for column %1! exceeds the maximum length defined for the column.
	109	There was an unexpected failure while setting key data.
	110	A valid count does not exist for the descriptor.
	111	This message should not be seen.
	112	%1! rows affected.
	113	The command structure given to this routine contains notification data or extended error data. This routine does not accept such a command structure.
	114	Extended error data does not exist for message %1!.
	115	A remote password cannot be set when a connection to a server exists.
	116	The server name/password combination supplied exceeds the 255 byte limit enforced by Client-Library.
	117	The CS_DISABLE_POLL property must be set to CS_FALSE when this routine is called.
	118	Unable to open file %1!.
	119	The data must be NULL when defining CS_INPUTVALUE parameters for a ct_cursor(CS_CURSOR_DECLARE) command.
	120	The buffer must be NULL when the current result set consists of format information only.
	121	There is no data associated with descriptor item %1!.
	122	Results are currently being fetched into this descriptor. A descriptor count of %1! is less than the result set size of %2!.

Value of layer	Value of Number	Meaning
	123	A descriptor has already been specified for the current command.
	124	ct_param() has already been used to define parameters for the command.
	125	A descriptor of size %1! is not large enough for a result set of size %2!.
	126	Another command structure is using the descriptor.
	127	This routine cannot be called if ct_bind() has already been called for the result set.
	128	The datatype field of a CS_IODESC must be set to either CS_TEXT_TYPE or CS_IMAGE_TYPE.
	129	An invalid locale was supplied in the %1! structure.
	130	An invalid precision or scale in the CS_NUMERIC or CS_DECIMAL value was supplied.
	131	A memory pool cannot be set or cleared if open connections exist on the context structure.
	132	The bind of result set item %1! resulted in truncation.
	133	No rows are affected. More result sets will follow.
	134	The specified id already exists on this connection.
	135	The specified id does not exist on this connection.
	136	A string of length 0 is not allowed for parameter %1!.
	137	A bind count of %1! is not consistent with the count supplied for existing binds. The current bind count is %2!.
	138	A data length of %1! exceeds the maximum length allowed for %2! data.
	139	Setting the precision or scale to CS_SRC_VALUE is allowed only if the corresponding result set column is of type numeric or decimal.
	140	Scale cannot be set greater than precision.
	141	%1! must be 0 or CS_UNUSED when %2! is NULL.
	142	This property can be used only in the appropriate Client-Library callback. This property cannot be used in main-line code.

Value of layer	Value of Number	Meaning
	143	The maximum number of connections cannot be set to a value less than the number of currently existing connections.
	144	This property can be used only if a cursor exists on the command structure.
	145	This property cannot be set when the command structure has results pending or has an open cursor.
	146	The CS_LOCALE structure supplied is not valid.
	147	This routine can be used only with the debug version of Client-Library.
	148	The Client-Library async manager was not able to continue. This connection has been marked dead.
	149	The current row's key has been partially set with ct_keydata().
		Every key column must be set with ct_keydata() before this operation can continue.
	150	This routine cannot be called because the context structure is in an undefined state. This is probably due to a ct_exit() failure.
	151	A connection to the server must exist on the connection structure before this routine can be called.
	152	A command structure must be supplied for a CS_CANCEL_CURRENT operation.
	153	This routine cannot be called when a connection to a server exists on the CS_CONNECTION structure.
	154	This routine cannot be called because the connection structure is in an undefined state.
	155	This routine cannot be called when the command structure is idle.
	156	This routine cannot be called when a command has been initialized but not sent.
	157	This routine cannot be called until ct_results() has been called for the command that was sent to the server.
	158	This routine can be called only if fetchable results are available to be read.

Value of layer	Value of Number	Meaning
	159	This routine can be called only if the command structure is idle.
	160	This routine can be called only if the cursor rows are available to be read.
	161	This routine can be called only if regular row results are available.
	162	A receive passthru operation is not legal while the connection is in the middle of processing results in the standard manner.
	163	This routine cannot be called until all fetchable results have been completely processed.
	164	This routine can be called only if compute results are available.
	165	This routine cannot be called when a nested cursor command is initialized.
	166	This routine cannot be called while the results of a nested cursor command are not completely processed.
	167	This routine cannot be called because the command structure is in an undefined state.
	168	This routine cannot be called because a receive passthru operation is in progress on this command structure.
	169	This routine cannot be called because a send passthru operation is in progress on this command structure.
	170	This routine cannot be called after ct_results() returns a result type of CS_DESCRIBE_RESULT.
	171	A cursor must be opened before this command type can be initialized.
	172	This routine cannot be called because the CS_COMMAND structure is in the middle of a send data operation.
	173	A return status of CS_PENDING must be returned from a completion callback if additional async operations have been initiated.
	174	A context structure must be supplied when setting/clearing this type of callback.
	175	There is not a callback handler installed for signal %1!.

Value of layer	Value of Number	Meaning
	176	The server does not support null parameters of type %1!.
	177	The length of the null-terminated string parameter %1! exceeds the maximum length allowed.
	178	This routine cannot be called until at least one call to ct_send_data() has been made.
	179	A cursor row must be fetched before this command can be initialized.
	180	This command must come immediately after a CS_CURSOR_DECLARE command has been initialized.
	181	This command is not allowed when the cursor is closed.
	182	This command is not allowed after all the cursor's rows have been fetched.
2	0	No error.
	1	Unknown error.
	2	The information being retrieved will not fit in a buffer of %1! bytes.
	3	Memory allocation failure
	4	The parameter %1! cannot be NULL.
	5	When %1! is NULL the %2! parameter must be 0.
	6	An illegal value of %1! was given for parameter %2!.
	7	The %1! parameter must be NULL.
	8	The %1! parameter must be set to CS_UNUSED.
	9	The property %1! cannot be set or cleared.
	10	An invalid locale pointer was passed in.
	11	The parameter %1! points to an illegal datatype value.
	12	An unknown locale name was passed in.
	13	A CS_GET operation cannot be performed on type %1!.
	14	Localization information could not be loaded.
	15	Error handling could not be initialized.
	16	Conversion between %1! and %2! datatypes is not supported.
	17	The format field of a CS_DATAFMT structure should be CS_FMT_UNUSED when the datatype is %1!

Value of layer	Value of Number	Meaning
	18	An illegal value of %1! was placed in the %2! field of the CS_DATAFMT structure.
	19	An illegal locale pointer was specified in the CS_DATAFMT structure.
	20	The conversion/operation resulted in overflow.
	21	The conversion/operation resulted in underflow.
	22	An illegal precision value was encountered.
	23	An illegal scale value was encountered.
	24	The conversion/operation was stopped due to a syntax error in the source field.
	25	The datatype value is outside the domain of legal values for the datatype.
	26	A division by zero is not allowed.
	27	WARNING: Existing error and message handlers have been deinstalled.
	28	There was not enough memory available to save messages. All previously stored messages have been cleared.
	29	In-line error handling must be initialized with the CS_INIT operation before any other cs_diag() action may be taken.
	30	The message limit cannot be set to a value less than the number of CS-Library messages currently saved.
	31	The context structure cannot be dropped because the application has not exited from %1!.
	32	When the type is CS_DT_CONFMT only a CS_SET operation is allowed.
	33	The requested translation is not supported.
	34	Some of the characters could not be translated.
	35	The conversion/operation stopped due to a style error.
	36	The result is truncated because the conversion/operation resulted in overflow
	37	cs_ctx_name failed to match the given keys.
	38	The string was not copied because this would result in overflow.
	39	The string could not be built. An illegal place holder was found in the text string.

Value of layer	Value of Number	Meaning
	40	Only 0, 1, or 2 stars are allowed in the format string.
	41	An unknown datatype token was found in the format string.
	42	The format string cannot be NULL.
	43	The custom format specifier is too long.
	44	A custom format specifier was not found to match the specifier in the format string.
	45	Bad locale handler for cs_locale on types CS_SYB_LANG, CS_SYB_CHARSET or CS_SYB_LANG_CHARSET.
	46	Can not access localization file %1!.
	47	%1! Connection exception—Connection does not exist.
	48	%1! Connection exception—Connection name in use.
	49	%1! Invalid cursor name.
	50	%1! Invalid SQL statement identifier.
	51	%1! cs_objects: error performing requested operation.
	52	An internal buffer overflow occurs.
4	1	There is a tds protocol error. Premature end of the datastream was encountered.
	2	There is a tds protocol error. An illegal tds version was received.
	3	There is a tds protocol error. An illegal login status was received.
	4	There is a tds protocol error. There are too many bytes in the datastream.
	5	memory allocation failure.
	6	There is a tds protocol error. Duplicate ALT ID was seen while processing results."
	7	There is a tds protocol error. Invalid ALT operator was seen while processing results.
	8	There is a tds protocol error. Invalid ALT id was seen while processing results.
	9	There is a tds protocol error. Invalid ALT column count was seen while processing results.

Value of layer	Value of Number	Meaning
	10	There is a tds protocol error. Invalid column number was seen while processing results.
	11	There is a tds protocol error. Invalid table index was seen while processing results.
	12	There is a tds protocol error. An illegal browse status was received.
	13	There is a tds protocol error. An illegal capability type was received.
	14	There is a tds protocol error. An invalid cursor name was received.
	15	There is a tds protocol error. A duplicate cursor id was received.
	16	There is a tds protocol error. An invalid cursor id was received.
	17	There is a tds protocol error. An invalid cursor row count was received.
	18	There is a tds protocol error. An invalid cursor status was received.
	19	There is a tds protocol error. An invalid done status was received.
	20	There is a tds protocol error. An illegal DONEINPROC token stream was received.
	21	There is a tds protocol error. An invalid dynamic status was received.
	22	There is a tds protocol error. An invalid dynamic statement length was received.
	23	There is a tds protocol error. An invalid dynamic type was received.
	24	There is a tds protocol error. An invalid dynamic id was received.
	25	There is a tds protocol error. An invalid packet size was received.
	26	There is a tds protocol error. An illegal ENVCHANGE type was received.
	27	There is a tds protocol error. An invalid message status was received.

Value of layer	Value of Number	Meaning
	28	There is a tds protocol error. An illegal token was received.
	29	There is a tds protocol error. An invalid option command was received.
	30	There is a tds protocol error. An invalid option type was received.
	31	There is a tds protocol error. An invalid order by stream was received.
	32	There is a tds protocol error. A PARAMFMT was received with no parameters specified.
	33	There is a tds protocol error. An invalid PARAMFMT stream was received.
	34	There is a tds protocol error. A ROWFMT was received with no columns specified.
	35	There is a tds protocol error. An invalid ROWFMT stream was received.
	36	There is a tds state machine error. An illegal tds token sequence was received
	37	There is a tds state machine error. Attempted operation with results pending. This is an internal error.
	38	There is a tds login error. Illegal number of parameters seen during negotiation.
	39	There is a tds protocol error. An invalid message id was received during login negotiation.
	40	There is a tds protocol error. An invalid column status was received.
	41	There is a tds protocol error. An invalid datatype was received.
	42	There is a tds protocol error. An invalid numeric precision was received.
	43	There is a tds protocol error. An invalid numeric scale was received.
	44	The attempt to connect to the server failed.
	45	There is an internal tds layer error. Access to the row buffer manager failed.

Value of layer	Value of Number	Meaning
	46	There is a tds login error. An attempt was made by the server to encrypt a password, but no encryption handler was installed.
	47	There is a tds login error. The installed encryption handler returned a status that was not CS_SUCCEED.
	48	There is a tds login error. An attempt was made by the server to issue a security challenge, but no challenge handler was installed.
	49	There is a tds login error. The installed challenge handler returned a status that was not CS_SUCCEED.
	50	There is an internal tds layer error. An error was returned from the server while processing an internal tds stream.
	51	There is an internal tds layer error. An unexpected error was returned from common library.
	52	There is an internal tds layer error. An unexpected error was returned from the async manager.
5	1	There was an error encountered while closing the connection.
	2	There was an error encountered while releasing the address.
	3	There was an error encountered while resolving the address.
	4	There was an error encountered while establishing the connection.
	5	There was an error encountered while executing the expedited write.
	6	There was an error while executing the network read.
	7	There was an error while executing the network write.
	8	There was an error encountered while opening the address dictionary.
	9	There was an error encountered while closing the address dictionary.
	10	A read was attempted on a connection already executing a read.

Value of layer	Value of Number	Meaning
	11	A write was attempted on a connection already executing a write
	12	State error: trying to write when connection is expecting a read.
	13	State error: trying to read when connection is expecting a write.
	14	Buffer is too small to fit a whole packet.
	15	Reading from the network while there remains unprocessed data from the last read.
	16	There was an error encountered while getting the address information.
	17	There was an error encountered while getting the address property.
	18	There is a protocol packet error. An illegal length was received.
	128	There was an error encountered while initializing network option recordkeeping.
	129	There was an error encountered while setting a network option.
	130	unused.
	131	There was an error encountered while initializing Net-Library.
	132	There was an error encountered while initializing Net-Library engine.
	133	There was an error encountered while setting Net-Library call-back.
	134	There was an error encountered while exiting Net-Library engine.
	135	There was an error encountered while exiting Net-Library.
	136	There was an error encountered while setting Net-Library callback mode.
	137	There was an error encountered while chaining signals in Net-Library.

Page Header Status Bits

Status Value	Description
0x0001	Data page
0x0002	Nonclustered index page
0x0004	Overflow page
0x0008	Page has an overflow page
0x0010	Free row number in offset table
0x0020	Text page Or Multi-column densities for distribution page
0x0040	Distribution page
0x0080	No variable length columns on page
0x0100	Last insert was at pfreeoff
0x0200	Page has disconnected overflow page
0x0400	All allocated extents on this log allocpg are in unbroken series from first on page to highest allocated
0x0800	For the future
0x1000	Page has offset table for binary search
0x4000	Distribution page has new style density Or First page of text fragment
0x8000	OAM page
0x0008	OAM page has attributes

0x0004	Sort bit is on in extents
0x0002	OAM needs garbage collection
0x0010	OAM has been deallocated

dbcc Commands

Command	Description
allocdump	Information about extents for an allocation page
bhash	Validate the integrity of the buffer hash table and display table entries
bufcount	Display up to the 10 longest buffer chains and the average chain length
buffer	Displays buffer headers and pages from buffer cache
bytes	Displays bytes in hex and ASCII from start address
checkalloc	Detects allocation errors in a database
checkcatalog	Checks the consistency of the system tables
checkdb	Validates the integrity of the data and index pages for each table
checktable	Validates the integrity of the data and index pages for a table
checkobjcache	Displays the cache bindings for an object and scans other caches for buffers in the wrong cache
connection_hangup	Closes a connection to another server
cursorinfo	Information for a specific cursor active for a spid
dbinfo	Displays the dbinfo structure
dbrecover	Run recovery on a database which has not been recovered
dbrepair	Updates or repairs database information
dbtable	Displays the dbtable structure
des	Display a descriptor structure (DES)

Command	Description
descount	Display the bucket number and chain size for the longest chains in the hash table
engine	Displays the network I/O tasks assigned to each engine
extentcheck	Display extents used by an object
extentdump	Display extent structure for a page number
findnotfullextents	Display extent ids for an object which has unused pages
findstranded	Display non-syslogs events on logsegment
fix_text	Update text for a new multi-byte character set
flushlog	Write all dirty log pages to disk
force_prefetch	Specify the global I/O prefetch value
gettrunc	Display the current status of the log transfer state for a database
help	Displays syntax of dbcc commands
indexalloc	Validate and/or fix integrity of an object's allocation for a specific indid
iosize	Set I/O size for an object
listoam	Display the OAM information for an object
locateindexpgs	Display references within an index to a specified page
lock	Display current table, page, address and semaphore locks
log	Display the transaction log
logprint	Write a message to the errorlog
logtransfer	Retrieve records to be formatted by the ltm and sent to Replication Server
memusage	Display server memory usage information
netmemshow	Display network memory fragments
netmemusage	display buffer size, buffer status and spid of the process for each memory fragment
object_stats	Display wait times for page locks on a per database/object basis
page	Display the contents of a page
pglinkage	Traverse and validate a page chain
pktmemshow	Display read, write and overflow buffers for active users
printaddress	Display information on each memory pool that has memory allocated to it

Command	Description
procbuf	Display procedure buffer headers and procedure headers from procedure cache
prtipage	Display page number pointed to by each index row in a page
pss	Display the contents of a process status structure
rebuildextents	Rebuild extents and OAM pages for an object
reindex	Validate and rebuild indexes after a sort order change
remap	Convert pre-10 procedure objects to system 10 format; also compresses procedure objects
resource	Displays configuration information
settrunc	Modifies the ltm information
show_bucket	Search the buffer cache for a page
showcache	Display the buffer pools for a cache
stacktrace	Print a stack trace for a process
tablealloc	Validate the integrity of an object's allocation
textalloc	Validate the integrity of an object's allocation for text/image columns
thresholds	Display the threshold cache and segment array for a dbtable structure
tune	Modify configuration run time values
update_tmode	Modify the current transaction mode for a stored procedure
usedextents	Display extents in use for a database or log device
user_stats	Display wait times for locks on a spid basis
xls	Display the ULC for a user or flush the ULC to syslogs

Adaptive Server 11.5

This appendix describes what I know about the next major release—Adaptive server 11.5. The majority of this information comes from an internal white paper dated July 1996 and a Sybase presentation in April 1997 and so it may not actually appear in the stated form but it is the current indication of what Sybase is putting into the next release.

The features may be summarized as:

performance

- Parallel processing
- Asynchronous prefetch
- Bi-directional index scans
- Partitioned clustered tables
- Index cache manager

security

- Integration with external security services
- User defined roles
- Proxy authorization

recovery

- Fault isolation at page level
- Point-in-time recovery

NT integration

- MAPI
- Event log
- Perfmon

extensibility

- Distributed query processing
- Logical process manager (task priority)
- Resource governor
- Extended stored procedures

Performance

Parallel processing

Adaptive server 11.5 provides parallel processing for select and utility commands. The operation uses multiple execution threads and also benefits by running on partitioned tables.

Parallel select

Adaptive server 11.5 supports parallel query execution for the following:

- Table scans
- Clustered index scans
- Nonclustered index scans
- Aggregates

- Joins

- Order by

- Select into

A parallel execution of a query uses multiple worker threads taken from a pool of work processes. Each worker thread accesses a portion of the data, depending on the command being executed and the type of access, and merges the results to create the query output to the client. The optimizer is aware of when parallel execution is possible and will check if a parallel plan is faster than a serial execution. Even if the optimizer chooses a parallel plan it may not be used if insufficient work processes are available to execute the command. The number of work processes chosen by the optimizer depends on the partitioning of the table and the type of plan chosen.

If a table scan of a partitioned table is being carried out, the number of work processes is set equal to the number of partitions. In this case, a work process cannot scan more than one partition and parallelism will not be used if sufficient work processes cannot be allocated. In all other cases, the number of work processes is determined by the optimizer. In this case, if a nonclustered index is used, each work process reads all of the leaf index pages but accesses a separate set of data pages. Hash-based scans of unpartitioned tables are rarely used; the principal exception being the outer table of a correlated join when the inner table rows are scanned once for each outer row in the nesting.

A number of new server-wide configuration parameters control parallel execution resources.

Work processes	Defines number of work processes available for use by parallel operations: default is 0 which disables parallel operation
Work process memory	Defines the amount of memory allocated to each worker thread
Maximum parallel degree	Defines the maximum number of work processes that may be assigned to perform an operation: set to 1 disables parallel operation
Maximum scan parallel degree	Defines maximum number of work processes that may be assigned to a table scan

There are also a number of new session based parameters to control parallel execution:

Set parallel degree	Specifies upper limit to number of work processes that may be used per query
Set scan parallel degree	Specifies upper limit to number of work processes that may be used per scan
Statement keywords	Allow individual query to specify parallel degree or serial execution with the "serial" or "parallel" keywords

Parallel utilities

The parallel processing support includes the dbcc, bcp, sort and create index utilities.

Parallel dbcc

This is implemented with a new dbcc command, **dbcc checkstorage** which can use multiple work processes to perform a joint **dbcc checkdb** and **dbcc checkalloc**. This new dbcc command uses a new system database, **dbccdb** to store error and statistics information about the command execution. Also, the dbcc checkstorage does not take a table lock when checking a table and so it allows higher concurrency then the checkdb.

Parallel index creation

The parallel index creation utilizes the parallel sort feature, which is also used to execute an **order by**. The parallel sort is carried out in three phases:

- The data is read and split into multiple disjoint ranges. This is carried out using **producer** threads.

- The disjoint ranges are then sorted by separate threads called **consumer** threads. For a clustered index, the number of **consumer** threads is equal to the number of partitions; for a nonclustered index the optimum number of threads is equal to the number of devices on the segment.

- The multiple sorted results are merged together.

Parallel bcp

Adaptive server 11.5 supports **slice assignments** which allows sorted data to be loaded into specific partitions of a clustered table.

Asynchronous prefetch

Adaptive server 11.5 supports asynchronous prefetch, which allows the task to issue physical reads in advance. Do not confuse this with the 11.0 prefetch which is a misnomer for large I/O buffers. This asynchronous prefetch will be an advantage for read intensive tasks such as scans, dbcc and recovery.

Bi-directional index scans

Adaptive server 11.5 supports scanning indexes in descending order. This allows an order by desc to avoid a sort. This is currently limited to single column indexes as it does provide for descending keys in a composite key index.

Partitioned clustered tables

Adaptive server 11.5 extends the ability to partition tables to clustered tables.

Index cache manager

Adaptive server 11.5 provides a cache of index descriptors to replace the current approach of tracking the last sysindexes page accessed in a single table object descriptor. This reduces spinlock contention in a multi-processor environment. The index descriptor cache is a configurable addition to the system memory requirements.

SECURITY

Support for external security services

Adaptive server 11.5 will support one-time login by supporting external security services such as DCE 1.1, CyberSAFE Kerberos and the NT Registry via a **security control layer**. The security control layer will be incorporated into the server to accept the login authenticated by the external security service. The client will login to the Security Service which authenticates the client and provides a "credential" to the client. Using this "credential," the client can then login to the server without having to supply a password. Where the authentication is carried out will be configurable with a new sp_configure parameter, **unified login required**.

Adaptive server 11.5 will also support the use of external security services to encrypt data between client and server and to ensure that the data is not tampered with during transmission. Detecting any tampering with the data includes verifying the origin of the data and out of sequence checks. Both encryption and tamper detect may be set at the server or requested by the client. Encryption and tamper detect are supported by DCE and Kerberos but not by NT.

User defined roles

Adaptive server 11.5 extends the administration roles to allow users to define custom roles. These roles can then have permissions granted and revoked and a user may belong to more than one role. This finally eliminates the single group restriction in privilege management. The 11.5 role-based access control provides the following:

Role hierarchies

Permissions or constraints of one role may be contained in another role. This is simply achieved by granting one role to another.

Role enablement

Roles may be turned on and off for a specific user on a connection.

Password protection

Roles may be password protected to prevent activation of a role. When password protected the **set role** command requires the password.

Mutual exclusivity

Roles may be defined as mutually exclusive to prevent a user having both enabled at the same time.

Proxy authorization

Adaptive server 11.5 permits the assignment of a proxy authorization so that client permissions can be maintained in a multi-tiered architecture. When clients do not login directly to the server, but to an application server which then logs into the server to execute the commands, the proxy authorization allows the application server to assume the identity of the client, and therefore executes the command with the permission of the client. This is illustrated in Figure D.1.

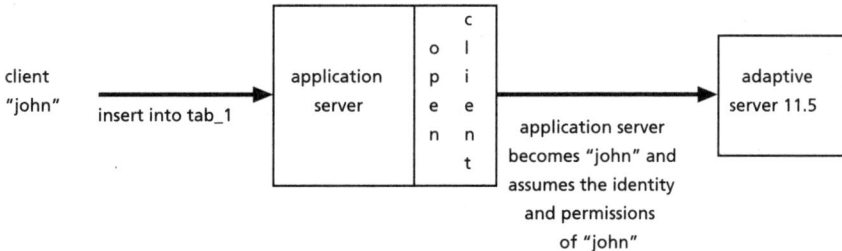

Figure D.1 Proxy authorization in a multi-tiered architecture

RECOVERY

Recovery fault isolation

In System 11.0, a recovery failure marks the complete database as suspect. Adaptive server 11.5 allows the recovery fault isolation level to be configured at the page level so that only the pages which are causing the recovery problem are marked as suspect: the rest of the database is available. Any query which attempts to read the suspect pages returns an error. The default fault isolation level is still the database level.

Point-in-time recovery

Adaptive server 11.5 allows transaction log recovery to a point-in-time.

```
load tran prod_db from log_dump1
        with until_time = "May 9, 1997 2:00 PM"
```

NT integration

MAPI

Microsoft Messaging API (MAPI) support is provided in Adaptive server 11.5 using the extended procedures feature. The server has an e-mail account defined and, using extended procedures to send, read, process and delete, the server may receive SQL queries via email and send the results out to the users in an email message.

perfmon

Adaptive server 11.5 will provide SQL Server counter and performance information to the NT Registry to allow this information to be viewed from the NT Performance Monitor GUI tool.

Event log

Adaptive server 11.5 is fully integrated with the NT event log and can send all error messages to the NT event log with suitable message tags to allow NT event log filtering.

EXTENSIBILITY

Distributed query engine

The OmniCONNECT engine has been incorporated into SQL Server to provide distributed joins across heterogeneous data sources. The OmniCONNECT integration will support the other 11.5 features and will optimize single source queries by passing them directly to the target data source. Clients connect normally to SQL Server which then has access to the Component Integration Layer which comprises the OmniCONNECT engine and the SQL Server Access Methods. Therefore, 11.5 supports distributed queries across any type of data source which is supported by OmniCONNECT and the SQL Server Access Methods.

Logical process manager (LPM)

Adaptive server 11.5 uses a logical processes manager to allow applications to have priorities assigned to them and then to limit the number of engines which may be used to execute each priority. The logical process manager consists of three components: **task priorities**, **engine groups** and **execution classes**.

Task priority

An execution priority may be assigned to a login, application or a stored procedure. The login priority takes precedence over the application which takes precedence over the stored procedure. Three priorities are available—high, medium and low. If a task is not assigned a priority it defaults to medium.

Engine group

Engines may be grouped so that they may be assigned tasks of a specific priority. The default group for an engine is the system defined ANYENGINE group which means that any available engine may process this task.

Execution class

The combination of engine group and priority is called execution class. A future release will include timeslice as a property of an execution class. An execution class has two attributes: a base priority of high, medium, or low and an affinity to an engine. There are three pre-defined execution classes: EC1 for preferred tasks (high), EC2 for normal tasks (medium: the default) and EC3 for low priority tasks. In addition to these three classes, you can define your own execution classes using **sp_addexeclass** and then bind the execution class to an engine with **sp_bindexeclass**.

This application priority and execution class allows non-critical processes to be assigned to a limited number of available engines. For example high priority tasks may be assigned to the ANYENGINE group and low priority tasks to a user-defined ENQUIRY_ENGINE group. The ENQUIRY_ENGINE group could be limited to 1 or 2 of the available engines. Therefore, the high priority tasks would be able to use any of the available engines but the low priority tasks would be limited to using 1 or at most 2 of the available engines.

The steps involved in assigning a priority are:

- Create an engine group

- Add engines to the engine group

- Define an execution class with a priority and affinity it to the engine group

- Bind the login, application or stored procedure to the execution class

Resource governor

The resource governor allows resource consumption limits to be set for a query, batch or transaction. These limits can be set on a distributed query across heterogeneous data sources, supported by the Adaptive Server integration of OmniCONNECT.

The resources which may be limited are execution time, number of rows returned or I/O cost. The I/O cost may be checked pre-execution; the execution time and number of rows are obviously run time limits. When a limit is exceeded, there is a configurable choice of actions:

- Issue and log a warning message

- Abort the transaction

- Abort the query batch

- Terminate the connection

The resource limits may be defined for a login name or an application name and may be defined over a time range so that different resource limits may be defined for during the day, overnight, weekend etc. The I/O cost may be defined as a pre-execution limit in which case the optimizer compares the weighted logical and physical I/O against the resource limit. This "unitless" resource I/O limit has been added to the **showplan** and the **statistics io** output.

Extended stored procedures

Extended stored procedures allow an operating system command or external program file to be executed from within the server. A number of system-defined extended procedures will be provided to execute functions such as electronic mail and operating system commands such as list directory.

FUTURE 11.G ENHANCEMENTS

Referential integrity

This includes increasing the maximum limit of 16 referential constraints for a table to 200.

Text search integration

Integration of the Verity full text search engine into SQL Server. This incorporates the normal text search operations such as boolean, fuzzy search, soundex, thesaurus, wild cards, weighting and search trees into SQL. A single SQL command may be issued against normal SQL Server datatype data and text data.

```
select invoice_no, invoice_date from invoices
     where inv_price > 10000
     and pertains (extra_info, "early delivery")
```

MIME datatypes

Support for MIME (Multipurpose Internet Mail Extensions) datatypes which allows an application to store and retrieve messages conforming to the MIME standard. This and the text search feature allow access via the Internet to large amounts of textual information with SQL analysis ability.

Support for external directory services

Support for access to external directory services such as DCE Directory Service or Novell Directory Service via a **directory control layer**. This removes the SQL Server use of the **interfaces** file and simplifies network administration.

DDL replication

Support for the replication of schema information.

Index

SyBooks™ Installation Guide

SyBooks Release 2.3

Document ID: 90002-01-0230-04

Last Revised: August 26, 1997

Principal author: Steven Cogorno

Document ID: 90002-01-0230

This publication pertains to SyBooks Release 2.3 of the Sybase database management software and to any subsequent release until otherwise indicated in new editions or technical notes. Information in this document is subject to change without notice. The software described herein is furnished under a license agreement, and it may be used or copied only in accordance with the terms of that agreement.

Document Orders

To order additional documents, U.S. and Canadian customers should call Customer Fulfillment at (800) 685-8225, fax (617) 229-9845.

Customers in other countries with a U.S. license agreement may contact Customer Fulfillment via the above fax number. All other international customers should contact their Sybase subsidiary or local distributor.

Upgrades are provided only at regularly scheduled software release dates.

Sybase Trademarks

Restricted Rights

Table of Contents

CHAPTER 8   Using the SyBooks Browser

CHAPTER 1

Welcome to SyBooks

Welcome to SyBooks™, the online documentation for Sybase® products. SyBooks online documentation is the standard method of document delivery for Sybase products. The advantages of using SyBooks include:

- **Distributed access to documentation** – When installed in a network environment, several SyBooks users can access the same book at once and no longer have to depend on a single set of documentation.

- **Instant access to information** – Links within and between individual books and comprehensive search capabilities enable instant access to related information.

- **Decreased reliance upon paper products** – Online documentation does not use paper, so it helps preserve resources.

New Features

To meet changing user needs, new features have been added to SyBooks distribution. These features include:

- The ability to read SyBooks directly off the CD-ROM.

- The ability to view SyBooks from a web browser and to integrate SyBooks with your existing intranet services.

Options for Accessing SyBooks

The following sections describe each of the ways you can access SyBooks.

Installing SyBooks on a Hard Drive

System administrators can install some or all of the collections and books in a central location, depending on disk space and information needs. This is the preferred method for accessing SyBooks. Books use the SyBooks browser, which is based on the *Dyna*Text browser from Electronic Book Technologies. The browser provides an interactive table of contents and advanced search capabilities for local and networked users. Individual users can add public or private notes, bookmarks, and hyperlinks. These features can be used by system administrators to communicate site-specific information and policies.

Using SyBooks Directly from the CD

With this release, you can view any of the books on the CD without installing them to a hard drive. To access SyBooks in this way, the user must have a copy of a SyBooks CD-ROM (release 2.3 or higher) and a CD-ROM drive. This option is useful for previewing new collections and books before installing SyBooks, or for situations where installing on a hard drive is not practical. Using SyBooks directly from the CD-ROM, may be slower than using it from a hard drive installation.

Installing SyBooks Web Server

The SyBooks Web Server provides access to SyBooks collections from a web browser such as Netscape, Mosaic, or Internet Explorer. This allows system administrators to integrate SyBooks with existing intranet services. Collections and books are stored in a single, central location. However, users cannot create annotations, and since there is no interactive table of contents, it may be more difficult to navigate. Using the SyBooks Web Server may be slower than using the standard SyBooks installation, because network traffic is generated for every HTML page. This solution is best for users who cannot access a standard installtion of SyBooks via NFS or network mounts. SyBooks Web Server is availible for Sun Solaris, SGI, HP-UX, IBM RS/6000 AIX, Digital UNIX, Intel Solaris, and UnixWare 2.0.

Printing PostScript

PostScript copies of all SyBooks books are included on the CD-ROM for those who prefer paper documentation. The books are fully indexed and are identical to bound Sybase books. Printing from PostScript may be useful to users who plan to read a book in its entirety. Sybase customers have limited rights to reproduce Sybase documentation.

Other Sybase Documentation Options

Sybase also offers the web-based and hard copy documentation.

SyBooks-on-the-Web

SyBooks-on-the-Web is Sybase's Internet documentation facility. It is based on DynaWeb from Electronic Book Technologies and is available to anyone with a web browser and World Wide Web access. The Sybase web site carries the latest copies of all SyBooks documentation. The URL is http://sybooks.sybase.com.

Hard Copy Documentation

Hard copy documentation is available for purchase as an alternative to using SyBooks online browsers or printing the PostScript files included on the CD-ROM. U.S. and Canadian customers and international customers with a U.S. license agreement should call Customer Fulfillment at (800) 685-8225 or fax (617) 229-9845 for information on how to order hard copy documentation. All other international customers should contact their Sybase subsidiary or local distributor.

Using This Guide

This guide covers the following topics:

- Procedures associated with installing and using SyBooks products on UNIX, Windows, and Macintosh systems.
- SyBooks browser.

For More Information

See the *DynaText Reader Guide* for complete information on the *Dyna*Text Browser.

Technical Support

Help is available for SyBooks through Sybase Technical Support.

Each customer site has one or more designated people who are authorized to contact Sybase Technical Support. If you cannot resolve your problem using the printed or online documentation, ask a designated person at your site to contact Sybase Technical Support.

CHAPTER 2

Installing SyBooks

This chapter describes how to install SyBooks on a hard drive. SyBooks uses *Dyna*Text, an online browser from Electronic Book Technologies. There are different browsers for each UNIX platform and for Macintosh and Windows. If you want to view SyBooks directly without installing it on the hard drive, see Chapter 4, "Using SyBooks Directly from the CD-ROM."

Installing SyBooks for UNIX

This section explains how to install SyBooks for UNIX.

Product Requirements

The following are required to run SyBooks:

*   Operating system: SunOS 4.1.3, Sun Solaris 2.4, IBM RS/6000 AIX, HP-UX, Digital UNIX, NCR, Intel Solaris, SGI 5.3, UnixWare 1.1, UnixWare 2.0.
*   Hard disk space: 15MB minimum, 400MB for full installation.

The Installation Process

The SyBooks Installer for UNIX is a Bourne shell script. You will be prompted for information to tailor SyBooks to your environment, including:

- The directory in which SyBooks will be installed.
- The UNIX platforms on which SyBooks will be viewed.
- The Sybase books and collections that will be installed.

You can quit the Installer at any time during installation, leaving the disk untouched.

Preparing to Install SyBooks

Before SyBooks can be installed, you must mount the CD-ROM drive. This often requires superuser privileges.

➤ *Note*

Mounting commands and mount points vary among different UNIX platforms. For mounting instructions, see your system administrator or consult the hardware documentation.

Installing SyBooks

To install SyBooks on any UNIX platform, follow these steps:

1. Change directories to the *sybooks/unix* directory on the SyBooks CD. For example, assuming that the CD-ROM drive is mounted as */cdrom*, enter:

   cd /cdrom/sybooks/unix

2. List the directory by entering:

   ls

3. If the file names appear in lowercase, enter:

   install.me

   If the file names appear in uppercase, enter:

   INSTALL.ME

4. The Installer will guide you through the installation process.

➤ *Note*

When choosing browsers to install, you must select the platforms of machines that will run SyBooks, **not** the platform of the file server where SyBooks is being stored. For example, if the NFS file server where SyBooks will be installed is a Sun Solaris machine and the clients are IBM AIX machines, you would install the IBM RS/6000 AIX browser.

Starting SyBooks

Users should either add the SyBooks directory to their path or use the full path name when starting SyBooks.

If SyBooks has been added to the path, start SyBooks by entering:

sybooks

If SyBooks has not been added to the path, start SyBooks by entering:

*sybooks_path/***sybooks**

This is a shell script that sets environment variables, determines the current platform and executes the proper browser binary. The first time SyBooks is run, the browser will create a directory in the user's home directory to store annotations.

To start SyBooks manually instead of using the script, see "Starting SyBooks Manually on UNIX" on page 29.

Installing SyBooks for Windows

This section explains how to install SyBooks for Windows.

Product Requirements

The following are required to run SyBooks:

- Operating system: DOS 4.01 or later and Windows 3.1, Windows 95, Windows NT 3.1 or later, OS/2 2.x or later (WinOS2).
- Hard disk space: 10MB minimum, 400MB for full installation.
- Memory: 4MB.

The Installation Process

The SyBooks Installer for Windows is a Windows application. You will be prompted for information to tailor SyBooks to your environment, including:

- The directory in which SyBooks will be installed.

- The Sybase books and collections that will be installed.

You can quit the Installer at any time during installation, leaving the disk untouched.

Installing SyBooks

To install SyBooks for Windows:

➤ *Note*

Windows 95 users can click the right mouse button on the SyBooks CD-ROM icon and select Install/Deinstall to start the Installer.

1. Insert the SyBooks CD into the CD-ROM drive.

2. Open the Windows File Manager. Change the current drive to the CD-ROM drive, and change the current directory to *drive_letter:\sybooks\windows*.

3. Double-click on the *setup.exe* file to start the Installer.

◆ *WARNING!*

If you intend to install SyBooks to or from a network drive, you must map the device to a drive letter before you begin the installation. Universal network connection paths are not supported.

Starting SyBooks

The SyBooks installation program creates a program group and icon for the *Dyna*Text browser. The browser is located in *bin\sybooks.exe* in the SyBooks directory. By default, a SyBooks icon is created in a group called SyBooks.

To start SyBooks, follow these steps:

1. Open the SyBooks group.

2. Double-click on the SyBooks icon.

Installing SyBooks for Macintosh

This section explains how to install SyBooks for Macintosh.

Product Requirements

The following are required to run SyBooks:

- Operating system: System 7.0 or later and AppleScript.
- Hard disk space: 10MB minimum, 400MB for full installation.
- Memory : 4MB.

The Installation Process

The SyBooks Installer for Macintosh will prompt you for information to tailor SyBooks to your environment, including:

- The directory in which SyBooks will be installed.
- The Sybase books and collections that will be installed.

You can quit the Installer at any time during installation, leaving the disk untouched.

Preparing to Install SyBooks

The SyBooks Installer for Macintosh requires AppleScript. If Apple Script is not installed, do the following:

1. Insert the SyBooks CD into the CD-ROM drive.
2. Open the SYBOOKS CD.
3. Open the *sybooks* folder.
4. Open the *mac* folder.
5. Copy *AppleScript* and *Scripting Additions* to the Extensions folder, located in the System Folder.
6. If you are using System 7.0 or System 7.1, copy *finderlib* to the Extensions folder.
7. Restart the computer.

Installing SyBooks

To install SyBooks for Macintosh, follow this procedure:

1. Create a folder by choosing New Folder from the File menu. You may choose any name for the folder; "SyBooks" is the default. Later, you will specify this folder as the "Destination folder" when running the installation program.

2. Insert the SyBooks CD into the CD-ROM drive.

3. Open the SYBOOKS CD.

4. Open the *sybooks* folder.

5. Open the *mac* folder.

6. Copy the *install.me* file to the same hard disk onto which SyBooks will be installed. Execute that copy.

7. Follow the instructions on the screen.

8. The installation program is finished when the screen displays the following message:

    ```
    SyBooks 2.2 Installation has completed successfully.
    ```

Starting SyBooks

1. Open the *sybooks* folder.

2. Open the *bin* folder.

3. Double-click on the SyBooks application.

CHAPTER 3

Updating SyBooks Installations

This chapter explains how to update an existing SyBooks installation. If you are installing SyBooks for the first time, go to Chapter 2, "Installing SyBooks."

Using Older SyBooks Discs

If you want to install books from an older SyBooks disc, you must install them before installing books from this release. The file and directory structures have changed and older SyBooks Installers will corrupt a 2.3 installation.

If you have an existing SyBooks installation that is older than release 2.3, the 2.3 Installer will update it to the current format.

The Update Process

The Installer does not overwrite any previously installed books. During the installation process, you can:

- Install new collections.
- Install new books in existing collections, if the book and the collection have the same release number.
- Delete previously installed collections from your installation.
- Update the *Dyna*Text Browser version and environment.

◆ *WARNING!*

If you install a newer version of a book that is already installed, you will not be able to copy annotations and links from the older book. If you wish to keep annotations, you will have to add them to the newer book manually.

Updating SyBooks for UNIX

This section explains the SyBooks update process for UNIX.

Preparing to Update SyBooks

Before running the Installer, you must set the SYBROOT environment variable to the location of the existing installation, if it is not already set.

Updating SyBooks

Start the Installer (see "Installing SyBooks for UNIX" on page 5). The Installer will ask you to select browsers and books to install or remove. The Installer will update the browser to the latest version. The Installer will also convert the *.ebtrc* file and the SyBooks directory structure to the format used with SyBooks Release 2.3.

➤ *Note*

If you are using SyBooks Web Server, remember to run the Server Configuration program after adding or removing books. See "Installing SyBooks Web Server for UNIX" on page 19 for more information.

Moving SyBooks to a Different Location

To move SyBooks to a new location, use the **mv** command. You will also need to update users' paths to point to the new location.

Updating SyBooks for Windows

Start the Installer (see "Installing SyBooks for Windows" on page 7). The Installer will ask you to select books to install or remove. The Installer will update the browser to the latest version.

Moving SyBooks to a Different Location

If you move the entire SyBooks environment to a different location, you must edit the contents of the *Dyna*Text configuration file, *dynatext.ini,* located in *SyBooks_root\bin.* All paths pointing to the **previous** *SyBooks_root* directory must be replaced with paths pointing to the **new** *SyBooks_root* directory.

You must also edit the *colls.cfg* files in *SyBooks_root\bin.*

Updating SyBooks for Macintosh

Start the Installer (see "Installing SyBooks for Macintosh" on page 9). The Installer will ask you to select browsers and books to install or remove. If you have an older SyBooks release installed, the Installer will automatically update it.

Moving SyBooks to a Different Location

If you move the entire SyBooks environment to a different location, you must edit the contents of the *Dyna*Text configuration file, *dynatext.cfg.* Or, use the SyBooks Installer to re-install SyBooks to the new location and delete the old copy.

CHAPTER 4

Using SyBooks Directly from the CD-ROM

This chapter explains how to view collections and books from the SyBooks CD-ROM without installing them to your hard drive.

Using SyBooks from the CD-ROM on UNIX

This section explains how to use SyBooks from the CD-ROM on UNIX machines.

Product Requirements

The following are required to run SyBooks from the CD-ROM:

- Operating system: SunOS 4.1.3, Sun Solaris 2.4, IBM RS/6000 AIX, HP-UX, Digital UNIX, NCR, Intel Solaris, SGI 5.3, UnixWare 1.1, UnixWare 2.0.
- Hard disk space: none.

Using SyBooks from the CD

To use SyBooks from the CD for UNIX follow these steps:

1. Mount the CD-ROM.

2. Change directories to the *sybooks/unix* directory on the SyBooks CD. For example, assuming that the CD-ROM drive is mounted as */cdrom*, enter:

   cd /cdrom/sybooks/unix

3. List the directory by entering:

    `ls`

4. If the file names appear in lowercase, enter:

    cdsybook

    If the file names appear in uppercase, enter:

    CDSYBOOK

➤ *Note*

On some UNIX platforms file names on ISO-9660 CD-ROMs appear in uppercase. SyBooks CD expects some of these file names to be lowercase. **CDSYBOOK** will automatically create symbolic links with lowercase file names on your hard drive that point to the file's uppercase counterpart on the CD-ROM. This takes about five minutes and requires 1–3MB of disk space on your hard drive. Once you are finished using SyBooks CD, you can remove the links or save them for future use.

Using SyBooks from the CD-ROM on Windows

This section explains how to use SyBooks from the CD-ROM on Windows machines.

Product Requirements

The following are required to run SyBooks from the CD-ROM:

*   Operating system: DOS 4.01 or later and Windows 3.1, Windows 95, Windows NT 3.x, OS/2 2.x or later (WinOS2).
*   Hard disk space: none.
*   Memory: 4MB.

Using SyBooks from the CD

To use SyBooks from the CD on Windows, follow these steps:

1. Insert the SyBooks CD into the CD-ROM drive.

2. Open the Windows File Manager. Change the current drive to the CD-ROM drive, and change the current directory to *drive_letter:\sybooks\windows*.

3. Double-click on the *sybooks.exe* file.

> ➤ *Note*

Windows 95 users can click the right mouse button on the SyBooks CD-ROM icon and select Run from CD to start SyBooks CD.

Using SyBooks from the CD-ROM on Macintosh

This section explains how to use SyBooks from the CD-ROM on Macintosh machines.

Product Requirements

The following are required to run SyBooks from the CD-ROM:

*   Operating system: System 7.0 or later.
*   Hard disk space: none.
*   Memory: 4MB.

Using SyBooks from the CD

To use SyBooks from the CD on Macintosh, follow these steps:

1. Insert the SyBooks CD into the CD-ROM drive.

2. Open the SYBOOKS CD.

3. Open the *sybooks* folder.

4. Open the *mac* folder.

5. Open the *bin* folder.

6. Open the SyBooks application.

CHAPTER 5

Installing SyBooks Web Server

SyBooks Web Server uses Electronic Book Technologies' DynaWeb, a web server that translates SGML to HTML. SyBooks Web Server must run on a UNIX machine. However, clients may use any machine that has a web browser. When installing SyBooks Web Server, use the platform on which the server will run.

◆ **WARNING!**
The License Agreement prohibits you from allowing any computer outside of your corporate intranet to access SyBooks Web Server.

Installing SyBooks Web Server for UNIX

This section explains how to install SyBooks Web Server for UNIX.

Product Requirements

The following is required to run SyBooks Web Server:

- Operating system: Sun Solaris 2.4, IBM RS/6000 AIX, HP-UX, Digital UNIX, NCR, Intel Solaris, SGI 5.3, UnixWare 2.0.
- Hard disk space: 15MB minimum, 400MB for full installation.

The Installation Process

The SyBooks Installer is used to install SyBooks Web Server. When installing SyBooks, you will have the option of installing the Web Server as well. See "Installing SyBooks for UNIX" on page 5 for information on the Installer.

Configuring SyBooks Web Server

1. Once the Installer has finished installing SyBooks, set the SYBROOT environment variable (the Installer will display the path).

2. Run the Server Configuration program by entering:

    `$SYBROOT/server/sws_cfg`

Starting SyBooks Web Server

Use the following command to start SyBooks Web Server:

`$SYBROOT/platform/sybk_ws`

➤ *Note*

If you specified a port below 1024 as the SyBooks Web Server port, you will need to have superuser privileges to start the SyBooks Web Server.

Shutting Down SyBooks Web Server

To terminate the SyBooks Web Server, use the UNIX **kill** command.

Migrating Existing Collections to SyBooks Web Server

If you have a SyBooks collection from release 2.2 or earlier, you must add styles to each book to enable the books for SyBooks Web Server. Collections from any release 2.3 book will include these styles.

If the styles have not been added to a book, SyBooks Web Server will display the following error message:

`Missing Stylesheet`

To migrate pre-2.3 release books by adding the necessary files, follow these steps:

1. Mount the SyBooks CD-ROM.

2. Change to the directory containing the styles by entering:

    `cd CD-ROM mount point/sybooks/unix/wsstyles`

3. Copy the styles by entering:

    `cp * $SYBROOT/collection/books/bookname/styles`

CHAPTER 6
Printing the PostScript Files

PostScript versions of all the Sybase documents included on this CD are located in the */sybooks/ps* directory. These files are organized in directories according to the *Dyna*Text collection in which they are located online. These files can be printed on PostScript printers, giving you the option to print high-quality paper documentation at no additional cost.

Sybase customers have limited rights to reproduce the Sybase documentation. For details, see the license agreement included with this CD.

Printing the Files

Keep the following in mind:

- PostScript files can be printed only on PostScript printers.
- All of the PostScript files are formatted to print on 8.5-by-11-inch or A4-size paper.
- You can also use an online tool like Adobe TranScript or GhostView to view the PostScript document and print selected sections.

Contact the vendor of your PostScript driver for information about printing these files on your system.

CHAPTER 7
Troubleshooting

Problems with SyBooks can often be fixed without calling SyBase Technical support. This chapter explains how to identify and fix some common problems. If you cannot fix the problem after exhausting the possible solutions, contact Sybase Technical Support.

In this chapter, SYBROOT is used to denote the location of the SyBooks installation.

A Word About UNIX Environment Variables

Before implementing any of these workarounds, set the SYBROOT environment variable to point to the location of the SyBooks installation. Throughout this section, SYBROOT is used in path names. If the variable is not set, the workarounds will fail.

➤ *Note*

Setting environment variables varies depending on the shell. Bourne shell (sh) users should use "VARIABLE=*value*; export VARIABLE". C-Shell (csh) users should use "setenv VARIABLE *value*". To make these changes permanent, add these variable definitions to the *.login* file.

Using the Log for Troubleshooting Installation Errors

If you encounter any problems or errors during installation, you can consult the *log.cur* file, which is located in the following places:

*   For UNIX: *$SYBROOT/config* or the home directory of the user that installed SyBooks.

*   For Macintosh: *$SYBROOT/config*.

*   For Windows NT: TEMP area (set in the System Control Panel).

*   For Windows: The directory pointed to by the TEMP environment variable or in *$SYBOOKS/config*.

Information in the *log.cur* file and other files in the *config* directory can be used for diagnosis and recovery purposes. Save these files, especially if you plan to contact Sybase Technical Support for further assistance.

Patches for Known Problems

Before calling technical support, look for a patch on the SyBooks Patches and Problems page on the World Wide Web. The URL is http://www.sybase.com/Offerings/Sybooks/problems.html.

If you do not have web access, patches can be obtained by FTP from *ftp.sybase.com* in the *pub/sybooks* directory.

Contacting Sybase Technical Support

If you cannot resolve a problem, gather the following information and call Sybase Technical Support:

*   **SyBooks Product Identification Number**–If you have a standalone version of SyBooks, this number will be listed on the CD-ROM and the CD package. If SyBooks was bundled on a product disk, the product ID is contained in an ASCII file named *prod_id*.

*   **Error messages displayed on screen** – Note the exact error messages given by the Installer or *Dyna*Text, or, create a printout or screen shot of the message(s).

*   **Log files and configuration files** – Locate the *log.cur* file and the *config* directory. The technical support engineer will need these files to assist you.

Diagnosing the Problem

The following sections describe problems you may experience and possible solutions. To resolve a problem, try the first solution. If it does not solve the problem, try the remaining solutions in the order listed.

Make sure that the platform listed matches the machine on which SyBooks is running. If the platform is listed as UNIX, it applies to all SyBooks UNIX platforms. Likewise, if the platform is listed as Windows, it applies to all version of Windows.

Problems with the Installer

Installer reports "Can't understand ..."

- Macintosh: Restart the computer to free up memory

Installer failed due to lack of memory or space

- Windows: See "Adjusting the Stack Space" (page 30)
- Windows: See "Defining the TEMP Directory" (page 30)

UNIX reports that "*install.me* not found"

- UNIX: Use the full path name or add "." to your path

Error Messages While Starting SyBooks

"can't open display"

- UNIX: See "Setting the DISPLAY Environment Variable" (page 28)
- UNIX: See "Allowing X Connections from Other Machines" (page 28)

"cannot convert string to type FontList"

- Sun Solaris CDE: See "Setting the XNLSPATH Environment Variable" (page 27)

"cannot find libX..."

- UNIX: See "Linking X Libraries" (page 29)

"cannot find file *.ebtrc*"

- UNIX: Use *$SYBROOT/sybooks* start-up script
- UNIX: See "Starting SyBooks Manually on UNIX" (page 29)

"translation table syntax error"

- UNIX: See "Setting the XKEYSYMDB Environment Variable" (page 27)

"x is not a valid book"

- Macintosh: See "Installing Missing Books" (page 30)

Problems Using SyBooks

Fonts in a book window display poorly

- UNIX: See "Installing X Window Fonts" (page 30)
- Windows: See "Installing Microsoft Windows Fonts" (page 30)

Pop-up menus do not work

- UNIX: See "Fix for the Motif 1.2.2 Menu Bug" (page 28)

When attempting to open a book, *Dyna*Text exits with a core dump

- UNIX: See "Setting the XNLSPATH Environment Variable" (page 27)
- UNIX: See "Setting the XKEYSYMDB Environment Variable" (page 27)

SyBooks windows do not resize or appear black

- Solaris: See "Fix for the Motif Resize Bug" (page 29)

Collection searches do not work

- UNIX: See "Creating Collection Indexes for UNIX" (page 31)
- Windows: See "Creating Collection Indexes for Windows" (page 31)
- Macintosh: Reinstall the collection using the Installer.

Error Messages While Starting SyBooks Web Server

"port xx: bind: permission denied"

- UNIX: Start a server with port number below 1024 as root
- UNIX: Change the port number to be greater than 1024

Server hangs or does not return a prompt

- UNIX: Set permissions on the *$SYBROOT/data/config/dynaweb.cfg* file to 755
- UNIX: Run the Server Configuration program

Error Messages While Using SyBooks Web Server

"Missing stylesheet"

- UNIX: See Chapter , "Migrating Existing Collections to SyBooks Web Server"

"Cannot open book"

- UNIX: See "Installing Missing Books" (page 30)

Possible Solutions

Setting the XNLSPATH Environment Variable

The *nls* directory is part of the X Window system. On some machines, most notably Sun Solaris CDE, *Dyna*Text cannot find this directory. An *nls* directory is included with SyBooks. Set XNLSPATH to *$SYBROOT/data/x11/nls*.

Setting the XKEYSYMDB Environment Variable

The *KeySymDB* file translates keys to symbolic mappings. On some machines, most notable Sun Solaris CDE, *Dyna*Text cannot find the *KeySymDB* file. A copy is included with SyBooks. Set XKEYSYMDB to *$SYBROOT/data/misc/keysym*.

Setting the DISPLAY Environment Variable

If a user is running SyBooks from a remote server instead of the local machine, the DISPLAY environment variable needs to be set so that *Dyna*Text knows which screen to use. Set DISPLAY to "*machine*:0.0" where *machine* is the name of the local X Workstation or X Terminal.

Allowing X Connections from Other Machines

If a user is running SyBooks from a remote host rather than the local machine, the server must be on the access control list. If it is not, have it added by the system administrator, or turn off access control. To turn off access control, use this command:

```
xhost +
```

Installing Sun OpenWindows Patches

All versions of *Dyna*Text for UNIX included with SyBooks are Motif applications. Starting Motif applications while running OpenWindows on SunOS 4.x or 5.x operating systems can introduce a variety of problems. The following patches, which are available from Sun, should resolve the OpenWindows conflicts:

- OpenWindows V3.0 Server Patch 3 (Patch #10044-58)
- OpenWindows 3.0 libXt CTE Jumbo Patch (Patch #100512-04)

Fix for the Motif 1.2.2 Menu Bug

A Motif 1.2.2 bug can prevent *Dyna*Text from mapping pop-up menus. If your UNIX environment supplies Motif 1.2 dynamically linked libraries, or if you are using the toolkit to link to Motif 1.2.2, add the following resources to the *Dyna*Text applications defaults file, *Dtext*, located in $SYBROOT/*data*/*x directory*/*defaults*/C:

```
dtext.motif122bug:        TRUE
*whichButton:             5
```

Fix for a "Widget Browser Scrollbar=0" Error

This indicates that an earlier version than Motif 1.2 is being used. Add the following lines to your .Xdefaults file.

```
*toc_scrollwin.width: 20

*toc_scrollwin.height: 20

*browser_scrollwin.width: 20

*browser_scrollwin.height: 20
```

Then type in the command:

```
xrdb .Xdefaults
```

If you continue to get the error, you may have to log out and back in to your UNIX environment to get the settings to take.

Fix for the Motif Resize Bug

If browser windows appear partially or completely black when using *Dyna*Text on Sun Solaris or Intel Solaris, add the following resource to the *.Xebt* file located in each user's home directory:

```
motifResizeBug:          TRUE
```

Linking X Libraries

*Dyna*Text uses dynamic linking and expects to find certain libraries in */usr/lib*. If you get an error similar to this:

```
can't find libX11.so.5
```

create a link called *libXt.so.1* in the */usr/lib* directory pointing to the most recent version of the library (for example, *libX11.so40*).

Starting SyBooks Manually on UNIX

To start SyBooks manually, do the following:

1. Set the SYBROOT environment variable to the directory path where SyBooks is installed.
2. Set the EBTRC environment variable to *$SYBROOT/.ebtrc*.
3. Set the XPLAT environment variable to match the X directory for your platform. The X directories are listed in the *$SYBROOT/data* directory.
4. Execute the SyBooks browser for your platform. The SyBooks binaries are located at *$SYBROOT/platform/bin/sybooks*.

Adjusting Book Window Sizes

If *Dyna*Text book windows are too large for your monitor, adjust the window geometry by changing the values in the parameter *fulltext.geometry* in the file *$SYBROOT/data/x dir/defaults/C/Dtext*.

Installing X Window Fonts

If *Dyna*Text browser text does not appear in the same font as on other UNIX platforms, or a font is rendered poorly, it is possible that all fonts were not installed when the X Window software was installed.

To resolve this problem, install all the fonts included with the X Window software.

Installing Microsoft Windows Fonts

SyBooks documents are **usually** displayed in Arial font, which is installed with Windows. If it is missing, characters may appear as strange symbols.

To resolve this problem, install the Arial fonts included with Microsoft Windows.

Installing Missing Books

When starting SyBooks or when opening a book in SyBooks Web Server, you may receive one or more of the following messages at the bottom of your screen:

```
Warning: '<book folder name>' is not a valid book
```

and:

```
"Unable to open book."
```

Both of these messages indicate that the book in question was not selected for installation. To install a specific book, run the Installer and add the missing book.

Adjusting the Stack Space

If you are using Windows 3.1.x or Windows 95, make sure you have enough stack space. The STACKS setting in the *config.sys* file should be:

```
STACKS=9,256
```

Windows NT users should see the operating system documentation for more information about adjusting stack space.

Defining the *TEMP* Directory

The SyBooks Installer for UNIX requires at least 1MB of temporary space. Windows and OS/2 users should add the following line to *autoexec.bat*.

```
SET TEMP=temp_directory
```

Windows NT users should use the System icon in Control Panel to set the TEMP variable.

Creating Collection Indexes for UNIX

If you need to rebuild the collection indexes for a collection, follow these steps:

1. Change to the collection directory.

2. Remove the *libidx* directory.

3. Run the Installer without adding or removing any books or browsers.

Creating Collection Indexes for Windows

If you need to rebuild the collection indexes for all collections, follow these steps:

1. After the installation program ends, go to a DOS prompt (native DOS or a DOS session).

2. Change to the drive where you installed SyBooks by entering:
   drive_letter:

3. Change to the SyBooks *config* directory by entering:
   cd \SyBooks_directory\config

4. To index the newly installed partial collections, enter:
   indexall

If you need to build a collection index for a single collection, follow these steps:

1. After the installation program has ended, go to a DOS prompt (native DOS or a DOS session).

2. Change to the drive where you installed SyBooks by entering:
   drive_letter:

3. Change to the SyBooks directory by entering:
   cd \SyBooks_directory

4. Look at the collection subdirectories by entering:
   dir /w

   Collection subdirectories begin with three letters and are followed by five digits. For example, for Open Client/Server™ release 10.0.2, the collection subdirectory is called *con10021*.

5. Change to the SyBooks binaries directory by entering:
   cd bin

6. To index the collection, enter:
   index collection_subdirectory

7. Repeat steps 3 through 6 for each collection you want to index.

If Indexing Fails

If the *mkcolidx.exe* collection indexing program fails due to insufficient memory, take the following steps:

1. Examine the *config.sys* and *autoexec.bat* files on the boot drive.

2. Increase the amount of conventional memory available (below 640K) by temporarily disabling unnecessary device or network drivers and TSRs.

3. Reboot and try to index the collection again. After you build the indexes for the collections, restore the driver and TSR configuration and reboot again, if necessary.

CHAPTER 8

Using the SyBooks Browser

SyBooks uses the *Dyna*Text browser to display online books. This chapter explains *Dyna*Text's basic functions. See the *DynaText Reader Guide* online book for more thorough documentation.

SyBooks Web Server uses DynaWeb to convert book data into HTML and deliver it to the Web browser client. For information about using DynaWeb, see the online help.

Opening a Book

When you start SyBooks, the *Dyna*Text library window appears as shown in Figure 8-1. The list of collections is shown in the left pane. The books that comprise the selected collection are shown in the right pane. In the figure, the *Transact SQL User's Guide* is selected; it is a book in the Sybase SQL Server Collection.

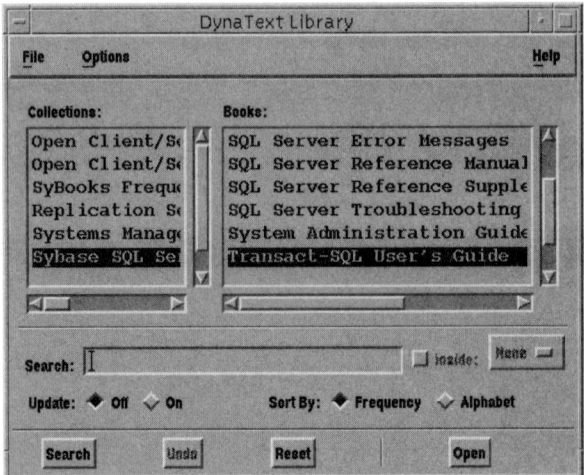

Figure 8-1: *Dya*Text collection window.

To view a book, first select the appropriate collection in the Collections pane, then select the book in the Books pane and click on the Open button. Or, after selecting the collection, simply double-click the book title in the Books pane. Figure 8-2 shows an example of a book window.

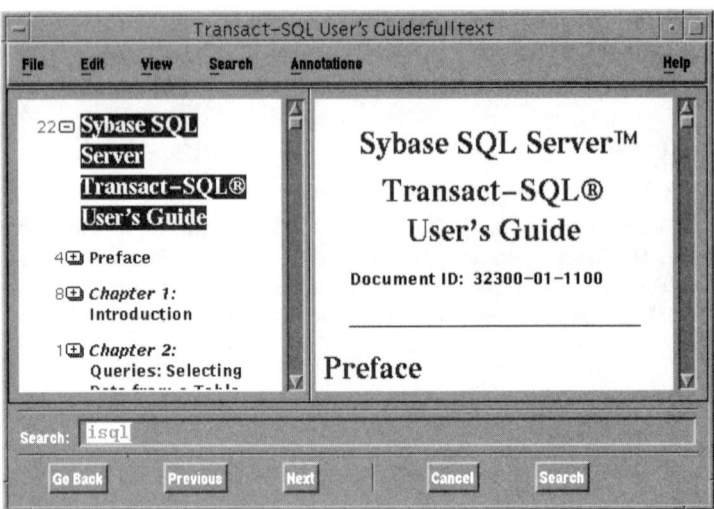

Figure 8-2: *Dyna*Text book window.

Using the Table of Contents

The Table of Contents (or TOC) pane in *Dyna*Text helps you navigate the book and find the information you need. When you move from one section of the book to another, *Dyna*Text highlights the TOC as a navigation aid. The icon to the left of the TOC entry controls the level of detail displayed. Clicking on the expand (+) icon displays the sections immediately below the heading. Clicking on the contract (-) icon hides the sections below the heading. The TOC pane normally displays book headings. To display a TOC of figures or tables, choose select view from the menu bar, then select TOC View and finally select Figures or Tables.

Viewing Figures and Tables

By default, SyBooks displays figures and graphics in pop-up windows which are activated by double-clicking the icon in the caption. If you would prefer that the graphics display inline, select the "inline" stylesheet (see "Using Alternate Stylesheets" on page 38).

Performing a Search

The search field displayed in the collection window is used to search the entire collection of books (see Figure 8-1). Once this search is completed, the number of hits will be displayed next to each book title.

If you perform a search in a book window, only that book is searched. Figure 8-2 shows an example of a book window with the search hits listed next to the book and chapter titles.

Understanding the Search Language

*Dyna*Text has an advanced query language that allows more flexible searches than traditional character string searching. The standard search is a word search. You can perform a specialized search by using Search Forms, which are listed under the Search menu and Forms submenu. For more information on the *Dyna*Text Query Language, see Chapter 8 of the *DynaText Reader Guide*.

Search Forms

Customized search forms have been created for each book. Though some books may not have all of the forms list in Table 8-1, you can use the query language. Note that in the table, "W" represents a word or multiple words and "N" represents a number. You can use these examples to make more complicated compound queries.

Table 8-1:   Search forms and the query language equivalent

Search Form	Query Language
Proximity	W within N words of W
AND	W and W
OR	W or W
NOT	W and not W
Title	W inside (<title>)
Procedure	W inside (<procedure>)
Example	W inside (<literallayout>)

Search Wildcards

*Dyna*Text recognizes the following wildcards:

- ? – Any single character.
- * – Zero or more characters, up to the end of the word.

➤ *Note*

*Dyna*Text indexes books based on words. This means that *Dyna*Text will not find words that have a substring that matches the search term. For example, searching for the word "select" will not find the word "selecting." If you want to find all words that contain a substring, use wildcards (for example, "select*").

Stop Lists

*Dyna*Text has a "stop list" which prevents you from searching for common words like "a" or "the."

When you enter a phrase with a word from the stop list, *Dyna*Text replaces it with the * wildcard character, which matches any word and reports that "a word is on the stop list." *Dyna*Text may have found occurrences of the phrase or expression. However, it probably also found other phrases with any other word appearing in the place of the stop list word.

Printing Documentation

If you are printing an entire book, use the PostScript files located in the *ps* directory on the SyBooks CD-ROM. These files will produce higher quality output than using *Dyna*Text's built-in print function. (See Chapter 6, "Printing the PostScript Files.")

To print selected sections of a book, use the *Dyna*Text print command. You will be presented with a table of contents. Select the sections you want to print and click Print.

Configuring a Printer for UNIX

*Dyna*Textfor UNIX platforms provides a PostScript printer configuration file located at *SyBooks_root/data/ps/config.dat*. Each printer listed in *config.dat* must have a separate entry. Entries must use the following syntax:

```
name width height print_command
```

where:

- *name* is the printer name to be displayed in the Printers menu.
- *width* is the width, in points, of the printer's page. Use 612 as an initial value, and adjust it as needed.
- *height* is the height, in points, of the printer's page. Use 792 as an initial value, and adjust it as needed.
- *print_command* is the UNIX printer command.

An example of a *config.dat* printer entry is as follows:

```
ps_sw_1 612 792 lpr -Pps_sw_1
```

Configuring a Printer for Other Platforms

*Dyna*Text for Windows and Macintosh uses the operating system printing services. For Macintosh, use the Chooser to select the printer. For Windows use the Print Manager. Refer to your operating system documentation for more information.

Changing the Way Text Appears

This section explains how to alter the look of text in a book.

Using Alternate Stylesheets

Some books may have alternate stylesheets. These are used to change the format and look of the text. To use an alternate stylesheet, select it from the Views menu and the Main submenu.

All books now include an "inline" stylesheet. If this stylesheet is selected, figures and tables will be displayed in the main text pane instead of appearing in pop-up windows.

Enlarging or Reducing the Font Size

You can enlarge or reduce the size of the text by choosing Enlarge or Reduce from the View menu. This remains in effect until the book is closed. Windows users may find that the default font size is too small or large for the resolution of the monitor. The SYBVIDEO environment variable can be used to change the default text point size. Try using different values between 10 and 20 until you find a satisfactory size.